Reading in Time

Reading in Time

Emily Dickinson in the Nineteenth Century

Cristanne Miller

University of Massachusetts Press   AMHERST AND BOSTON

LC 2012004379
ISBN 978-1-55849-951-1 (paper); 950-8 (library cloth)

Designed by Dennis Anderson
Set in Adobe MinionPro by Westchester Book
Printed and bound by Thomson-Shore, Inc.

Library of Congress Cataloging-in-Publication Data

Miller, Cristanne.
Reading in time : Emily Dickinson in the nineteenth century / Cristanne Miller.
    p. cm.
Includes bibliographical references and index.
ISBN 978-1-55849-951-5 (pbk. : alk. paper)—
ISBN 978-1-55849-950-8 (library cloth : alk. paper)
1. Dickinson, Emily, 1830–1886—Criticism and interpetation.
2. Literature and society—United States—History—19th century.
I. Title.
PS1541.Z5M485 2012
811'.4—dc23

                                                    2012004379

British Library Cataloguing in Publication data are available.

Figures 1, 2, and 4–6 are reproduced by permission of The Houghton Library, Harvard University, MS Am 1118.3 (36 d), (11 c), (47 b) (174 b) (56 a) © The President and Fellows of Harvard College. Figures 3 and 7 are reproduced courtesy of the Archives of the Lyman & Merrie Wood Museum of Springfield History, Springfield, Massachusetts.

CONTENTS

ILLUSTRATIONS

ACKNOWLEDGMENTS

ALTHOUGH QUICKLY written, this book both builds on ideas about Dickinson I have been developing since graduate school and has enjoyed the assistance of numbers of people that would imply a longer period of gestation. First my deep thanks to the University at Buffalo for granting me a year's leave to conduct the required research and write a draft of the book, and to the English Departments at both Harvard and Boston Universities for extending affiliate faculty status to me during 2009–2010—extended to 2010–2011 by Harvard to enable my continued use of their library facilities. Thanks also to Leslie Morris, curator of Modern Books and Manuscripts at the Houghton, and the reference librarians at the Houghton, especially Susan Halpert, for assistance in making materials available to me. I am also grateful for the enthusiastic support of Bruce Wilcox, director of the University of Massachusetts Press.

In Cambridge during my year of leave, it was a pleasure to talk with several people about my project or poetry generally, including Paula Bennett, Lawrence Buell, Stephen Burt, Virginia Jackson, Mary Loeffelholz, Polly Longsworth, and Anita Patterson. Several others, in and outside of the Boston area, commented on one or more drafted sections or chapters of my manuscript and deserve special thanks—including Faith Barrett, Catherine Corman, Bonnie Costello, Martin Greenup, Jennifer Leader, Maurice Lee, Victoria Morgan, and Sandra Runzo. Faith Barrett, Melanie Hubbard, Vivian Pollak, and Sandra Runzo also generously shared unpublished materials on Dickinson with me. Two people read more broadly with enormously useful commentary: Domhnall Mitchell read three chapters and Vivian Pollak read most of the manuscript.

In Buffalo, I have enjoyed the stimulation of conversations about poetry and about innovation with the affiliated faculty of the Poetics Program, especially Myung Mi Kim, with Marta Werner, and with many students. Special thanks also go to three research assistants: Elizabeth Miller took extensive notes on the *Springfield Republican* and helped me proofread poems; Andrew Rippeon and Sushmita Sircar checked (and re-checked) my own counts and calculations about poems retained, circulated, sent to various correspondents, and lengths of poems written, retained, and circulated. While Susan

Howe and I never spoke about this work, her influence on thinking about Dickinson has been so pervasive in Buffalo and among contemporary poets that it feels as though conversations about Dickinson here are in effect conversations with her ideas. Hence she has been a kind of indirect interlocutor throughout. Her ideas, sensitive ear, and committed feminism have resonated deeply even when my conclusions differ from hers.

With such assistance, this book should no doubt be stronger than I have been able to make it. All flaws and any remaining errors or inconsistencies are my own. Here I would also like to express gratitude to Jerold Frakes, for the "Sweet Debt of Life" entailed in his support of my busy work schedule and the uneven trials and exhilaration of writing since our first dance together, over twenty-five years ago.

DICKINSON'S POEMS are reproduced by permission of the publishers from *The Poems of Emily Dickinson: Variorum Edition,* edited by Ralph Waldo Franklin, Cambridge: Belknap Press/Harvard University Press, © 1998 by the President and Fellows of Harvard College. Dickinson's letters are reproduced by permission of the publishers from *The Letters of Emily Dickinson: Variorum Edition,* edited by Thomas H. Johnson, Cambridge: Belknap Press/Harvard University Press, © 1958 by the President and Fellows of Harvard College. Dickinson's "The Sleeping" and "The Snake," published in the *Springfield Republican,* are reproduced courtesy of the Archives of the Lyman & Merrie Wood Museum of Springfield History, Springfield, Massachusetts.

ABBREVIATIONS

AM   *Atlantic Monthly*

EDJ   *The Emily Dickinson Journal*

EDL   Emily Dickinson's Lexicon, http://edl.byu.edu/lexicon.

EDR   Emily Dickinson Family Library, Houghton Library, Harvard University

EmEL   Ralph Waldo Emerson, *Essays and Lectures,* edited by Joel Porte. Library of America, 1983.

F   *The Poems of Emily Dickinson,* edited by Ralph Waldo Franklin, 3 vols. (Cambridge: Belknap Press/Harvard University Press, 1998). Unless otherwise indicated, poems are cited as Dickinson writes them in her manuscript books, with the number Franklin assigns.

Fas   Fascicle, a bound manuscript booklet made by Dickinson

L   *Letters of Emily Dickinson,* edited by Thomas H. Johnson and Theodora Ward, 3 vols. (Cambridge: Belknap Press/Harvard University Press, 1958). Letters are cited with the number Johnson and Ward assign.

LOG   Walt Whitman, *Leaves of Grass,* Walt Whitman Archive, http://whitmanarchive.org/published/LG/1855/whole.html.

S   Set, Dickinson's unbound folded pages, constituting a manuscript booklet

SR   *Springfield Daily Republican,* newspaper subscribed to by the Dickinsons

WFH   *Words for the Hour: A New Anthology of Civil War Poems,* edited by Faith Barrett and Cristanne Miller (Amherst: University of Massachusetts Press, 2005).

Reading in Time

Reading in Time = Reading in context of antebellum culture

2. Reading as though Dickinson had different periods of writing

1

Reading in Dickinson's Time

The secret of the poetic art lies in the keeping of time.
Robert Duncan, 1961

congruent - in agreement or harmony

Almost a Heroine
AM June 1862

EMILY DICKINSON wrote the large majority of her poems during and in at least partial relation to antebellum culture and the Civil War, partaking in popular discourse, experimenting with form in ways congruent with her peers, and both accepting and experimenting with basic genre assumptions of her era. To the extent that Dickinson's poetry responds to its cultural context, it is primarily to this period, not the postbellum decades, and indeed Dickinson's poetry marks the culminating peak of experiment with stanzaic and metrical structures in short-lined verse popular during this period. As this study documents, Dickinson's writing practices also change remarkably after 1865. While one might chart several different kinds of changes in the poet's writing practices from those I trace here, the shifts in her writing, retaining, and circulating of poems that occur around 1865 are dramatic and notable, making it reasonable to think of Dickinson as writing in two major periods—earlier and later.[1] In this book, I focus on the earlier period, and especially on her prolific years between 1860 and 1865.

I began this project of reading "in time"—that is, historically and with attention to Dickinson's rhythms and forms—by asking myself what counted as reasonable evidence for responding to the essentially unanswerable questions about Dickinson: how did she compose? why did she keep manuscript books and how did she use them? how did she conceive of the poem, specifically the lyric poem? why did she choose not to publish? These questions led me through many books in the Dickinson family library housed at the Houghton Library at Harvard and then back to Dickinson's manuscript books and other poems that she retained in her possession. Where others might have looked primarily to biography or theory, my questions led me to an increased alertness to patterns in Dickinson's writing, circulating, and retaining poems and in the material she was reading. At least in the years up through 1865, such patterns indicate that we learn most significantly about her poems of this period through careful attention to the poems she retains. This focus on the poems she kept stands in direct contrast to arguments like Marietta Messmer's that "it is her letters and letter-poems—rather than her (fascicle) poems alone or in isolation—which seem to be most representative of Dickinson's fundamental choices about literary production" (3). Generally, the patterns of writing, circulation, and retention I have found in Dickinson's poems, and what I have learned from reading her schoolbooks, personal library, and periodicals, point toward the correction of some assumptions and the rethinking of some scholarly hypotheses about Dickinson's aesthetic and practices. My goal here is not to claim definitive answers in place of hypotheses but to provide different kinds of information by asking more rigorous questions of the material we already know well and suggesting new contexts for thinking about it. I trust that the practices I document and my hypotheses will generate both new questions and further study.

First and foremost, I argue that Dickinson was vitally engaged with multiple aspects of her culture—literary, social, cultural, religious, and political—a fact altogether congruent with her physical reclusiveness and her periodic claim that her life and thoughts did not follow normative grooves.[2] Faith Barrett, Paula Bennett, Paul Crumbley, Jed Deppman, Virginia Jackson, Mary Loeffelholz, Domhnall Mitchell, Aife Murray, Daneen Wardrop, and Shira Wolosky are among the critics who have contributed recently to scholarship in this area. Unlike these scholars, I focus primarily on what we learn from her periodical reading and from attention to the formal properties of poems we know Dickinson read with enthusiasm. She wrote in an innovative and idiosyncratic response to contemporary styles, events, and idioms while sharing their cultural base. Moreover, while most of her poems were never circulated, she seems to have written with a contemporary audience in mind that was (or would have been, to the extent that the audience remained imagined) alert to her allusions to news and popular authors as well as to culturally central texts like the Bible and Shakespeare. Newspapers, periodicals, popular song and poetry, and the most famous poets of her day provided plots, phrases, metrical and stanzaic forms, and other stimulus for her writing.

While Dickinson sometimes, especially in early letters and poems, used quotation marks to indicate such allusion, more often her borrowing was thoroughly absorbed within her own thinking; as she writes to Thomas Wentworth Higginson, "[I] never consciously touch a paint, mixed by another person" but when she does become conscious of such borrowing "I do not let go it, because it is mine" (L271). Once made her own, words and ideas no longer belonged to others who used them first. As I discuss in Chapter 4, this at-

idiosyncratic - peculiar or individual

titude toward lifting or recirculating what is useful resembles general attitudes of the antebellum culture of reprinting, as analyzed by Meredith McGill. Dickinson is less directly influenced by the individual writers of her time than she is an absorptive reader: everything goes into the mix of her own fertile imagination and becomes "mine," as she says.[3] Chapters 2, 3, and 4 contribute to understanding Dickinson's receptive reading and refashioning through attention to the genres and formal structures of her poems in relation to those of her contemporaries, in particular the genres of the lyric, ballad, and free verse. Chapters 5 and 6 explore especially Dickinson's periodical reading as providing a basis for her revisions of popular American Orientalism and, in 1860, focus on foreign travel as the impetus for becoming a poet, and on the range of her poetry written in response to the Civil War.

Evidence illuminating Dickinson's conceptions of the poet and poem comes from her poems, letters, what we know she read, and the more nebulous influences of the dominant institutions in her life: schools, the church, and her family. Substantial scholarship already exists on Dickinson's reading of the Bible and a few authors like Shakespeare, Emerson, and Elizabeth Barrett Browning. Scholarship is currently underway on Dickinson's reading of other favorite writers, such as Robert Browning, George Eliot, and the Brontes.[4] Other critics have shown that even ostensibly intimate phrases of letters are sometimes directly lifted from popular literature—for example, her phrase "My business is to love" appears in *Miss Gilbert's Career*, a novel written by Josiah Gilbert Holland, the husband of one of her closest friends and co-editor of the *Springfield Republican*. Two aspects of her self-description to Higginson echo descriptions in stories by Harriet Prescott (Spofford) and Rose Terry (Cooke) published in the *Atlantic Monthly*.[5] Scholars are also now beginning to take seriously the influence of periodicals on Dickinson's verse, in particular the *Republican* and the *Atlantic*, both publications to which her family subscribed. As a devoted reader of newspapers and periodicals, she was a more than usually active observer of the cultural energies of her time.

The Atlantic Monthly is of particular importance to my study because its contributions best represent what I believe was the level of Dickinson's aspiration for her art and she began reading it with its first issue in November 1857, shortly before beginning to preserve her own poems in fascicles in 1858. Dickinson's letters demonstrate that she was familiar with the *Atlantic*'s contents and that she knew who had written many of its anonymously published stories, essays, and poems—that is, what has appeared as blanket anonymity to twentieth- and twenty-first-century readers was more of an open secret to her and to many nineteenth-century readers. Starting in December 1860, the back or front matter sometimes listed the journal's regular contributors; a February 1860 cover lists authors published in the previous and the current issue; and some issues contained articles "by the author of" work that is advertised under "Literary Notices" in that or another issue's back pages with the author's name. From December 1862 on, the *Atlantic* also published a bi-annual index of contributions, including names of authors—except for those few pieces published truly anonymously. In April 1862, Dickinson knew that Higginson had written the "Letter to a Young Contributor" because she recognized his style from earlier essays. The *Atlantic* was also particularly hospitable to women writers, including contributions from several female novelists, poets, and essayists in its pages.[6]

More significant to the question of evidence for judging what mattered to the maturing poet, not all pages of Dickinson family copies of the *Atlantic* were cut, indicating that neither Emily nor any other member of her family read those essays; for example, the entire volume of April 1863 is uncut. Scholars claiming that Dickinson knew particular essays simply because they were published in the *Atlantic* will need to check whether relevant pages of the journal were cut to know whether Dickinson might in fact have read them.[7] Among the essays with cut pages, some contain marks of having been read, including a few virtually certain to indicate the poet's own enthusiasms and revealing something about her style of reading. At the trivial end, some pages in the issues between 1857 and 1865 have smudges, perhaps from spills, ash, or dead bugs; the February 1861 cover was used for a math problem; and two pages were used to blot fresh ink (November 1861 and 1862): some letters are visible but no words can be read. More significantly, the essay "Elizabeth Barrett Browning" by Kate Field (September 1861) has been excised—evidently by Dickinson, a conclusion based on her known love of Barrett Browning and proclivity for cutting things out of texts.[8] Two Civil War poems have more than one passage, or stanza, marked in pencil—one by Oliver Wendell Holmes in March 1862 and another by Josiah Holland in August 1864—and two stories are marked with light pencil, including a February 1861 installment of "The Professor's Story," also by Holmes.[9] Moreover, one of Sam Bowles's calling cards, dated "Amherst Sunday Oct 21," calls attention to "page 615—2d paragraph left column / page 616 1st paragraph" of a November 1860 installment of this story; this card was left in the November issue. Both paragraphs describe a woman's performative mourning apparel through literary comparison: "Gray's Elegy was not a more perfect composition"; she is "the very picture of artless simplicity,—as represented in well-played genteel comedy" (615, 616). While we cannot know whether these marks or this card are Dickinson's, they match those made in books we know she read enthusiastically and coincide with her known interests, including an interest in constructing speakers of apparently "artless simplicity" (see Chapter 4). The card also provides clear evidence that Dickinson and her friends shared passages they enjoyed with each other.[10]

Dickinson's well-known cut-outs appended to a few letters, and some-times to scraps of paper on which she later drafted poems, make it highly likely that she was also the person who cut two phrases out of an 1862 essay by Harriet Prescott, providing a retrospective on the career of Elizabeth Sara Sheppard. Dickinson outlines rectangularly in pencil and then cuts out the phrase "'Almost a Heroine',," a few pages later also outlining and then incis-ing the running header for the essay, "The Author of 'Charles Auchester'" (763, 769). There is no record of what she did with these cut-out phrases, but one could imagine that in the middle of 1862, two months after having first written to Higginson, Dickinson felt herself to be at the height of her poetic powers, hence may have felt a kind of adventurous hopefulness, in addition to her frequently discussed sorrow over the war. Her clipping of these words suggests some identification with them, which in turn suggests that she may at least occasionally have seen herself as the protagonist of her own story. This phrase may particularly have appealed to her because the capitalized "Almost" provides a tongue-in-cheek check on the larger claim ("Heroine"), making it self-ironizing as well as potentially grand. Here is a fact (the cut-out) about which we can only know that Dickinson is likely to have been responsi-ble for it. The more we learn about what are either probably or indubitably her marks and cuttings, the firmer basis we will have for interpretive specu-lation about what they imply.

Such marks and cuttings in the *Atlantic* and other evidence about Dickin-son's reading practices definitely indicate that Dickinson was an interactive reader, at least sometimes responding physically to reading she enjoyed. She was also apparently not a great respecter of the sanctity or integrity of printed literature, or perhaps of any textuality. Martha Nell Smith reads Dickinson's cuttings from the Bible, a *New England Primer,* and her father's copy of Dick-ens as "irreverent . . . opportunities" for Dickinson "to exert control over ex-pression by remaking supposedly fixed utterances and thereby challenge authorities"; Dickinson "overturns the dicta of her day" ("Poet as Cartoon-ist" 71, 72). Dickinson seems, however, to have had no more respect for the textual integrity of ephemeral periodicals like the *Atlantic* or texts owned by non-patriarchal others than for the Bible or her father's books, given the ex-tensive pencil markings and page-folding almost certainly made by her in books owned by her mother, her brother, and her best friend and sister-in-law Susan Huntington Gilbert Dickinson, and in books of her own.[11] More-over, we now know that many nineteenth-century Americans exchanged books with marked passages and kept scrapbooks with cut-out articles and written-in items. Dickinson writes: "A Book I have – a friend gave – / Whose Pencil – here and there – / Had notched the place that pleased Him –"; cutting from and marking in books was a widespread cultural practice, not unique to her or her family ("Death sets a Thing significant" F640).[12] Dickinson family copies of the *Springfield Republican* have not been kept so we cannot know whether Dickinson similarly marked, folded, or cut articles from the daily newspaper, but references in poems and letters indicate that she kept current in national and international news.[13] Her willingness to mark and cut out lines or phrases that interested and amused her call into question whether she regarded all texts—including copies of her own poems—to be fair game for her own and others' plunder and transformative use.

While others have written about particular aspects of Dickinson's usage or style that change over the years, there has been relatively little attention to changes in the formal properties of her poetry. After mapping the stanzaic and metrical structure of every entry in Franklin's 1998 reading edition of the *Poems,* I have found that Dickinson writes in an extraordinary variety of rhythmic forms, many of them inconsistent within a single poem, and some written distinctly in the loosened rhythms of ballads or even, a few, in free verse, rather than in the stricter syllabic count of hymn meters (see Chapter 3). These patterns vary over the years—despite some continuous characteristics, like Dickinson's compressed syntax, disruptive use of dashes, wide-ranging registers of diction, and use of radically disorienting metonymy and metaphor. After 1865, Dickinson writes a smaller percentage of poems that are formally innovative (although some late poems are radically innovative in form) and, starting in 1865, she writes an increasing percentage of poems that are four lines or shorter (around 22 percent in 1865).[14] It is partly for this reason that the later work is less innovative, since much of her radical play with formal structures occurs through the disruption of established rhythmic patterns within a single poem, as I discuss in Chapters 3 and 4. After 1865, Dickinson writes a greater proportion of verse in fully realized alternating iambic tetrameter and trimeter (8686)—again, no doubt in part because the poems are shorter, but she is also choosing to write in fewer distinct forms, centering more on hymnal Common Meter.[15] In short, while hundreds of her poems can (as the cliché goes) be sung in whole or part to "The Yellow Rose of Texas" or any other simple ballad tune, this is true for far fewer than half of her poems written through 1865 and only around half after that date. Moreover, especially in her most productive years, Dickinson writes in as many as twenty to forty distinct stanzaic patterns per year, not including the poems that shift from one pattern to another, use variant lineation within an established pattern, or conclude with truncated lines or stanzas.

After 1865, Dickinson's writing of poetry drops precipitously. According to Franklin's dating, she wrote 295 poems in 1863, 98 in 1864, and 229 in 1865. She then wrote ten poems in 1866; twelve in 1867, eleven in 1868, and eleven again in 1869. Thereafter, she never wrote more than forty-eight poems in a year and in several years her output was in the teens or twenties—that is, she was often writing one or two poems a month, on average, rather than a poem every one or two days, and many of these later poems were only a few lines long. During the twenty-one years from 1866 until the end of her life, she wrote 669 poems. In the eight years leading up to 1866, however, Dickinson had written 1120 poems, 937 of them since 1861, or around 63 percent of the poems she would write in her life (52 percent since 1861).[16] These numbers cannot be exact since Dickinson did not date manuscripts and there is only indirect evidence for most dating: dates of letters, occasional references, and the approximated date of handwriting in a poem's earliest extant copy— although the striking changes in her handwriting over the years provide good evidence for general dating of these copies. Everything we know about her mode of composition and copying, however, suggests that at least through 1865 the poet typically copied poems to retain or circulate fairly soon after writing them. Although dates must be less certain for her poems written after 1865 and not retained in clean copy, Dickinson also circulated far more of her poems during these years, and many of those have been dated by recipients. We can, then, treat Franklin's dating with reasonable certainty, at least within the year assigned. Moreover, it is abundantly clear that Dickinson's primary output occurred between 1860 and 1865, and that there are marked changes in her patterns of writing after 1865.

Similarly, it is only between 1860 and 1865 that Dickinson retains almost every poem she writes. Both Johnson's and Franklin's editions include poems that Dickinson circulated but did not herself preserve, hence that we have only through her letters.[17] In 1861, she saves around 91 percent of the poems we know that she wrote; in 1860 and 1862, around 98 percent; between 1863 and 1865, Dickinson saves 99 percent of her poems. In contrast, after 1865 she saves an average of 77 percent and in several years less than this: she saves 68 percent of the thirty-one poems written in 1876, a mere 56 percent of the thirty-four poems written in 1883, 62 percent of the thirteen written in 1885, and one of the two poems from 1886.[18] After 1865, Dickinson circulates a higher percentage of her poems than during the war, even though she also continues to send out poems written during her earlier more productive years. After 1875, she never circulates less than 34 percent of what she has written, and in some years she circulates as much as 59, 70, or 100 percent (in 1883, 1884, and 1886 respectively), all but one poem within a year or two of its composition—as judged by the earliest extant draft. Between 1861 and 1865, in contrast, she circulates only between 15 and 37 percent of her poems (with an average of 24 percent), some long after initial composition.[19] Rather than writing primarily poems of irregular structure preserved in fair copy in carefully constructed booklets and shared with no one, after 1865 Dickinson

So there may be many others lost.

increasingly writes very short poems in regular meter and circulates them without keeping a copy. We have 119 of Dickinson's poems written after 1865 only because she mailed them to people who kept them, not because she preserved copies herself. Moreover, after 1866, around 62 percent of the poems she circulates are five lines or shorter, and many are occasional or seasonal.

As I discuss in the following chapters, these patterns have significant implications for the ways we understand Dickinson's particular conceptions of the poem, her writing practices, and her attitudes toward publication over the course of her lifetime. We cannot reasonably, for example, use patterns of her writing from the late 1870s and 1880s to explain the very different patterns of composition, preserving, and circulating her poems in the early 1860s, when she writes most of her poems. On the other hand, generalizations about Dickinson's creative process based on poetry written between 1860 and 1865 will describe her writing not just of the majority of her poems but also the very great majority she deliberately retained and that are obviously not occasional and more than five lines long. While one might also distinguish poems of 1858 to 1860 from those of 1864 and 1865, or in other shorter periods (as I do in Chapter 5, through attention to poems of 1860), my primary interest here is in reflecting on major patterns of her writing through 1865 and significant differences that take place thereafter. The idea that Dickinson writes a foundationally hybrid poetry, responsive to the materials on which she writes or in interaction with such materials, depends entirely on her preservation of drafts and fragments after 1865—as Marta Werner notes in speculating that in her late years Dickinson discards the idea of a finished poem.[20] Since the poet saved very few drafts during the years of her most extraordinary productivity, we must conclude either that they meant nothing to her during this period or that she only later began writing on envelopes, cooking wrappers, and other fragments of paper—whether or not such a practice is epistemologically significant.

Dates matter. Aife Murray's scholarship on the correlation between Dickinson's astonishing productivity in the 1860s and domestic help in the house also makes this crucial point (*Maid* 10, 78–81). Yet reliable domestic help alone does not persuasively account for differences in her ways of composing, copying, and circulating poems. For example, although (as Murray informs us) the Dickinsons had steady servant help from December 1856 until October 1865 (Margaret Ó Brien Lawler), Dickinson preserves no poems of her own until 1858 (81, 244). Though Murray claims that Dickinson "steadily averaged about seventy-five poems and letters per year" after 1869, when after an almost four-year hiatus the Dickinsons again have long-term domestic help (Margaret Maher), taken alone this average disguises the fact that Dickinson does not reach this number of combined letters and poems per year until 1877 and that in every year after 1869 she writes more letters than poems as well as shorter poems than previously, less often preserved. Both letters and poems require time to write but not an intense urge to write verse. Murray's claim that the poet writes more compositions on scraps of paper like shopping lists and food paper after 1869 than before also cannot be proven since we cannot know whether she first begins writing on scraps then or only preserves scraps because she is no longer making fair copies.[21] When Dickinson returns sporadically to making sets between 1871 and 1875, she rarely saves drafts for poems copied into sets. Such tabulation of domestic help also does not account for the marked decrease in the intensity of experimentation with metrical and stanzaic forms after 1865. Murray's research on the relationship between Dickinson's productivity as a writer and periods when the family enjoyed the reliable ongoing employment of a maid significantly establishes the poet's closeness to household rhythms and must be a factor contributing to the sudden drop in her productivity with Ó Brien Lawler's departure in October 1865, but no generalization based on patterns of Dickinson's life after Maher enters the household in 1869 can account for her productivity in the preceding decade. Nonetheless, such scholarship underlines the importance of attention to dates and context when generalizing about Dickinson's writing.

Dickinson's enthusiasm for antebellum literature was far warmer than that of most twenty-first-century readers. Reading her poems in tandem with those she read in school books, published volumes, and periodicals makes it clear that her poetry is also closer formally to that of her peers than has been assumed. While there is considerably more attention to popular nineteenth-century verse now than there was a decade ago, many critics still dismiss it as more or less uniformly dismal. Lyndall Gordon's recent biography refers to periodical poetry by Dickinson's contemporaries as "sentimental tosh," and to literary editor Fidelia Cooke as "clueless about poetry" because of the selections she makes for the *Republican,* echoing Richard Sewall's earlier claim that the newspaper's taste was "thoroughly conventional" (Sewall, "Perfect Audience" 207; Gordon 10).[22] Shannon Thomas agrees, and implies the same of the *Atlantic* (62). Both the *Atlantic* and *Republican,* however, published poetry by John Greenleaf Whittier, Henry Wadsworth Longfellow, James Russell Lowell, Ralph Waldo Emerson, Elizabeth Barrett Browning, and other well-known poets regarded as innovative in their time, and the *Atlantic* published one poem of Whitman's. Despite her enthusiastic reading, Dickinson at times represented herself as outside the mainstream, perhaps because she was unconscious of aspects of her indebtedness to popular literature, while consciously adapting, playing off of, or manipulating others. Her own exaggerations of her individuality ("the only Kangaroo among the beauty"), however, need not be ours.[23] Put differently, one can acknowledge her distinctness without seeing her as unique or anomalous to a culture that in fact seems to have provided her with profuse and powerful models.

A corollary critical assumption holds that there is little change between antebellum and post-bellum poetry, and that what little difference there is lies in increased tendencies toward innovative forms and the acceptance of more widely varied styles of verse in the second half of the century. Certainly by the 1890s American poetry had begun to take on strong signs of modernist concision, skepticism, and irreverence formally and in its topics and diction. Even casual reading of the poetry volumes Dickinson and other family members owned and the poetry published in the periodicals the Dickinsons subscribed to, however, reveals that the antebellum period enthusiastically embraced a variety of innovative formal structures, including poems with a high degree of structural irregularity (see Chapter 2). While much verse of the period is predictable in its language and sentiments (as is much verse in every age), many poems are not. More important, the antebellum period lionized poets who were masters of sonic harmonies and rhythm. Dickinson's sensitivity to nuanced variation in metrical forms and interest in formal innovation were encouraged by her school books, by her reading at home, and by literary commentary in journals like the *Atlantic.* Moreover, many if not most of the stanzaic forms Dickinson used can be found in poetry by at least one of her contemporaries in a venue she would have known.

The evidence of her reading and of her contemporaries' writing establishes that Dickinson was an enthusiastic and appreciative reader of the literary culture of the 1850s and 1860s; hence her decision not to publish is unlikely to have been based primarily on the idea that formal elements of her work would not be accepted or would be radically rewritten by interfering editors, as I discuss in my conclusion. Scholarly claims that Dickinson's most significant sense of the poem is that on the page and that she collages her handwritten words with visual elements are in part the topic of my Chapter 4, where I find that Dickinson writes a poetry of implied orality and that her writing out of poems is their least stable aspect. This textual instability corresponds to other aspects of her poetry—such as its epistemological and syntactic openness, experimentation with metrical norms, inclusion of variant words on fair copies, and revision over the course of several years. Such factors point to the conclusion that at least through 1865 Dickinson's poetic is more crucially attuned to the ear than to the eye.

The idea that Dickinson's poetic is foundationally epistolary is also seriously challenged by evidence revealing the patterns of Dickinson's circulation of poems to her contemporaries, before and after 1865, as previously indicated. During her most creative years, Dickinson shows no one the great majority of poems she writes. Perhaps more surprising is that Dickinson

---

Handwritten marginalia:

corollary - a proposition that follows from one already proved

concision - using only the words necessary to convey an idea

irreverence - a lack of respect for people or things that are generally taken seriously

lionize - give a lot of public attention and approval to (someone).

sonic - denoting, relating to, or of the nature of sound or sound waves.

circulates no poems with direct mention of the Civil War, few that invoke the war indirectly, and relatively few of her poems most frequently anthologized and regarded as among her most important for understanding her thought and art today. Knowing that she never circulated the majority of her most serious poems suggests that her inclusion of poems in letters may often be more conventional than has been thought. Franklin hypothesizes that when retained and circulated copies of a poem are written at about the same time, Dickinson typically circulates the poem before entering it into a fascicle or set (page 20). He provides no evidence, however, that this is the case—that is, we cannot generally know that circulating a poem is a step toward Dickinson's deciding to keep it rather than following a decision that it will be retained. Over the course of her lifetime, we have a record of 530 poems that Dickinson sent to friends, family, and acquaintances. Of these, she sent 90 to more than one person, some to several people.[24] It is indeed striking that Dickinson frequently sends poems that constitute the entire message or that are accompanied by at most a line or two of prose. Toward the end of her life, she is sending such missives to many people. At the same time, Dickinson's repeated sending of the same poem to more than one person indicates that she regarded her poems as isolatable from a particular personal or epistolary context and is therefore unlikely to have considered them generically as a "letter." Her patterns of revision—often several years after having preserved a copy—point to the same conclusion, namely, that she composes, revises, and uses her poems in ways she does not treat prose.[25]

Most debate on Dickinson's letters has focused either on their aesthetics or on the look of manuscript pages. Most prominent has been the defensive position that the letters are of a quality and significance to be regarded as "art" in and of themselves and that their artfulness is "poetic." Scholarship focused on the manuscripts is summarized in the introduction to the recent volume *Reading Emily Dickinson's Letters* edited by Jane Eberwein and Cindy MacKenzie: "many poems consistently merged with their prose context, thus forming letter-poems or poem-letters" (ix).[26] As noted earlier, however, Domhnall Mitchell's precise measurements of Dickinson's manuscripts reveal that she consistently began first lines of poetry with capital letters and spaced lines of poetry differently from lines of prose on the page, although these distinctions break down in the last three or four years of her life, as her handwriting becomes extremely large and loose (*Measures* 177). My reasoning leaves aside all question of the look of the manuscript page and instead focuses on Dickinson's different patterns of use of poems and letters.

Dickinson never sends a prose letter to more than one recipient—although she occasionally repeats an isolated phrase. She also sends several poems—sometimes with just an address at the top of the page and a signature afterward, if even that—to one or more persons without retaining a copy. For example, in 1861, Dickinson sent a note addressed "Mr. Bowles" and containing as its entire missive the lines: "The Juggler's *Hat* her Country is – / The Mountain Gorse – the *Bee's* –" (F186); in 1869, Dickinson sent Sue the quatrain, "The Work of Her that went, / The Toil of Fellows done – / In Ovens green our Mother bakes, / By Fires of the Sun –" (1159), without address or signature; in 1876, she sent a note signed "Emily" to her pastor, Jonathan Jenkins, or his wife Sarah, consisting of the quatrain: "To his simplicity / To die was little fate / If Duty – live – / Contented, but her Confederate." (F1387 B)—concluding a letter to Higginson with the same lines at about the same time (L449). She retained no copy of any of these lines for herself. Most of Dickinson's uses of such poems (or letter-poems) were like these: brief occasional or aphoristic expressions, fitting entirely nineteenth-century practices of acknowledging gifts, expressing consolation or affection, or clothing any astute observation in verse. This is especially the case after 1866, as previously indicated. Dickinson also sent apparently intimate verse to more than one person. For example, she mailed a poem beginning "Pass to thy Rendezvous of Light," (F1624) to Sue after the death of her son (and Emily's adored nephew) Gilbert in 1883, and then sent the same lines two years later to Higginson in response to George Eliot's death (L868, L972). No copy of these lines remains among her papers. Given this doubled use, these lines cannot be understood restrictively as a private message, in the way we expect of letters, as a genre. Like poems, they are meaningful beyond a single context.

Because she sent so many poems to more than one person, at times to as many as six or seven, we know that for her a poem was separable from its initiating context—personal or textual. Moreover, the fact that she did not send the majority of her poems (and the vast majority of her most serious poems) to anyone supports the hypothesis that the letter and the poem were for her, for the most part, distinct genres. It is certainly significant that the language of Dickinson's letters shares many of the characteristics of the language of her poems, and that she circulates so many poems. The patterns of such circulating and the kinds of poems generally sent, however, indicate that before 1866 she was writing relatively few missives that could be considered letter-poems or poem-letters; hence this practice cannot be taken as a model for understanding her composition or aesthetic generally.

To my mind, Dickinson regarded the poem as an essentially aural structure, which could be performed or mapped in distinct and various ways in writing—a conclusion supported by ways that Dickinson writes about poetry, about the poet, and by the extreme significance of aural or sonic features to her verse. The written poem, like the spoken poem, is a performance, whether as dramatic lyric, meditative or philosophical speculation,

apostrophe, or occasion of direct address.[27] As Jed Deppman has persuasively argued, Dickinson also used poetry as a way of thinking through a
variety of subjects. Consequently, she writes poems that present contrasting
perspectives on a large number of subjects—another aspect of performance,
or dramatic presentation. Similarly, while Dickinson's use of multiple registers of language and wildly diverse linkages through metonymy or metaphor
make some poems highly allusive, almost all her poems provide at least some
narrative, epistemological, or psychological point of reference and make
good sense within the context of their historical moment, just as they are
typically comprehensible at the level of syntax.

Especially with a poet like Dickinson, the test of any pattern or theory is
its usefulness in reading the poems, individually and as a whole. The following chapters of this book focus largely on Dickinson's writing practices
or broad cultural points of engagement rather than on individual poems,
although each chapter engages with particular poems and Chapters 5 and 6
analyze distinct topical subsets of her poetry. Every chapter assumes that
attention both to Dickinson's reading and to her patterns of writing and
circulating verse is revelatory. For the remainder of this chapter, I turn to
interpretation of a single poem to demonstrate ways that attention to historical context and to patterns of Dickinson's language can matter in reading her poems.

"The Black Berry – wears a Thorn in his side –" (F548) was apparently
never circulated and exists only in fair copy as inscribed in Fascicle 27 in the
summer of 1863, as was typical of poems she wrote during this year. There
Dickinson proposes two alternatives for the word "offers" in line 3, both of
which maintain the iambic meter and line length she first writes out in the
poem; she does not later revise the poem in any way.

	syllables	beats		
The Black Berry – wears a Thorn in his side –	10	4		
But no Man heard Him cry –	6	3		
He offers His Berry, just the same	9	4	[spices	flavors
To Partridge – and to Boy –	6	3		
He sometimes holds upon the Fence –	8	4		
Or struggles to a Tree –	6	3		
Or clasps a Rock, with both His Hands –	8	4		
But not for sympathy –	6	3		
We – tell a Hurt – to cool it –	7	3		
This Mourner – to the Sky	6	3		
A little further reaches – instead –	9	4		
Brave Black Berry –	4	3		

Written in a loosened ballad meter, this poem shifts to a different structure of beats in its final quatrain, calling the reader's attention to this moment in the poem (see Chapter 3 on meter). The first stanza contains multiple unstressed syllables between beats; the second stanza maintains the same rhythm of 4343 beats but without variation from its iambic meter; and the last stanza shifts to a 3343 beat structure, again with the looser rhythms of the ballad measure in the final two lines—where Dickinson includes extra unstressed syllables between beats in the penultimate line, then reduces the final line to just four syllables.[28] Both in its rhythms and in its tale of private suffering loosely analogous to Jesus' crucifixion, this poem resembles several poems of the period. Similarly, the poem's speaker resembles the apparently artless speaker of traditional ballads, in its use of simple narrative and diction (see Chapter 4).

The single line that most marks this poem as Dickinson's is the first line of the final stanza, the line responsible both for the shift in stanzaic structure (away from the 4343 established pattern) and for the shift outside the narrative of the "Brave" berry. With "We – tell a Hurt – to cool it –," Dickinson alters the focus of this poem from a tale of martyrdom to the question of how one chooses to deal with pain: if telling "cool[s]" a hurt then it is most painful to suffer without speaking.[29] The "Berry" is either silent or unheard, or both: the speaker's claim that it is unheard by "Man" implies that the sufferer of this poem may complain in a way heard by God or some other non-human entity. The poem ends with the berry's eschewal of sympathy—an action presented as its striving to reach "further" or higher but also as an act of isolation. This berry creates ("spices," "flavors") and "offers" himself, in anthropomorphized form, to animal or human hunger without complaint either for being eaten or for the pain of wearing "a Thorn in his side –," acts that are presented indirectly as choices that refuse the comfort of human community based on "tell[ing]."

This poem received little attention until recent readings that interpret the "Black Berry" as referring to African Americans.[30] Given its composition in 1863, Dickinson's writing of "Black Berry" rather than *blackberry,* and the anthropomorphism of presenting the berry as a human-like sufferer, such an interpretation has obvious appeal. A reader of the phenomenally popular 1851 novel *Uncle Tom's Cabin,* as Dickinson was, would have been familiar with the trope of the black man as Christian martyr to slavery's torment. Put into more precise historical context and the patterns of Dickinson's writing, however, this reading becomes improbable as a primary interpretation. Every detail of this poem makes sense in relation to blackberries, which grow wild on extremely thorny vines in the mid and late summer throughout New England, and in relation to a romanticized Christian martyrdom but not to any human subject. Dickinson's conceit makes the berry itself rather than the picker the one who suffers from its thorns. Like Christ, the "Black Berry" "of-fers" his fruit to others, asking not even "sympathy" for himself, but merely reaching "to the Sky" as if to some spiritual salvation.

Neither the story of creative (or fruitful) production while under such tor-ment nor Dickinson's concluding reflection about silence would seem to have much to do with African Americans or racial politics by the summer of 1863. While Dickinson herself may have heard relatively few or no African Americans speak in person about the suffering of slavery, such suffering was depicted repeatedly in the *Springfield Republican* and (less often) in the *Atlantic,* and had been for years—although with greater intensity and fre-quency since the war began. The *Republican* ran frequent articles on escaped slaves, on the treatment of slaves in various parts of the South, and on partic-ular incidents having to do with individual slaves or slave-owners. Moreover, by the summer of 1863, the Emancipation Proclamation had freed slaves in the Confederate states and African Americans were now fighting in the Union armies—as Dickinson well knew; Higginson had been commanding the First South Carolina Volunteers, a regiment recruited from former slaves, since November of 1862. In other words, by mid-1863, the suffering of the enslaved was not a silenced or silent tale. This was instead a historical moment for focus on the strengths and intelligence of people of African descent, as Dick-inson knew from her periodical reading.[31] Moreover, Dickinson does not use the adjective "Black" to describe people of color in any letter or poem until 1881, when she refers to a new servant as a "Black Man" (L721).[32] National attitudes toward African Americans changed in the nearly twenty years between 1863 and 1881. The latter period was more openly racist in the Northern states, as David Blight and other historians have argued, given the repressive and nostalgic politics dominant in the North following the war and especially following Reconstruction.[33] Dickinson may have intended her "Black Berry" as a Christian romanticization of the formerly enslaved, but the allusion is not persuasive as a primary anchor for understanding the poem and seems to me more likely as an unintended potential allusion in what is otherwise a largely playful poem about blackberries.[34]

In seeking evidence for a reading of the poem understanding the berry as African American, one would also need to ask whether other of Dickinson's poems, or poems by her contemporaries, reveal associations among (black) berries and African Americans. Dickinson does anthropomorphize an ani-mal as a black man in another poem also written in 1863: the line "No Black bird bates His Banjo –" must allude to African Americans, since no bird plays a banjo and stereotyped black men do, as depicted on sheet music for minstrel tunes Dickinson owned ("It makes no difference abroad –"; F686).[35] On the other hand, only berries, bees, and birds are "Black" in Dickinson's poems—all common sights in New England—and there was no strong association of berries with people of color in popular culture as there was with banjos and crows.[36]

In "It makes no difference abroad –," Dickinson reflects that "The Seasons – fit – the same –" no matter what disasters are occurring in the human world. As evidence, she refers to several aspects of nature, each time using a metaphor inappropriate to the thing described: "Mornings blossom . . . flowers – kindle . . . Brooks slam . . ." In this context, the alliterative "No Black bird bates His Banjo – / For passing Calvary –" fits the established pattern of natural indifference to human suffering. The racist or (as Sandra Runzo argues) trickster image of the black minstrel varies Dickinson's portrait of blooming, flaming, and lustful nature to include the bird/musician, abetting a derogatory stereotype of black people as always cheerful, or at least as appearing always cheerful to cultural outsiders, since it is not stated why the bird refuses to "bate[] His Banjo" for an unidentified sufferer.[37] Moreover, because the focus on the "Black"-ness of the bird rests largely on Dickinson's writing "Black bird" as two words rather than the usual one, one must note that Dickinson always writes "Blue Bird" equally distinctly and that she anthropomorphizes animals and other life forms in hundreds of poems; in other words, anthropomorphization is not reserved for birds or plants standing for (and dehumanizing) African Americans.[38] The possibility that Dickinson manipulates racial codes based on historical context opens ranges of reference previously unconceived, but many of her poems suggest multiple avenues of conjecture that veer away from or outright contradict the primary statement or narrative of the poem, typically through the isolation of single metaphors, words, or phrases. Such interpretation may enrich our understanding of Dickinson and her culture but should not, to my mind, overwhelm or ignore the poem's obvious directions.[39]

Read in its entirety and with attention to its historical context, "The Black Berry – wears a Thorn" seems to me primarily concerned with the fact that telling a hurt "cool[s]" its pain, therefore reflecting on the choice a sufferer makes who eschews the possibility of such sharing. From the beginning of this poem, the anthropomorphized "Black Berry" makes choices: he "wears" his thorn, rather than being pierced by or inflicted with it; he "offers" his fruit without protest—either at his thorn or at the fact that "no Man heard Him cry," suggesting that he is unheard, or that he cries when no one can hear him, or that he seeks succor or support only from the inanimate: the fence, a tree, a rock, the sky. "We," presumably "we" people, unlike this berry, talk when we are in pain. "We – tell" somebody, and presumably (at least when we are lucky) we "clasp[]" something besides a rock "with both [our] Hands." This berry is "Brave" but pathetic. If it alludes to African Americans, it is already

→ Penny Press Puzzle Books
   (not word search)
→ Banana Cream Pie
→ Socks (Warm + Fuzzy)
     or Slippers
→ Ginger Lolipops

anachronistic, since the bravery of African Americans in 1863 was actively in the news and loud, as they fought in battles such as the much publicized charge at Fort Wagner (July 1863). There is, moreover, a kind of playfulness in this tale of excessive martyrdom enacted by the delicious berry that would seem out of place in a poem on racial politics in 1863 and tone-deaf in a way inconsistent with other of Dickinson's poems—although this is always a possibility with issues of cultural sensitivity. Particularly during the Civil War, as I discuss in Chapter 6, Dickinson takes on a variety of tones and situational or dramatic perspectives for considerations of death and suffering, from the irreverently playful to the profoundly grim. While a few poems consider questions of race or speak from positions suggestively including newly freed men and women, none portray a distinctly African American speaker or articulate explicit sympathy for the (previously) enslaved.

The following chapters focus on the dynamics of sound, form, and thought in Dickinson's poetry in ways that mark it as distinctly lyric, as understood by her immediate predecessors and contemporaries, and on patterns of her borrowing or adoption of popular poetic forms, modes, and idioms. Dickinson is a poet of patterns, not of systems or codes. She does not use particular formal structures (say shorter- or longer-lined poems, particular metrical or stanzaic structures, more or less innovative forms, or dramatic rather than reflective or descriptive lyrics) for particular topics, moods, or themes.[40] Her practice is more nuanced, variant, and complex than any codifying theory. The chapters detailing lyric properties of Dickinson's writing, her borrowings from ballad form and aspects of the ballad speaker, her use of Orientalist idiom and travel metaphors, and her experimentation with various popular modes in Civil War poems do not constitute a grammar of forms or seek to depict Dickinson as always writing from a particular aesthetic or cultural perspective. Instead, they provide information about patterns of practice that enable greater attentiveness to the unique intersections of form, sonic quality, speaking position, cultural resonance, and content in individual poems, based on what we know about Dickinson's poems and what we know of the cultural and historical moment in which she wrote them.

Scholarship of the last thirty years has transformed critical perception of the Dickinson poem. Whereas in 1980 the Dickinson poem was regarded as at least relatively stable and entirely iconoclastic in having been bound into handsewn manuscript booklets and circulated through letters to friends, it is now known to be unstable in primary ways and to have taken popular and common form: handsewn manuscripts and private portfolios were typical modes of stabilizing, collecting, or preserving writing of various kinds; self-authored poems were frequently circulated by post and in private manuscripts; and poetry was frequently quoted or written impromptu in every kind of writing, including personal letters.[41] By refocusing attention on the patterns of Dickinson's writing, copying, and circulating of poems during her period of most prolific creativity, and on the poems themselves as testimonials of what Dickinson cared for most when writing, this study seeks to provide new information for understanding the structures most significant to Dickinson's poetry, how she thought of her activity as a poet during her most prolific years, and the relation of her writing to that of her antebellum contemporaries. Through such focus, it hopes to shift the terms of popular and scholarly debate by creating more precise and detailed frames for reading Dickinson as a learned and enthusiastic participant in many of the cultural discourses of her century.

2

Lyric Strains

> Who is a poet but he whom the heart of man permanently accepts as a
> singer of its own hopes, emotions, and thoughts? And what is poetry but
> that song?
>
> George W. Curtis, 1863

> As all the Heavens were a Bell,
> And Being, but an Ear,
>
> "I felt a Funeral, in my Brain," F340

GENRE CRITICISM is dominated by transhistorical definitional distinctions,
albeit distinctions determined by the critical assumptions of the period in which
they are made. This makes sense; a genre must be inclusive in its defining
characteristics. In contrast, while poets may set themselves a particular generic
task (to write a sonnet, an ode, an epic), their engagement with form is distinctly embedded in a historical moment and their understanding of genre is
historically and locally framed. To read a genre historically in relation to a particular poet's work, therefore, requires knowing when we retroproject contemporary genre, or other, expectations for reading upon earlier norms and how
our norms differ from those of, say, the mid-nineteenth century in the United
States. Since the rise of New Criticism, nineteenth-century American poetry
has been read almost wholly through retroprojected norms. At the level of
genre, those norms stem from finely articulated taxonomies for the lyric poem
based on British romantic poetry and German and British romantic aesthetics.
At the level of literary study, those norms have more to do with the general
predispositions of twentieth-century criticism than with either the aesthetics
or, more important, the practice of nineteenth-century American writers.[1]
This chapter proposes an alternative approach to mid-nineteenth-century poetry in the United States, more inductive than deductive and identifying characteristics of the lyric through study of the practice of a particular time and
place. It asks not what a lyric "is" but how the lyric was written and understood
in the 1840s and 1850s through examining the reading we know Dickinson
engaged in from childhood to young adulthood, thereby mapping how she (or

[handwritten margin note: can't separate a poet from his context]

19

any New England poet) would have been likely to understand the lyric in the late 1850s, when she began writing poetry in earnest.

No major genre is a definitively set or coded form. As Wai Chee Dimock puts it, genres are like "runaway reproductive processes," always changing, morphing, compounding, and receiving input from other genres (1378). Poetry is particularly "supple" in this receiving, she notes. The lyric was perhaps the most supple of all, in that for centuries it seemed to be defined as a kind of default mode including dozens of poetic types—the ode, elegy, paean, psalm, dirge, and short dramatic poem, to name a few—and in effect encompassing all poetry not constituting a play, novel, or epic. According to Gérard Genette, and unlike other poetic genres whose distinct taxonomies can be traced back to Ancient Greece, the lyric as such was first defined in the late eighteenth century, and even eighteenth- and nineteenth-century theories were not restrictive of form.[2] In the twenty-first century, many innovative poets seek to redefine the lyric in ways reminiscent of its earlier inclusiveness. Lyn Hejinian writes that the lyric has "maximum vertical intensity (the single moment in to which the idea rushes)" and is focused not on "expression" but on an "interest in free knowing"; "Writing forms are not merely shapes but forces; formal questions are about dynamics—they ask how, where, and why the writing moves" (*Language of Inquiry* 44, 235, 42). Julia Bloch writes that "lyrical musicality" and "sonic texture," or the formal features of "address and sound get us closer to a working formulation [of the genre] for the contemporary moment" than "theoriz[ing] individual acts of speech" (37). Brian Reed writes that in work of "the twenty-first century avant-garde" genres "cease to be defined by disciplinary rules of inclusion or exclusion; they become jumbled [and "labile"] archives of examples and habits of reading" (157). This chapter, in part, creates such an archive of examples from the mid-nineteenth century in order to clarify the extent and inclusiveness of its lyric strains.

Following this exercise in criticism both enforces greater accuracy for thinking about a genre in a particular moment of time and revolutionizes the way we need to understand Dickinson's writing in relation to that of her contemporaries by revealing patterns of verse and thought at odds with continuing stereotypes of early nineteenth-century poetry. First, antebellum American verse cherished originality, often described as wildness, and encouraged what we might call a fluid relationship between European or traditional forms and innovative poetic practice. Dickinson grew up reading poetry of (for that time) experimental and at times markedly irregular forms; her own numerous variations from standard ballad and hymn meter are in tune with this aspect of her contemporaries' poetry, although they push farther in the degree and frequency of the irregularity and combine these features with a strikingly original compression of syntax and meaning. Second,

Dickinson's education at Amherst Academy encouraged by rule and example the idea that form should be driven by content, not by any kind of rule. Third, nineteenth-century American definitions of and references to "lyric" rarely mention subjectivity, address, or temporality—the characteristics centering virtually all twentieth- and twenty-first-century discussion of this genre.[3] Instead, despite the fact that nineteenth-century American poets and critics were well versed in British (and, typically, German) romanticism, they tended to understand the lyric in relation to song, which is to say sound, music, harmoniousness, "Beauty." Lyric, in short, was scarcely distinguished from the lyrical. Reading Dickinson with attention to the properties of lyric valorized by her contemporaries returns us to features of her verse currently largely ignored or interpreted simplistically: in particular the sonic qualities of rhythm, assonance, alliteration, rhyme, and repetition.

The aspect of nineteenth-century American verse most often overlooked or thinly understood by current readers is the formal. For Dickinson and her peers, poetry was an art conceived in relation to rhythm, figure, and sound, although these elements were regarded as secondary to the extent that they were assumed to enable the thought and feeling of the verse. The metrical structures and properties of sound of Dickinson's poems both link her more closely to the art of her generation than has been acknowledged and distinguish her as a great poet. Although aesthetic norms had changed by the end of the century, Dickinson's poetic practices remained within the formal range extolled as exemplary according to the praise her poems received when they were first published in 1890—in contrast to the widely held assumption that Dickinson was roundly condemned by her first reviewers. As Willis Buckingham summarizes, within the decade following the publication of *Poems,* five hundred commentaries on Dickinson's work appeared in print, most of them written by critics on average fifteen years her junior—that is, readers educated in the 1860s and 1870s, not, like her, in the 1840s and 1850s ("Poetry Readers"). One of the two most frequently used words in these reviews was "genius"; moreover, despite the fact that these reviewers were primarily of a younger generation, Buckingham asserts that their "desired poetical goals remain thought and feeling, to the poetic expression of which some critics believe song and sound are indispensable." "When Dickinson is faulted," in these 1890s reviews, "it is almost always for her technical irregularities," and yet, Buckingham notes, "a surprising number of nineties reviewers, admitting the absence of conventional metrics, nevertheless rejoiced in her *wilding* music" (166, my emphasis). In her own day, this appreciation would have been less "surprising"—and indeed the fact that Dickinson was compared to ninety-five other writers in these early reviews indicates that she was far from unique in bending conventional forms.[4]

In 1862, Thomas Wentworth Higginson does not condemn Dickinson's verse as being out of line with that of their contemporaries: he calls it "spasmodic"—the name given to a group of radical and controversial poets Dickinson admired—including Keats, Shelley, Byron, Barrett Browning, the young Tennyson, De Quincy, Alexander Smith, and Emily Bronte.[5] Dickinson's admiration of both the Brownings, Keats, and Tennyson is well known; she also extolls Smith's "exquisite frensy," claiming that his *Poems* contains "some wonderful figures, as ever I met in my life," although they "are not very coherent"—all characteristics of the Spasmodics (L128, 19 June 1853). Similar writers were described by Henry James as belonging to an "Azarian School" of writing, named after Harriet Prescott Spofford's novel *Azarian*.[6] Dickinson praised Spofford's early stories to Susan Gilbert, precisely the stories James protests against in his 1865 review.[7] Spofford herself later comments that she stopped writing in this style because "the public taste changed. With the coming of Mr. Howells as editor of the *Atlantic* [in 1866], and his influence, the realistic arrived. I doubt if anything I wrote in those days would be accepted by any magazine now."[8] Even in the 1890s, enough of a taste for poetry that played against standard metrical and rhyming forms remained (or had developed anew), however, for sales of Dickinson's *Poems* to reach 10,000 by 1900, not including an additional 10,000 cumulative sales of the second and third series of her poems and a volume of letters.[9]

Despite decades of cultural and historical criticism to the contrary, Dickinson is still frequently described as anomalous and unique in her formal aesthetic, hence (with Whitman) as a solitary forerunner of modernist and later avant-gardist poetics. Because the majority of nineteenth-century verse maintained a type of diction, syntax, and descriptive detail that sounded stilted or overblown to the twentieth-century ear and because it focused on topics and emotional registers already dropping from high regard by the end of the nineteenth century, other aspects of this verse have also inaccurately been heard as stodgy or without significant variation. A reader of the nineteenth century, accustomed to sentimentality and the diction of neo-classical, Romantic, and Victorian verse, however, would have perceived an impressive variety of formal structures, topics, tonal registers, and types of audience addressed. Although it seems counter-intuitive, mid-nineteenth-century innovation in the lyric functions as a direct forerunner to modernist rejection of fixed form and poetic closure, as practiced generally and especially as combined in Dickinson's poems with terse philosophizing and great syntactic compression. Dickinson's contemporaries offered her useful models for manipulating popular forms and experimenting with ways of understanding the relation of language, thought, and patterned form.

Dickinson grew up in a world of verse—from prayers in the *New England Primer* and the verse alphabet she rewrote with the names of her friends to hymn-singing in church and an extensive range of poetry owned by her family and bearing marks of her attention.[10] Although pentameter verse had the greatest status, short-lined verse was ubiquitous during the antebellum period. Even narrative poems like Longfellow's *Hiawatha* or serious British verse like Tennyson's "In Memoriam," use tetrameter, or sometimes a looser 4-beat line, and the most popular short-lined form was the ballad or ballad-style poem that used some variation of 3- and 4-beat lines. Narrative poems were popular during this century and poets blended lyric and narrative properties in various ways. In 1789 in England, Wordsworth and Coleridge touted their blending of lyric and narrative genres in *Lyrical Ballads.* In the United States, Dickinson enthusiastically recommended Longfellow's 1847 *Evangeline* to a friend in an 1848 letter, and both it and his 1855 *Hiawatha* sold thousands of copies. In the same letter, Dickinson also mentions that she is reading Tennyson's verse narrative *The Princess.*[11] Later, Elizabeth Barrett Browning's 1857 *Aurora Leigh* was among her favorite poems. Dickinson also marked extensively "Spasmodic" poet Alexander Smith's popular 157-page poem "A Life Drama" (1852), and two other long poems (around 35 pages each) by Barrett Browning, "The Poet's Vows" and "A Vision of Poets." Although not fictional, James Russell Lowell's *A Fable for Critics* evidently also entertained Dickinson, since it is extensively marked.[12] Poe could not have been more mistaken in his 1850 essay "The Poetic Principle" when he claims that the "long poem" will "never be popular again" (*Selected Writings* 465).

Dickinson wrote no long poems and there is little evidence that she conceived of her poems in significant relation to thematic or narrative clusters or sequences, given that she never revised fascicle booklet arrangements in the way she does the wording of individual lyrics.[13] She nevertheless experiments in her poems with the boundaries of narrative, dramatic, and lyric properties, all of which undermine the notion of a personally subjective lyric speaker and hence also of the lyric poem as a private reflection, "overheard" by its readers—as John Stuart Mill put it in 1833.[14] As is frequently noted, many of her poems use the diction of gothic or sentimental fiction, and her admiration of Robert Browning and of long narrative poems may have influenced the dialogic quality of her verse. In contrast, there is little acknowledgment of the very wide variety and number of dramatic lyrics that Dickinson composed in her experiments with lyric strains. Long poems typically contained several set pieces: riddles, songs, dialogue, apostrophes, elegies—again a fluidity of boundary that may have inspired Dickinson's lyrics. Because lyric theorizing is particularly active at present, I linger on the implications of current genre criticism for thinking about Dickinson's poetry.

If the lyric expresses in its intensest form the subjectivity of the poet him or her self (the most common definition), or follows any of the more complex equations having to do with time, deixis, and address developed in the mid and late twentieth century, then Dickinson's multiple definition poems and patently fictitious uses of the pronoun "I" must call into doubt whether her poems are lyric—leading to claims like Virginia Jackson's in *Dickinson's Misery* that Dickinson does not in fact write lyric poems.[15] Lyric has indeed become nearly synonymous with "poetry," as Jackson argues, but this is not a new phenomenon. New is only the distinctly narrowing effect of such synonymity during the twentieth century.[16] Marjorie Perloff goes so far as to say that interest in poetic sound has been dampened by the "continuing dominance of Romantic lyric theory, with its equation of 'poetry' and 'lyric,' coupled with an understanding of 'lyric' as *the* mode of subjectivity—of self-reflexiveness, the mode in which a solitary I is overheard in meditation or conversation with an unnamed other" ("Sound of Poetry" 750). In contrast, in the early and mid nineteenth-century United States, "lyric" described any poetry that was not distinctly dramatic, epic, or narrative, that was harmonic or musical in its language, or that was conceived as song. Dickinson's poetry fit this model.

Gender also significantly affects critical definition of lyric in ways directly linked to Dickinson's era and poetics.[17] The scholars contributing to Laura Mandell's *Poetess Archive Journal* and database represent nineteenth-century writing in relation to "the poetess tradition." Mandell focuses on the late eighteenth- and nineteenth-century production of poetry "written in what came to be designated an 'effeminate' style, whether written by men or women" and primarily associated with female poets who called themselves or were called poetesses; in the United States the dates for such identification and practice are given as 1773 to 1865 (Archive "Introduction"). Mandell frequently refers to "poetess" verse as "flowery" and "sentimental," noting that it uses "easily imitable forms" (primarily ballad-style).[18] More specifically, under "Uses of the Archive," she claims:

> There are a number of poetic conventions characterizing the poetess tradition: artificial diction, tetrameter and trimeter metric systems, conventional and apparently uncritical sentiments, direct quotation of other poets, salient rhyme schemes, linguistic transparency, and a focus on the themes of patriotism and domesticity. The term thus links gender to poetic style. As feminine, the poetess tradition has been continuously maligned. An early nineteenth-century reviewer remarks that female poets 'disregarded the high art of poetry.'

While Mandell does not conflate this tradition of writing with the lyric, the association between lyric and the short-lined forms she describes is strong, hence she implies that the lyric also is a primarily "effeminate" or female-associated genre during the nineteenth century. Margaret Dickie makes this association explicit, arguing that the lyric's "brief, repetitive, and figurative" properties "articulate a sense of the self as particular, discontinuous, limited, private, hidden" (537, 539). Hence she claims that the genre as a whole is "publicly degraded," a form associated with women and "considered insufficient to express the grandness" of the U.S. or of American individualism (537, 539).[19] In contrast to Mandell, Paula Bennett argues that the "poetess" model was far more pervasive in Britain than in the U.S. and that it does not accurately represent even early nineteenth-century American poetry, let alone that written over a period of ninety years (*Public Sphere*). Similarly, Shira Wolosky stresses the range of political, religious, and otherwise public, socially significant and acclaimed poetry written by women during this century (*Poetry and Public Discourse*).[20]

The gendering of genre is an under-theorized aspect of genre criticism. For at least two centuries, the lyric has been associated in broad terms with Sappho and the feminine just as the epic has been associated with masculine heroics and makers (Keller and Miller; Prins, *Victorian Sappho*). Perhaps because of the popularity of nineteenth-century poetry, there has also been some conflation of verse with popular culture generally. Critics like Andreas Huyssen have persuasively argued that political and aesthetic discourse in the late nineteenth century gendered mass culture as feminine. Indeed, the nineteenth-century popular imagination increasingly regarded all artists and writers, not just lyric poets, as feminine. Powerful cultural spokesmen pushed back against this characterization. Early in the nineteenth century, Sir Walter Scott masculinized the ballad tradition by collecting Scottish martial ballads. Longfellow attempted to professionalize the calling of the poet in part by establishing the poet as masculine (Rubin 29).[21] An 1860 review of Lowell's *Fresh Hearts that Failed Three Thousand Years Ago* calls "The Brave Old Ship, The Orient" a "truly masculine poem, full of vigor and imagination" (760). David Atwood Wasson compares one of Whittier's poems to a battle in its importance—surely the most masculinizing analogy possible: "'Barbara Frietchie' is the true sequel to the Battle of Gettysburg, is that other victory which the nation *asked* of Meade the soldier and obtained from Whittier the poet" (338). In the same spirit of devaluing stereotyped femininity, an anonymous reviewer praises a volume of poems by Anne Whitney for its:

> absence of all 'female' lamentations. [Whitney] evidently does not belong to the sisterhood of weeping poetesses. She does not cry out on every page that she is a woman, and particularly distressed, abused, and wretched, solely on that account. There is no arrogant vaunting of strength, no sickening display of 'weakness,' no

questioning, no apologizing for thinking, or doing, because she is a woman . . . but as a soul she addresses herself to souls in a higher region, alike independent of sex or condition. ("Poets and Poetry," *SR* 2 July 1859)

Gender association with the lyric functioned differently for men like Long-fellow or Whittier, who had an investment in the public status of the profession of the poet, and for women like Dickinson, for whom there was no question of public professionalism. Moreover, from Dickinson's perspective, writers such as Tennyson, Longfellow, Bryant, Lowell, and Whittier were lionized by an adoring public, not demasculinized. Lyrics were also used to espouse the most serious and public causes of the 1840s and 1850s—for example, abolition. And poetry remained the most prestigious literary form throughout the nine-teenth century. Even when Oliver Wendell Holmes characterizes the "glitter-ing lyric" as gleaming "like a diamond on a dancing girl," he calls his own poems "Lyrics" and describes "Anacreon's numbers" as "glid[ing]" from "Saxon lips," using an ethnic designator signifying masculine prowess and pointed reference to Anacreon, not Sappho, as the great classical lyricist.[22]

It is clear from her correspondence and from her poems on poetry that Dickinson regarded the poet as powerful and poetry as an expression rival-ing divine epiphany in its ability to inspire, not as effeminate. In 1851 she writes to Sue that "we are the only poets"—clearly a mark of their distinc-tion, not their limitation or weakness (L56). In "reckon[ing]" the worth of poetry, Dickinson compares it with the Sun, Summer, and the "Heaven of God," then concludes "Poets – All –," or that poets are above the rest (F533). "To pile like Thunder" represents poetry as "coeval" with love and as having the same power on a reader as "see[ing] God" (F1353). Such effusions do not point toward her regarding poetry as a secondary genre. For Dickinson, all language has power, and language that "live[s]" through the crafted forms of poetry rivals the force of divinity and nature: poetry "stun[s] . . . With Bolts – of Melody!" (F348).[23] When Dickinson represents herself as a poet or constructs figures of creative force in her poems, she often uses feminine meta-phors, and primary elements of her diction come from domestic or other-wise feminized spheres or respond to gendered constructions of the natural (Miller, *Poet's Grammar* 158–59, 166–70). Similarly, her favored form is a brief short-lined variant of popular ballad or hymn structures—albeit typically without the other elements identified by Mandell as "effeminate." As a genre, however, poetry for her is synonymous with acts and conditions of power.

Perhaps Dickinson chooses indeterminate reference in many poems to prevent the possibility of friends or future readers identifying her with the personalized "sisterhood of weeping poetesses," instead blending impersonal forms like definitions, philosophical speculation, and dramatic lyrics with poems of distinct but unplaced sentiment and experience.[24] In 1862, Dickinson writes to Higginson that her "I" is "the Representative of the Verse – it does not mean – me – but a supposed person"—that is, she rejects the position of expressing personal subjectivity in her poems (L268).[25] A few years earlier, in 1856, Julia Ward Howe similarly distinguishes the "I" of her verse from personal expression: in her poem "The Lyric I," Howe writes that "The philosophic I, is not / The I that any man may meet / On errands of familiar use, / Or held to greetings in the street . . . Is not the I that wastes the meal, / And leaves hiatus in the shirt" (6). Both Howe and Dickinson make this categorical distinction unapologetically and with the assumption both that the distinction needs to be made and that it does not require elaboration.

Giorgio Agamben surprisingly echoes nineteenth-century American understanding of the lyric in writing that poetry exists "only in the tension and difference (and hence also virtual interference) between sound and sense"; "verse is the being that dwells in this schism":

> it is as if, having met each other, each of the two movements [language's movement toward sense and a discourse . . . moving from comprehension to sound] then followed the other's tracks, such that language found itself led back in the end to language, and comprehension to comprehension. This inverted chiasm—this and nothing else—is what we call poetry. This chiasm is, beyond every vagueness, poetry's crossing with thought, the thinking essence of poetry and the poeticizing essence of thought.[26]

This definition of poetry as moving simultaneously toward both concrete properties of language and comprehension resembles the focus of Dickinson's peers on the qualities of "Beauty" and "Truth," also called "argument" or "sense," in poetry. An appreciation of nineteenth-century American aesthetics requires a decisive return to "Beauty" or "sound," that is, the lyrical aspect of the lyric poem, and acknowledgment that didactic and philosophical argument were fully compatible with "lyric" practice.

Arguing from Dickinson's readings of philosophy, schoolbooks, and lexical debates, Jed Deppman proposes that Dickinson's poems of thought, or of trying-to-think, constitute a "new generic shape for the lyric" (62). This new poetic form attempts to "force the mind to do something extremely difficult"—as in "I tried to think a lonelier Thing / Than any I had seen –" (F570), or "I think To Live – may be a Bliss" (F757), or "I many times thought Peace had come" (F737).[27] According to Deppman, Dickinson felt that "lyric poetry was the best language game in which to pursue . . . difficult projects of thought" (5). As Erika Scheurer puts it, Dickinson "sets up an exploratory mode of discourse—the mind thinking, not the mind having thought" ("Epistolary Voice"). My research indicates (as do Deppman and Scheurer) that Dickinson had ample models in the mid-nineteenth century for thinking of poetry—and in particular the relatively brief, short-lined poem—as a genre open to formal experimentation and "projects of thought."[28] She foregrounds this process of thinking in a way that makes it effectively new, but both thinking and sonic qualities ground nineteenth-century definitions of the lyric.

Dickinson writes about "poetry," not the "lyric," a word she never uses in extant letters or verse. Mid-nineteenth-century educational texts, common reference, and poetic practice, however, provide a sense of the contours of the lyric as she is likely to have understood it. Richard Green Parker's *Aids to English Composition* consists of numerous short sections defining genres, rhetorical figures, tropes, and aspects of grammar and punctuation including examples and exercises for the student under each category.[29] He defines the lyric briefly and restrictively as "that kind of poetry which is written to accompany the lyre, or other musical instrument. The versification may either be regular, or united in fanciful combinations, in correspondence with the strain for which it is composed" (284). This definition is followed by entries on the ballad, ode, sonnet, cantata, epigram, logogriph (riddle), madrigal, pastoral, elegy, and epitaph, among others. Parker later states that "The higher species of poetry embraces the three following divisions, namely: 1. Tales and Romances. 2. Epic and Dramatic Poetry. 3. Didactic and Descriptive Poetry" (294) but defines "Romance" in relation to minstrel verse, and gives Milton's "L'Allegro" and "Il Penseroso" as examples of descriptive poems, as well as noting "another class of poems, uniting the didactic and the descriptive classes, . . . which are called the Sentimental" (295, 298, 299). In short, while the lyric is not listed as a "higher species of poetry" two of the three "higher" categories are presented as including poetry associated with lyric.[30] In some ways Dickinson strained the boundaries of the contemporary lyric, but those boundaries were capacious.

Parker's definition of lyric is consistent with other definitions of the time, although general usage of the word was more inclusive. For example, Dickinson's 1842 Webster's defines "lyric poetry" as "such as is sung to the harp or lyre," mentioning Anacreon, Alcæus, Stesichorus, Sappho, and Horace as "distinguished" practitioners (EDL). Pond's Murray's *Grammar,* also used at Amherst Academy, describes the "three objects of verse" as "melody, harmony, and expression" (202).[31] In an 1831 *Church Psalmody,* editors Lowell Mason and David Greene write at length on "lyric poetry" both as "Matter" and "Structure" in their preface, in ways that clarify the musical reference in Parker, Webster, and Pond's Murray's *Grammar:* "The aim of all lyric poetry," Mason and Greene write, "should be to express *emotion,* and the *sentiments* should be such as are adapted to this end. This is the original and natural office of all poetry; and it is more especially the natural office of all poetry which is designed to be used in connection with music. Poetry itself is the language of emotion; and that only is good lyric poetry, which requires the aid of music to produce its full effect." The authors then distinguish merely "didactic" hymns that "preach," despite the fact that they can be set to music, from those that "sing": "This forcibly bringing syllables and notes into contact, and pronouncing them together, is not singing, any more than noise is music"—that is, the lyric quality of the hymn inheres in the poem's harmonic strains, not in setting it to notes. Mason and Greene later describe Isaac Watts, whose compositions make up a good percentage of their volume, as having "written more good psalms and hymns of a highly lyrical character, than any other author, . . . [and] probably . . . nearly half of all the valuable lyric poetry in the language" (viii). On the secular side, the *Atlantic Monthly* provides a similar definitional range. Over half the uses of the word "lyric" appearing in its first twelve issues suggest something harmonious or graceful and the others are basically interchangeable with "poetry" that is not specifically a drama, epic, or verse novel.[32] A June 1860 review praises a poem as the best in the volume because it is "embodied with true lyric feeling" (760); W. L. Symonds writes that modern literature begins with troubadour songs: "Europe became vocal in every part with fantastic poems, lyrical in the South epical in the North" (132). In an 1863 retrospective on "Longfellow," George W. Curtis writes, "Who is a poet but he whom the heart of man permanently accepts as a singer of its own hopes, emotions, and thoughts? And what is poetry but that song?" (770). According to these uses, the lyric included tavern singing, occasional poems, and sea ballads as well as more elite verse associated with music, feeling, and beauty.

Emerson and Poe, poets significant to Dickinson during her youth, see lyric qualities as definitive of all poetry, although not surprisingly, they evaluate what constitute lyric qualities and their importance to the poem differently. In "The Poet," Emerson distinguishes a "writer of lyrics" or mere "lyrist" from a "poet," proposing that "it is not metres, but a metre-making argument that makes a poem"—a passage on a page Dickinson appears to mark in her own volume by folding it in half (EDR 21; *EmEL* 450).[33] Poets should be both "children of music" (presumably "lyrists") and "Language-maker[s]" for whom thought drives the rhythm (*EmEL* 450, 456–57). Consequently, meter-making "argument" is not simply rational or didactic; it is based on an "abandonment to the nature of things"; "the poet knows that he speaks adequately . . . only when he speaks somewhat wildly, or 'with the flower of the mind'" (459), inspired by and creating "Beauty" (468). Or as Emerson writes in "Nature," borrowing from Keats's famous lines, "Whilst thus the poet animates nature with his own thoughts, he differs from the philosopher only herein, that the one proposes Beauty as his main end; the other Truth. But the philosopher, not less than the poet, postpones the apparent order and relations of things to the empire of thought. . . . The true philosopher and the true poet are one, and a beauty, which is truth, and a truth, which is beauty, is the aim of both" (*EmEL* 36). Thought, then, is indivisible from "music" or "Beauty" for the poet.

Emerson's poem "Merlin" makes much the same argument: the poet "shall not his brain encumber / With the coil of rhythm and number; / But, leaving rule and pale forethought, / He shall aye climb / For his rhyme." The poet's "mighty line" can "bereave[] a tyrant of his will"; it makes "the wild blood" of the reader "start"; but the poem must discard "efficacious rhymes" to reach this power (*Poems* 182, 180, 183). Similarly, in his 1841 "Lecture on the Times," Emerson complains that in "the current literature and poetry" the "thinker gives me results, and never invites me to be present with him at his invocation of truth, and to enjoy with him its proceeding into his mind"; Emerson wants thought or argument that are in process, precisely the form Deppman claims that Dickinson creates in her poems (*EmEL* 165–66). Understanding the importance of an active intelligence within the poem, for Dickinson and some of her contemporaries, may also help to distinguish her work from the "poetess" model ridiculed by Mark Twain, whose Emmeline Grangerford "could rattle off poetry like nothing. She didn't ever have to stop to think" (140).[34]

In partial contrast, in "The Philosophy of Composition" and "The Poetic Principle," Poe defines "poetry" as synonymous with the lyric. A poem, he claims, cannot last longer than it would take one to read in a "single sitting." Consequently, *Paradise Lost* is "essentially prose"; "a long poem does not exist" (*Selected Writings* 455, 464).[35] Moreover, "Beauty is the sole legitimate province of the poem" (455)—or, as he puts it in another essay, we "correctly deduce the *novelty,* the *originality,* the *invention,* the *imagination,* or lastly the *creation* of BEAUTY . . . as the essence of all Poesy."[36] This claim underscores the primary argument of Poe's "Principle" and primary point of contrast with Emerson: for Poe, the true "heresy" among nineteenth-century writers of poetry is that "the ultimate object of Poetry is Truth" or "*The Didactic*" ("Philosophy" 468). While Emerson is suspicious of the "jingling serenader's art" or merely musical poem, and calls Poe "the jingle man," Poe subordinates all else to the aesthetic.[37]

Like Emerson, Dickinson regards the process of thinking as central to her poetry—an idea she may have grown up with: her father writes in an 1828 piece in the *New England Inquirer* that "Wordsworth is one of the few poets who will be read in the next generation" because "[a]long with the delicious melodies which he pours forth, he has *thought* on every page" (in Fisher and Rabe 52). In her poems, Dickinson ponders whether one can, or dares to, articulate truth; "Tell all the truth but tell it slant – . . . The Truth must dazzle gradually / Or every man be blind –" (F1263), she famously writes.[38] A form like the lyric that proceeds by "meter-making" or slant "argument" may have been ideal for her attempts to process and communicate "truth." The speaker who "preached about Breadth till it argued him narrow" also preached "of Truth until it proclaimed him a Liar / The Truth never flaunted a sign –" (F1266A).[39] Unlike opinion, "Truth, outlasts the Sun –" (F1495) but it is frightening: "The truth I do not dare to know / I muffle with a jest." (F1750). Facing truths, for her, is as much a narrative as a philosophical activity; historical or biblical tales, parables, and anecdotes from daily life allow contemplation that does not necessarily lead to conclusive thought. For example, in "Tell as a Marksman – were forgotten" (F1148) she relates the story of William Tell, one of several stories of European national liberation heroes popular in her day. William Cullen Bryant's version of this story, "William Tell. A Sonnet" (marked in the table of contents of his *Poems*), predictably stresses Tell's "great work to set thy country free"; Dickinson's tale is far less clear about what point it moves toward.[40] While neither Emerson nor Dickinson understands truth in the form of Poe's italics, as *The Didactic*," they see part of the work of poetry as provoking and engaging in risky thought.

Holmes represents the lyric as giving body to "thought" in his March 1858 "The Autocrat of the Breakfast Table," his regular *Atlantic Monthly* feature. Quoting his fictional "friend, the Poet," Holmes writes: "A lyric conception . . . hits me like a bullet in the forehead. I have often had the blood drop from my cheeks when it struck . . . then a sudden flush and a beating of the vessels in the head, —then a long sigh, —and the poem is written." This poem is not "impromptu," however, since Holmes's fictional poet immediately distinguishes between the poem "written" and the poem "*copied*"—between what he calls the poem's "soul" and its "body" that "men read and publishers pay for." The poem's soul is "born in an instant in the poet's soul," but it exists only "potentially" in that state and cannot with certainty be copied into "stanzas" (614). Moreover, the poem comes "as a thought, tangled in the meshes of a few sweet words,—words that have loved each other from the cradle of the language, but have never been wedded until now" (614). Presumably, the poem's thought cannot be disentangled from that original and "sweet" combination of words as they are written into the requisite "stanzas" or meter. Julia Ward Howe also suggests that thought is a provenance of the lyric poem; in the last lines of "The Lyric I" she hopes her poem will be "a boon / For all who weep, and think, and love." Parker's *English Composition* claims that "True poetry consists in the idea, and it may be presented even in the form of prose. It addresses itself to the imagination and to the feelings" (245–46n). As these various accounts suggest, the mid-nineteenth-century American conception of the lyric was not based on formal, optative, or topical exclusions but had to do with concepts like music, beauty, the imagination, and thought. The poem referred to as lyric was typically brief, beautiful or musical, and articulated its point in a fitting and "sweet" form, combining words "never . . . wedded until now." In his preface to Dickinson's 1890 *Poems,* Higginson similarly praises both the "glimpses of a lyric strain" and her poems' "main quality . . . of extraordinary grasp and insight, uttered with an uneven vigor sometimes exasperating, seemingly wayward, but really unsought and inevitable. After all, when a thought takes one's breath away, a lesson on grammar is an impertinence" ("Preface" vi).

While Dickinson's originality is manifest both in the thoughts or expressions of her poems and in her formal inventiveness, there was a general proclivity for innovation in short-lined verse in every publishing venue she knew during her youth and through her period of greatest productivity. To return to Dickinson's schoolbooks, Ebenezer Porter's *Rhetorical Reader* provides a selection of 59 poems or poetic excerpts among its elocutionary exercises, the majority of which (34 out of 59) use pentameter lines.[41] The twenty-five shorter-lined poems or excerpts, however, occur in twenty-two distinct formal patterns, differentiated by line length, construction of verse stanza, and rhyme scheme, with some following no consistency in proceeding from one stanza to the next. This plethora of forms and level of inconsistency are utterly at odds with twentieth- and twenty-first-century representations of nineteenth-century verse. While such inventiveness is associated historically with the ode, many of these examples share no other feature of this form.[42] As Parker's textbook put it in defining "lyric," their "fanciful combinations" are "united" through the poem's rhythmic strain and its narrative or argument (284). Charles Sprague's "Fathers of New England," for example, consists of five stanzas of 20, 14, 10, 20 and 18 lines respectively. The arrangement of line lengths varies in each stanza and the rhyme scheme varies from couplets and abab sequences to aabccb and abba, also in varying sequences and patterns in each stanza (Porter 215–17). Fitz-Greene Halleck, another American author, writes the frequently anthologized "Marco Bozzaris" in stanzas of varied lengths and varying rhyme schemes, using a tetrameter base, but concluding each major syntactic unit with a trimeter line. The first stanza has eleven lines and rhymes ababccdeeed, while the second has fourteen lines and rhymes abccaabddeffe, and so on (122–23).[43] Fifteen of the twenty-two examples of short-lined verse represented in Porter's instructional *Reader* combine distinct variations of iambic or trochaic trimeter, tetrameter, and catalectic meter.

Breaking away from ruled forms, a practice associated with natural "wildness," figured largely in American aesthetics. According to Sandra Runzo, "wild" and "irregular" Irish music was highly popular in the early nineteenth

century (chap. 2). Part of the popularity of ballads was their "natural" style—
characterized by Sir Walter Scott as providing "emancipation from the rules"
of dramatic unities and strict verse form, and "reliev[ing] from shackles" poets
who followed their model "to present life in its scenes of wildest contrast, and
in all its boundless variety of character" (45).[44] In this 1830 essay, Scott stresses
the bold and sublime "wildness" of the ancient forms. In the *Atlantic*, Lowell
ridicules poems with predictable rhyme and meter, and Holmes calls them "pi-
ous plums."[45] Charles Halpine praises Tennyson as having a muse "wild and
wilful . . . defiant of rules, and daringly insubordinate to arbitrary forms" such
as the sonnet or "other such Procrustean moulds into which poetic thought is
at times cast"; he could write well only when allowed full innovative rein, Halpine declares (463).[46] Curtis's review praises Longfellow's "Saga of King Olaf"
as using "every variety of measure, heroic, elegiac, lyrical" in telling "the wild
old Scandinavian tradition" (773). In 1854 Henry David Thoreau famously proclaims, "I love the wild not less than the good" and Whitman's 1855 argument
for free form is in this sense entirely in step with the times; as he writes in his
"Preface," "The rhyme and uniformity of perfect poems show the free growth
of metrical laws and bud from them as unerringly and loosely as lilacs or roses
on a bush" (*Walden* 149; *LOG* v). The *Springfield Republican* strongly endorsed
Aurora Leigh by printing lengthy sections of the poem on the first page of its 1
January 1857 issue, commenting that the poem will not be popular because "its
materials are drawn from a realm of thought which is bathed in too subtle an
atmosphere for common breathing, and from forms entirely unfamiliar to the
common eye." And indeed Barrett Browning herself echoes Emerson's call for
a poet to follow a meter-making argument, not "form" itself:

> What form is best for poems? Let me think
> Of forms less, and the external. Trust the spirit,
> As Sovran nature does, to make the form;
> For otherwise we only imprison spirit,
> And not embody.[47]

Barrett Browning here champions some element of formal experimentation, in
lines markedly varying from iambic pentameter. As these examples demonstrate, Porter is not alone in representing poems of varied and irregular forms
as exemplary, thereby implicitly instructing students to write in innovative
forms, trust their "spirit," or be "defiant of rules"—at least in short-lined verse.

Other instructional texts echo Porter's implied message and his selection.
As previously noted, Parker's *English Composition* not only asserts that "true
poetry" adheres in the "idea" of the poem but distinguishes between "perfect" and "allowable" rhymes, thereby encouraging at least some deviation
from strict rhyming practice, and indeed many of Dickinson's peers use slant

rhymes (245–46).[48] William H. McGuffy's popular *Reader* contains fewer but equally varied short-lined poems. These include an unrhymed poem by Robert Southey in which every stanza has a different arrangement of line lengths, varying from 6 to 10 syllables, an excerpt from William Collins's "The Passions," even more varied in stanza lengths and line lengths within stanzas, and ten biblical passages written in unrhymed, unmetered verse lines of highly varied length.[49] Rufus Griswold's 1843 *Readings in American Poetry,* "designed principally for the use of schools," suggests that American authors may have been particularly apt to write in short-lined verse with a loose metrical norm and variant rhyme scheme (3). Out of the 130 poems in this collection, 68 are short-lined, and of the remaining 62 written partly or wholly in pentameter or longer lines, 15 contain as many short lines (usually trimeters) as long. These "essentially American" poems, "in spirit as well as by origin," favor tetrameters, followed closely by variations on the ballad meter combination of tetrameter and trimeter. Again, the inclusion of six poems highly irregular in stanza length, meter, and rhyme scheme indicates that irregularity is compatible with excellence and, in this case, "essentially American" spirit. Irregularly structured poems appear in standard elocutionary readers from the time Dickinson entered school through the period when she had written the majority of her poems. The impression Dickinson or any other teenager learning from such readers would receive is that poetry is written in multiple forms and that short-lined and relatively brief poems allow for particularly fertile formal innovation. They would also infer that formal innovation is admirable and contributes to the excellence of the poem.

Dickinson's reading at home would only have strengthened these lessons. The family's 1849 volume of Bryant's *Poems*—which includes pencil markings throughout the table of contents and on several poems—contains many short-lined poems, and several poems with lines of varying length: "Hymn to the North Star," for example, has lines from six to twelve syllables in a 6-line stanza (EDR 246). Out of the eighty-three poems in Adelaide Anne Proctor's *Legends and Lyrics,* all but seventeen are short-lined, and several of those seventeen combine long and short lines—for example lines of alternating three and eleven syllables in "Because" or ten and four syllables in "A Comfort" (EDR 405)—a pattern Dickinson also experiments with, for example, in "One Crucifixion is recorded – only –" (F670).[50] Next to Dickinson, Longfellow is the master of his age in metrical inventiveness, and his 1850 collection of *Poems* contains eight poems of highly irregular form—differing line lengths, stanza lengths, rhyme schemes, and organization of line lengths within stanzas. Longfellow also uses the greatest variety of forms, from poems written entirely in lines of four to six syllables ("Afternoon in February") to the long-lined "To the Driving Cloud," which constructs its 6-beat lines from a combination of dactyls and trochees, in ballad style. In this volume's eighty-two poems not including "Translations" or a verse novel and verse drama, Long-fellow uses thirty-nine distinct forms, and he repeats only eight metrical patterns in the whole volume.[51] Longfellow's interest in formal innovation and irregularity is marked in his headnote to "The Elected Knight" a poem "trans-lated from the Middle Ages," where he remarks that "The irregularities of the original have been carefully preserved" (*Poems* 193).[52] This is a far cry from current critical assumption that nineteenth-century editors as standard prac-tice edited out "irregularities."

Holmes, another favorite poet of Dickinson's, writes frequently in a variety of short-lined forms. In his 1851 *Poems,* the section titled "Lyrics" includes eighteen distinct metrical structures, most in some variety of tetrameter and trimeter in quatrains or double quatrains; only six poems in this section in-clude lines ten syllables or longer. Bayard Taylor's *Romances, Lyrics, and Songs* (1852) includes twenty distinct metrical forms in sections titled "Lyrics" and "Songs and Sonnets"; these forms range from the sonnet and ballad to poems like "Love and Solitude," which combines lines from four to twelve syllables in inconsistent patterns with irregular rhyme schemes, and rhyming lines of different lengths (EDR 311). In an 1853 volume of Tennyson's *Poems,* Dickin-son marks a poem with a very unusual sequence of line lengths: "Song" has 12-line stanzas with line lengths running 885(10)(10)3958(10)89 syllables, and a rhyme scheme of aabccbbadefe. A few pages later, the poem "Adeline" con-tains stanzas of irregular length (from nine to sixteen lines) and an irregular rhyme scheme.[53] Similarly, Barrett Browning's 1852 *Poems* includes poems with variable stanza and line lengths—for example, "Isobel's Child," a heavily marked poem, contains stanzas varying from two to fifty-three lines.[54]

Dickinson's newspaper reading similarly supported the lessons of her schoolbooks and favorite volumes of poetry that innovation and formal ir-regularity were sanctioned. The *Republican* frequently published poetry in its pages, especially on Saturdays. In the first five months of 1857, it printed a majority of poems using some version of a 4-beat line, or combination of 3- and 4-beat lines. Eight of these poems are irregular in both sequence of line length and stanza lengths (those that observe stanza divisions), and typically use irregular or no rhyme—like "The Sweet Uses of Adversity," a 23-line poem with lines of three to thirteen syllables, without rhyme (16 May 1857). "Lost and Won" by J. W. N. Jr. has seven stanzas varying in length from two to eight lines, differing line-lengths within stanzas, and various rhyme schemes (10 January 1857); "Deborah Lee," by the pseudonymous Fuzzy Guzzy, has irregu-lar stanza length (from six to eleven lines), line lengths (from 5- to 10-syllables), and no rhyme (21 February 1857).[55] And Dickinson would surely have appreci-ated a poem printed on the same day as her "The Sleeping" ("Safe in their

Alabaster Chambers –"), namely Emily Judson's "Growing Dark," where a lizard

> . . . ventures boldly out,
> And looks about,
> And with his hollow feet
> Treads his small evening beat,
> Darting upon his prey
> In such a tricksy, winsome sort of way,
> His delicate marauding seems no sin.
>
> . . . .
>
> The beetle's drone
> Turns to a dirge-like solitary moan;
> Night deepens, and I sit, in cheerless doubt, alone.

(SR 1 March 1862)

This poem moves from lines of four to twelve syllables in an irregular pattern, following both the movements of small creatures and thoughts of the speaker. The *Republican* publishes poems by famous writers (Longfellow, Whittier, Barrett Browning, Byron, Shelley, Schiller) and unknowns, such as "Dubioso" and "Flirtuoso," who exchange love poems on 7 and 14 February.[56] My point here is that every venue in which Dickinson read poetry during her youth at least occasionally printed poems using non-standard metrical forms, including some verse of irregular meter and rhyme scheme.[57] Much if not all of this verse would have been understood within the broad category of "lyric."

In "Listening to Dickinson," John Shoptaw maps the fertile variation of Dickinson's metrical patterns in 1863, the year of her most active writing, observing that Dickinson "often invent[ed] a meter for a poem and us[ed] it just that once. The number of poems Dickinson composed in 1863 in patterns rare or unheard of in religious or secular lyric poetry, including her own, surpasses even those [she writes] in common meter"—the form Dickinson used most often (39). Reading her varied forms in conjunction with the contemporary verse she was reading, however, reveals that Dickinson's forms were not at all "unheard of"; such variation was presented as a model in rhetorical readers that sold thousands of copies in hundreds of editions throughout her youth and adulthood. Dickinson's poetry was unusual in its radical concision and disjunction, its yoking of strikingly disparate realms of thought or registers of language through metonymy and metaphor, and in its social, philosophical, and religious acuity. Before 1866, she also uses irregular forms for many of her poems. The practice of formal innovation and her understanding of form in relation to sense or argument, however, was thoroughly a product of her time.

From her early schooling, Dickinson would have understood the genre of poetry to be almost infinitely capacious and fluid as to subject matter, address, tone or register of language, and form. Early to mid-nineteenth-century poets apparently regarded especially the short-lined, non-narrative poem as a free field for experimentation. Dickinson's poetic, then, is not striking because it is formally innovative; her innovations simply occur in a larger percentage of her poems and result in better poems because they link more profoundly a "trying to think" or "meter-making" process with highly crafted properties of rhythm and sound. And I would say this is not just because Dickinson is a better poet but because she is a better *lyric* poet, as she would have understood these terms—that is, Dickinson's poetry achieves its thinking and effects through the work of its music, or rhythms and sounds.

Dickinson indicates in several poems that for her sound is a, if not the, key element of poetry and that it is directly linked to thinking and feeling. "The Spirit is the Conscious Ear – / We actually Hear / When We inspect –" she writes (F718). In "The saddest noise, the sweetest noise," the poet concludes, "An ear can break a human heart / As quickly as a spear. / We wish the ear had not a heart / So dangerously near." (F1789). In an 1873 letter, she writes, "The Ear is the last Face" (L405), and later writes again of the "ear of the Heart" (L807, 1883). In "I think I was enchanted," the effect of reading Elizabeth Barrett Browning's poems is at first "Lunacy of Light" but then the poet fills three stanzas imagining the "Titanic Opera" of all creatures in nature and "Days" stepping to "Mighty Metres" (F627). Similarly, in "I cannot dance upon my Toes –," the poet demonstrates "Ballet Knowledge" by parodying that highly visual art before celebrating her verse as having the fullness of "Opera" (F381 B). Most famously, she defines poetry as the sound of a storm: "To pile like Thunder to it's close / Then crumble grand away . . . would be Poetry –" (F1353). In "I would not paint – a picture –" she explains "Nor would I be a Poet –" because "It's finer – Own the Ear –"—or, better yet, combine creativity and "Ear" hence "stun myself / With Bolts – of Melody!" (F348). For Dickinson, as for most readers and writers of the mid-nineteenth century, poetry electrifies through the "Ear." The musicality of Dickinson's verse and the importance of music to her conception of poetry have been commented on by others—especially Judy Jo Small and Sandra Runzo, who writes that music is Dickinson's "trope for the quintessence of life, for the source and harmony of the self" (Runzo, ms 45). In a 1933 review of Dickinson's letters, Marianne Moore refers to "the behavior of an ear that lives on sound" as characterizing Dickinson's verse (*Prose* 292). For nearly a century, composers have demonstrated their sense of her poems' musicality by setting them to music. The critical turn toward cultural studies and historicism since the 1980s and the more particular turn toward materiality as a point of focus in Dickinson studies have downplayed the importance of sound to her verse. Reading Dickinson's poetry

according to the primary concerns of her own era, however, requires attention not just to poetic form but to elements of form that manifest themselves
aurally.

Even were one unable to distinguish poetry from prose in Dickinson's letters through her patterns of capitalization and spacing, there is in all but a
few exceptional cases a difference between the aphoristic concision or even
playful brilliance of her prose and the consistent concentrated sound pat-
ternings of her verse. The central property of all her poems is their structural,
aural, rhythmic, syntactic patterning. From a nineteenth-century perspective, Dickinson's poetry would have been "lyric" because her thoughts were
articulated through significant patterns of rhythm and sound—the "sweetness," "beauty," and originality of their language, their "words that have loved
each other from the cradle of the language, but have never been wedded until
now." While talking about sound is a little like talking about humor—to
analyze it can kill its effect rather than demonstrate its power—I will attempt
to demonstrate the extent to which sound directs the emphasis of Dickinson's
"Titanic Opera" (F627).[58]

Readers of "I felt a Funeral, in my Brain," (F340) debate the extent to which
the brain's "Funeral" is metaphorical; they argue that it refers to death, a mi-
graine, a psychic break, or Dickinson's witness of an actual funeral—perhaps
Frazar Stearns's, who was killed in the Civil War. Similarly, critics debate the
meaning of the poem's inconclusive final "then –": does it mark the utter collapse of life or sense, or does it suggest some unpredictable next step in its sequence of perceptions? The poem, which was never circulated, does not answer any of these questions, but it does create a clear point of greatest aural
emphasis that may affect understanding and that, I think, would have been
perceived more readily as key to the poem in an age that read lyrically, or with
attention to the way sound directs reader attention, than in our age, which
reads for the most part with attention to narrative, biography, page space, or
in relation to theory. Moreover, the poem's point of greatest aural emphasis
identifies hearing with consciousness.

> I felt a Funeral, in my Brain,
> And Mourners to and fro
> Kept treading – treading – till it seemed
> That Sense was breaking through –
>
> And when they all were seated,
> A Service, like a Drum –
> Kept beating – beating – till I thought
> My mind was going numb –

And then I heard them lift a Box
And creak across my Soul
With those same Boots of Lead, again,
Then Space – began to toll,

As all the Heavens were a Bell,
And Being, but an Ear,
And I, and Silence, some strange Race
Wrecked, solitary, here –

And then a Plank in Reason, broke,
And I dropped down, and down –
And hit a World, at every plunge,   ]Crash –
And Finished knowing – then –   ]Got through –

This poem is written in alternating lines of tetrameter and trimeter, rhyming abcb—with the exception of the second stanza, which has 7686 syllables. Its iambic metrical norm, however, is repeatedly syncopated by two-syllable words with a falling rhythm—not just the repeated "treading – treading" and "beating – beating" but nearly every two-syllable word in the poem, from the opening "Funeral" (which functions metrically as a two-syllable word *fun'ral*) and "Mourners" to the final "Finished knowing." Consequently, the poem is dominated by falling beats (trochees) in an overall design that is consistently iambic.

The poem plays these rising and falling rhythms against each other brilliantly. The rhythmic counterpoint may suggest the disjunction of traditional forms and experience: because the meter is iambic, every trochaic word necessarily crosses a foot boundary, such that its first syllable ends one iambic foot and its second less-stressed syllable begins the next iamb, creating a kind of urgency of falling rhythms against the highly regular rising undertone. Simply marked, the poem's rhythms read:

I félt | a Fún|eral, ín | my Bráin,
And Móurn|ers tó | and fró
Kept tréad|ing – tréad|ing – tíll | it séemed
That Sénse | was bréak|ing thróugh –

And whén | they áll | were séat|ed,
A Sér|vice, líke | a Drúm –
Kept béat|ing – béat|ing – tíll | I thóught
My mínd | was gó|ing númb –

And thén | I héard | them líft | a Bóx
And créak | acróss | my Sóul

With thóse | sáme Bóots | of Léad, | agáin,
Then Spáce – | begán | to tóll,

As áll | the Héav|ens wére | a Béll,
And Bé|ing, bút | an Ēar,
And Í,| and Síl|ence, sóme | stránge Ráce
Wrécked, sól|itár|y, hére –

And thén | a Plánk | in Réas|on, bróke,
And Í | drópped dówn, | and dówn –
And hít | a Wórld,| at év|ery plúnge,
And Fín|ished knów|ing – thén –

This play of dual rhythms is made more complex by a number of pauses within metrical feet (between the initial relatively unstressed and concluding relatively stressed syllable), which also syncopate the basic rising rhythm. Such interplay might suggest the suppleness of traditional forms: iambic meter does not break down in the presence of falling word rhythms and frequent pauses. Or the dual rhythm might hint at the paradox of the speaker's extraordinary lucidity in describing a process of mental collapse, or the tension pushing against such lucidity. Or there may be no meaning as such at all in this patterning, which enacts the heaviness appropriate to a funeral in its repeated polysyllabic words of falling rhythm while maintaining a syntactic urgency and general metrical upbeat supporting its narrative of suspense. Sound patterns are not translatable as interpretive argument. Nonetheless, the iambic pulse, with its syncopating and heavier counter-beat, the repeated line-initial "And [then]," and enjambment across line and stanza boundaries ("Space – began to toll, // As all the Heavens were a Bell . . .") make the poem's narrative forceful and tense, while the multiple pauses slow the reader's progress.

The only exceptions to this pattern in which all two-syllable words have a falling rhythm occur in stanza 3, with a surprising three two-syllable words with a rising rhythm that occurs within foot boundaries: "across," "again," and "began." Not coincidentally, other elements of sound manifest growing intensity in this stanza. It ends with an enjambed line, contains the poem's first spondee ("same Boots"), and accelerates the repetition of "s"s leading to the poem's climax. Stanza 3's quicker and lighter beats and enjambed final line speed us into the mysterious stasis of stanza 4, beginning with its first two words of liquid expansiveness and wonder: "As all . . ." Stanza 4 is aurally, rhythmically, syntactically, and metaphorically remarkable. Each line contains a strong internal assonance and the long third line contains two such echoes: Heavens/Bell, Being/Ear, I/Silence *and* strange/Race in line 3, and solitary/here in line 4. Following the previous stanza's "same" and "Space," this stanza reverberates with long *a*'s (strange Race . . . solitary), *s*'s (Heavens, Silence, some strange Race, solitary) and *r*'s (strange Race / Wrecked, solitary). Most remarkably this stanza includes five relatively stressed syllables in a row: "some strange Race / Wrecked, solitary . . ."

Stanzas three and four together build to an extraordinary climax, where the long vowel sounds and liquid word endings beginning with "Space – began to toll" make the lines (and the experience) seem to stretch out in a timeless way. In the midst of the poem's sequential narrative ("And when . . . And then . . . And . . . And"), we enter a realm of paradoxically heard space rather than time, where the experience of alienation is so profound it seems biological: "Being" ceases to be human and becomes instead metonymic, an "Ear," a category of listening, or perhaps of solitude: "I" becomes racially indistinguishable from "Silence." Moreover, its open vowel ("I") registers as a mere subset of the longer word and larger category, I / Silence. This stanza's spondees climax, however, not with "Silence" or "Race" but with "Wrecked"—a word reminding the reader that this state has not been chosen. Listen to these two stanzas again:

And then I heard them lift a Box
And creak across my Soul
With those same Boots of Lead, again,
Then Space – began to toll,

As all the Heavens were a Bell,
And Being, but an Ear,
And I, and Silence, some strange Race
Wrecked, solitary, here –

After the word "Wrecked," the rhythm pauses with the comma and then decrescendos: "solitary" lets us down easily with its multiple relatively unstressed syllables, and the concluding deictic "here" grounds us reflectively in our own—not just the speaker's—present. We, too, may be "Wrecked" "here," in the solitude of our own obsessions or pain.

The final stanza, in this aurally focused reading, is distinctly anti-climactic. The narrative resumes: "And then." The moment of epiphany has passed. We have now only to witness the results: reason gives way—a result we could have predicted. Dropping "down, and down" seems logical, and although each "plunge" brings some further "World" or revelation, none is as extraordinary as having been arrested in alienated "Being" with "Silence." And "then"—well, then whatever it is that occurs when we at least temporarily "Finish[] knowing." Aurally, the poem does not ask us to linger on this inconclusive ending but instead on that earlier uncanny, suspended and highly stressed moment of clear "knowing." Consequently, it suggests that what matters most when you feel a funeral in your brain is not what happens afterwards, or how closely this feeling resembles actual funerals, but the moment of psychic awareness, of intensified consciousness, that such a feeling inevitably leads to—that moment when we feel fully our own astonishing and dislocated strangeness, an experience focused in that internal chamber receptive only to sound.

While the concept of "Being" as "but an Ear" is unique to this poem, Dickinson's interweaving of sound patterns with epistemological reflections recurs. Dickinson has an extraordinary versatility in creating patterns of sound that build to points of felt but not easily explicated emphasis. In "I felt a Funeral," repetition, enjambment, metrical variation, assonance, and alliteration combine to stunning effect in portraying an uncanny moment of consciousness. Dickinson uses similar techniques in "The Soul selects her own Society –" (F409), a poem that reaches its climax in its final stanza, where the speaker moves from generalizing about the agency of all souls ("The" soul) to reminiscing about a particular extreme example:

> The Soul selects her own Society –
> Then – shuts the Door –
> To her divine Majority –   ]On
> Present no more –   ]obtrude
>
> Unmoved – she notes the Chariots – pausing –
> At her low Gate –
> Unmoved – an Emperor be kneeling
> Opon her Mat –   ]On her Rush mat
>
> I've known her – from an ample nation –
> Choose One –
> Then – close the Valves of her attention –]   lids –
> Like Stone –

While all souls choose, only the exceptionally selective close out all but "One" intimate companion. The poem ends in a tone of wonder at the possibility of such extremity.

The tonal force of this poem's final stanza results from metrical variation and sound play. Whereas lines 1 and 3 of each stanza maintain between eight and ten syllables throughout the poem, lines 2 and 4 reduce from the 4-syllable line of stanzas 1 and 2 to a 2-syllable spondee in stanza 3: "Choose One . . . Like Stone – "—each word a monosyllable and capitalized. Equally contributing is the crescendo of assonance and rhyme. In this poem, long lines conclude with syllabic rhyme: each ends in a polysyllable rhyming on its final syllable, respectively "y"; "ing"; and "tion." In contrast, the short lines end with monosyllables and a stronger rhyme, although the rhyme is full only in the first stanza. By the time we arrive at the poem's last word, "Stone," we both notice the lack of full rhyme with "One" and hear full rhymes with "Stone" reverberating from earlier in the poem: "own" and "known." Moreover, the poem contains repeated long *o* sounds: Soul/own/Society/Door/no/more/notes/low/known/ close/Stone—the dominant tone in a remarkable eleven out of the poem's fifty-two words. The last word resonates, then, with a sound pattern that has been echoing since the first line of the poem, and that dominates the first stanza (Soul, own, Society, Door, no, more). Like a stringed instrument that vibrates sympathetically to certain pitches, these key words of the first line vibrate sonically all the way to the end. "Stone" also vibrates with the poem's echoing *n*'s—in the last stanza alone: "One," "known" "an," "nation," "Then," and "attention." *O* is the most open of sounds. Paradoxically, its repetitions lead to a chilling state of closure: the Soul's autonomous self-possession in selecting its community of intimates is as absolute as the grave; the heart is a living entity to those whom it selects but "Like Stone" to all who remain outside its "attention."

Assonance and word rhythms play a role of extraordinary significance in Dickinson's lyric strains, although they have not received much attention in critical literature on her work. Another poem never sent to anyone, "Wild nights" (F269), gains some of its force from the repeated long *i* and monosyllables in those two opening words, echoed in the three long *i*s of the poem's penultimate line: "Might I but moor – tonight – / In thee!" Carol Maier illuminates the power of such a pattern through her discussion of a Spanish translation of (or poetic response to) this poem, beginning with the words "noche loca" (crazy night), a translation that does not literally reproduce "Wild nights" but which Maier persuasively argues is more forceful than the literal "noches tempestuosas" because its repetition of the long *o* and of word structure (in Spanish, the grammatical trochees of *noche loca*) more closely imitates Dickinson's assonance and structural repetition in "Wild nights" (85).

In other poems, full rhyme is a more significant element in the poem's lyric effect. Also never circulated, "A Toad, can die of Light –" (F419), maintains no consistency in line or stanza length or in syllables or beats per line, which vary from two to ten and two to five, respectively. Its strong rhyming and aural effects, however, link the stanzas and culminate in a powerful cadence:

	rhyme scheme	
A Toad, can die of Light –	a	
Death is the Common Right	a	]mutual – equal –
Of Toads and Men –	b	
Of Earl and Midge	c	
The privilege –	c	
Why swagger, then?	b	
The Gnat's supremacy is large as Thine –	d	

Life – is a different Thing –	e	]Another
So measure Wine –	d	
Naked of Flask – Naked of Cask –	f(f)	
Bare Rhine –	d	
Which Ruby's mine?	d	

In the first stanza of this poem, the rhyme of lines 3 and 6 cuts across three sentences to create an aural chiasmus (bccb, Men Midge privil*ege* then) leading up to the pentameter line at the end of this stanza—which sounds wonderfully contemptuous in its length and its introduction of a new rhyme sound ("Thine") but also echoes the strong vowel (the long i) of the first two lines. This contemptuousness is also suggested by the repeated short *a* in "swagger" and "Gnat" and polysyllabic elongation, first in the 3-syllable "privilege," then in the 4-syllable "supremacy." From the perspective of sound, Dickinson is absolutely right to keep "Common" rather than the variants "mutual" or "equal"; their liquid sounds and longer vowels would interfere with the crispness of the poem's opening hard syllables (*Toad can die Light Death Common Right Toads*) echoed later in "Toads," "Mi*dge*," "different," "Naked," "Cask," and "Flask."

Like the last line in the first stanza, the first in the second begins without a rhyme: "Life – is a different Thing –." Even while proclaiming difference, however, this line echoes the syntactic structure (X is Y) and sounds of the preceding line: the "l" of "large" and "i" of "Thine" in "Life" and the "th" of "Thine" in "Thing." "Thing" at the end of the line sounds oddly conclusive, because of the lack of rhyme, and perhaps because it returns us to the opening trimeter line-length. From this point on, the poem makes an increasing number of aural connections. The second stanza rhymes edf(f)dd—picking up and repeating the sound of the final pentameter line of stanza one, bringing the conclusively final and unrhymed word of that stanza and line of thought into a new set of rhymes. Line 10 contains internal rhyme and dashes that make it sound like a pair of dimeter lines and move quickly, exactly the opposite of the final 2 lines, where Dickinson writes what would more normally have been a trimeter (with internal rhyme) as two poetic lines. Dickinson probably separates these final short phrases onto two rows of print because "Bare Rhine" concludes the rhyme, thought, and syntax begun two lines earlier and could therefore logically conclude the poem; as I discuss in Chapter 4, she follows syntax and rhyme in splitting metrical lines. In contrast, the phrases "Naked of Flask – Naked of Cask –" repeat the same thought and phrase structure. The question of the final line is syntactically independent, hence also more unexpected—perhaps the reason Dickinson gives it its own line. Yet it returns us to the "u" of "supremacy" in "Ruby" and consolidates the long "i's" that the poem has been playing with throughout (die, Light, Right, Why, Thine, Life,

Wine, Rhine, mine). What the speaker claims through these rhymes is her "Life" ("mine"), not her death. In a poem written during the Civil War, at a time when martyr deaths were mourned and glorified repeatedly in public forums, and in a religious culture that saw mortal life as merely preliminary to afterlife, Dickinson may be asking "Why" glorify death?

Yet "Life" is a curiously objectified "Thing"—albeit a different kind of thing from Death. According to the analogy with wine, "Life" intoxicates; it is a kind of artisanal or artistic product varying in quality according to the skill of its maker and the luck of contingencies, like the weather. Logically, then, the value of life is far from intrinsic; it is made, a "Thing," a product of effort, knowledge, work, often cooperative labor, perhaps devotion. Again, following the analogy with wine, Dickinson may imply that one person's "Ruby" cannot be utterly distinguished from another's. Like vintners depending on others to produce their wine, we are implicated in the "Bare Rhine" of our neighbors. Clearly, Dickinson uses "Rhine" for the rhyme with "wine" and "mine," but the geographical marker for wine also encourages the idea that we do not produce the quality of our lives sui generis. As Dickinson says in "The Robin's my Criterion for Tune –," we "discern[] . . . Provincially" according to where we "grow" or were "born" (F256). Rhymes emphasize these implied connections: *Thine, Wine, Rhine,* and *mine* interlink questions of community or co-dependency (thine/mine) with the principal words of the first line of each stanza: *Light* and *Life.* This trajectory of sound pulls "Thine" away from comparison with the dying gnat's "supremacy" to the question of choice: confronted with life at its most "Naked" and "Bare," what quality do you choose? How do you distinguish your "Life," or "Wine," from the animal "Common Right" to "die"? That which gives life (light) "can" as easily lead to death, the poem implies, but for an individual's determination to make "Life" indeed a "different Thing." This is a brilliant, and brilliantly simple, poem in its multiple political, cultural, and ontological implications, structured in two stanzas of iambic meter and insistent rhyme, syncopated by inconsistent line lengths. The dominant rhythmic figure of the poem is chiasmus or inverted parallelism, repeated in the UsuS stress patterns at the beginning of lines 2, 8, and 10 and repeated in the second half of line 10, as well as in the chiastic rhyme pattern of lines 3 through 6 and 9 through 11 (Men, Midge, privilege, then and Wine, Flask, Cask, Rhine).[59] Chiasmus is a pattern of return, balance. While the poem ends with a question, it also suggests the possibility of order through its building consonance of rhythm and sounds. And this order is associated not with an afterlife or with spiritual or doctrinal truths but with the pleasure and labor of "Life."

Dickinson is a poet of sounds. Where Marianne Moore defines poetry through an organic metaphor as "'imaginary gardens with real toads in them,'" Dickinson may, in "I felt a Funeral, in my Brain," in effect define poetry as language that brings us to the experience of "Being [as] but an Ear" (*Becoming Marianne Moore* 73). Reading Dickinson requires affiliation with that "Silence" of attentive listening, which alone situates us in the moment, in the poem's "here," although any reader's response to a poem will inevitably move out from that "here" to the "And then" of his or her contextual understanding, often being struck by lines that both illuminate ways of thinking and implant tunes in our brains. Such reading is encouraged by approaching Dickinson as a poet of lyric strains in the implied definitions of her century, whether or not in relation to critical definitions of ours.

Dickinson's poetry is not Poe's—that is, "Beauty" is not for her "the sole legitimate province" of the poem. Dickinson also goes farther than Emerson: her poems not only contain a "meter-making argument" but an argument that typically functions in ways as unpredictable or "defiant of rules" as her metaphors and verse forms. Who could guess that "I felt a Funeral, in my Brain,"—a surprising enough conceit from the start—would lead to a moment of isolated racial identification with "Silence," yet the logic of the poem feels equally astonishing and right, perhaps in part because of the tense urgency of its rhythms and sounds. Another poem begins with the definitive statement that "This World is not conclusion." (complete with line-end period) but concludes with a striking metaphorical admission that we will always doubt this conviction, and the paradoxical combination of a full rhyme with an open dash: "Much Gesture, from the Pulpit – / Strong Hallelujahs roll – / Narcotics cannot still the Tooth / That nibbles at the soul –" (F373). A poem ostensibly about beetles or June bugs that drop from the ceiling in summer contains the unanticipated reflection that "A Bomb opon the Ceiling / Is an improving thing – / It keeps the nerves progressive / Conjecture flourishing –" (F1150). Another begins with its speaker irritated by spiders in what appears to be an outhouse: "Alone and in a Circumstance / Reluctant to be told / A spider on my reticence / Assiduously crawled"; then with one of those astonishing and logical turns, it becomes the occasion for a profound meditation on God's role in what she calls the "Larceny" of the "marrow of the Day"—the substance that gives meaning to and enables competent functioning in our lives. "[W]hat redress can be," she asks, "For an offence not here nor there / So not in Equity – / That Larceny of time and mind / The marrow of the Day / By spider, or forbid it Lord / That I should specify –" (F1174). Dickinson not only engages in a process of thinking in her poems; uncharacteristically for the nineteenth century, she also truncates and compresses that process so radically that the syntax and sound of every line or stanza plays a dramatic role in developing its force or logic.

If we read genre through a process that is both definitional and historically sensitive, we hear not just Dickinson's nineteenth-century verse but also twenty-first-century innovative engagement with lyric differently and in ways that may inform each other. As suggested earlier, the romantic/post-romantic genre definition has been aggressively challenged, and is being newly theorized. In 1988, Ron Silliman, Carla Harryman, Lyn Hejinian, Steve Benson, Bob Perelman, and Barrett Watten's "Politics of Poetry" manifesto criticizes the "narrowness and provincialism of mainstream literary norms" that have held up "the personal, 'expressive' lyric . . . as the canonical poetic form," and in 1999 Marjorie Perloff declares that poets like Silliman and Susan Howe "have no interest in the closural first-person metaphoric model of mainstream poetry." "[P]erhaps *the* cardinal principle of American Language poetics," Perloff states, "has been the dismissal of 'voice' as the foundational principle of lyric poetry" ("Language Poetry" 419, 405).[60] Some of this writing emphasizes sound. Elizabeth Willis muses that "If the lyric's defining characteristic is the priority of its sonic patterns . . . then it depends on being heard; it hangs everything on the presence and engagement of its audience . . . a social context of which the writer is a part" ("Lyric Dissent" 229, 230). More recently, in a discussion of the lyric in Buffalo, New York, Myung Mi Kim stated that for her the most urgent question about the lyric was what work it enabled the poet to do. In writing, she looks for the "opening" in that "combinatory system" we call language that allows for innovation or newness—a statement that calls to mind Dickinson's claim in "I dwell in Possibility –" that poetry is "A fairer House than Prose –" because it is "More numerous" of windows and doors (F466).[61] According to Kim, lyric involves "sounding," and "sounding" is an "event" or "activating force." Because sounding occurs "at the cusp of the viable and the as yet unavailable," lyric has the "potential to create a language-based, rhythmical space for the viable [or, Kim says, "maybe for the unviable"] as part of a cultural and historical process"; to this extent, lyric in effect "creates ontological openings." Giving even greater emphasis to sound, Denise Riley regards the lyric as "thought being made in the ear" (66).[62]

Obviously, Dickinson is not a twenty-first-century experimentalist poet; Kim's vocabulary would have been foreign to her in the same way that Holmes's diction of sweetness is to us. Nonetheless, such comments may provide a more useful vocabulary for articulating how the genre of lyric enabled certain kinds of work for Dickinson in the late 1850s than now-canonical definitions of the romantic/post-romantic lyric insofar as they emphasize dynamics of sound, form, and thought rather than expressions of individual subjectivity or a particular relation to time. And such comments may also reveal ways in which Dickinson's verse continues to be useful as a model for reading (and writing) contemporary lyric verse—not because she anticipated later formulations but because the practice of poetry in her era allowed openings in some ways similar to those of turn-of-the-twenty-first-century innovative poetries.

Dickinson wrote to Higginson that she "could not drop the Bells whose jingling cooled [her] Tramp" (L265) and later to her cousins: "Let Emily sing for you because she cannot pray" (L278). Such messages suggest that the lyric ("Bells" / "sing[ing]") enabled work Dickinson could do in no other way. Given what we are learning about the surprisingly progressive quality of her education and the formally innovative poetry she read as a girl, it appears that she found a particular openness to innovation in the lyric strains of short-lined verse that made it the most capacious mode of "sounding" her thought (Kim), or through which to "generate and shape knowledge of the world" (Dimock 1383). Lyric strains may have linked Dickinson, in her writing practice, not just to other women who wrote poetry in her age, or to those men and women to whom she mailed poems, but generically with the wide range of poets she had read who were also experimenting with lyric verse. Wai Chee Dimock suggests that the stability of traditional genres helps prevent a fixation on originality; for Dickinson, it may have been the combination of traditional aspects of the lyric poem and her contemporaries' innovative manipulations of lyric form that made the short-lined lyric such a fitting genre for working at that "cusp" of the "viable and the as yet unavailable," as Kim says, or in her own words "trying to think" in ways that enabled her to "stun [herself] / With Bolts – of Melody!"

3

Hymn, the "Ballad Wild," and Free Verse

Bear with the Ballad –
"Sang from the Heart, Sire," F1083

As the previous chapter demonstrates, although a great variety of verse was considered lyric, from sea chanties to verse of highly irregular rhyming and stanzaic structure, the lyric poem as such was not a much discussed genre in the mid-nineteenth-century United States. In contrast, the ballad had been the topic of active public debate for decades by the time of Dickinson's youth. Following the late eighteenth-century ballad revival in the British Isles, with its defining impact on Romantic poetry, the ballad had become a popular form for imitation and experiment—no doubt spurring the American enthusiasm for departures from set form, especially for short-lined poems. While there is ample evidence that Dickinson wrote with the rhythms of hymns in her ears, several aspects of her verse suggest that a more accurate formulation would be that she wrote in relation to song. Song, in this context, includes the hymns and ballads she sang, the poetry she read, and the popular music she played on the piano.[1]

I do not mean by this that Dickinson imagines her poems literally as sung or even as oral—in distinction to their significant aurality: Dickinson knew traditions of oral and communal poetry like the ballad through a combination of print and recitation or song, and she understood the integrity of the page. At the same time, her poetry leans strongly toward what might be called a secondary or written orality: like Robert Browning, Whitman, and others of her contemporaries, she creates the fiction of a speaking presence with great attention to inflections and rhythms of speech, but speech that she assumes will be known primarily through the page (see Chapter 4).[2] Many prose writers of the 1840s and 1850s experimented with dialect and regional idioms—famously in *Uncle Tom's Cabin* and in travel or humorous sketches—and dialect poetry was written frequently during the Civil War. Dickinson writes in an idiom familiar to her New England ear, combining the verve and idiosyncrasies of speech with the measures of song, perhaps one reason

49

for her apparent simultaneous delight in the patterned opportunities afforded by short-lined verse and in the loosening or disrupting of those patterns to make her language more "alive."[3]

There is a long tradition of permeable boundaries between poems and songs: songs have "lyrics" and poems are often set to music or titled "Song" or "Hymn"—as in Longfellow's "The Song of Hiawatha" or Bryant's "Song of the Stars" and Emerson's "Hymn: sung at the completion of the Concord monument, April 19, 1836"—all poems Dickinson knew.[4] Writing of the "lyrical productions" selected for his poetry anthology *Songs of Three Centuries*, John Greenleaf Whittier exclaims that "the last century has been prolific in song" (*Whittier on Writers* 202). Dickinson herself frequently refers to poems as songs and imagines birds as like poets in "The Robin's my Criterion for Tune –" (F256), "The Robin is the One" (F501C), "The Birds begun at Four o'clock –" (F504 B), "The Robin for the Crumb" (F810 B), and "At Half past Three, a single Bird" (F1099 B), to give just a few examples of poems where birds produce "reports," "Miracle," "Chronicle," or "Experiment." Michael Cohen writes that in the early nineteenth century "songs, stories, and poems come from a surprisingly wide array of sources" and "cannot be located precisely in any one cultural domain." Ballads in particular, he argues, constitute a hybrid form of oral and print cultures and a "'folk' form" that was associated with medieval troubadours but often used contemporary events as subject matter ("Peddlars" 12, 28).[5] Both ballads and hymns reveal aspects of their oral base as sung, shared, and shaped communally.

The extraordinary fertility of Dickinson's stanzaic and metrical forms arises from these intersections of elite and popular, printed and sung, religious and secular short-lined forms prevalent in the 1840s and 1850s. Her experimentation with loosened meter, shifts in stanzaic form mid-poem, and testing of free verse rhythms also reveals the influence of the eighteenth-century ballad revival as it had filtered into American popular poetry. Following this revival, fascination with traditional ballads brought renewed interest in the accentual rhythms of medieval verse and a vogue for imitating such forms. According to Albert Friedman, the ballad revival broke the "tyranny" of the iamb in the nineteenth century by (re)introducing poets to the option of tri-syllabic substitution for the two-syllable foot (248–49, 346).[6] Sir Walter Scott claimed that James Macpherson's 1760 collection of Ossian poems gave "new tone to poetry throughout all Europe."[7] Goethe, Robert Burns, Blake, Wordsworth, Coleridge, and Tennyson were influenced by ballads; Wordsworth wrote that ballads "emancipate 'new poets'"; Christopher North wrote that "perhaps none of us ever wrote verses of any worth who had not been more or less readers of our old ballads" (Friedman 292).[8] In the United States, Whittier claims that the "sturdiest and homeliest Scottish simplicity" of ballads has been among the key influences on "the modern lyric" (*Whittier on Writers* 205). Steve Newman more strongly states that the ballad changed lyric poetry by transforming it from "polite" into "imaginative writing" (1).[9] Since the early nineteenth century, poets and scholars have seen the ballad revival as having a transformational effect on nineteenth-century lyric verse, including a loosening of metrical form. Dickinson used the ballad's forms and associations as both a foil and a model for her own innovative and dramatic lyric poems.

Michael Cohen identifies the ballad as "arguably the most important genre in nineteenth-century poetic discourse" in the United States; before the Civil War, the ballad was understood to include not just adventurous or uncanny tales but also didactic verse ("Whittier" 3).[10] Contemporary ballads could be contemplative, sensational, satirical, political, or comic, and were extremely popular for reading and recitation and as set to music and sung. The *Springfield Republican* published many poems in ballad form—such as Luella Clark's "On a Sunny Summer Morning" set to music by Carl Hanse, and the traditional "Love me little, love me long," first published in 1659.[11] During the Civil War, a good part of the poetry that was published and most popular song was described as "ballads."[12] This included poems of widely variant formal properties; for example, poems shaped more like what we might call an ode (with stanzas combining lines of varied length, devised to fit the poet's mood or refrain) were called "ballads." Such loose nomenclature leads Cohen to hypothesize that the term "ballad" was used as a "sign of [the poet's] ability to reach thousands of readers" and of "a poetic culture only indirectly under the control of legitimating social forces" ("Whittier" 26).[13] Certainly at the level of practice, early and mid-nineteenth-century American literary culture showed less concern with formal definition and more with a broad conflation of qualities for omnibus genres like the lyric and ballad.

Dickinson's exact repetition of short-lined accentual-syllabic patterns in many poems stems from the kind of regularity required for the communal singing of hymns. In contrast, her use of a looser running rhythm or accentual (as opposed to accentual-syllabic) meter follows the model of balladic verse. These models are distinctly different in structuring principles even though often not in description or practice. Neither the hymn nor the ballad models an interrogation of philosophical questions but their easy rhythms, pungently idiomatic address, and loose narrative structures seem to enable Dickinson's densely metaphorical and epistemological turns. Fluctuating between the precise tunes of hymns, the ballad's "wild" looseness, and her own musical sense of cadence in language, Dickinson's poems and process of composition are illuminated by understanding more about both her musical practice and the musical culture of the United States during her formative years.[14]

Dickinson refers to ballads in six poems between 1858 and 1881—from the early "I had a guinea golden –" (F12) where the speaker laments the loss of a Robin "Troubadour" who sings "ballads" and "Heart not so heavy as mine" (F88 C) where a passing stranger whistles "A careless snatch – a ballad –" to "Sang from the Heart, Sire" (F1083), where the speaker refers to her own bloody "Tune" as a "Ballad."[15] These poems feature traditional aspects of ballads associating the genre with carefree people of the "street" or folk culture in contrast to a more modern and troubled speaker, who is separated from nature by being indoors (F88). "Sang from the Heart, Sire," however, also overturns the traditional expectation that the expressive wanderer or troubadour is male and the indoor, more conventional listener female through its aggressive address of undying love to a "Sire."[16] According to Virginia Jackson, Dickinson quotes from a traditional ballad in what may have been an early comic valentine, complete with pasted-on illustrations (*Misery* 140–41).[17]

In letters, Dickinson frequently refers to the music she sang or played, including several ballads. When her family bought a piano she announced it proudly in letters to Abiah Root: she practiced the piano two hours a day in Amherst and "only one hour a day" at Mount Holyoke (L7, 8, 9, 18, 23). She and Abiah exchange information about their mode of instruction (the Bertini method) and the "beautiful pieces" they've learned, including the popular tunes "The Grave of Bonaparte," "Lancers Quick Step," "Wood Up," "Maiden Weep No More" (L7), "Lady of Beauty," and "Susanah" (L29). Piano playing was a form of shared pleasure; she wishes "to see you [Abiah] and hear you play" (L7) and comments coyly that "S.S. . . . is as handsome, entertaining, and as fine a piano player as in former times" (L9). One night in 1848, after returning from a party at 10:00, "Father wishing to hear the Piano, I like an obedient daughter, played & sang a few tunes, much to his apparent gratification" (L20). Carlton Lowenberg calls Dickinson an accomplished pianist, judging from the difficulty of pieces she owned (13).[18] As frequently noted, Kate Scott Turner recalls "those blissful evenings at Austin's" when "Emily was often at the piano playing weird & beautiful melodies, all from her own inspiration"—evenings that evidently continued into 1859.[19]

Song was also an ongoing part of Dickinson's life. In February 1845, Dickinson refers to going to "singing-school Sabbath evenings to improve my voice" (L5), and at Mount Holyoke she sang for thirty minutes a day, presumably hymns (L18). Musical enthusiasms at school were not entirely religious: Sandra Runzo relates the story of Mary Lyon inviting the popular abolitionist Hutchinson Family Singers to Mount Holyoke for a private concert for the student body in spring or summer of 1848, while Dickinson was a student there, and Dickinson owned sheet music for Hutchinson Family and several other popular songs. Her classmate Mary Lyon recalls a day when Dickinson fetches her "singing-book in hand" to walk with her to a sequestered spot outdoors where they could sing "tune after tune . . . carrying two parts, and by snatches three or four" as a "remedy for depression, repression, suppression and oppression."[20] In a playful letter to her Uncle Joel Norcross, Dickinson represents the "fun" of her life as a song: Amherst, she writes, is a "great town . . . Chorus – 'a still greater one is this.' 'Now for the jovial bowl,' etc. You are fond of singing – I think – and by close, and assiduous practice may learn ["Lady of Beauty" and "Susanah"] before I see you again" (L29). Dickinson's letters to Austin often mention music or use musical metaphors, as in an October 30, 1851 letter, where family life on a stormy night involves musical counterpoint: "the orchestra of winds perform their strange, sad music"; Vinnie diverts their father "with little snatches of music"; and she hopes that Austin's "stove is singing the merry song of the wood" (L60). A nostalgic and fanciful letter to John Graves in April 1856 mentions three songs, a troubadour, a roundelay, a ballad, humming, and playing the piano! For example, she hopes that he "as a ballad hummed, and lost, [may] remember . . . and drop a tear, if a *troubadour* that strain may chance to sing," namely "Lang Syne." Later she notes, "I play the old, odd tunes yet, which used to flit about your head after honest hours – and wake dear Sue, and madden me, with their grief and fun" (L184). In letters like these, it appears that Dickinson imagines life as a succession of musical moments and in relation to a succession of songs that she hears, hums, or that "madden" her, presumably by being stuck in her head. In her letters, she mentions music over one hundred times, not counting references to bird or insect song.[21]

Such frequent reference is hardly surprising in this era given the huge popularity of music, in and out of the home. According to E. Lawrence Abel, by 1850 owning a piano was de rigueur for the middle-class family and every accomplished girl knew how to play—both for solo performance and to accompany herself and other singers (140). The appetite for songs, however, went far beyond bourgeois parlor practices and hymn singing. Minstrel shows, popular throughout the States, included considerable music, as did most theatrical performances.[22] Dickinson's critical review of a Jennie Lind concert she heard in Northampton indicates her familiarity with high-quality singing (L46).[23] The love of music was particularly prominent in public life during the Civil War. There are innumerable stories about the songs sung by Confederate and Union troops as they marched. Especially in regiments made up from colleges and small towns, the men were almost certainly accustomed to singing as well as to studying or working together. General Robert E. Lee reportedly said, "I don't believe we can have an army without music" (Abel 1). Encamped armies enjoyed concerts and impromptu singing, and nearly every regiment had at least the rudiments of a band. A Confederate band played waltzes and polkas during Pickett's Charge at Gettysburg, and Union and Confederate bands often competed against each other in neighboring encampments, and sometimes even on battlefields (Abel 190).

Army music, parlor songs, hymns, and poems were not strictly separable. Poems were set to music and became available as sheet music to huge populations virtually overnight. Poet and singer Harry McCarthy's "The Bonnie Blue Flag" was greeted with wild enthusiasm and demands that he sing it over and over when he first performed it. According to an 1862 account, within twenty-four hours of a concert in New Orleans, "The Bonnie Blue Flag" had become the rallying song of the Confederacy.[24] James Ryder Randall composed "My Maryland" to the rhythm and meters of James Clarence Mangan's "Karamanian's Exile"; almost immediately following its first newspaper publication, according to E. Lawrence Abel, "virtually every Southern newspaper reprinted it" and within a few days of its publication in Baltimore, Hetty and Jennie Cary had set the poem to "O Tannenbaum" (68, 70).[25] This poem written to the rhythm of a popular poem and revised to fit the tune of a popular song was widely distributed as sheet music. General Beauregard had copies of "My Maryland" distributed to any soldier who wanted it (Abel 71).

"Psalm," like "hymn," was used interchangeably with poem or song, again suggesting an understanding of "lyric" that crossed the boundaries of saying and singing and the religious and secular.[26] In letters, Dickinson refers to the popular "Lady of Beauty" and bird song as hymns (L29, 269), as well as poems by Holland, Higginson, and herself (L307, 674, 182, 418), and she calls Austin's attempt at poetry a "psalm" (L110).[27] "Musicians wrestle everywhere –" refers to a sermon as a "Hymn from pulpit read –" (F229 B, 1861). Similarly, *The Household Book of Poetry* contains fourteen hymns by Isaac Watts among its "poems." Easily the most popular Northern song of the Civil War was Julia Ward Howe's "Battle Hymn of the Republic"—a poem written to replace the lyrics of "John Brown's Body" (sung to an already well-known tune), printed in a literary magazine, and then sung as a marching song to which soldiers added a "Glory Hallelujah" chorus.[28]

This fluidity matches that with which Dickinson refers to all kinds of daily sound as "tunes" or music in both letters and poems. As noted earlier, in depicting her "enchantment" at first reading Barrett Browning, Dickinson presents its effects as musical: "The Days – to Mighty Metres stept –" and "the meanest Tunes // That Nature murmured to herself / To keep herself in Cheer – / I took for Giants – practicing / Titanic Opera –" (F627). Nature's humming "to keep herself in Cheer" may be modeled on the poet's own behavior; Dickinson describes herself as going "round my work, humming a little air till mother had gone to sleep" and then crying "with all my might" (L36, 7 May 1850). Another poem uses "poesy" and "melody" as alternatives: "They have a little

Odor – that to me / Is metre – nay – 'tis melody"—or "poesy," as sent to Ger-
trude Vanderbilt; both poesy and melody have "metre" and indicate the "Habit
– of a Laureate –" (F505 B). In "To learn the Transport by the Pain –" (F178 B),
"patient 'Laureates'" have "voices – trained – below" that after death "Ascend
in ceaseless Carol – / Inaudible . . . To us – the duller scholars / Of the Mysterious Bard!" Or, as Dickinson puts it in a copy sent to Sue, they sing a
"stanza, hushed, below – // [that] Breaks in victorious Carol" once they join the
"mysterious 'Band'," presumably in heaven. In both versions, we earthly "Laureates" learn "Transport" from life's "Pain" through vocal training or stanzas
that become full song only after death. On earth and in heaven, life is characterized as both music and poetry. In "Better – than Music!" (F378), Dickinson
uses a similar motif: here a transformational moment in the speaker's life
provides a new "tune" or "strain" that "'Twas'nt contained – like other stanza –"
and functions as a "Translation – / Of all tunes I knew – and more –." After
exclaiming for five stanzas about the extraordinary newness of this strain the
poem concludes:

> Let me not spill – it's smallest cadence –
> Humming – for promise – when alone –
> Humming – until my faint Rehearsal –
> Drop into tune – around the Throne –

Life's music is hummed as if in "Rehearsal" for the fuller music of spiritual
afterlife. Melody is the structure of both this life and its spiritual continuation, and melody is conceived in "stanza[s]," just as the "Opera" of "Day"
moves in "Metres."[29] Religious, secular, poetic, and metaphorical music min-
gles for Dickinson in a foundation of metered, stanzaic time and tunes. context →
                                                                        creation
    Hymns had a privileged place in nineteenth-century musical culture be-
cause of the dominant Protestant culture and widespread ritual of church
singing. Like ballads, hymns also have a hybrid quality insofar as they articulate both an innate presupposition of individuality and what Victoria Morgan calls "interrelation" or community. As Morgan traces the development
of hymn culture, the genre presumes a speaker-God or I-Thou structure of
prayer, invocation, or praise, hence some level of individuality, at the same
time that it is associated with communal performance through congrega-
tional singing. Dickinson, she argues, uses the hymn form to emphasize a
heterologous poetics of relation or "being-in-relation" in opposition to the
traditional "I-Thou" hierarchy of hymnal address.[30] Similarly, it seems to me
that Dickinson found meter itself generally enabling because it was a shared
system of cultural givens that she could manipulate in individualistic, innovative ways without departing from its cultural base or sense of writing in
relation. This dialectic between individuality and relation or community

bears some resemblance to the ballad's hybridity as part of both print and oral culture, or a modern manifestation of poetic making presumed to stem from oral traditions. Dickinson attended church until around 1860, after she had begun writing seriously and eschewing other public appearances. In *A Poet's Grammar*, I suggest the attraction Watts's use of slant rhymes and idiomatic diction would have had for her (141–43).[31] We also know that in at least one instance, Dickinson substitutes words of her own for a hymn tune. She writes to Sue in 1852 that thoughts of a reunion so filled her head that when the pastor "read the 100th Psalm I kept saying your precious letter all over to myself, and Susie, when they sang . . . I made up words and kept singing how I loved you, and you had gone, while all the rest of the choir was singing Hallelujahs" (L88). Vivian Pollak persuasively reads this letter as part of a "passionately subversive courtship" between Dickinson and Susan, but it may also be read as an early model for one of the ways that Dickinson composes, following a song she's just heard, or "old, odd tunes" stuck in her head, or the rhythms of poems she remembers (*Anxiety of Gender* 60–61). As the models of "Oh Maryland," "The Battle-Hymn of the Republic," and Longfellow's *Hiawatha* indicate, composition according to the rhythms of other poems or tunes was widespread.

Rhythmic tunes seemed to function for Dickinson as the compositional foundation for her poems. Many of her poems use more than one stanzaic pattern but they rarely lapse from stanzaic into non-stanzaic form, suggesting that she composed through a conjunction of ideas or phrases and stanzaic rhythm or tune. As Michael Manson writes, Dickinson "cultivated the strongest most insistent rhythmic form available in English, one that binds lines together into one felt unit, and then she used syntax, enjambment, and visual form to push and frustrate that sensation of rhythmic completion in new ways" (390, 375).[32] The stanza, as he notes, is a form of "rhythmic completion," and precisely because it functions so powerfully as a unit of completion Dickinson's enjambments across stanzas and metrical play within stanzaic boundaries are commensurately forceful. What we know of Dickinson's life makes it probable that she composed in her head, matching rhythms that "madden" her with words—in the same way she attached words to a hymn when anticipating Sue's return.[33] We also know that Dickinson had quite extraordinary recall: not only does she quote extensively in letters, but she apparently either never or only once sent the same poem twice to the same person—although she mailed over 500 poems, and 252 to Susan alone over the course of nearly thirty years.[34] Remembering a composition until she had leisure to write it out, or to complete it, would not have been difficult. Dickinson may especially have composed in her head while suffering problems with her vision. She underwent eye treatment in Boston between late

April and 21 November in 1864 and again from 1 April to October in 1865. Yet she copied 98 poems into fascicles or sets during 1864 and 229 in 1865, according to the evidence of her handwriting. As Alfred Habegger notes, "one reason for thinking [Dickinson] continued composing in Cambridge and then brought her rough drafts home at the end of her treatment is that a huge number of perfect copies in ink—her unstitched 'sets'—have been assigned to early and late 1865," the periods after each of her two rounds of treatment (489). It is equally possible that Dickinson worked from memory rather than drafts in writing out some of these poems; metered stanzas are powerful mnemonic devices.

Norms provided structure for Dickinson's poetic composition, but neither she nor her contemporaries regarded them as rigid, and she obviously did not find them confining—just as syntax is a normative structure that does not limit creativity in making sentences.[35] David Porter, Annie Finch, and others have argued for a metrically coded interpretation of Dickinson's use of hymn forms, reading her rejection of the authority of iambic pentameter as signaling her rebellious rejection of religious and masculine orthodoxy.[36] Morgan regards Dickinson as parodying some elements of Watts's hymnody but argues that she followed in the steps of Watts and even more of female hymnists in using hymn form to articulate dissent and to create a communally based or relational understanding of divinity. While there may be some element of critical commentary in her widely secular use of hymn forms, Mitchell correctly points out that the hymns she was reading and singing were themselves extremely varied; she did not need to challenge orthodoxies to find in them models for her own formal experimentation.[37] In all Dickinson's poems comparing poetry to prose, poetry—the form involving rhythmic and accentual norms—is the more liberating. Poetry is the realm of "Possibility," "A fairer House than Prose –" (F466), whereas prose is like a "Closet" one can be "shut . . . up in" (F445).

Hymnal common meter (8686 syllables) varies from standard ballad meter (4343 beats) in that its quatrains typically rhyme abab rather than abcb, although poems were called ballads that used an abab rhyme, and hymns sometimes rhymed abcb. Dickinson's favored rhyme scheme is abcb, that is, the typical ballad, not hymn, pattern.[38] As previously stated, hymns have greater metrical regularity than ballads, eschewing both multiple unstressed syllables (for example, where a 4-beat line might have ten or more syllables) and the omission of unstressed syllables (giving a 3-beat line as few as three syllables).[39] In their 1831 *Church Psalmody* under the headings of "lyric poetry" and "structure," Mason and Green claim that "the several stanzas of a hymn should possess a good degree of uniformity, as to measure, accent and pauses. . . . as they are all to be sung to the same tune" (vii).[40] Hymns differ from ballads also in their precise syllabic definition: hymns are classified according to syllables per line in stanzas, as, for example "8s" or "7s" (a stanza of repeated eight- or repeated seven-syllable lines) or as "6 & 5" (a stanza alternating 6- and 5-syllable lines), with distinct patterns of line-end stress for lines with odd and even numbers of syllables.[41] Ballads, in contrast, organize lines accentually by numbers of strong beats in a line without regard to the patterns of unstressed syllables between beats or at the end of a line. Exactly repeated numbers of syllables per line ensure that hymns of any metrical pattern can be sung to the tune of any other hymn having that same pattern—hence, a congregation would need to know only a small number of tunes in order to sing an infinite number of hymns. While ballads are also often sung to well-known tunes, there is greater leeway for truncated or extended lines because traditionally their verses are not sung chorally.

As Mitchell points out, hymns occur in a wide variety of forms—not just common meter (8686), long meter (8888), and short meter (6686). *Village Hymns* ends with a "Table of Tunes" including among many other structures 8 & 7; 7 & 6; 8, 7, 4; and 5, 6, 11.[42] Isaac Watts occasionally uses highly singular forms—for example 88688(14), repeating the form precisely from stanza to stanza. Similarly, "ballads" were written in a great variety of meters throughout the antebellum period. Richard Green Parker's *Aids to English Composition* defines the ballad as loosely as it does the lyric: the ballad is "a rhyming record of some adventure or transaction which is amusing or interesting to the populace, and written in easy and uniform verse, so that it may easily be sung by those who have little acquaintance with music" (249). Generally, poems with anecdotal, narrative, or comic focus using relaxed diction in clearly accented meter were called ballads. According to Francis J. Child, a "narrative song" or "short tale in lyric verse" was a ballad (464). Stephen J. Adams regards all combinations of tetrameter and trimeter lines in a quatrain as "variants" of the "basic ballad stanza"; Dickinson's poems, he briefly notes, use different versions of the ballad stanza interchangeably within the same poem (40–41).[43] More precisely put, the fact that Dickinson uses more than one stanzaic form in a single poem links her poetry distinctly with ballads, since such alteration of rhythmic pattern cannot be tolerated in hymn singing; on the other hand, the fact that Dickinson repeats precisely defined stanzaic structures like 8787 or 7686, not varying even one syllable per line, indicates without question the strong influence of hymn form on her meter. While, as I indicate later, some of her poems in ballad meter engage with popular idioms like the gothic, there is not a consistent difference in tone or topic between Dickinson poems using hymnic or balladic rhythms, especially if one considers her free verse poems as a further loosening of, or experimentation with, the ballad form—although Dickinson does not write any simple sentimental verses in free verse irregularity. To repeat a previous claim, Dickinson does not write in rhythmic or formal codes. She seems instead to find all forms flexible to her thought or design.

By far and away, Dickinson's most often repeated form is the accentual-syllabic quatrain 8686 abcb; she writes some of her greatest poems in this form, including "The World – stands – solemner – to me –" (F280), "A solemn thing – it was – I said –" (F307), "'Heaven' – is what I cannot reach!" (F310), "If you were coming in the Fall," (F356), "I heard a Fly buzz – when I died –" (F591), "I meant to have but modest needs –" (F711), "Pain – has an Element of Blank –" (F760), "My Life had stood – a Loaded Gun –" (F764), "One Blessing had I than the rest" (F767), "Suspense – is Hostiler than Death –" (F775), "This Consciousness that is aware" (F817 B), "Perception of an Object costs" (F1103 B), and "Alone and in a Circumstance" (F1174).[44] These poems follow precisely their accentual syllabic pattern in all stanzas, in itself a proof that Dickinson need not disrupt metrical patterns to write poems of extraordinary force and distinction. Dickinson's second most frequently used form across all years of her writing is short meter, 6686 rhymed abcb—precisely realized, for example, in "A Bird, came down the Walk –" (F359 C), "It would have starved a Gnat – " (F444), "They shut me up in Prose – " (F445), "The Heart asks Pleasure – first –" (F588), "On a Columnar Self –" (F740), and "Essential Oils – are wrung –" (F772 B). Both these forms are common in elite and popular, religious and secular poetry and song.

Dickinson uses other hymn-meter forms that also appear frequently in popular poetry; for example, she uses common particular meter (886886, aabccb,) in "Not in this World to see his face – " (F435)—a form J. Mason Good uses in "Watch," included in Ebenezer Porter's *Rhetorical Reader* (194).[45] She uses long meter (8s) in "The Martyr Poets – did not tell –" (F665) and "My Soul – accused Me – And I quailed –" (F793)—both rhymed aabb, a form Bryant uses in "To the Fringed Gentian," marked in his *Poems* (EDR 246).[46] "Kill your Balm – and it's Odors bless you – " (F309) uses stanzas of 9898, rhymed abab, where the odd-numbered lines involve syllabic, assonantal, or otherwise slant rhymes (for example, "bless you . . . perfume" in stanza 1), a pattern also used by Whittier in "A Memorial M.A.C."[47] Longfellow uses an 8787 stanza in "A Psalm of Life," "Footsteps of Angels," and "To the River Charles" as Dickinson does in "He forgot – and I – remembered –" (F232), "Rearrange a 'Wife's' Affection!" (F267), and "Her – last Poems –" (F600 C).[48] The *Republican* prints "The May Flower" by Edward C. Goodwin on 16 May 1857 in 7686—a form Dickinson uses in "The Doomed – regard the Sunrise" (F298), "She sights a Bird – she chuckles –" (F351), "There is a pain – so utter –" (F515), "The good Will of a Flower" (F954), and "I sing to use the Waiting," (F955), among other poems. Other stanzaic patterns Dickinson uses with some regularity include 8585, 7676, 7575, and (less often) 9595—all forms also found in the poetry she was reading in the 1840s and 1850s.[49]

The majority of Dickinson's 8686 poems contain some marked variation from the norm, for example, including a stanza in a different metrical form—especially those written before 1866. Across the years, her most precisely realized stanzaic form is short meter (6686).[50] *Church Psalmody* praises short meter as more lyrical and forceful than long meter (8s) because "it expresses as much of thought and feeling in twenty-six syllables, as the stanza in long metre does in thirty-two."[51] In principle, "Every line should be *full of meaning* . . . An unmeaning line or word thrown in to make out the rhyme or measure, is like a dead limb on a living body . . ." Therefore, as editors, they rewrite several "hymns in long metre . . . into common or short metre, by merely disencumbering the lines of their lifeless members" (v). Even the revered Isaac Watts's hymns were shortened in some hymnals, as Dickinson probably knew because Samuel Worcester excuses the abridgment made by his father (also named Samuel) of some of Watts's hymns (iii–iv). The younger Worcester taught at Amherst College and edited several volumes of hymns, including *Psalms, Hymns, and Spiritual Songs,* owned by Edward Dickinson. Dickinson might well have been attracted to the touted concision of the short meter form and certainly shared the belief that every word and line should be alive.

In keeping with hymn structure's mandate to maintain regular rhythms, Dickinson is extraordinarily resourceful in creating unusual accentual-syllabic patterns—such as 11/4s, in "Unto like Story – Trouble has enticed me – / How Kinsmen fell –" (F300), or 4s in "Answer July / Where is the Bee –" (F667), or 8/2s in "A word is dead, when it is said / Some say –" (F278), or 5585 in "I never saw a Moor. / I never saw the Sea –" (F800). Some of her more unusual stanza structures occur in poems just a single stanza long; others are repeated, sometimes with slight variation—as in "Unto like Story," where in a 24-line poem she uses a 10- or 9-syllable substitution for the expected 11-syllable line four times and a 2-syllable line instead of 4-syllable line twice. Most of these variations occur in the last stanza, a site where Dickinson frequently shortens lines. She also echoes the hymn-meter's precision in her frequent patterned use of polysyllabic line endings and catalectic lines, which create complex rhythmic patterns that are neither distinctly falling nor rising.

In "How the old Mountains drip with Sunset" (F327), for example, the 9-syllable first and third lines of each stanza scan as iambic with a final unstressed, unrhymed syllable, whereas the 5-syllable second and fourth lines are catalectic, beginning with a stressed syllable and ending on stressed monosyllabic rhymes.[52] For Dickinson, a 9-syllable line is relatively long, hence its use here may suggest the excess of the sunset's beauty, or of the speaker's chutzpah in recreating such visual extravagance in metaphor. The length of the first and third lines also gives a bolder punch to the 5-syllable lines (in contrast to the alteration of 8- and 6-syllable lines, which also form 14-syllable two-line units, but with a different internal rhythm). Almost every line begins with a stressed then an unstressed syllable, hence falling rhythm, but the first and third lines switch immediately to an iambic or rising rhythm, creating the common iambic-verse chiastic pattern of stressed, two unstressed, and then another stressed syllable (as marked in the last stanza below), emphasizing the repeated exclamatory "How."[53]

How the old Mountains drip with Sunset
How the Hemlocks burn –
How the Dun Brake is draped in Cinder
By the Wizard Sun –

How the old Steeples hand the Scarlet
Till the Ball is full –
Have I the lip of the Flamingo
That I dare to tell?

Then, how the Fire ebbs like Billows –
Touching all the Grass
With a departing – Sapphire – feature –
As a Duchess passed –

How a small Dusk crawls on the Village
Till the Houses blot
And the odd Flambeau, no men carry
Glimmer on the Street –

How it is Night – in Nest and Kennel –
And where was the Wood –
Just a Dome of Abyss is Bowing
Into Solitude –

Thése are | the Ví|sions flítt|ed Guí|do –   Us | uS | uS | uS | u –
Títian –| néver | tóld –   Su – | Su | S –   [_S |u – S | uS]
Dómen|ichí|no drópped | his pén|cil –   Us | uS | uS | uS | u
Pára||lýzed, with | Góld – [54]   Su | S,u | S –   [_S |uS, | uS]

As in "I felt a Funeral, in my Brain," Dickinson here also places two-syllable words in falling rhythms across foot boundaries so that they both support and syncopate an iambic rhythm, as seen in the last stanza's *Visions, flitted, Guido,* and *pencil.*[55] In this poem of competitively fanciful description, where the speaker flaunts verbal skills surpassing the representational art of Italian masters, the tension of her wonder at nature's beauty and her glee at "dar[ing]" to describe something beyond the ability of the greatest painters may be reflected in the poem's competing rhythms, emphatic line beginnings, and uneven line lengths.

Dickinson is brilliant in creating rhythmic combinations of odd- and even-numbered-syllable lines. "She sights a Bird – she chuckles –" (F351) constructs the comic suspense of its narrative through a 7686 iambic quatrain; one hears the difference between this stanza's shorter and longer, even- and odd-syllable lines distinctly:

	syllables	beats	
She sights a Bird – she chuckles –	7	3	
She flattens – then she crawls –	6	3	
She runs without the look of feet –	8	4	
Her eyes increase to Balls –	6	3	
Her Jaws stir – twitching – hungry –	7	3	]mouth stirs – longing –
Her Teeth can hardly stand –	6	3	
She leaps, but Robin leaped the first –	8	4	
Ah, Pussy, of the Sand,	6	3	
The Hopes so juicy ripening –	7	3	
You almost bathed your Tongue –	6	3	
When Bliss disclosed a hundred Toes –	8	4	] wings –
And fled with every one –	6	3	

(F351)

[handwritten margin notes: no dashes illustrates the cat's quickness as opposed to the careful deliberation inspired by the dashes in the 1st 2 in the lines]

Here the cat's cautious stalking is set up in the initial alteration of unstressed and stressed line endings, necessitating a brief pause in enunciating the consecutive unstressed syllables at the end of line one and beginning of line two. This effect is heightened by the fact that line two begins a new syntactic unit but also by the short phrases, punctuated by dashes, that characterize both lines: " – she chúckles – / She fláttens –" (- uSu – / uSu –). The long (8-syllable) third line of the stanza, however, is a single phrase without punctuating interruption or metrical variation, suggesting the cat's quickness in contrast to her earlier deliberation ("She rúns withóut the lóok of féet –"—uSuSuSuS). This pattern of contiguous unaccented syllables at the end of the 7-syllable and beginning of the 6-syllable lines, followed by the uninterrupted 8-syllable line, is almost exactly repeated in the second stanza, where the first line of the stanza is again broken into short segments, ends on the unaccented syllable of a polysyllabic word, and the third line again has a more continuous flow. In both cases, we hear the third line as fuller because of its greater length, smooth rhythmic progression from the previous 6-syllable line (ending with a stressed syllable), and iambic conclusion.

In the third stanza, the long vowels of the first two lines, in stressed and unstressed syllables (H*o*pes *so* j*u*icy r*i*pening – / *You* almost b*a*thed y*ou*r), again have the effect of slowing the reader's pace, continuing the suspense of the cat's anticipated spring. In speaking them, one can almost feel the mouth watering, a sensation interrupted by the crisper, longer, comic third line: "When Bliss disclosed a hundred Toes –." The internal rhyme of "disclosed" and "Toes" emphasizes the long *o*s of the previous lines while the consonantal cluster of "Bli*ss* di*scl*osed a hu*ndr*ed *T*oes," sounds that can't be elided, suggests the scampering of small feet. The punchline—"And fled with every one –"—rounds off the released narrative tension of the preceding eight-syllable line, bringing a lightly cadenced closure to the tale. The anticlimax of the final line is heightened by the fact that the poem ends on a rhyme that is less resonant than the echoing and internally rhyming long *o*s of the dramatically more intense preceding lines: *Tongue/one* following *Hopes/so/almost/disclosed/Toes*. Together with sound play and syntax, the 7686 stanzaic structure of this poem contributes to its comic effect—both in its constructed suspense and in the relief of comic closure: the eight-syllable line brings narrative balance, giving each stanza the familiar 86 conclusion. All's well with this world, even though the poem instructs us that we, like the Pussy, may find our source of keenly anticipated "Bliss" to be "fled" more often than not.[56]

I do not mean to say that any meter functions only to create one kind of effect in Dickinson's poems. Far from it! In "He fumbles at your Soul," Dickinson uses the same predominantly 7686 structure to present an encounter with an unspecified, fearful but seductive power. This extraordinary poem begins with a stanza in 6686, moves to 7686 for the middle two stanzas, and concludes with a refrain-like stanza of 86. As copied into fascicle 22, it reads:[57]

	syllables	beats	
He fumbles at your Soul	6	2	
As Players at the Keys –	6	2	
Before they drop full Music on –	8	4	
He stuns you by Degrees –	6	2	
Prepares your brittle substance	7	3	]nature
For the etherial Blow	6	2	
By fainter Hammers – further heard –	8	4	
Then nearer – Then so – slow –	6	3	
Your Breath – has chance to straighten –	7	3	]time
Your Brain – to bubble cool –	6	3	
Deals One – imperial Thunderbolt –	8	4	
That peels your naked soul –	6	3	]scalps

When Winds hold Forests in their Paws –	8	4	]take
The Firmaments – are still –	6	2	]Universe – is

(F477 B)

"He fumbles" begins decisively: the 6-syllable line has only two key words and sounds, or two fully realized beats—as do the other two 6-syllable lines of this stanza; in fact, all three lines have the same uSusuS rhythmic pattern. This is minimalist reporting, giving the reader news that is shocking and wholly un-expected even though it describes an event that apparently happens repeat-edly ("He fumbles") and to an undefined "you"—which might well mean *us*. In contrast, the 8-syllable third line introduces the fullness of four anticipated metrical beats as well as a fifth semantic stress: "Befóre they dróp fúll Músic ón –," or uS|uS|US|us. The sequence "drop full Music" doesn't disrupt the iambic undertone but suggests the authority of the player in its variation of rhythm and anticipates the violence of his climax. This line also introduces a temporal note to the poem's anticipation: there is a "Before . . . full Music" and therefore by implication also an after. These lines move with ominous deliberation—the third line in part because of its unanticipated stresses.

In the next two stanzas, the rhythm varies slightly, as what "He" does and how "you" respond continue their inexorable progress. As in "She sights a Bird," the 7-syllable line opening stanzas two and three ends on the unstressed syllable of a polysyllabic word, which causes a slight glottal stop before the un-accented syllable at the beginning of the following line, even while the syntax demands continuation. Generally in this poem, Dickinson plays the tension of enjambed complex syntax against the hesitations and elongations of the poem's meter, punctuation, drawn-out vowels, and soft consonants (r's). The 8-syllable third line in the second stanza contains no extra semantic stress but instead an arresting internal dash and parallel alliteration, in effect breaking the line in two ("fainter Hammers – further heard –"), preparing the reader for the extreme retardation of the final line in this stanza, with its two internal dashes and repetition of *n*'s, *r*'s, *s*'s, and *o*'s: "Then nearer – Then so – slow –." This stanza's 8-syllable line is also the first to move the reader into the experi-ence of the poem's "you" through the comparatives "fainter" and "further," shifting the focus away from what "He" does to how "you" feel and hear. Be-cause of its enjambment, this second stanza is the most tense of the poem. The reader has to hear the continuation of both the poem's introductory clause ("He fumbles . . . stuns . . . Prepares" building in the next stanza to ". . . Deals . . .") and its secondary clause: "so – slow – [that] // Your Breath – has chance to straighten." The syntax balances his action with "your" response.

The third stanza of the poem, again structured 7686, brings both clauses to conclusion and the narrative to its climax: once "you" have prepared yourself through enduring these preliminary "Blow[s]" in parallel to His preparatory fumbling, "He . . . Deals One – imperial Thunderbolt – / That peels [scalps] your naked soul –." This stanza again contains so many internal pauses that each line functions both to continue the urgent syntactic thrust of the narrative and to retard that progress, making us linger in the immediate combined horror and wonder of "His" power and "your" experience. Again, one hears a difference between the opening 7-syllable line and the markedly more active 8-syllable line—in this case further lengthened by the eliding of "ial" into one syllable in "imperial." Like "Befóre they dróp fúll Músic ón," "Déals Óne – impérial Thúnderbólt" has an unexpected point of semantic and grammatical stress (US – uSuSuS). Both these lines (as also "When Wínds hóld Fórests in their Páws"; uSUSusuS) fulfill their four-beat expectation but with significant variation of the rhythm. In each case, a sequence of two or three strongly stressed and syntactically significant syllables gives the lines ponderous heft (drop full Music; Deals One; Winds hold Forests). Far from comic in tone, "He fumbles" narrates a scene of primal encounter with a force that may be divine, sexual, or imaginative, and of suspense that is simultaneously fear and expectation. Its metrical structure and the differing realization of stressed syllables in each stanza's one 8-syllable line help to create a sense of disequilibrium, the edginess of not knowing whether this is a state "you" desire or fear, or both, but knowing that once the fumbling begins the "Thunderbolt" will inevitably follow, as will that post-orgasmic moment of "still[ness]." Here Dickinson's complex syntax and enjambment over more than one stanza are not consistent with hymn structure, nor is the shift of stanza pattern between a 6686 and a 7686 structure. Yet her general use of rhythmic patterns based on the difference of a single syllable between paired lines links her verse to hymns, as does her remarkable variety of repeated patterns in the range of 4- to 9-syllable lines.

Dickinson's most common alteration of stanzas within a poem is from her first to her second most frequently used form, or 8686 to 6686. This shift occurs in an 1862 poem, "The Whole of it came not at once –," where the 8686 form of stanza one changes to 6686 for the rest of the poem:

line		syllables	
1	The Whole of it came not at once –	8	
2	'Twas Murder by degrees –	6	
3	A Thrust – and then for Life a chance	8	
4	The Bliss to cauterize –	6	]The certain prey to teaze –
5	The Cat reprieves the mouse	6	
6	She eases from her teeth	6	
7	Just long enough for Hope to teaze –	8	]stir
8	Then mashes it to death –	6	crunches

9	'Tis Life's award – to die –	6	
10	Contenteder if once –	6	
11	Than dying half – then rallying	8	
12	For consciouser Eclipse –	6	totaller

(F485)

We hear this rhythmic shift immediately in the brevity of line 5, and the unanticipated sequence of three lines of 6 syllables beginning with line 4, emphasizing by contrast the 8 syllables of line 7. Perhaps Dickinson makes this shift because she hears a particular conjunction of syntax and rhythm at the beginning of a poem and then at some point a more concise or truncated rhythm; or this shift may be a part of her general move toward greater concision as poems progress—most marked in line length and number of lines per stanza as a poem concludes. Exactly the same pattern of change occurs in "That first Day, when you praised Me, Sweet," (F470), "The Birds begun at Four o'clock –" (F504 B), and "I think To Live – may be a Bliss" (F757). "I found the words to every thought" (F436) instead changes from an 8659 pattern to 8686; "I felt my life with both my hands" (F357) moves from an 8686 stanza to 8668, then 8956, finally returning to 8686. "A Burdock twitched my gown" (F289 B) shifts twice, from 668 to 6664 to 664. "If I may have it, when it's dead," (F431) begins with an 8686 pattern but uncharacteristically moves into long meter (8s) for its final five stanzas. Clearly Dickinson is writing in stanzas but not by any rule.[58] She shifts from one stanza form to the next as seems most appropriate to her topic or as she hears the rhythms of her words, but not with any predictable tonal association with a particular form. Perhaps the fact that so many of her poems involve thinking through an implied question or a process of reflection encourages movement from one rhythmic structure to another.

In some poems, Dickinson shifts to a new pattern for a single stanza mid-poem—as demonstrated earlier in "I felt a Funeral, in my Brain," where the repeated 8686 pattern is interrupted in the second stanza by 7686. The transition reads:

I felt a Funeral, in my Brain,
And Mourners to and fro
Kept treading – treading – till it seemed
That Sense was breaking through –

And when they all were seated,
A Service, like a Drum –
Kept beating – beating – till I thought
My mind was going numb –

And then I heard them lift a Box . . .

(F340, lines 1–9)

"It was not Death, for I stood up," (F355) includes a single stanza of 6686, and "Because I could not stop for Death –" (F479) one stanza of 6886, within their 8686 patterns. In other poems, Dickinson uses more than two stanza forms. "There's a certain Slant of light" (F320) makes brilliant use of an opening 7575 catalectic quatrain, shifting to a trochaic and catalectic 6585 measure in the penultimate stanza, then to 8585 at the end of the poem. This movement to lines alternating even- and odd-numbered syllables gives a fuller and softer tone to its bleak observation through its inclusion of unstressed line-final syllables in contrast with the first stanza's juxtaposition of relatively stressed syllables at the beginning and end of each line. One hears this difference as Dickinson moves from the opening, ponderous lines to the final two stanzas:

1	There's a certain Slant of light,	SuSuSuS	7
	Winter Afternoons –	SuSuS	5
	That oppresses, like the Heft	suSusuS	7
	Of Cathedral Tunes –	suSuS	5
5	Heavenly Hurt, it gives us –	Su(u)SuSu	7(6?)
	We can find no scar,	SuSuS	5
	But internal difference –	SuSuSu(u)	7(6?)
	Where the Meanings, are –	SuSus	5
	None may teach it – Any –	SuSuSu	6
10	'Tis the Seal Despair –	SuSuS	5
	An imperial affliction	suSusuSu	8
	Sent us of the Air –	SusuS	5
	When it comes, the Landscape listens –	SuSuSuSu	8
	Shadows – hold their breath –	SuSuS	5
15	When it goes, 'tis like the Distance	SuSusuSu	8
	On the look of Death –	suSuS	5

Line 11, the first eight-syllable line, introduces the first two-line sequence without a phrasal break. This smoother progression, however, does not abate the poem's feeling of oppressive weight, and the mid-line caesurae in lines 13 to 15 intensify the poem's disjunction.

The poem's final lines and images—the listening landscape and "Distance" as death's image—feel suspended, an effect created in part through the longer-lined rush of syllables in lines 11 and 12, followed by the next lines' staggered syntactic breaks, and by the poem's repeated invitation to elongate the enunciation of syllables in polysyllabic words. In stanza two, "Heavenly" and "difference" ambiguously invite full pronunciation, as "imperial affliction" definitely does in stanza three, although we unthinkingly elide syllables of such words in other poems to maintain the meter.[59] The hard consonants and *s*'s of the final stanza (it, Landscape, listens, Shadows, goes, it, 'tis, like, Distance, look, Death) similarly slow the speaking of these lines despite their lighter stresses than in stanza one, marking the uncanny precision of this oppression, pervasive as the air but aimed to create "internal difference" in each soul. Everything in the poem seems to contribute to the simultaneous ephemerality and heaviness, the vagueness and deeply felt effect of this phenomenon of light. This poem about the cold and niggardly brightness of winter skies as manifesting the indifference of a punishing God moves seamlessly from the short, bleakly end-stopped lines of its first stanza to the longer but equally despairing lines of its conclusion.[60]

More radically, Dickinson at times moves from an apparently accentual-syllabic stanzaic pattern into the ballad's accentual, or more irregular, patterning—usually by shortening lines at the end of a poem. In "The Soul selects her own Society –" such shortening in the final stanza maintains the two beats of the previous 4-syllable lines, but uses only two monosyllabic words: "Choose One" and "Like Stone"—(F409).[61] Dickinson also often truncates final stanza structure. The previously discussed "He fumbles" ends with two lines rather than a quatrain. "The Love a Life can show Below" (F285 B) begins 886886 then shifts to an 8686 quatrain in conclusion. "It ceased to hurt me, though so slow" moves from quatrains of 8s to 8844 in stanza three and then a final stanza of 886, concluding: "Nor what consoled it, I could trace – / Except, whereas 'twas Wilderness – / It's better – almost Peace –" (F421). Judy Jo Small finds "metrical deficiency" in the "calculated shock" of such truncated conclusions, but I believe that Dickinson finds expressive flexibility rather than a rigidity she must distort in metrical patterning (Small 86, 192, 193). She often varies closing structures to intensify a poem's ending. For example, in "It ceased to hurt me, though so slow" the penultimate stanza of 8844 sounds cut off, since it works rhythmically as three lines of 8, but it also sets up a new aural expectation for a tercet, fulfilled by the closing stanza's 886 pattern.[62] With its slant aaa rhyme (trace/Wilderness/Peace) and standard tercet form, this 886 stanza brings the poem to a cadenced, indeed peaceful, conclusion. Again, such variation among stanzaic forms and use of truncated lines or stanzas is impossible in a hymn model.

Dickinson's expressive freedom in moving among stanzaic forms and in truncating concluding stanzas and lines must have been influenced by her familiarity with isochronic forms, like that of the traditional ballad. Although she does not write a large number of overtly ballad meter poems in any given year, she writes them throughout her life. These poems sometimes maintain a consistent number of beats and sometimes shift patterns mid-poem, although with less precision than when Dickinson shifts from one accentual syllabic stanza form to another. "We dream – it is good we are dreaming-" (F584) proceeds according to beats in a line; all but two lines have three beats, although the syllable count varies from six to nine.[63] The first stanza reads:

	syllables	beats	
We dréam – it is góod we are dréaming –	9	3	]We should dream
It would húrt us – wére we awáke –	8	3	
But sínce it is pláying – kíll us,	8	3	]They
And wé are pláying – shríek –	6	3	

This is classic ballad meter in its indiscriminate inclusion of unstressed syllables between major beats, and Dickinson makes powerful use of its loosened measure in this poem of reflection about the nightmare of living, ending every stanza with a 6- or 7-syllable comparatively compact line, anticipating the curt finality of her conclusion: "It's prudenter – to dream –."

Similarly, "Did you ever stand in a Cavern's Mouth –" (F619) provides a classic example of ballad meter in its first two stanzas, where the poem is gothic in its narrative:

	syllables	beats
Did you ever stand in a Cavern's Mouth –	10	4
Widths out of the Sun –	5	3
And look – and shudder, and block your breath –	9	4
And deem to be alone	6	3

When Dickinson's poem leaves the "Goblin" "horror" of flight from the dark behind, however, its rhythm turns to even 8686 iambic meter:

	syllables	beats
Did you ever look in a Cannon's face –	10	4
Between whose Yellow eye –	6	3
And your's – the Judgment intervened –	8	4
The Question of 'To die" –	6	3

(stanza 3)

Once stanza 3 poses its initiating question, shifting focus from melodrama to war, the poem's rhythm changes and remains evenly iambic throughout the fourth stanza.[64] The altogether gothic psychological ghost story of "One need not be a chamber – to be Haunted –" (F407 A) is not in ballad meter, however; it has an irregular structure of line lengths (11 to 2) and beats (5 to 2) but follows a regular meter of alternating catalectic and iambic lines, with only one line including extra-metrical or additional unstressed syllables—the patently poetic or archaically imitative, "Than unarmed, one's a'self encounter."

"Blazing in Gold – and / Quenching – in Purple!" (F321 A) uses loosened ballad meter throughout in a repeated chiastic rhythm (SuuS):

	syllables	beats
Blazing in Gold – and / Quenching – in Purple!	10	4
Leaping – like Leopards in the sky –	8	4
Then – at the feet of the old Horizon –	10	4
Laying it's spotted face – to die!	8	4
Stooping as low as the kitchen window –	10	4
Touching the Roof – / And tinting the Barn –	9	4
Kissing it's Bonnet to the Meadow –	9	4
And the Juggler of Day – is gone![65]	8	3

The agile and ecstatic activity of "Day"—or day's "Juggler"—is here represented through the excess of quickened, unaccented syllables between the poem's four beats (three beats in the concluding line). Dickinson syncopates the rhythm of her fascicle copy of this poem through dashes and the splitting of metrical lines (marked above with a slash) but not in the copy published in *Drum Beat* in 1864 or the 1866 copy to Higginson, which contain no stanza division, split lines, or dashes. In either form, one hears the ballad rhythm. Dickinson would have read hundreds of such poems, but may have given particular attention to Emerson's "Each and All," a poem she marked both in the table of contents and along one margin in her volume of his *Poems* (EDR 21), and which includes several lines with additional unstressed syllables between beats, or in Longfellow's "The Happiest Land. Fragment of a Modern Ballad"—one of several of his ballad-style poems, which she (or someone) marks by folding the page in half (EDR 288).

"Did we disobey Him?" (F299) introduces the balladic model through reduction rather than increase of syllables in its falling rhythm.[66] The poem's second line contains just three words but three strong beats—a technique Dickinson rarely uses near the beginning of a poem:

	syllables	beats	
Did we disobey Him?	6	3	SusuSu
Just one time!	3	3	SUS
Charged us to forget Him –	6	3	SusuSu
But we could'nt learn!	5	3	SusuS
Were Himself – such a Dunce –	6		3 (2?) SuS – uuS
What would we – do?	4	3	SuS – U
Love the dull lad – best –	5	3	SuSu – S
Oh, would'nt you?	4	3	S,UsU

The unevenness of this poem lies in part in its heavy semantic and syntactic emphasis within the few words of each line. Only three of the poem's eight lines have the six syllables that would be anticipated in a standard 3-beat line, and some of those lines might be spoken with only two beats, in an anapestic rhythm (uuSuuS): "Were Himself – such a Dunce –." This poem indirectly pleading with a lover to love "the dull lad" who refuses to "forget Him" is awkward in nearly every respect—from its use of inconsistent and distancing pronouns to its use of extremely short syntactic units, punctuated by dashes, and uneven rhythms. Consequently, although its beats are relatively constant, the poem resists a ballad's anticipated flowing rhythm. Instead, the emphatic and disjointed phrases enact the speaker's simultaneous self-abasing apology, defiant declaration, and instruction. The regularity of the beat in counterpoint with the poem's syntactic and semantic fits and starts suggest with what difficulty any speech issues.

"I went to Heaven –" (F577 B) uses a 2-beat ballad line and has an even more dramatically uneven rhythm:

	syllables	beats
I went to Heaven –	5	2
'Twas a small Town –	4	2
Lit – with a Ruby –	4	2
Lathed – with Down –	3	2
Stiller – than the fields	5	2
At the full Dew –	4	2
Beautiful – as Pictures –	6	2
No Man drew –	3	2 (3?)
People – like the Moth –	5	2
Of Mechlin – frames –	4	2
Duties – of Gossamer –	6	2
And Eider – names –	4	2
Almost – contented –	5	2
I – could be –	3	2
'Mong such unique	4	2
Society –	4	2

(577)

This poem's rhythm varies from iambic in its opening and closing lines ("I wént to Héaven –" and "'Mong súch uníque / Socíetý –") to more broadly rising ("'Twas a smáll Tówn –"), with some distinctly falling rhythms ("Béautiful – as Píctures –" and "Dúties – of Góssamer –") and some lines that might be read as catalectic with three beats rather than two, especially because of the caesura following the first two syllables: "Stíller – thán the fíelds" and "Péople – líke the

Móth –." These nuanced shifts in rhythm prevent this poem from having a strong rhythmic drive (hence open it to various ways to hear its rhythms) until the last four lines, which function like a rhyming couplet of iambic tetrameter. The final "Society" playfully, almost parodically, elevates the secondary stress of its final "y" to provide the expected final beat and rhyme, but on the whole this poem resists "easy" rhythms (to return to Parker's definition of the ballad), a resistance underlined by the mid-line dashes, interrupting the syntax every few words.

Clearly, Dickinson departs from the regularity of balladic meter just as she changes hymn stanzas within a poem. "It dont sound so terrible – quite – as it did –" (F384) departs even more dramatically than "I went to Heaven –" from its basic 4-beat rhythm. Here again the uneven rhythm may call attention to the speaker's distress: it was written following the death of Frazar Stearns in battle on 14 March 1862, an event deeply disturbing to all the Dickinsons.[67] No stanza matches any other and the final stanza closes down to primarily 2-beat rather than 4-beat lines. Again, there is nothing "easy" in this poem's rhythms, and its last two stanzas push strongly toward free verse:

		syllables	beats
1	It dont sóund so térrible – quíte – as it díd –	11	4
2	I rún it óver – "Déad", Brain – "Déad".	8	4 (5?)
3	Pút it in Látin – léft of my schóol –	9	4
4	Seéms it dont shríek so – únder rúle.	8	4
5	Túrn it, a líttle – fúll in the fáce	9	4
6	A Tróuble looks bítterest –	7	2
7	Shíft it – júst –	3	2
8	Sáy "When Tomórrow cómes this wáy –	8	4
9	Í shall have wáded dówn one Dáy".	8	4
10	I suppóse it will ínterrúpt me sóme	10	4
11	Till I gét accústomed – but thén the Tómb	10	4
12	Like óther new Thíngs – shows lárgest – thén –	9	4 (5?)
13	And smáller, by Hábit –	6	2
14	It's shréwder thén	4	2
15	Pút the Thóught in advánce – a Yéar –	8	4 (3?)
16	How líke "a fít" – then –	5	2
17	Múrder – wéar!	3	2

This poem's opening exclamation is disrupted through punctuation and semantically by the isolated and stressed "quite," (the death is not "quite" as "terrible" as it first sounded). The effect of disruption is intensified by the concentration of stressed words and pauses in line 2, "'Dead,' Brain – 'Dead',"

the extremely uneven line lengths, and enjambment: "[F]ull in the face" begins a new sentence unit mid-line (full in the face / a trouble looks bitterest),
although "full" has no capital. The last stanza also discards the established
aabb rhyme scheme for an abab rhyme. Such variation in rhythm, rhyme,
and stanza structure makes clear how little of a "fit" the speaker finds this
death.

Dickinson also writes poems that have no predictable pattern of line
length or stanza structure but nonetheless maintain a regular meter—such
as "A Toad, can die of Light –" (F419). This poem begins with two lines of six
syllables then four lines of four syllables—a kind of pattern, but not one that
anticipates the 10-syllable line concluding this stanza or the varied line
lengths of its second stanza (64826). Yet the meter is so evenly iambic that it
cannot be considered free verse, despite the abrupt variation in line length
and beats, as we see in the first stanza:

A Toad, can die of Light –	6	3	
Death is the Common Right	6	3	]mutual – * equal –
Of Toads and Men –	4	2	
Of Earl and Midge	4	2	
The privilege –	4	2	
Why swagger, then?	4	2	
The Gnat's supremacy is large as Thine –	10	5	

Similarly, "Delight is as the flight – " (F317) has irregular line lengths in its
9-line stanzas (eight lines in the final stanza) but is iambic throughout and
features frequent full rhymes. Dickinson would have been familiar with published poetry following a metrical rhythm through otherwise unpredictable
line and stanza patterns—for example, the previously quoted "Growing
Dark" by Emily Judson (SR 1 March 1862). The poem begins:

The lizard, with his mouse-like eyes,	8	4	a
Peeps from the mortice with surprise	8	4	a
At such strange quiet after day's harsh din;	10	5	b
Then ventures boldly out,	6	3	c
And looks about,	4	2	c
And with his hollow feet	6	3	d
Treads his small evening beat,	6	3	d
Darting upon his prey	6	3	e
In such a tricksy, winsome sort of way,	10	5	e
His delicate marauding seems no sin.	10	5 [3?]	b

This anthropomorphic description of a "tricksy" lizard uses a variation of
line length and rhythms resembling Dickinson's.

Dickinson covers the full spectrum of metrical realization in her verse. Some poems repeat precise metrical patterns in every stanza; some use more than one stanza type but each type is exactly realized and familiar; others use a loosened balladic beat throughout, or shift from one pattern of beats to another. Still others move from a regular accentual syllabic or accentual pattern into rhythmic irregularity. It is primarily in the frequency with which she departs from set stanzaic patterns, however, that Dickinson's use of metered forms differs from that of her peers, and such variation is most pronounced before 1866, although it remains a distinctive element of her verse. Of the 522 poems she wrote in 1862 and 1863, 61 are highly irregular in stanzaic structure, line length, and rhyme, and another 68 use more than one stanzaic form, for a total of 129 markedly irregular poems or close to a quarter of the poems written during these two years. She also uses 20 distinct stanzaic or metrical forms during these years (and in others years before 1866 over 30 distinct forms). If one counts as "irregular" poems that include an extra-stanzaic line or shortened stanzas and lines, the total of irregular poems written during 1862 and 1863 is 156, or around 30 percent. In contrast, in 1877, Dickinson uses 16 different forms in her 42 poems, but only 3 are markedly irregular and only an additional 2 change stanzaic form mid-poem (12 percent). Moreover, over half (24 of 42) follow a metrical pattern precisely, mostly common or short meter. Similarly, in 1876, 57 percent of Dickinson's poems follow a single metrical/stanzaic pattern precisely from beginning to end, whereas in 1862, only 21 percent do.[68]

As suggested earlier, Dickinson's use of both hymn and ballad models has interesting implications for understanding her process of composition. Her occasional imitation of popular registers appears to be self-conscious, suggesting that she may have set herself exercises—as in "now I will write a Scottish-style ballad," resulting in "Poor little Heart!" (F214) with its repeated "dinna care," quoting Robert Burns.[69] She may also at times have decided to experiment with combining different stanzaic forms. Primarily, however, it is my sense that Dickinson's composition began with the rhythm of a stanza in her head, a rhythm that might be stimulated by her reading, a poem she knew, or a song—typically a unit of rhythmic completion involving multiple lines and rhyme, or a stanza.[70] A beginning stanza set a pattern. The next stanza might establish a different pattern without apparently disrupting Dickinson's conception of appropriate form—or perhaps more perfectly fulfilling her sense of form for that continuing thought process or observation. Composing to a stanzaic rhythm did not mean slavishly adhering to a pattern; stanzas gave force and shape to thought through their anticipated rhythmic and syntactic closure—even when altered, or forestalled by enjambment. If Dickinson had composed primarily by the line, or the phrase, it is unlikely that so much of her verse would be written in stanzas, and that so much of her syntax and rhyme would follow stanzaic models, even when she writes her lines without stanza division. Similarly, it is unlikely that her shifts away from an initial pattern would themselves take stanzaic form, as they so often do. Dickinson's variant words and phrases are almost without exception metrically and grammatically identical to the word she first writes, hence also fit the governing rhythmic structure.[71]

In those instances where there is no apparent stanzaic or metrical organization, Dickinson's composition by tune or rhythm may correspond more clearly to the "weird & beautiful melodies, all from her own inspiration" Kate Anthon mentions than to the "old, odd tunes" Dickinson described as "madden[ing] me, with their grief and fun" (L184). These are free verse compositions—if by free verse we mean poems possibly involving meter and rhyme but without any pattern predicting line length, meter, stanzaic structure, or rhyme scheme from one line to the next.[72] T. S. Eliot's "Prufrock" could serve as an example of a free verse poem using both meter and rhyme; the poem begins with rhymed catalectic lines followed by an unrhymed line of trochees: "Let us go then, you and I, / When the evening is spread out against the sky / Like a patient etherised upon a table" (3). Eliot's repeated description of women's pretentious chatter similarly occurs in a rhymed and metered (iambic) couplet: "In the róom the wómen cóme and gó / Tálking of Míchelángeló."

Through her reading in the 1850s, Dickinson had some familiarity with free verse. She apparently admired the work of Martin Farquhar Tupper, a British poet who preceded Whitman in writing long-lined, unrhymed, and unmetered verse; his *Proverbial Philosophy* was owned by the Dickinsons and heavily marked.[73] Although there is no record that she admired Whitman, she would have read his "Bardic Symbols," an early version of "As I ebb'd with the ocean of life," in the April 1860 *Atlantic* (445–47), and the *Republican* printed both a lengthy negative review of *Leaves of Grass* and a skillful parody, beginning "I happify myself" (*SR* 16 June 1860, 4). It is also possible Dickinson had seen biblical passages lineated as verse—not just the Psalms but books like Job and Isaiah. As mentioned in Chapter 2, McGuffey's 1841 *Reader* prints ten biblical passages as poetry in unrhymed, unmetered lines of varying lengths. For example, a passage from Revelations was printed as:

And after these things, I saw another angel descending from heaven,
Having great power: and the earth was enlightened with his glory:
And he cried mightily with a loud voice: saying
She is fallen! she is fallen!
Babylon the great!
And is become the habitation of demons
And the hold of every impure spirit . . .

(McGuffey 257)

Formally irregular popular poems and the few examples of free verse Dickinson knew might have encouraged her to experiment with leaving all patterned structures behind.

While Dickinson's free verse never wholly abandons meter, stanza, and rhyme, it does at times abandon rhyme and depart markedly from even the loosened beats of ballad meter, creating rhythms that correspond to no consistent pattern. "It is dead – Find it –" (F434) is unrhymed and without a metrical norm:

1	It is dead – Find it –	5	2
	Out of sound – Out of Sight –	6	2
	"Happy"? Which is wiser –	5	3
	You, or the Wind?	4	2
5	"Conscious"? Wont you ask that –	6	3
	Of the low Ground?	4	1 (2?)
	"Homesick"? Many met it –	6	3
	Even through them – This cannot testify –	10	4 (5?)
9	Themself – as dumb –	4	2

All but the penultimate 10-syllable line vary between 4 and 6 syllables, and 2 or 3 beats, but the strong internal caesura in every line except the sixth and the multiple mid-line questions disrupt any metrical flow. Even the normal grammatical stresses on the words "Happy," "Conscious" and "Homesick" become ambiguous: whereas each of these words normally has a falling rhythm, Dickinson's question mark emphasizes the final syllable, either shifting the stress entirely or evening it out between the two syllables. Moreover, the many pronouns, helping verbs, and conjunctions that normally take relative stress depending on their context and the metrical norm contribute ambiguously to this poem's rhythmic pattern, especially because there are so many of them: it, Out, Out, You, Wont, you, that, it, through, them, This. This poem's multiple disruptions and fitful stops and starts may mimic the frustrated confusion of anyone attempting to question or find the dead.

The short syntactically determined lines and ambiguously stressed monosyllables in the first stanza of "While it is alive" (F287 B) similarly disrupt a clear sense of meter, perhaps not coincidentally again in dealing with the question of what happens at death.

While it is alive	5	2
Until Death touches it	6	3
While it and I lap one Air	7	4 (?)
Dwell in one Blood	4	3
Under one Sacrament	6	3
Show me division can split or pare –	9	4

Love is like Life – merely longer	8	4
Love is like Death, during the Grave	8	4
Love is the Fellow of the Resurrection	11	4
Scooping up the Dust and chanting "Live"!	9	5 (4?)

Beginning with the first line, the poem's rhythms are unclear. One might read "While it is alive" in ballad rhythm (usuuS), as a line with two beats (one weak), or instead as a catalectic line (SusuS), with three stresses.[74] The next two lines do not clarify the rhythm. Given the semantic and grammatical stress on "Death" and "touch[es]," "Until" is most logically read as two relatively unstressed syllables followed by two stresses (uuSSus), giving a strongly rising rhythm, but a super-iamb is unusual in the "easy" rhythms of ballad measure. The final four words of line three ("I lap one Air") might all take semantic stress, especially given the line's opening iambic rhythm: "While it and I" (uSuS). Reading either "and *I lap* one *Air*" (uSSuS) or "and *I* lap *one Air*" (uSuSS) disrupts an iambic norm, a disruption potentially repeated in the echoing patterns of the next two lines—"Dwell in one Blood / Under one Sacrament"—where the "one" might or might not be read as stressed. The final line in the first stanza returns to a loose ballad measure ("Show me division can split or pare –": SuuSuuSuS), yielding a catalectic line with falling rhythm at odds with the preceding lines' excess of stressed syllables. This poem's first stanza is rhythmically complex in a way suggesting that its lines are organized by syntax, not meter.

The unrhymed first stanza of "I can wade Grief – / Whole Pools of it –" (F312) also proceeds in a rhythm determined more clearly by syntax and semantic and interpretive emphasis than by metrical norm—again in part because of its many ambiguously stressed monosyllables. Although the poem's final lines settle into unmistakable iambs ("Give Himmaleh – / They'll carry – Him!"), up to that point the poem's strongest organizational unit is syntactic. The seven-stanza, 32-line poem "I'm saying every day / 'If I should be a Queen, Tomorrow'-" (F575) can also be scanned in a way producing a semblance of a ballad line with rising rhythms, but the scansion becomes so complex and the inconsistency of beats (as well as syllables) from line to line so great that free verse seems a better way to describe its procedure. With rhythms of from two to five beats, stanzas of four to twelve lines, no rhyme scheme (although periodic rhymes—sometimes in alternate, sometimes in consecutive lines), and lines organized by syntactic juncture, this poem's playful preparation for being "Summoned – unexpectedly – / To Exeter –" paradoxically presents its preparation for the conventions of elite status by rejecting conventions of verse. The speaker claims to "perch my Tongue / On Twigs of singing – rather high –" but is more influenced in her rhythms by "Put[ting] from my simple speech all plain word – " and taking on "other accents," different from those "heard" around her than by adopting the presumably ordered rhythms of royalty. Similarly, in "The Robin's my Criterion for Tune –" (F256), the line lengths and the rhyme patterns are so irregular (including one line that fits no part of a rhyming pattern) that even the iambic beat throughout does not prevent it from sounding uneven, perhaps in tongue-in-cheek parody of the assumed roughness of American "Provincial[]" verse in comparison with that of "The Queen."[75]

It is this tension between repeated patterns and differentiation from them that may make sense of the fact that Dickinson asserts to Higginson that she "could not drop the Bells" of meter at the same time that she acknowledges his criticism of her verse as "'uncontrolled'" and "'Wayward,'" asking "are these more orderly?" (L265, 271). And indeed her poetry takes on more "orderly" patterns after 1865, demonstrating greater reliance on the quatrain although perhaps in other ways departing from stanzaic norms.[76] In the 1880s, she may have composed by the phrase or line, although her completed poems from this period are typically more regular than her earlier compositions in metrical and stanzaic patterns, suggesting that the stanza continues to be the dominant form she hears. For the most part and definitely through her spectacular productivity before 1866, Dickinson distinctly ordered words and phrases into stanzas.[77] Shoptaw proposes that "poetic sound . . . helps produce poetic meaning" ("Cryptography" 222). Tunes in her head apparently helped Dickinson to filter or process out everything inessential so that what emerges is compact "amazing sense" ("This was a Poet –" F446).

The patterns of her verse also indicate that Dickinson composed her first stanzas first—unlike Marianne Moore, who composed her syllabic verse by the stanza but often did not compose the beginning stanza first. As Moore wrote to Ezra Pound in 1919, "the form of the original stanza of anything I have written has been a matter of expediency, hit upon as being approximately suitable to the subject," although this stage of stanzaic expediency occurs well after Moore has begun to play with phrases and lines (*Selected Letters* 122). In an interview with Donald Hall, she adds: "Words cluster like chromosomes, determining the procedure" (*Reader* 263). For Dickinson, the organizational process may also have been a clustering of words with a rhythm that "determin[ed] the procedure," or gave a structuring impulse, enabling her to work out an expression or thought. Her poems take shape as metered phrases within the patterns of a stanza, much like the lyrics of a song, which do not need to be written in prescriptive lines in order to be heard as distinct rhythmic units. Jane Eberwein notes that some of Dickinson's poems "go nowhere" after a "strong beginning," suggesting that she composes first stanzas first (*Strategies of Limitation* 128).[78] The well-documented history of "Safe in their Alabaster Chambers –" (F124 B, 1859) supports this hypothesis, as does her composition of "It sifts from Leaden Sieves –" (F291 B), where Dickinson revises all but the first stanza over a period of twenty-one years. Similarly, in the much later "The Mind lives on the Heart" (F1384, 1875), Dickinson maintains the first four lines intact (with one slight revision) as first written on a fragment of wrapping paper, but initially writes the last four lines with multiple corrections and variants and then later dramatically revises them.[79]

As already noted, starting in 1865, Dickinson begins writing a larger percentage of single-stanza (usually quatrain) poems. In later years, this percentage increases, or we have only a single stanza extant of what may at some point have been a longer poem. During the years when Dickinson did not make clean copies of her poems, the only source for many of her poems is her letters, and we know that she often sent only a single stanza or a few lines of a longer poem to correspondents.[80] It was common Victorian practice to quote excerpted lines of poetry in literature and letters. Especially if she composed in her head, it is possible that after 1865, she may have written a poem on a scrap of paper she did not preserve—or she may never have written out a poem from which she sent a few lines to a friend. In either case, Dickinson's tendency both to quote her work by groups of lines, often a stanza, and to write poems a stanza long in later years underline her propensity to compose in metrical units longer than the line, defined by a conjunction of, or the tension between, meter, rhyme, and syntax.

In contending that Dickinson writes in free verse lines, Susan Howe reports correspondence with Ralph W. Franklin in which he queries "What happens to [your argument] if the form lurking in the mind is the stanza?" Howe famously responds: "As a poet, I cannot assert that Dickinson composed in stanzas and was careless about line breaks. In the precinct of Poetry, a word, the space around a word, each letter, every mark, silence, or sound volatizes an inner law of form—moves on a rigorous line" (*Birth-mark* 134, 145). While I agree entirely with Howe that Dickinson was not "careless about line breaks" or any aspect of sound, I am convinced that in fact the rhythm lurking in her mind as she composed was most often the stanza, even when she was composing in what we might call free verse. To my mind, this is the only explanation consistent with her repeated rhythmic units, especially given her tendency to vary these structures by the stanza.

The arrangement of Dickinson's poems in fascicles further underlines both the importance of the stanza to her compositional practice and the idea that Dickinson had a conscious interest in experimentation with form: she often uses a particular stanzaic form several times in quick succession. For example, during 1863, Dickinson wrote only four poems in Common Particular Meter (886886), two of them written or copied in close succession in fascicle 36: "Behind Me – dips Eternity –" (F743) and "Sweet Mountains – Ye tell Me no lie –"

(F745). During the same year, she wrote fourteen poems in an 8585 rhythm (with some variation), seven of them copied consecutively or nearly so in Fascicle 37: "Autumn – overlooked my Knitting –," F786; "Bloom opon the Mountain stated –," F787 C; "Publication – is the Auction," F788; "All but Death, Can be adjusted," F789; "Growth of Man – like Growth of Nature –," F790; and "So the Eyes accost – and sunder," F792. As noted in Chapter 1, earlier in the year, she wrote three poems beginning with a ten-syllable line not repeated in the poem: "There's been a Death, in the Opposite House," (F547), "The Black Berry – wears a Thorn in his side –" (F548), and "The One that could repeat the Summer Day –" (F549 B), copied consecutively into fascicle 27. More remarkably, she copied two poems into fascicle 37 beginning with a stanza of highly irregular construction, namely lines of (11)492 syllables: "Four Trees – opon a solitary Acre –" (F778) and "Renunciation – is a piercing Virtue –" (F782)—the only times she ever uses this structure.[81] If Franklin's reconstruction of Dickinson's manuscript books corresponds at all to order of composition, she frequently writes several poems in succession in common meter: in Fascicle 24 (F512, 514, 516, 518, 519, 521, 522, 523, 524), fascicle 28 (F525), and Fascicle 26 (F589, 590, 591, 593, 595, 596, 597). Similarly, she at times writes more than one poem of highly irregular construction—for example, in Fascicle 29 ("Forget! The lady with the Amulet" F625, and "Undue Significance a starving man attaches" F626); Fascicle 31 ("What I can do – I will –" F641, "A Secret told –" F643, "For Death – or rather" F644 B, "To fill a Gap" F647); and Fascicle 36 ("Grief is a Mouse –" F753, and "Let Us play Yesterday –" F754). She does not, however, write poems successively with the same unusual end patterns, and poems that begin similarly (like "Four Trees" and "Renunciation") proceed quite differently. This tendency to repeat a pattern relatively quickly after using it once suggests that Dickinson may have had a particular rhythm or tune in her head for days, or that composing one poem in relation to a particular structure may have interested her in following up that trial with others in the same mode. Even if fascicle organization allows us to conclude nothing about composition, such patterns of arrangement suggest that Dickinson thinks of her poems in terms of formal patterns in addition to or rather than in thematic clusters.

Dickinson's verse marks a culmination of innovation with antebellum American poetic forms, a full mastery of short-lined verse patterns familiar in the 1840s and 1850s, written with exquisite ear and extraordinary rhythmic invention, as well as with a strikingly original syntactic concision and metaphorical range in the service of sometimes profound, sometimes playful philosophical and psychological enquiry. Such metered verse continued and continues to be written, but no other poet has manipulated its forms in more strikingly various ways, with greater sensitivity to the possibilities of short-lined expressivity, or perhaps with greater patterned irregularity. For

Dickinson, short-lined, metered, rhyming verse, as influenced by the loosened rhythms of balladic poems and songs, provided a form of enormous flexibility and capacity for thought experiments because it enabled composition through set and shifting, competing and interlocking rhythms and tunes. While this flexibility has something to do with the forms themselves and much to do with the nature of Dickinson's imagination, it is also a function of the cultural context in which hymns, ballads, popular songs, and poems by the most prestigious poets of her day enjoyed wide circulation, using similar forms with great variety. Dickinson apparently found it fruitful and inspiring to work out from communal norms, shared rhythms of thought and expression, well-known "tunes," in creating her own distinctive poems. The communal base must have been reassuring, anchoring her thought in a culture of exchange even while she chose not to publish. Dickinson's extraordinary accomplishment was to recognize the possibilities for an ambitious, complex, and powerfully expressive lyric poetry offered by this range of popular short-lined verse and song. Her work in turn opened new possibilities for further experimentation with concision in short-lined verse departing altogether from the hymn and ballad forms Dickinson heard as the foundation for nature's and her own meter.

4

Spoken Poetry and the Written Poem

"The Garrison of Cape Ann" would have been a fine poem but it has too much of the author in it . . .

AM November 1860

A word is dead, when it is said
Some say –
I say it just begins to live
That day

F278, 1862; transcribed by Frances Norcross 1894

THE TWO preceding chapters present evidence of Dickinson's closeness to her antebellum peers in valuing forms of verse that reveal some strain of wildness and in playing out the innovative rhythmic possibilities of both hymn and ballad forms and the intersections between them. Both these forms have a strong association with orality or performance—the ballad through its roots in oral tradition and the hymn through its assumed direct address to God in praise or prayer and its leaning toward plain language. Many of the elements characterizing Dickinson's verse also characterize speech: namely, its frequently paratactic structure; use of disjunction, questions, exclamations, and mid-sentence pauses; repetition; and use of colloquial idiom. Brita Lindberg-Seyersted calls Dickinson's illocutionary syntax and diction the single most important characteristic of her language.[1] Dickinson was also, however, unquestionably interested in how one writes a poem on the page. Unlike her meter, which does not change from one copy to the next, Dickinson's writing out of poems is largely unstable. Some aspects of inscription are invariable, as they are for her contemporaries: capitalization of the first word in a poetic line and strong line-endings, generally coincident with at least a minor syntactic juncture, so that a poetic line never concludes with an article or other minor function word. In contrast to these invariable features, Dickinson frequently alters capitalization within the line, punctuation, the use of space between stanzas, and the writing out of metrical lines. In short, while her poetry proceeds through sonic patterns, it is "oral" only in a secondary, written sense. As I will demonstrate in this chapter, the combination of a strong speaking presence with features that can only be seen on a page is most dramatically observed in Dickinson's experimentation with the writing out of metrical lines, so that one hears clear metrical units but sees poetic lines that do not correspond to the heard structure.

Dickinson's experimentation with formal elements of the page resembles those of other antebellum poets and publishers in that others use irregular or innovative divisions of metrical lines and multiple dashes or other nonstandard punctuation—although, to my knowledge, none as disjunctively as Dickinson. According to Jay Fliegelman, there was also a long-established practice in the United States of using written texts to communicate oral textures: "orality can be and in the eighteenth century often was, a defining characteristic of print, a set of cues within a text that signal it is to be heard by the ear (as performance) as much as it is to be read by the eye" (218n. 50). Dickinson's dashes, for example, would fit well-known patterns of using punctuation as a paralinguistic feature to signal hesitation, emphasis, or other rhetorical modes without having distinct elocutionary coding. According to Fliegelman, written orality was understood as both "public-oriented" and as representing an "inner voice of emotion," the same paradoxical or ambivalent combination seen in many of Dickinson's poems. Tom Paulin sees "dissenting Protestantism" as the key model for Dickinson's distinctive and antiauthoritarian "orality," describing both its and her language as "impatient of print"; Dickinson would learn from dissenting Protestant texts, he contends, "to communicate an overwhelming sense of the present moment, the now of utterance" in writing.[2] In *The People's Poetry,* Tyler Hoffman writes about a tradition of secondary orality in American poetry, or poems written for print publication but implying spoken performance.[3] In an age when oratory was among the most popular forms of public entertainment it is hardly surprising that writers of various kinds would compose for the ear, with an astute sense of audience and the effects of performance, whether the text was written, performed publicly, or both.[4] This chapter explores the extent to which Dickinson's speakers resemble the ballad-style speaker of many nineteenth-century poems and how the dramatic or performative element of her poems may help us understand the instability of her poetic inscription.

The tension between the material idiosyncrasies of Dickinson's punctuation, capitalization, lineation, and very occasional illustration, on the one hand, and the colloquial register and direct address of her language, on the other, is in part an extension of romantic poetry's negotiation between balladic orality and published verse. This negotiation was often represented in the romantic poet's appropriation of an untutored speaker who is close to nature and gives rise to the poet's reflection—like Wordsworth's leech gatherer and

solitary reaper in poems by those titles. Dickinson follows this model in constructing a "tired and sore" speaker soothed by a carefree whistler in "Heart
not so heavy as mine" (F88 C). According to Maureen McLane, in the early
nineteenth century the imitation of traditional ballads resulted in "the emer-
gence of a new multivalent literary orality," and a cultural logic that made
"the oral . . . virtually coextensive with the primitive"; orality offered literate
British poets "the romance of fled music," while offering cultural theory "the
primitive within" (*Balladeering* 21, 42, 41). Steve Newman similarly refers to
the ballad's hybrid textual and oral status, as a traditional form assumed to be
transmitted orally but collected, printed, and widely distributed from the
mid-eighteenth century on, and composed in writing by nineteenth-century
poets adopting elements of balladic form.[5] Dickinson heightens such negotiation or hybridity by constructing informal speakers and representing poetry
itself as ephemeral in ostentatiously written texts. And yet one can also interpret the instability of her poems' written forms as undercutting the iconic or
definitively inscribed elements of the writing, thereby again bringing the
written form closer to the impulsive impermanence of speech: Dickinson's
writing may be as performative as any spoken iteration of a poem. Writing
out her texts in different ways would seem to demonstrate both Dickinson's
lack of commitment to particular instantiations of a poem and her ongoing
interest in experimentation with the writing out of verse. In her fascicles and
sets, Dickinson constructs poet-speakers using the dramatic fiction of a
speaking presence, while inscribing that immediacy in the implied but also
fictional stability of a written poem. In letters and in her late draft copies,
there is less evidence of attachment even to the inclusive stability of fascicle or
set poems, with their variant words and revisions. Interestingly, Dickinson
also uses a first-person speaker less often in her late poems. This tension,
then, between a dramatized but indeterminate speaker and what may also be
a performative writing act in retaining the poem pertains primarily to poems
written before 1866 or those copied into sets between 1871 and 1875.

An 1862 poem takes the difference between talking and writing as part of
its topic while calling attention to the divergent possibilities for the writing
out of metrical lines in its first stanza:

	syllables	beats
We talked as Girls do –	5	2
Fond, and late –	3	2
We speculated fair, on every subject, but the Grave –	14	7
Of our's, none affair –	5	3
We handled Destinies, as cool –	8	4
As we – Disposers – be –	6	3

And God, a Quiet Party	7	3	
To our authority –	6	3	
But fondest, dwelt opon Ourself	8	4	
As we eventual – be –	6	3	
When Girls, to Women, softly raised	8	4	
We – occupy – Degree –	6	3	[too – partake –
We parted with a contract	7	3	
To cherish, and to write	6	3	[recollect –
But Heaven made both, impossible	8	4	
Before another night.	6	3	

(F392)

Talking "as Girls do," these young women "speculated . . . on every subject" having to do with life and particularly on their own future lives as "Women," when they would be "raised" to "occupy – Degree." Their "authority" as girls, in contrast to such "Degree," seems to come from innocence—for example, in their assumption that "the Grave" is irrelevant to them and that they can "handle[] Destinies," regarding God as no more than a "Quiet Party" to their "cool" decisions. The intimacy of this talking leads to a "contract / To cherish, and to write"—suggesting, as the variant "recollect" indicates, that the writing enacts the cherishing in a recollection of their "late" hours of talking.

Written when she was thirty-two, no longer a "Girl," this poem might be read as Dickinson remembering occasions of talking late into the night with Vinnie, or any girlhood friend; it is easy to imagine a young Dickinson "cool[ly] . . . Dispos[ing]" of the fates of her acquaintances. There is, however, no record of an intimate friend of hers dying the day after they have spent long hours together—in other words, there is no evidence that this poem is in fact a recollection. Never sent to anyone and preserved only in a manuscript book (Fas 19), this poem deals with a common sentimental tale: two loving girls do not suspect that within twenty-four hours one of them will die. Three of its four stanzas, however, focus instead on what the girls talked about, presented in a chatty style echoing the girls' late-night talking. Whatever interests Dickinson enough to preserve this poem in fair copy, then, seems to have more to do with this speaking act than with the tale per se. Jed Deppman calls Dickinson's conception of the poem "profoundly conversational" and "other-dependent," observing that a number of her poems "thematize conversation" (28–29). "We talked as Girls do" both thematizes conversation and takes a conversational tone toward a presumed or fictional interlocutor.

This poem structures relationship through language. While writing is a secondary choice in the narrative, chosen only when the friends can no longer talk, Dickinson's writing out of the opening metrical line as two short lines followed by an unusually long third line suggests that writing is also of interest here. These naïve, "Fond," fearless talkers are characteristically Dickinsonian: they talk because this is the way to establish and maintain contact, and they hubristically, unreservedly assume an "authority" they know they cannot publicly hold: girls are, after all, the least authoritative members of nineteenth-century society. The principal talker is also pragmatic, acknowledging frankly her loss and their mistake in ignoring death as a topic of concern. This is also characteristic of Dickinson's speakers: the language of many poems makes the speaker seem young, relatively powerless, undifferentiated from others of her class, but shrewd, acutely speculative, and eager to enter into "Degree." These girls are also comfortably literate and take writing for granted as a substitute for speaking.

As suggested earlier, Dickinson probably developed such non-individualized dramatic speakers articulating both a presumed innocence and an incisive critical view of life, theology, human psychology, and politics partially in response to the ballad's traditionally unsophisticated speaker, echoed in much Romantic poetry—although her speakers are typically educated, as in "We talked as Girls do."[6] Especially as a woman, Dickinson could adopt this popular guise of innocent marginality to the world of political and historical events in ways that fit the cultural script of modesty while indirectly engaging with them.[7] Moreover, her speakers represent both their own reflections and poetry itself as the products of intense curiosity, experience, playful or crafty thinking, and of luck, not of genius or extraordinary creativity. "I'm Nobody!"—as one of Dickinson's speakers famously exclaims (F260), or "I reckon – When I count at all –" another speaker offhandedly begins, using a rural colloquialism to indicate her or his general unattentiveness to precise thought or figuring while introducing a complex and ambitious comparison between a heaven "too difficult" to attain and poetry (F533). While Dickinson participated enthusiastically in the culture of poetic greatness through requesting author photographs and reading biographies, and while some of her poems regard poetry as implicitly divine, her speaking poets and poetic speakers more closely resemble the anonymous ballad singer than the writers she idolized. Here, again, we see Dickinson's poetry balancing a paradox. As previously discussed, she both writes in well-known popular forms and experiments with a wide range of innovative structures; she experiments with spoken perspectives and writes poems out in experimental ways on the page; and she writes a philosophically profound poetry drawing on vocabularies of contemporary scientific, mathematical, and political knowledge while frequently representing her speaker as naïve and the poet as unexceptional.

Ballads may also have appealed to Dickinson as providing a general model for her dramatic speakers because, unlike hymns, they were strongly associated with a region or nation, through dialect or distinctive colloquialisms and through the kinds of tales they tell. Johann Gottfried von Herder and Sir Walter Scott wrote influentially about ballads as a touchstone for the revival or rejuvenation of a powerful poetry of a "folk."[8] More significant for the United States, the converse assumption developed simultaneously: namely, that a common or indigenous local population is naturally poetical and will produce ballad-like verse. Alexis de Tocqueville follows this logic in associating a ballad-like literature with the U.S., claiming that "democratic ages" will produce a literature of "fantastic, incorrect, overburdened, and loose" forms and identifying such forms with the American "people," not with educated and style-conscious poets (61).[9] Perhaps in mockery, J. J. Trux writes in 1855 that the plantation songs of "Negro Minstrelsy" constitute such a true national poetry.[10] In 1867, Higginson makes this claim seriously in relation to spirituals. Calling himself "a faithful student of the Scottish ballads," he sees himself as a second Walter Scott in his collection of these "unwritten songs, as simple and indigenous as the Border Minstrelsy . . . and often as essentially poetic" ("Negro Spirituals" 685).

Later in the century, American ballad collector and theorist Francis James Child and his student Francis Gummere identify balladic form with community or democracy. The traditional ballad, Child writes, is "a truly national" form, in which "there is such community of ideas and feelings that the whole people form an individual. Such Poetry . . . will always be an expression of the mind and heart of the people as an individual, and never of the personality of individual men" (464). In *Democracy and Poetry,* Gummere further argues that traditional poetry contains both "the democratic mystery of convention" and the rhythms and "instinct of union, coherence, sympathy": the ballad is the most democratic of poems in its reflection of "currents of communal sympathy which circle the globe" (218, 219, 256).[11] As noted in Chapter 2, Griswold's *Readings in American Poetry* (1843) indicates more broadly that formal irregularity is compatible with an "essentially American" spirit in poetry. Dickinson owned sheet music for a ballad that articulated such nationalism openly: "Our Native Song," dedicated to "The People of the United States," celebrates "The Anthem chant, the Ballad wild, the notes that we remember long, The Theme we sing with lisping tongue, 'Tis this we love, our native song" (EDR 469). Both Dickinson's formally irregular poetry and her shrewdly naïve poet-speaker manifested qualities familiar to the antebellum public as at least theoretically characteristic of an American and democratic poet.[12]

Several poets in the United States associated local geography or nature with poetic voice, often in ways suggesting the childlike or naïve ballad speaker. Most influentially, Emerson celebrated an innate poetic language in the natural world, hence a language simultaneously universal and manifested in a particular region or nation. In nature "we hear primal warblings and attempt to write them down"; poets are "the men of more delicate ear [who] write down these cadences more faithfully, and these transcripts, though imperfect, become the songs of nations"; logically, then, "America is a poem in our eyes; its ample geography dazzles the imagination, and it will not wait long for its metres" (*EmEL* 449). Following Emerson's lead, Whitman identifies "the United States themselves as essentially the greatest poem," implying that this "poem" is written by all Americans, a communal product par excellence (*LOG* 1855, iii). Longfellow follows balladic discourse of natural and national speech more conventionally in introducing a Swedish poem he has translated, claiming the poem's "tone" comes from the country itself; "There is something patriarchal still lingering about rural life in Sweden, which renders it a fit theme for song. Almost primeval simplicity reigns."[13] Others note the same simplicity in Longfellow's own poems. Curtis praises his mind as "tak[ing] a simple, child-like hold of life" (773) and even Poe praises "The Wreck of the Hesperus" for its "*beauty* of child-like confidence and innocence." Longfellow's translation of "The Luck of Edenhall," Poe further asserts, "has all the free, hearty, *obvious* movement of the true ballad-legend" ("Longfellow's Ballads," *Works* 368, 370). The anonymously authored "Songs of the Sea" describes fishing ballads as "lyric blessings" in that they may be a source for an American national poetry (*AM* July 1858, 155). Dickinson bows in the direction of this discourse when she writes that "A faded Boy – in sallow Clothes / Who drove a lonesome Cow" is "A statesman's Embryo –" (F1549); country boys become national leaders, but it is their "extinct" boyhood and the cows they drive that are "Remanded to a Ballad's Barn," hence become the stuff of (presumably national) ballads.[14] A review of Whittier's *Home Ballads and Poems* praises the fact that the author "smacks of the soil"; he writes among the "best of the modern ballads . . . embodying native legends. . . . We have had no more purely American poet" (AM November 1860, 637, 639). Somewhat more grudgingly, this reviewer then comments that "The Garrison of Cape Ann" "would have been a fine poem, but it has too much of the author in it." The American bard speaks most appropriately not as a singular maker but when giving form to the land and its people, without "too much of the author in it."[15]

As a folk poetry, ballads were associated with nature and the rustic as well as with regional or national voice. Wordsworth's claims for the originality of *Lyrical Ballads* participate in this discourse: the newness of his volume lies, he writes, in its depiction of "incidents and situations from common life" related "as far as was possible, in a selection of language really used by men." In "low and rustic life," the "essential passions . . . speak a plainer and more emphatic language" (*Preface* 156). The poet's role is to give crafted and written form to that "plainer" language. The ballad speaker, like Wordsworth's rustic, is presumed to be more or less identical with nature, hence incapable of the debilitating self-consciousness associated with cosmopolitanism and the marketplace. As Child put it in 1874, "The fundamental characteristic of popular ballads is . . . the absence of subjectivity and of self-consciousness. Though they do not 'write themselves,' . . . still the author counts for nothing, and it is not by mere accident, but with the best reason, that they have come down to us anonymous" (464).[16] Consequently, even when there is an "I," the ballad's point of focus (unlike the romantic ode's) is not the speaker. Like nature itself, the ballad both provided the ground for historical and national identification and was assumed to stand outside the self-conscious process of reflecting upon or constructing its history.

Like Child and others, James Russell Lowell saw ballad makers as standing "face to face with life in a way that is getting more and more impossible for us"; but he also understood ballads to be "renewers of youth in us" and insisted that their themes were not "the monopoly of the dead" ("The Ballad"). Ballads arise from "whatever moves the heart and inspires the soul of man," hence the exceptional modern poet could also hear in the present "the tones of joy as clear and of wail as deep as ever thrilled him in history or poem" (140).[17] Child writes that ballads "are extremely difficult to imitate by the highly civilized modern man, and most of the attempts to reproduce this kind of poetry have been ridiculous failures" (214); in contrast, Lowell defines originality as based in "imaginative power. Given your material, in other words, the life in which you live, how much can you see in it? . . . Nothing is so simple and straightforward, nothing so sure to reveal an unexpected sympathy with every change of our mood, a profounder meaning with every enlargement of our experience."[18] Dickinson is no balladeer and no scholar of the form, but popular as well as scholarly discourse on the virtues of "simple and straightforward" speech may have influenced her development of the pithy, sagacious, informal speaker.

Like ballads, hymns and popular songs undercut the romantic model of poetry featuring a self-conscious observer/creator. The "I" of a hymn is indeterminate and presumed to include every believer, doubter, and sufferer; all who sing a hymn's words implicitly adopt its singular speaking position while participating in its choral or communal performance. Ballads and other popular songs were not sung communally but their "I" was imagined as a shared position, representing a class of speakers rather than an individual. In Dickinson's sheet music collection—mostly pieces published in the 1840s—a few songs list no author for the lyrics and others are advertised most prominently "as sung by" particular performers.[19] A song's imagined first-person speaker was often portrayed on the cover of the sheet music—for example, showing banjo-playing African Americans or wistful-looking young women.[20] To the extent that Dickinson's poems focus on the intensity of an articulated feeling or dilemma rather than an individualized biographical frame for that experience, they resemble songs waiting for a singer, someone to step into the "I" provided as a staged performance, although with greater self-consciousness and irony than typical of ballads and hymns.

Gary Stonum has written persuasively about Dickinson's deemphasis of the kind of poetic authority characterizing British romanticism, while constructing a version of the sublime that does not foreground an individualized psyche.[21] Dickinson, he states, was interested in the impact of poetry on an audience, not in the cult of the poet-genius or the individualizing implications of subjective reflection (*Dickinson Sublime* 10). Christa Vogelius has similarly argued that Dickinson valued the art of photography as resistant to "pure subjectivity, to the seamless equation of the lyric 'I' and the poet's self," in contrast to painting, which—like romantic poetry—emphasized the genius of an individual maker (33). Dickinson's poems deemphasize individuality even when using language that is ostentatiously distinctive. As discussed previously, in "How the old Mountains drip with Sunset" (F327), Dickinson's speaker remains indeterminate while tak[ing] on the "lip of the Flamingo" to "dare to tell" about the setting of the "Wizard" sun ("a Dome of Abyss . . . Bowing / Into Solitude –")—a phenomenon that Titian "never told –" and that "Paralyzed" Domenichino. In "I send Two Sunsets –/ Day and I – in competition ran –" (F557 B) an apparently even more naïve and equally undifferentiated speaker engages in an open contest with "Day"—a metonym for nature, or perhaps for God since Dickinson uses the masculine pronoun, unusual in nineteenth-century reference to nature. Here the speaker asserts the advantage of multiple quickly made sunsets and stars over "His" (the master maker's) "more ample" "one" because hers are "convenient"; they can be "carried in the hand."[22] Although "Essential Oils" must be "wrung" from the rose's natural bloom by "Screws," the resulting "Attar" of poetry makes eternal "Summer" "in Lady's Drawer" long after the woman's (poet's?) death (F772). "Screws," not inspiration, are the required factor for artistry and the resulting product is treasured in part for its usefulness—for example, in scenting the undergarments, or daily aspects, of women's lives. There is no poet as such in this poem and no authority of genius. One of Dickinson's two poems adulating Barrett Browning focuses solely on the effect of her poems, not the writer: "I think I was enchanted" celebrates a poet whose work "enchant[s]" (F627). Similarly, in "To pile like Thunder to it's close" there is no agent of creation (F1353). It is poetry—not a maker—that is "coeval" with love and God.

When Dickinson's poet is extraordinary, it is because of temporary miraculous transformation, like that of popular Orientalist tales. "It would never be

Common – more – I said –" (F388) reads like a fairy tale in which the speaker does nothing to deserve either the initial transformation or her later loss of "Palaces" and "word[s] of Gold." Dickinson's poet is occasionally inspired in finding the right word (a revelation of "Cherubim") but such a gift follows struggle and seems based in part on luck ("Shall I take thee, the Poet said" F1243). Generally, Dickinson adores words, not word-crafters: "The Poets light but Lamps – / Themselves – go out –" (F930). She "would not" be a poet but instead wonders "what would the Dower be, / Had I the Art to stun myself / with Bolts – of Melody!" (F348). For her, the poet is the instrument for staging the poem, and it is the poem, the enactment of communication, that matters. Yet even the poem may be ephemeral: "True Poems flee –," like bird song and like all performance ("To see the Summer Sky" F1491). Whether it captures the essence of something ordinary or sublime, the poem is both comparable to the divine and "convenient."

Dickinson provides stronger evidence of this conviction in her few poems about an author-centric poet. "This was a Poet –" acknowledges that "He" (that is, the singular maker) "Distills amazing sense / From Ordinary Meanings –" and is a "Discloser" of immense "Pictures" but it also accuses "Him" of entitling us "To ceaseless Poverty" in contrast to his "Fortune" and generally of being "unconscious" of his relation to the world; she concludes not with the greatness of poetry but with distancingly capitalized reference to the poet: "Himself – to Him – a Fortune – / Exterior – to Time –" (F446). This poet's ostentatiously personal "Fortune" is a far cry from Dickinson's preservation of poems in uncirculated booklets or poems that celebrate poetry, not the poet. In "Her – last Poems – / Poets ended –" (F600 C), also about Barrett Browning, the awkward shifting in the first stanzas between references to music (the "Silver" that "bubbled," "Flute," "Robin" that "Gushed") and the poet ("Not on Record . . . Other . . . Woman – so divine –") may suggest Dickinson's discomfort with this style of praise. More characteristically, in "Besides the Autumn poets sing" the speaker notices "A few prosaic days" that follow the fuller glories of "Mr Bryant's 'Golden Rod' – / And Mr Thomson's 'sheaves'." (F123 B). This speaker's theme and audience are limited to something "Besides" what famous poets "sing," and claim only a squirrel "Perhaps" as audience.[23]

With those to whom she sends poems, Dickinson similarly deemphasizes the craft and self-consciousness of her art, implying that the embedded or appended poem merely continues her message, providing a more expedient form of communication. In those instances where she calls explicit attention to her switch from prose to poetry, the fiction is of efficacy: Dickinson writes "I have no Saxon, now" before writing out a poem in a letter to Higginson in June 1862 (L265). To her Norcross cousins, she writes: "Let Emily sing for you because she cannot pray" (L278) and "the night is falling, so I must close with a little hymn. I had hoped to express more. Love more I never can" (L307); to Samuel Bowles she writes, "Here's what I had to 'tell you' – You will tell no other?" (L250) and "Because I could not say it – I fixed it in the Verse – for you to read –" (L251). Later, to Higginson, she writes "Please, Sir, Hear" (L282), and "You asked me if I wrote now? I have no other Playmate," and then lists poems she's including as a "Gale . . . Epitaph . . . a Word to a Friend, and a Blue Bird" (L513). Not a grand author, she merely sings, prays, tells, or plays. Such phrases occlude the possibility that the poems she sends have been (or will be) preserved in other contexts or sent to other readers and call no attention to the poems' intertextual dialogue with other literature or with national and international news. Such language might seem deceptive in that it disguises Dickinson's experimentation with form, prolific writing, and multiple copies of her poems. On the other hand, it is consistent with the fiction of her speakers' naturalness or lack of authority.

The sheer number of Dickinson's poems written from the perspective of an unindividualized sage or gnomic yet naïve speaker indicates the significance of this stance to her work. Moreover, her cryptically aphoristic style also gives her verse without a first-person speaker the edge of frank wonder or uninhibited honesty attributed to children and others regarded as uncivilized or unlearned—although relatively little of her poetry has what Poe calls the "hearty, obvious movement of the true ballad-legend" and it is worth repeating that Dickinson frequently uses registers of particular knowledge (economic, legal, scientific, philosophical). For Dickinson, the ballad seems to provide a mode rooted in the colloquial and eschewing individual positioning as a counterpoint to the complexity of her highly self-conscious reflections, questions, and observations. At the same time, tracing Dickinson's reference to ballads demonstrates that she moves from imitation of the ballad's archaic patterning and romantic poetry's balladic clichés to transformative use of the fiction of the natural, uninhibited speaker. Barton Levi Saint Armand writes that "Dickinson, like Blake, was . . . a deliberate naïf. . . . [B]oth these poets turned orthodoxy's weapons against itself" (165).[24] Blake was first published in the United States in abolitionist and other social radical journals in the 1840s; while Dickinson might have read his verse, even without this direct influence they both borrowed from ballad tradition in constructing poems of performed innocence.[25]

"I meant to have but modest needs –" (F711) makes the naïve speaker's increasing astuteness its topic. The poem begins by using the frugal register of domestic economy to mock gently the speaker's younger self, who imagines "modest needs – / Such as Content – and Heaven –" can be kept "Within my income –" and therefore confidently asks God for "A Heaven not so large as Your's, / But large enough – for me –." After noting God's amusement at her "honest" belief in the "Tale" that "'Whatsoever Ye shall ask – / Itself be given You' –" the speaker becomes cynical. "[G]rown shrewder," she tells her own more believable tale of disillusionment, maintaining the diction of the child but mixing registers of frugality and the law ("stipulate," "grant," "extant," "Judgment") with colloquial expression ("showed their dimples," "I left the Place – with all my might –," "swindled"). With its precise 8686 meter and abcb rhyme scheme, the poem narrates a story unusual for a ballad but using the ballad's "easy and uniform" rhythms and façade of simple wisdom.[26] Similarly, "The Sun kept setting – setting – still" (F715) uses even and "easy" rhythms (8686, abcb) to imagine the process of dying through the guise of simple observation of immediate facts: "No Hue of Afternoon – / Opon the Village I perceived –. . . . The Dusk kept dropping – dropping – still / No Dew opon the Grass –." The poem's present-tense conclusion—"'Tis Dying – I am doing – but / I'm not afraid to know –"—maintains this tone of alert attention to small details, as though "Dying" involves no more than the loss of "Light" and "sound," eschewing all theological, cultural, and philosophical conclusions.

The more famous "It was not Death, for I stood up," (F355) follows the same pattern of apparently simple, logical, and precise observation. Here the speaker grasps at common distinctions (standing up, or at what time the bells "Put out their Tongues") to distinguish his or her misery from states of being easier to name—"not Death . . . not Night . . . not Frost . . . Nor Fire" but "like Chaos." Such distinctions lead to the conclusion that whatever its name, the condition described does not even leave sufficient evidence of itself to "justify – Despair." Like others, this speaker maintains the fiction of innocence in part through repeated uncommon or even uncanny metaphors and grammatical or idiomatic coinages, as though she or he is so unlearned as to have to invent ways to express complex thoughts from the plain language of everyday: the dead "lie down," bells "Put out their Tongues," winds "crawl," "space stares"; "Chaos" is not infinite but "Stopless"; and this unknown state ("It") does not seem or feel but "tasted, like" other conditions. Through repeated assertion of the inability to name what "It" is, Dickinson brilliantly represents a condition without naming it, thus creating the desired intensity of precisely defined experience, maintaining the fiction of an unknowing speaker's or poet's awed inability to find an appropriate name, and also suggesting a psychological condition so intense that there is in fact no language to name it.

Many of Dickinson's poems using a loosened ballad measure speak from this position of innocent shrewdness. To return to poems discussed in Chapter 3, "We dream – it is good, we are dreaming-" (F584) uses the unconventional phrasing of children's games ("it is playing – kill us, / And we are playing – shriek –") to point toward a state of "hurt" too terrible to bear while "awake." "Did you ever stand in a Cavern's Mouth –" (F619) proceeds slowly toward the "horror" of "look[ing] in a Cannon's face" through gothic melodrama and what might in other circumstances seem like playful personification: "Judgment" intervenes between the cannon's "Yellow eye – / And your's" to answer "The Question of 'To die' –." In "I went to Heaven – / 'Twas a small Town –" (F577 B), Dickinson uses the language and landscape of her own community to anticipate the "Society" of afterlife. Even "It dont sound so terrible – quite – as it did –" (F384) uses the language of "school," putting the fact of death "under rule" in order to "get accustomed" to it, and thereby learn to wear the fact of "Murder" "like 'a fit'."

Emerson writes that "The meaner the type by which a law is expressed, and the more pungent it is, the more lasting in the memories of men; just as we choose the smallest box or case in which any needful utensil can be carried" ("The Poet" *EmEL* 455). Dickinson manifests this rule of concise pungency in the mixed registers of diction of her speakers—sometimes to comic effect, as in "I send Two Sunsets –," and sometimes with what Emerson called "terrible simplicity," as in the profoundly baffled perspective of "It was not Death" and "It dont sound so terrible –." Dickinson's "I" sees through the shams of adult politeness, pretense, and rationality.

The guise of unselfconsciousness in written forms has historical roots familiar to Dickinson from models besides the ballad. Logan Esdale links the performed naturalness and immediacy of Dickinson's speaking voice with a tradition of letter writing: from the eighteenth century on, there was an accepted fiction that letters were written as if spontaneously and for private reading while in fact many were composed with circulation, if not publication, in mind. Published letters were popular reading. A brief article on "Female Authors" in the *Republican* claims that "women excel men" in epistolary writing because they talk and "write freshly, naturally, vivaciously"; the author then proves this point with reference to published work by Harriet Beecher Stowe, Jane Austen, Maria Edgeworth, Charlotte Bronte, and others, confusing the "fresh" style they cultivated for publication with nature, just as Esdale describes (14 February 1857). In poems and letters, Dickinson's faux simplicity participates in this fiction of naturalness, with its concomitant fiction that "you" are the author's only reader and her words are spontaneous. Dickinson must be seen as present to some degree in the speaker of her poems: she could not write so profoundly about grief, pain, love, desire, and spiritual questioning without experience of these states. Similarly, some of her verse in letters is written only for its recipient, probably impromptu—for example, the quatrain "To own a Susan of my own" (F1436, 1877) to Susan, or a three-line verse "We wear our sober Dresses when we die," to Sarah Tuckerman (F1619, 1883), or the quatrain "Within that little Hive" (F1633, 1884) to

Elizabeth Holland—none of which she preserved. Yet many of her letters and poems play with the fiction of spontaneous intimacy and freshness Esdale describes, especially those poems she sends to more than one person.

The most striking instance of multiple uses of a poem occurs in the love poem addressed but not sent as "Going – to – Her! / Happy – Letter!," mailed to her Norcross cousins as "Going to them, happy letter!" and then copied out as though to send to someone else as "Going to Him!" (F277).[27] Equally strik-ing is Dickinson's previously mentioned recycling of lines sent to Sue after Gilbert's death in 1883 ("Pass to thy Rendezvous of Light,") and to Higginson two years later (L868, L972). Franklin and Johnson print these lines as poetry, as the doubled use in different contexts suggests, but Dickinson does not pre-serve them among her own records.[28] If poems of romantic flirtation and condolence can be sent to multiple recipients on different occasions then they are not uniquely private messages. As previously stated, Dickinson circulated at least ninety poems or parts of poems to more than one person, not count-ing compositions like "Going to Her!" (or "Him!") found among her papers but unsent. Meredith McGill refers to lyric poems of unspecified address (such as Poe's "To———") as a "tremendously popular technology for the pro-duction of print-intimacy"; the dislocation of the unspecified address "strikes the keynote both of the intimate manuscript circulation of polite verse and the anonymous and unbounded culture of reprinting" (*Culture of Reprinting* 160). Dickinson's decontextualized uses of "I" and "you" enact similar ambi-guities of intimacy and anonymity, heightened by the apparent trustworthi-ness of a simple speaker—although no recipient of such a poem in a letter could have known this was the case.

According to McGill, the eschewal of an author-centered perspective was widespread as part of the culture of reprinting dominant in the United States from the early nineteenth century into the 1850s. The lack of copyright pro-tection for American authors was justified largely on the grounds that de-centralized mass production supported values appropriate to a democracy, where what mattered most was the accessibility of literature to a wide audience, not the economic gain of individual authors (1–4). The prevalent system of re-printing texts without authors' approval or, often, even knowledge of where and how their texts were issued, placed authorship "under complex forms of occlusion," McGill states (39). This system stressed the rights of the public over those of an author. Given her father and brother's legal profession, it is likely that Dickinson knew about debates over copyright and that most American authors desired a copyright law that would define literary texts as intellectual property, giving them greater economic return from publishing and more firmly establishing the author as the central literary authority (83).[29] Dickinson knew that periodicals borrowed freely from each other's pages since she frequently saw material from the *Atlantic* and other periodicals re-printed in the *Republican*. An 1859 anonymous review of Anne Whitney's poetry even judges it by "venture[ing] to predict that comparatively few of Anne Whitney's poems will be copied, and go the rounds of the press. They are not of the kind which take their seat in the corners of newspapers, and so go forth on their mission of love and blessing, to the ends of the earth"—in contrast to Adelaide Proctor's poems, which "have greeted us almost every-where" ("Poets on Poetry" *SR* 2 July 1859). She must also have been aware that her own poems were reprinted, since some reappeared in local papers.[30] As McGill summarizes it, American arguments favoring international copyright agreement typically invoked "the romantic conception of the isolate artist" (92)—perhaps a reason Dickinson would not have supported her fellow artists in this debate. At the same time, by not publishing, she retained exclusive control over the poems she did not circulate and some control over those she sent to particular recipients.

Were Dickinson primarily interested in a stable poetic text—either as manifest in its words and rhythms or as written on the page—then such con-trol would be of crucial significance to her. All evidence suggests, however, that Dickinson did not value stability over other elements of her poetic. Her poems and letters reject authoritative authorial positioning through their de-emphasis of poetic artistry, construction of non-referential and deceptively unselfconscious speakers, and manipulation of disjunctive language struc-tures and metaphors that make them function more like epistemological puzzles than instances of concluded thought. As is well known, her manu-script book poems often contain alternative phrases or words, and she revises some poems years after first preserving them. Further, when she writes out more than one fair copy of a poem, she often changes the lineation, punctua-tion, capitalization, and space between stanzas of the text.[31] As argued previ-ously, the points of stability for Dickinson in a poem are its idea or thought and its fundamental rhythm. Revisions indeed make subtle, or sometimes more substantive, changes in a poem's effect, but they are variants within what Dickinson seems to regard as the basic poem.

Dickinson's portrayal of her poet as deceptively simple, as though without self-consciousness or aesthetic design, creates the fiction that the particular elements of any given poem are a result of impulse and spontaneity rather than deliberation; this portrayal of the poet fits representations of the poem through ephemeral forms such as song, dance, light, scent, or thunder. As in Whitman's poetry, the fiction of such portrayal is that the poet produces un-premeditated speech, whether or not the words are written. Knowing that this is a fiction, knowing that Dickinson also deceptively represents the po-etry in her letters as uniquely targeted, and knowing that she writes out her poems differently from one occasion to the next, it seems reasonable to conclude that for her poetry is not essentially iconic but creates a sense of performed presence.[32] As Dennis Tedlock writes, "there is nothing about writing, in and of itself, that requires a text to be fixed for all times and places. Writing, like speaking, is a performance" and "no single performance in print . . . is definitive" (Tedlock 178). This would in particular be the case for poets who are engaged in what Tyler Hoffman describes as poetry "written to be experienced as oral" (5). The artifact of Dickinson's page both matters as a performance and does not appear to be an exclusive representation of any poem. Following this logic, the instability of Dickinson's writing out of poems is consistent with her representation of a non-authoritative or balladic poet: each performance is accurate and excludes all other interpretive possibilities at the moment of its expression so that taken in isolation it would seem to be the only way to manifest its rhythmic or expressive patterns. Only cumulative evidence demonstrates that she did not define a poem by its inscription, as she did by its meter, rhyme scheme, or controlling conceits. Dickinson did not write clusters of poems experimenting with particular aspects of lineation or capitalization as she did with meter and stanza structures, and she does not use the physical page or line as a regular feature of harmonic organization as she does the stanza. She does, however, significantly experiment with a range of ways of writing out poems, most interestingly in variations of the metrical line.

From the time she begins preserving her poems, Dickinson occasionally splits metrical lines or, less often, combines two metrical lines into a single poetic line.[33] In Manson's terminology of "staves," she often writes hemi-stiches on individual rows of print or writes two stiches in a single row of print; one nevertheless hears the stanza or stave. Dickinson's split metrical lines call attention to what would otherwise be an internal rhyme or foreground syntactic or thematic patterns. She never splits a metrical line between an article and noun or in the middle of a prepositional phrase, just as she does not end metrical lines in this way, although occasionally she enjambs a line-ending with a conjunction such as "then" or "as." Run-on lines, in contrast, do not occur as part of a pattern within the poem, do not coincide with phrase boundaries, often leaving a dangling "the" or "of" or "a" at the end of a row of print, and do not mark rhymes. Moreover, run-on lines occur only when Dickinson has reached the far right-hand edge of the page. The fact that Dickinson's poems with split metrical lines sound more conventional than they look is important and has always been so to Dickinson's reception. Mabel Loomis Todd records in her diary that she first persuaded Higginson to agree to publish Dickinson's poems by reading them aloud to him; he was "greatly astonished," having had "no idea there were so many in passably conventional form" (Sewall, *Life* 220)—convention being, for Higginson as for many in his generation, a matter of the ear. One cannot hear a split metrical line in the way one hears meter, rhyme, and syntax.[34] Lowell praises the ballad-maker's art by claiming "It is only by the ear that the true mother-tongue . . . is learned" ("The Ballad"); even when written in irregular poetic lines, Dickinson's poems have the sound of that "mother-tongue that knows the short way to the heart" learned by "the ear."

Dickinson most often splits a metrical line at the beginning of a poem: in "Of Bronze – and Blaze – / The North – tonight –" (F319), she divides the first metrical line into two parts, then writes the rest of the poem in the expected 8686 quatrains. The same pattern occurs in "They dropped like Flakes – / They dropped like stars –" (F545), "Her – last Poems – / Poets ended –" (F600 C), "I went to thank Her – / But She Slept –" (F637), "I gained it so – / By Climbing slow –" (F639), and "Always Mine! / No more Vacation!" (F942), among many others. Such division also occurs frequently in a poem's last stanza—for example in " 'Tis Opposites – Entice," which ends, "Be only / Me –" (F612), "A Toad, can die of Light –" (F419), which ends "Bare Rhine – / Which Ruby's mine?," "The Sun and Moon must make their haste –" (F1063), which begins its last stanza "Oh Poor and Far – / Oh Hindered Eye / That hunted for the Day –," or "There came a Wind like a Bugle – ", which splits its tetrameter penultimate line: "How much can come / And much can go," before the expected trimeter ending: "And yet abide the World!" (F1618).[35]

"It cant be 'Summer'!" (F265; see Figure 1) splits an eight-syllable metrical line into consecutive five- and three-syllable lines both at the beginning and near the end of the poem: "It cant be 'Summer'! / That – got through!" and "It cant be 'Dying'! / It's too Rouge –." The poem maintains its 8/6 pattern in the other six lines of the poem and the entire poem is evenly iambic, if one reads the split metrical lines as an aural unit (uSuSu / SuS)—as is true of all Dickinson's split metrical lines.

"Safe in their Alabaster Chambers –" (F124 B; see Figure 2) splits metrical lines twice in its first stanza and once in the second as written in Fascicle 6: "Untouched by morning / And untouched by noon – . . . Rafter of satin, / And Roof of stone. // . . . Light laughs the breeze / In her Castle above them –." These splits occur at a phrase boundary, making poetic lines with two beats each (in a 4-beat ballad-style rhythm). In each case they also begin the new poetic line with a word rarely capitalized in her verse except at line beginnings ("And . . . And . . . In . . ."). There is no ambiguity that Dickinson intends a new line: the split line begins with a capital letter and coincides with a syntactic juncture; spacing also makes the intention of these divisions clear.

This writing out of "Safe in their Alabaster Chambers –" is particularly interesting because in every other manuscript she writes "Rafter of Satin – and Roof of Stone" as continuous, and the poem is published as "The Sleeping"

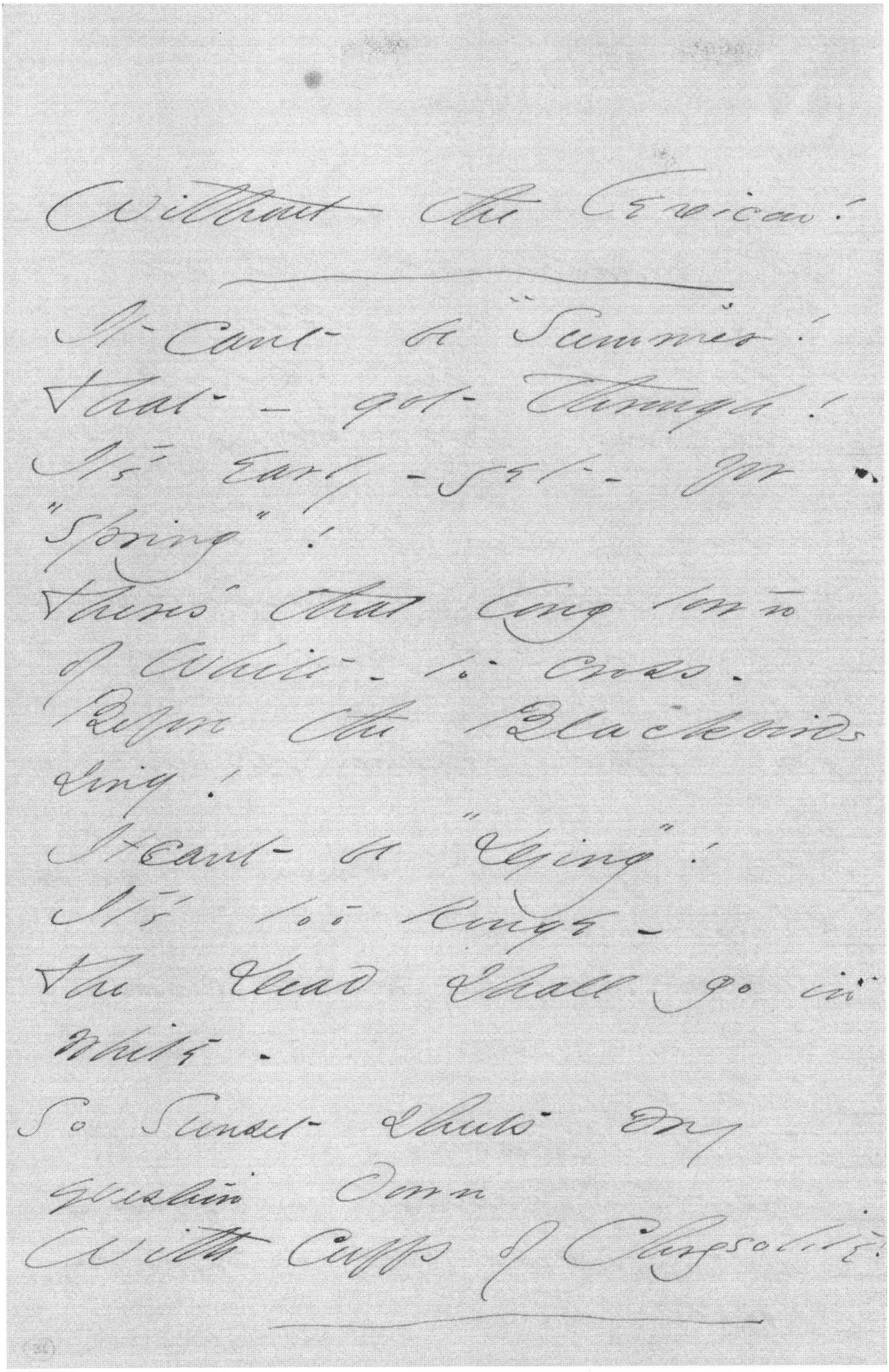

Figure 1. "It cant be 'Summer'!" (F265, Houghton Library MS Am 1118.3; 36 d)

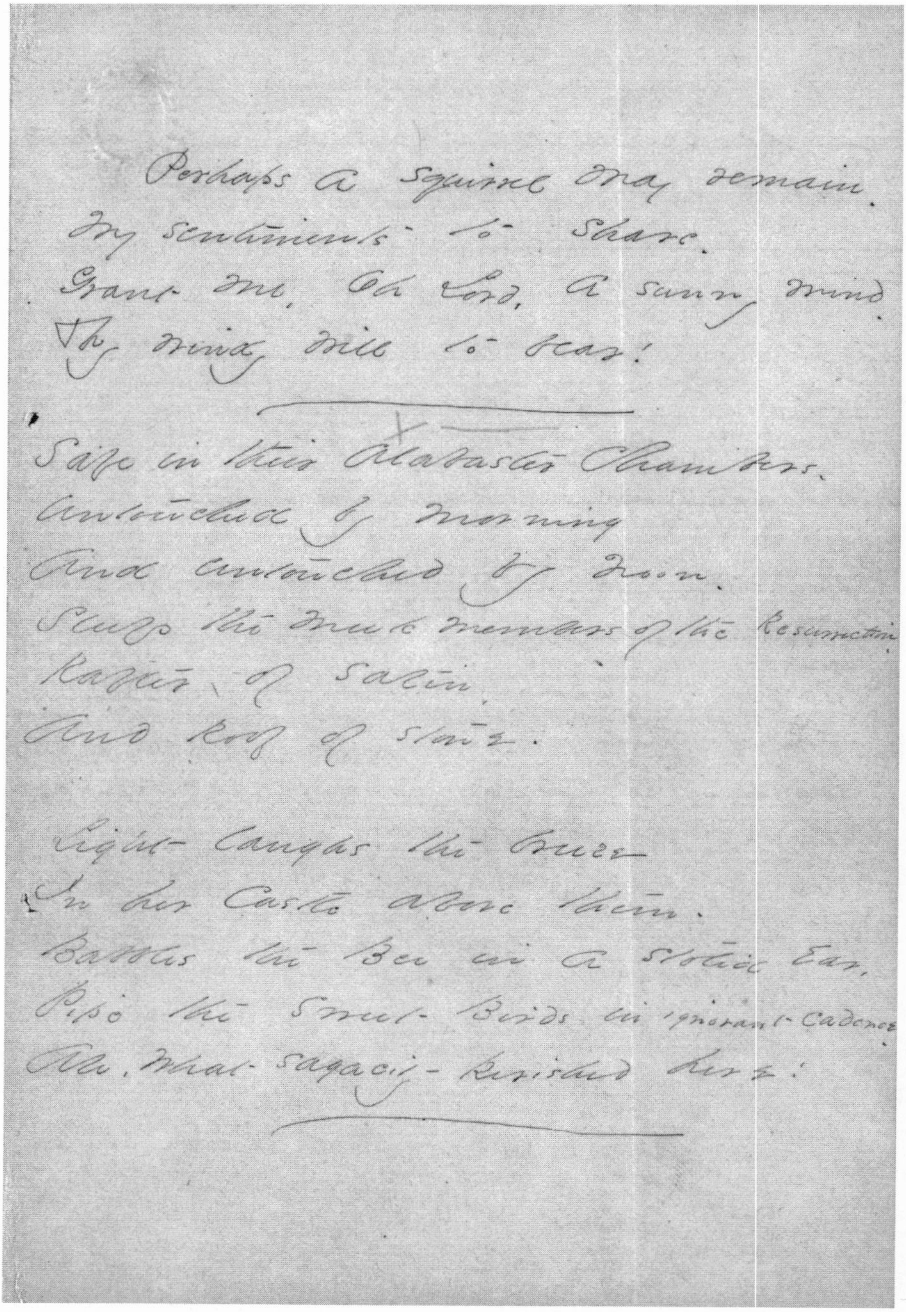

Perhaps a squirrel may remain
My sentiments to share.
Grant me, Oh Lord, a sunny mind
Thy windy mill to bear!

Safe in their Alabaster Chambers.
Untouched by morning
And untouched by noon.
Sleep the meek members of the Resurrection
Rafter of Satin,
And Roof of stone.

Light laughs the Breeze
In her Castle above them.
Babbles the Bee in a stolid Ear,
Pipe the Sweet Birds in ignorant Cadence
Ah, what sagacity perished here!

Figure 2. "Safe in their Alabaster Chambers" (F124, Houghton Library MS Am 1118.3; 11 c) with these phrases in a single line in the *Republican* on 1 March 1862 (see Figure 3).

This poem provides ample evidence of the instability of Dickinson's textual transcriptions and her apparent lack of concern about such instability. In every version she writes, she capitalizes "Alabaster Chambers," but neither she nor Susan complains that both words are written small in the *Republican*'s printing or that "cadence" (as written in Fas 6) has apparently been changed to "cadences," to create penultimate 11-syllable lines in both stanzas. Nor do they mention the indentations marking the rhyming lines. At the same time, the *Republican* printing demonstrates editorial tolerance for irregularity: the first stanza has a long first line (9 syllables) followed by two shorter lines (5 syllables each), whereas the second stanza begins with two short lines (4 and 6 syllables) followed by a 9-syllable line. Sue responds to this publication with enthusiasm: *"Has girl read Republican? It takes as long to start our Fleet as the Burnside,"* she writes. Although we can't know if Dickinson shared Sue's enthusiasm, there is no evidence she was dissatisfied.[36]

As indicated in Chapter 3, other poems experiment with lineation independently of conventional meter but unambiguously marking poetic lines. In "A Toad, can die of Light –" (F419; see Figure 4) the meter and line length are irregular, yet every line but one ends with a rhyme and every poetic line participates in a syntactic pattern:

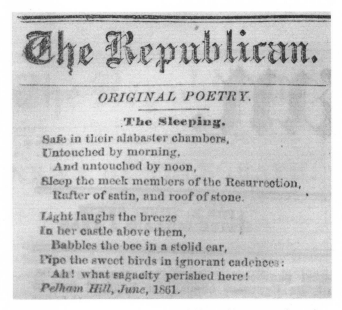

Figure 3. "The Sleeping" (F124, *Springfield Republican* 1 March 1862)

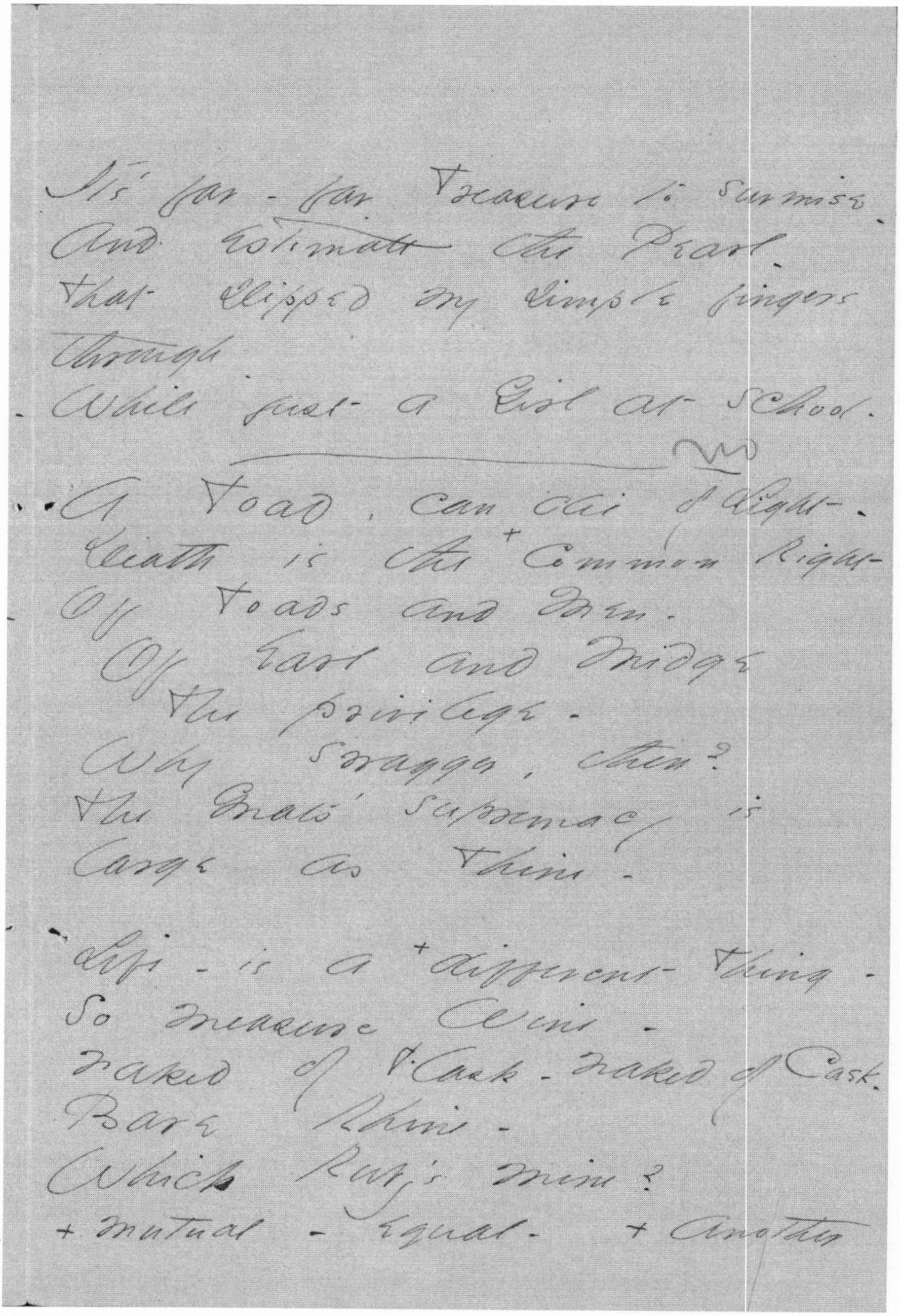

'Tis far - far Treasure to surmise -
And estimate the Pearl -
that slipped my simple fingers
through
- While just a Girl at School.

A Toad, can die of Light -
Death is the + Common Right
Of Toads and Men -
Of Earl and Midge
the privilege -
Why swagger, then?
the Gnat's supremacy is
large as Thine -

Life - is a + different thing -
So measure Wine -
Naked of + Cask - Naked of Cask.
Bare Rhine -
Which Ruby's mine?
+ mutual - Equal.   + Another

Figure 4. "A Toad, can die of Light" (F419, Houghton Library MS Am 1118.3; 47 b)

	syllables	rhyme	
A Toad, can die of Light –	6	a	
Death is the Common Right	6	a	]mutual – equal –
Of Toads and Men –	4	b	
Of Earl and Midge	4	c	
The privilege –	4	c	
Why swagger, then?	4	b	
The Gnat's supremacy is large as Thine –	10	d	
Life – is a different Thing –	6	e	]Another
So measure Wine –	4	d	
Naked of Flask – Naked of Cask –	8	(f)f	
Bare Rhine –	2	d	
Which Ruby's mine?	4	d	

The splitting of "Of Toads and Men – / Of Earl and Midge" establishes a syntactic parallel; similarly, the continued succession of dimeter lines with "The privilege –" emphasizes a rhyme.[37] "Bare Rhine – / Which Ruby's mine?" repeats this pattern and echoes the precedent of "Why swagger, then?," which gives a full poetic line to a four-syllable question. As mentioned in Chapter 3, this poem has no stanzaic norm, although each line supports the iambic rhythm. Except the 10-syllable line 7 (run-on after "is"), every row of print functions as its own poetic line: all begin with capitals and participate in syntactic or rhyming patterns. The poem distinguishes types of "measure"— the "supremacy" of dying to the "Naked[ness]" of "Life." Both formally and rhetorically, Dickinson promotes a "measure" associated not with hierarchies but with unadorned pleasure ("Bare Rhine") and the intoxication of rhythm as well as of wine.

"You'll know it – as you know 'tis Noon –" (F429; see Figure 5) displays even more clearly the difference between split and run-on lines. The second stanza of this poem is a standard quatrain of 8s—the poem's basic rhythmic pattern, although the rhymes are at best slant; the first stanza, in contrast, includes two split metrical lines and the last stanza contains one.[38]

1	You'll know it – as you know 'tis Noon –	8 [3 – 5] syllables
	By Glory –	3
	As you do the Sun –	5
	By Glory –	3
5	As you will in Heaven –	5
	Know God the Father – and the Son.	8
	By intuition, Mightiest Things	8
	Assert themselves – and not by terms –	8
	"I'm Midnight" – need the Midnight say –	8
10	"I'm Sunrise" – Need the Majesty?	8

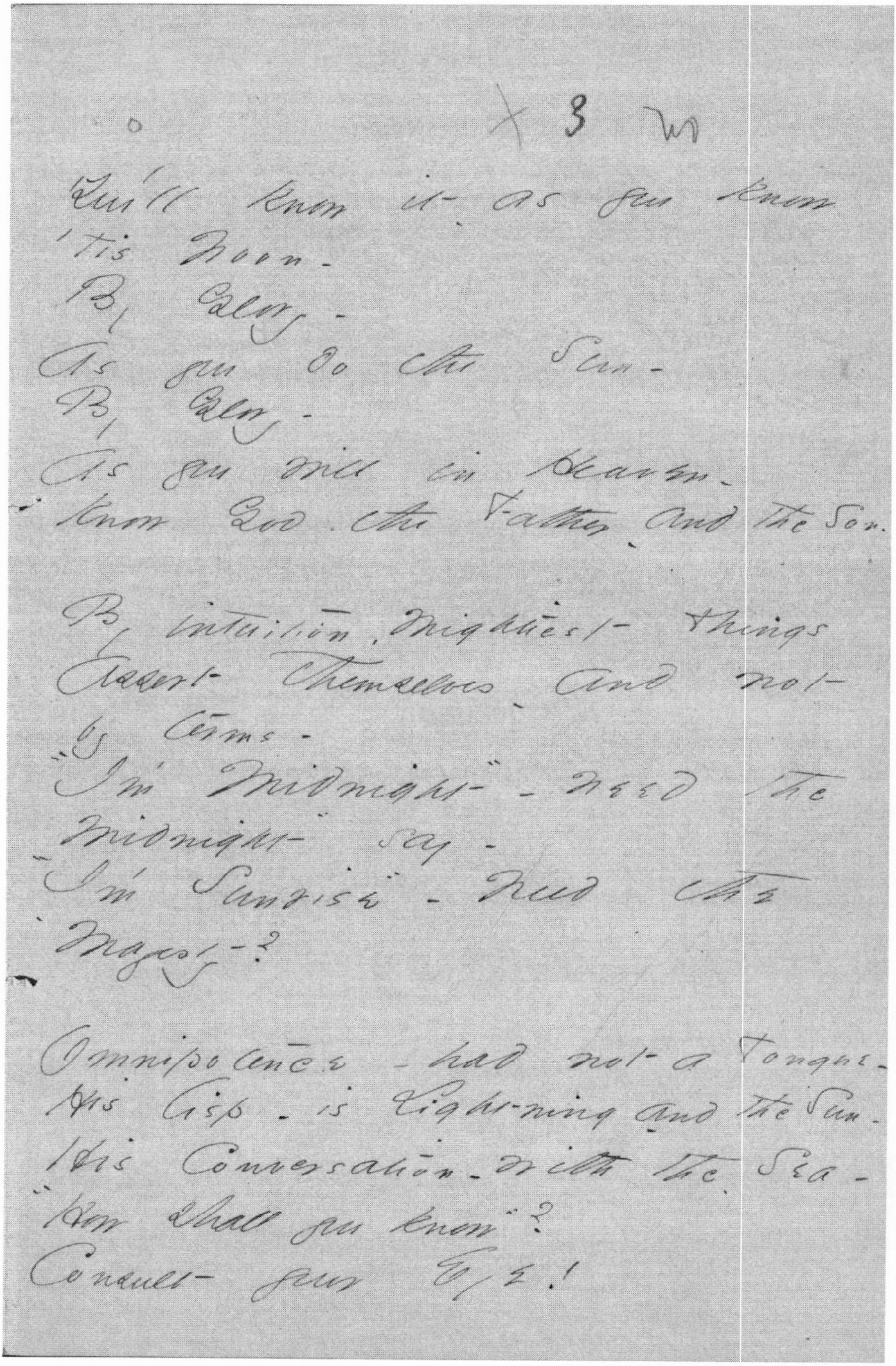

o × 3 m

You'll know it – as you know
'tis Noon –
By Glory –
As you do the Sun –
By Glory –
As you will in Heaven –
Know God the Father – and the Son.

By intuition, Mightiest Things
Assert themselves – and not
by terms –
"I'm Midnight" – need the
Midnight – say –
"I'm Sunrise" – Need the
Majesty –?

Omnipotence – had not a Tongue –
His lisp – is Lightning – and the Sun –
His Conversation – with the Sea –
"How shall you know"?
Consult your Eye!

Figure 5. "You'll know it – as you know 'tis Noon –" (F429, Houghton Library MS Am 1118.3; 174 b)

	Omnipotence – had not a Tongue –	8
	His lisp – is Lightning – and the Sun –	8
	His Conversation – with the Sea –	8
	"How shall you know"?	4
15	Consult your Eye!	4

In line 1, Dickinson establishes a syntactic precedent for her split lineation through the pause, marked with a dash, after "You'll know it –." This dash sets up the 3- and then 5-syllable syntactic units occurring later as separate poetic lines of parallel syntax ("You'll know it – as you know . . . By . . . As you do . . . By . . . As you will"). The second stanza contains three run-on lines, where a metrical line laps onto a new row of print, breaking twice at the word "the." Such division clarifies that "Majesty" ("Need the | Majesty"—line 10) does not begin a new poetic line despite its capitalization. Predictably, the poem's other variation of metrical lines occurs at its conclusion, again splitting an 8-syllable line following a significant syntactic break, in this case both emphasizing a quoted question and its answer and echoing earlier phrases about knowing. Cumulatively, the poem's split lines emphasize questions about what we "know" and underline the speaker's claim that such knowledge will come "By intuition." Here power is tongueless and term-less but not without language. In the poem's formal logic, however, we are led most powerfully neither by our intuition nor our "Eye" but by syntactic patterns. This poem about the recognition of power is precisely organized in ways emphasizing the fluidity of poetic form while realizing a metrical norm and establishing a rhetoric of knowledge.

Dickinson also composes a handful of poems that might be regarded as hovering around a pentameter norm using split lines. The quatrains of 'We'll pass without the parting / So to spare" (F503 B) alternate 7- and 3-syllable lines, rhyming abcb. Had Dickinson written the verse out differently it would consist of pentameter rhyming couplets:

We'll pass without the parting
So to spare
Certificate of Absence –
Deeming where

I left Her I could find Her
If I tried –
This way, I keep from missing
Those that died.

Or written as pentameter couplets:

We'll pass without the parting So to spare
Certificate of Absence – Deeming where

I left Her I could find Her If I tried –
This way, I keep from missing Those that died.

The fact that Dickinson gives this poem precisely the same line structure in a set fair copy and in a letter indicates her intention to split what might otherwise be pentameter lines; perhaps she hears this rhythm as syncopated by line breaks.[39]

Dickinson less frequently combines lines. One crystalline example of this phenomenon occurs, however, in "On this wondrous sea – sailing silently –" (F3 B, 1858), which she had sent to Susan in 1853 as "On this wondrous sea / Sailing silently," a lineation consistent with the 5-syllable lines of the rest of the poem. In either lineation, the reader hears distinct syntactic and rhyming units "On this wondrous sea –" and "sailing silently." Dickinson similarly combines a poem's first lines in "Drama's Vitallest Expression is the Common Day" (F776; see Figure 6), giving a 13-syllable first line and 3-line first stanza followed by quatrains of 8/5 in the next three stanzas.

Drama's Vitallest Expression is the Common Day
That arise and set about Us –
Other Tragedy

Perish in the Recitation –
This – the best enact   ]more exert
When the Audience is scattered
And the Boxes shut –

"Hamlet" to Himself were Hamlet –
Had not Shakespeare wrote –
Though the "Romeo" left no Record   ]leave
Of his Juliet,

It were infinite enacted   ]tenderer –
In the Human Heart –
Only Theatre recorded
Owner cannot shut –   ]Never yet was shut –

In this poem, again, the difference between run-on and poetic lines is distinct. The irregular initial stanza of (13)85 syllables is followed by three stanzas of regular 8585 syllables. In distinction to the combining of two metrical lines into a single long poetic line in stanza one, the several run-on lines are signaled by the fact that Dickinson does not capitalize "about," "scattered," "wrote" and "no." Although the second "Hamlet" (beginning a run-on line) is capitalized, as a proper noun, Dickinson rarely ends a poetic line with a helping verb such as "were," while she frequently ends lines with active verbs such as "wrote." Other poems combining lines include "If *He dissolve* – then – there is

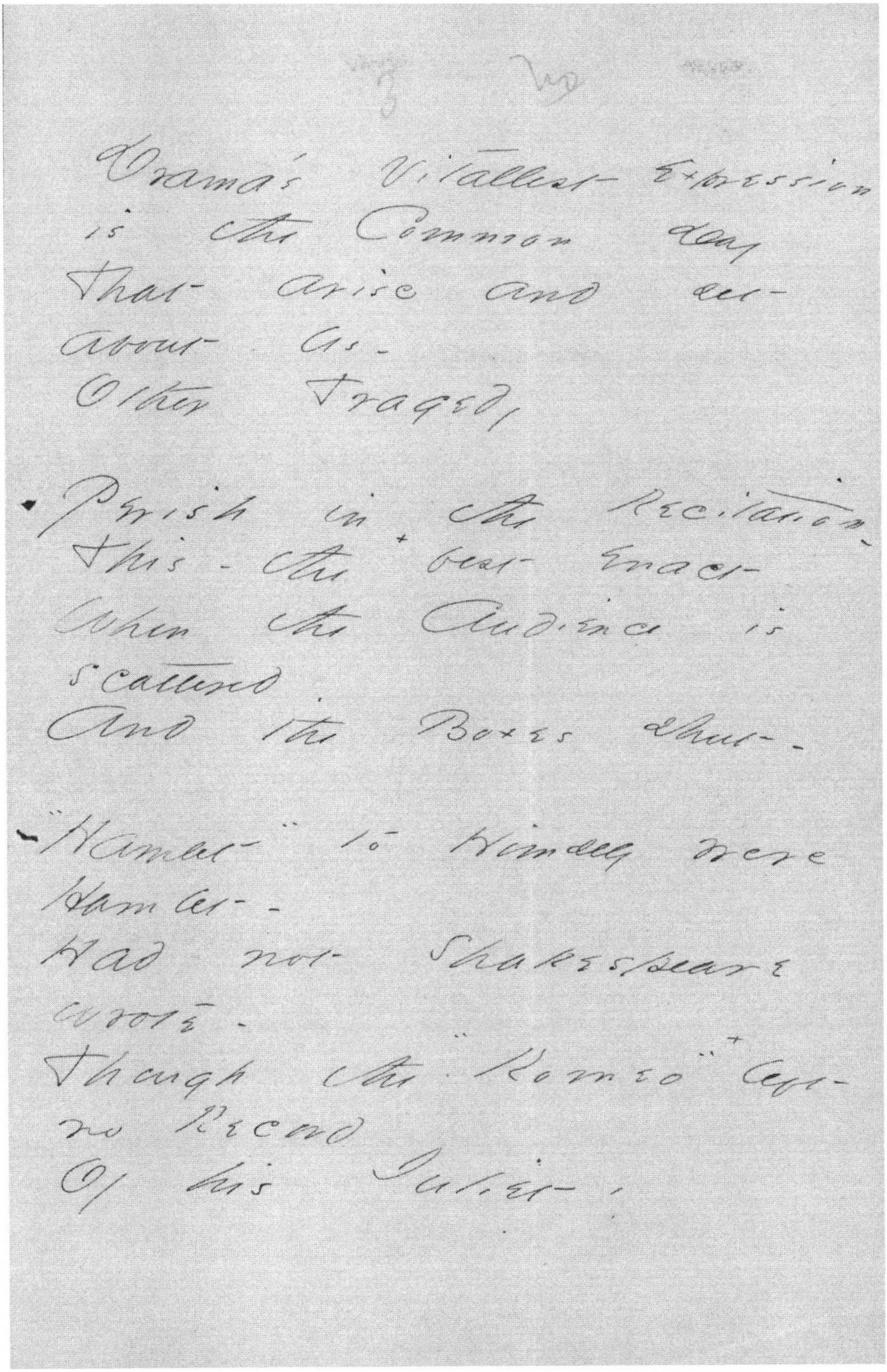

Drama's Vitallest Expression
is the Common day
that arise and set
about Us—
Other Tragedy

Perish in the Recitation—
this—the best Enact
When the Audience is
scattered
And the Boxes shut—

"Hamlet" to Himself were
Hamlet—
Had not Shakespeare
wrote—
Though the "Romeo" left
no Record
Of his Juliet,

Figure 6. "Drama's Vitallest Expression is the Common Day" (F776, Houghton Library
MS Am 1118.3; 56 a, first page)

nothing – more –" (F251), where the opening 10-syllable line is followed by
four lines of five syllables, before a more irregular pattern sets in; and "Read
– Sweet – how others – strove –" (F323), where the 11-syllable fifth line ("How
many times they – bore the faithful witness –") interrupts what is otherwise
primarily a 4/6-syllable sequence of syntactically paired unrhymed lines.[40]

Split and combined lineation of metrical lines was relatively common in
the 1840s and 1850s. Emerson divides metrical lines in "Merlin," for example,
where "He shall aye climb / For his rhyme" follows four lines of tetrameter.
Dickinson marks the first page of Emerson's "Give All to Love" by folding it
in half lengthwise, a poem irregularly combining roughly 2- and 4-beat
lines: "Leave all for love;— / Yet, hear me, yet, / One word more thy heart
behoved" (*Poems* 141). Similarly, in "Rain in Summer," where line length is
highly irregular but sequences of lines often pair accentual-syllabic structures, Longfellow writes: "He can behold / Aquarius old / Walking the fence-
less fields of air. . . . He can behold / Things manifold / That have not yet
been wholly told,—" in a pattern of parallel phrasing and 448 syllables, assuming conventional elision of unstressed vowels in "Aquarius" (*Poems*).
The *Springfield Republican* frequently prints poems with split-line patterns
that vary the rhythm and rhyme—for example, the comic "Papa, What is a
Newspaper, & What Does it Contain?" published on 11 April 1857, which
breaks its basic quatrain into five-line stanzas of 9955(10), with an aabbc
rhyme scheme. Bryant writes rhyming couplets of fourteen syllables in "The
Death of the Flowers" and "The Conjunction of Jupiter and Venus"—poems
Dickinson marks in Sue's book of his *Poems;* both use syntactic breaks suggesting an 8686 abcb pattern. The same pattern occurs in Holmes's "The Ballad of the Oysterman," Longfellow's "The Belfry of Bruges" and "Nuremberg"
(*Poems*), Bayard Taylor's "Manuela. A Ballad of California," and Samuel Ferguson's "The Forging of the Anchor," another poem Dickinson apparently
marks for attention.[41]

While there are ambiguous instances of split lineation or run-on lines in
Dickinson's late manuscripts, where her handwriting is so large that she
rarely has more than a few words on any row of print, it is typically obvious
when Dickinson writes a run-on line and when she splits a metrical line
into two poetic lines. On the other hand, Dickinson's inclination to split
lines to foreground syntactic junctures or internal rhyme does indicate a
way of thinking about lineation closer to free verse than to meter per se,
since free verse lineation tends to be syntactically structured.[42] This syntactic organization is also distinct from run-on lines, because of its structuring emphasis on the end of the line. For Dickinson, the end of the line is
a more significant consistent point of emphasis than the beginning, as even

a cursory glance at the poems composed in any year reveals. Line-end words are the basis for her rhymes and are typically words of semantic force; in contrast, many lines begin with an article, conjunction like "And," or preposition.

In several poems, Dickinson departs radically from metrical organization in a single stanza or pair of lines. To return to "We talked as Girls do –" (F392), three of its four stanzas move fluidly from one familiar hymn-stanza form to another: 8686, to 8676, then 7686. The poem begins, however, with a stanza of 53(14)5—or in which an initial 8-syllable metrical line is divided 5/3, followed by a line combining 6- and 8-syllable metrical units and thereby swallowing the initiation of the first stanza's rhyme, then concluding with a slightly shortened but otherwise predictable (rhyming) last line. Read aloud, one hears 8685 with an abcb rhyme, but this is far from what one sees on the page:

We talked as Girls do –	5	2
Fond, and late –	3	3
We speculated fair, on every subject, but the Grave –	14	7
Of our's, none affair –	5	3

We handled Destinies, as cool –
As we – Disposers – be –
And God, a Quiet Party
To our authority.

But fondest, dwelt opon Ourself
As we eventual – be –
When Girls, to Women, softly raised
We – occupy – Degree –

We parted with a contract
To cherish, and to write
But Heaven made both, impossible
Before another night.

This stanza's third line includes a syntactic pause marked with a comma at "fair," where one would anticipate a new row of print to mark what one hears as the anticipated 6-syllable metrical unit initiating a rhyme—that is, it marks the unit even while swallowing it in a longer poetic line. By starting a new row of print after "on," Dickinson emphatically eschews metrical lineation, since she was near the end of a row of print with "fair," and she does not divide poetic lines between a preposition ("on") and its object. Perhaps this unexpectedly long poetic line mimics the exuberant flow of talk between "Fond" "Girls"—as though such a rush has no patience with formal rules. The opening split metrical line—"We talked as Girls do – / Fond, and late –"—emphasizes both the word "Fond" through its unanticipated line-initial position and isolation from the following adjective by a comma, and the verb "do," even more emphasized by its occurrence at the end of a line: "We talked" the way that girls universally and throughout time "do." As noted previously, this activity or presumed agency of their talking (what they "do") is the poem's key point of focus until we reach the turn of the final stanza. Dickinson presents this poem's narrative turn in a stanza of regular iambic meter, with full rhyme (write/night), no dashes, concluding with a period, and containing only one unconventional capitalization, on "Heaven"—a word popularly capitalized. Perhaps the split and then elongated lines of the first stanza serve in advance to anticipate the poem's— and indeed all humanity's predictable—turn to "the Grave," the word concluding her exceptionally long line, hence impossible for the reader to ignore as the girls do.

The last stanza of "Of nearness to her sundered Things" (F337) similarly disrupts metrical for syntactic organization. After four stanzas of 8686 iambic abcb verse, Dickinson writes:

	syllables
As we – it were – that perished –	7
Themself – had just remained till we rejoin them –	11
And 'twas they, and not ourself	7
That mourned –	2

Heard according to metrical expectations, the stanza yields a structure fairly consistent with its first four, complete with slant rhyme and also following logical syntactic divisions. One hears:

	syllables
As we – it were – that perished –	7
Themself – had just remained	6
till we rejoin them – And 'twas they,	8
and not ourself That mourned –	6

Dickinson's one copy of this poem, however, makes clear that "till" is written small and there is no break between "they" and "and not." There is a narrative logic in Dickinson's metrically disruptive organization of this stanza, emphasizing our mourning and the odd reversal of "Themself" (not us) as waiting—in an unusually long line beginning with the coined pronoun "Themself" and ending with "them," thereby emphatically shifting the poem's focus from "we" to "them." The following poetic line then establishes the oppositional parallel uniting "they" and "ourself" through contrast ("they, and not ourself"). These pronouns are divided by a comma and by "not"—as "we" are divided from "them" by that larger negating force, death. This lineation powerfully maintains a heard familiar rhythm while structurally foregrounding the complex relationship of the living with the dead and, again, demonstrating Dickinson's sense of scriptural fluidity. "We" can imagine the dead only through knowing "ourself," as though all living are one in this mortality, hence at times of "special" sensitivity we feel a closeness to "them," displacing our acute longing for reunion by imagining that it is in fact the dead who mourn for us.[43]

The disruptive lineation in "Publication – is the Auction" (F788) resides in the shifting of a single monosyllabic word in the poem's penultimate stanza:

Thought belong to Him who gave it –	8
Then – to Him Who bear	5
It's Corporeal illustration – sell	9
The Royal Air –	4

Here, in the one extant copy of a poem of otherwise consistent 8585 quatrains, Dickinson shifts the first word of a new clause from its expected syntactic and metrical position at the beginning of a line ("Corporeal illustration / [S]ell The Royal Air") to the end of the preceding line, giving a startling emphasis to the word "sell," isolated by punctuation, syntax, and irregular metrical positioning and strongly emphasized by its position at the end of a line.[44] Such variation cannot be accidental—unless one would conclude that Dickinson pays no attention at all to the writing out of her poems, a conclusion at odds with the evidence of her clean copies and the indisputably metrical organization of the vast majority of her poems as well as her repeated experimentation with lineation that restructures the metrical. She might not have kept this inscription, however, if she wrote the stanza out again.

John Shoptaw distinguishes between a poet's *"textual intent"* or "intention to produce a poem" and *"textual act,"* the writing by which poets "set the text," "declare the poem a poem." This textual act occurs, he proposes, both throughout the poem's composition and at the end of the writing process, concluding as the poet decides to "let it stand" ("Cryptography" 223). With Dickinson, the emphasis is not on text but on making: she has a making intent and a making act, the latter taking textual form but not, I believe, essentially defined as a written document. Moreover, once Dickinson has made a fair copy of a poem there is no evidence that she intends to let it "stand." Like other poets (one thinks immediately of Walt Whitman and Marianne Moore), she revises over decades. For example, Dickinson copied "I – Years – had been – from Home –" (F440) into a manuscript booklet in 1862. Ten years later she revised it in a fair copy on notepaper, unfolded, unaddressed, and unsigned. While Dickinson makes several changes in wording and punctuation in the poem's first two stanzas, the most dramatic change occurs in its final stanza, which she writes out irregularly in 1862 but as a regular 6686 stanza in 1872:

> I moved my fingers off, as cautiously as Glass –
> And held my Ears – and like a Thief
> Stole – gasping – from the House.

(F440A, 1862)

> Then moved my Fingers off
> As cautiously as Glass
> And held my ears, and like a Thief
> Fled gasping from the House –

(F440B, 1872)

The later copy might be considered a correction or it could demonstrate Dickinson's general move toward more regular meters after 1865. As usual, she marks the implied metrical break even in 1862 with the comma after "off."[45]

Dickinson keeps draft copies of many poems after 1866, leaving us more complete records of her composing and revising processes for these years. "After all Birds have been investigated" (F1383), for example, exists in two fair copies and four drafts. The first fair copy, written about 1875, had highly irregular lineation: (11)49264(10), in the first stanza and 4646468 in the second stanza. Dickinson then radically revised the second stanza in two stages, sending a version of this stanza alone to Samuel Bowles in 1877. A few months later, after further revisions to stanza 2, she sent both stanzas written out in quatrains of (15)(11)(10)(10) and (10)(10)(10)8 to Higginson, changing what used to be capital letters marking the beginning of a poetic line to small letters wherever previous lines were combined. Here Dickinson demonstrates almost every form of her textual instability: in lineation, radical verbal revision, capitalization, punctuation, and by sending only one stanza to a correspondent.

Dickinson's inscriptions of "Through the Strait Pass of Suffering" (F187 C) indicate that her revisions are not always progressive. She sends this poem to Sue and to Samuel Bowles, apparently with two differences in wording, in 1861. (We can only surmise the wording of Sue's copy from the 1891 publication of this poem in the *Independent*.) Dickinson then copied the poem into a fascicle two years later, using the words sent to Sue but maintaining the alternative wording sent to Bowles by using marginal variants, suggesting that in 1863 she still wanted to keep both possibilities for word choice in play. Additionally, punctuation and capitalization in the fascicle copy are distinctly different from those in the copy to Bowles.[46] In this poem, revision is not conclusive; the text remains open to possibilities of change.

A few poems are revised to the point where they must be considered new poems. "Knows how to forget! / But – could she teach – it?" (F391 A), a poem

Dickinson recorded in 1862 (Fas 19), is almost entirely rewritten three years later (S7). In 1862, the poem has four stanzas; three are quatrains containing 2-beat lines but one stanza combines these metrical lines into longer poetic lines, giving two 4-beat (10-syllable) lines.[47] In 1865, "Knows how to forget! / But could It teach it?" (F391 B) maintains only the first two lines from the original poem and has six stanzas, all written in 2- (or 3-) beat quatrains. Although the poems pursue the same idea, it is surely a stretch to call them the same poem when only two lines out of a potential sixteen are the same, and one of those two is variant. On the other hand, Dickinson's four new second stanzas for "Safe in their Alabaster Chambers –" do not constitute wholly new poems because of the metrical and linguistic stability of its first stanza, even though she writes that stanza out differently, as previously shown.[48]

More typical seems to be "The Mushroom is the Elf of Plants –" (F1350 F), a poem that exists in three successive drafts and six copies (one lost), all written "around 1874." According to Franklin, this poem's first draft consists of a single stanza of iambic 7686 (later the second stanza of the poem); what he identifies as the next draft has the poem's first eight lines, in 86867686, without stanza division. The third copy, written in two 8-line stanzas, maintains the 7686 iambic structure after the poem's first four lines and includes a number of revisions on the page, including an interpolated 4-line stanza that Dickinson mailed alone, in slightly revised form, to Higginson in late May or early June. At about the same time, she made a fair copy of this poem, written out in quatrains, including one new variant but without indication of the poem's previous stages (S13).[49]

In another variation of progressive revision, Dickinson writes out a fair copy of "As imperceptibly as Grief" "about early 1865" (F935 B, S5) The poem here contains eight quatrains, beginning with a stanza of iambic 8686 and then moving to 6686 for all following stanzas. About 1866, she makes another fair copy of the poem and also sends a copy of just four of the eight quatrains to Higginson. In 1882, Dickinson makes another fair copy of these sixteen lines, written without stanza division. There is one variant marked in the set copy, adopted by all later fair copies, but several changes in punctuation occur from that initial copy, to the second round of fair copies a year later, to the final truncated copy, after another sixteen years—which includes some punctuation used in the set but not in the 1866 copies and some different from any earlier copy. Moreover, the two copies made in 1866 are not identical in wording and the 1882 copy introduces a new verbal variant. To our knowledge, after 1866, Dickinson makes no further use of the omitted four middle stanzas of the poem, describing the late summer behavior of "The Maple ... the Bird ... The Winds ... [and] The Cricket." Here is an example where one word revision once made is kept but others change and the inscription and punctuation of the poem continue to change over seventeen years.

Such instabilities in Dickinson's recopying and revising may have manifested her own version of the instabilities of print culture. Just as poems were reprinted, set to music, excerpted and revised by various hands, thanks to the lack of copyright and a culture of reprinting, Dickinson revised her poems in their various inscriptions. Her "making act," to return to Shoptaw's distinctions, was extended, but we cannot know that this is only because the poems were not published; publication did not stop Whitman or Moore from revising. Seeing poems by many of her favorite authors reprinted in periodicals, anthologies, or special volumes of verse—lines differently indented and in various fonts, sometimes illustrated, occasionally with altered titles—may have encouraged Dickinson to think of textuality both as the medium of potential immortality through publication and as allowing for varying choices of instantiation.

Lineation in Dickinson's free verse poems is distinctly patterned by syntax. The unrhymed "Victory comes late –" (F195 B) maintains a rough iambic undertone, but the combination of highly irregular line lengths, no pattern of even- and odd-numbered syllables, and the unevenness of the meter prevent all sense of metrical regularity.

	syllables	approximate beats
Victory comes late –	5	3
And is held low to freezing lips –	8	4
Too rapt with frost	4	2
To take it –	3	1
How sweet it would have tasted –	7	3
Just a Drop –	3	2
Was God so economical?	8	4
His Table's spread too high for Us –	8	4
Unless We dine on Tiptoe –	7	3
Crumbs – fit such little mouths –	6	3
Cherries – suit Robins –	5	2 or 3
The Eagle's Golden Breakfast strangles – Them –	10	5
God keep His Oath to Sparrows –	7	3
Who of little Love – know how to starve –[50]	9	4

As with the free verse poems examined in Chapter 3, the lack of a rhythmic pattern makes it difficult to determine beats per line. The first line might give "Victory" a traditional metrical alternation of stresses (Víctorý comes láte) or it might treat "Victory" more colloquially, giving greater stress to "comes":

"Víctory cómes láte –" sounds more like free verse. Moreover, from "Was God so economical" to the end, Dickinson's line breaks disrupt an iambic norm in following syntax. In contrast, "To fill a Gap / Insert the Thing that caused it –" (F647) contains lines of equally diverse length, organized by syntactic juncture, but the meter is unbroken iambic throughout. "Four Trees – opon a solitary Acre –" (F778) has lines of variant length, organized by syntactic juncture and a long-short pattern that undercuts a metrical norm, although its even-numbered lines are (with one exception) unambiguously iambic: "Without Design . . . Maintain . . . The Wind . . . But God . . . Or Boy . . . What Plan . . . Unknown." These punctuating short lines provide a flavor of iambic "Design" throughout, thereby strengthening the implied possibility of some "Plan" behind the trees' spacing as well.[51] Nonetheless, the poem sounds like free verse.

Dickinson's variant metrical lineation and free verse are both markedly different from her use of enjambment across lines and stanzas because enjambment is most forceful when it pushes across a clearly determined boundary. Syntax is the basis of all everyday language use. Hence its cultural valence differs from that of meter, a system associated only with poetry. In some poems, the impetus of Dickinson's syntax creates competing systems of order and rhythm within the poem through enjambment. For example, in "When I was small, a Woman died –" (F518), the woman's son "Went up from the Potomac – / His face all Victory // To look at her –"—an enjambment across a stanza boundary radically redefining our expectations of what constitutes "Victory" for this soldier. In "No Bobolink – reverse His Singing" (F766), the bobolink sings even when his home tree "By the Farmer be – // Clove to the Root –" an enjambment that gives forceful emphasis to the violence of "Clove." In "Publication – is the Auction" (F788), as noted earlier, "sell / The Royal Air – // In the Parcel –" crosses three lines and one stanza break and begins with the final word in the third line of a stanza, an extremely unusual non-coincidence of syntactic and metrical boundaries for short-lined verse. The unexpectedness of this rhythm appropriately introduces the speaker's closing parry, that regardless of how one markets "Heavenly Grace" one should "reduce no Human Spirit / To Disgrace of Price –" (F788). Such disruption, paradoxically, underlines the fact that the poem's patterning meter and rhyme are as crucial to its articulation as any departure from its norms. This poem also provides a powerful example of Dickinson's speech-like diction (with its imperatives, and the modifier "Possibly") while maintaining a high rhetorical style and including an instance of radical metrical play through non-standard lineation.

Dickinson experiments broadly with the rhythmic variation offered by meter and syntax, frequently creating a tension between a poem's colloquial, illocutionary diction and syntax, the heard patterns of meter and rhyme, and the variously written poetic line. While some of her contemporaries also experiment with variant lineation of metrical lines and irregular metrical structures, I know of none who do so as frequently, at such extremes, or with the instability Dickinson demonstrates in the multiple ways she writes out the same poem. This lack of commitment to a particular inscription is as interesting as the fact of the experimentation itself. Sharon Cameron coined the phrase "choosing not choosing" to describe Dickinson's use of variant words in the margins of poems she preserved: in these manuscripts, she chooses not to choose between words, keeping all in play. We know, however, that Dickinson also repeatedly chose to choose—particularly in sending poems in letters, where no variants of any kind appear, or in writing out multiple copies, where she repeatedly chooses differently. While Dickinson enters variant words into margins only of poems she preserves at home, she seems not to have a distinctive private and presentation or public sense of a poem's other written features, since she does not consistently use or reject stanza breaks or regularize or disrupt metrical lineation, punctuation, or capitalization for either use.

Other words for instability might be openness or fluidity—terms more affirmative in their critical valence. The question this choice of terminology broaches is whether or not Dickinson imagines the variant written versions of particular poems to be a key aspect of her poetic and hence definitional, the way meter and rhyme are. The evidence of the manuscripts leaves this question open. Reading manuscript patterns through ways that Dickinson defines herself as a poet, however, leads me to see the evidence as suggesting that visual aspects of her poetic are more like ways of presenting or performing a poem than like definitional constructions. At the same time, to the extent that Dickinson conceives the poem as performative—dramatic, implicitly spoken, staging a perspective or attitude—then all performative aspects are definitional. Textual instability or fluidity as a practice is fully commensurate with the characteristic openness of Dickinson's verse, as established by her variant word choices, indeterminate referentiality, syntactic deletions, and complex metonymies. Yet while her indeterminacy and riddling language play characterize even her many poems that adhere strictly to accentual syllabic forms, linear instabilities come less frequently into play. Hence they contribute to the ongoing tension between heard and written, shared and singular aspects of Dickinson's poems, just as her circulating poems in letters contributes to Dickinson's sense of a poem's use. In neither case, however, do these practices define Dickinson's conception or use of poetry, at least through 1865.

Ballads, and to a lesser extent hymns, provided Dickinson with highly flexible metrical forms and speaking positions grounded in the apparently naïve authority of an indeterminate speaker, often implicitly representative of some larger community and of ordinary life. As Lowell put it, ballads "show how full of poetry and beauty our daily life is, if it can only be looked at poetically" (Bell, "Only True Folk Songs" 140). In her own poems, such a speaking position may both have encouraged and resulted from Dickinson's conception of her poet as producing ephemeral performances, the "essence" of lived experience or daily phenomena. This artistry of daily invention was in harmony with a poetic of process, thinking, revision, engaged in reflection or enquiry rather than in pronouncement, conclusions, or iconic texts.[52] Her inventiveness with stanzaic and metrical rhythms took multiple forms, as did her play of rhythms in relation to syntax. Similarly, she experimented with the written line in relation to metrical and stanzaic norms, balancing the implied emphasis on her poetic as essentially aural or based on heard rhythms with the indication that a poem's inscription may be a guide to its logic, even if in unstable ways.

Such experimentation does not constitute a radically new conception of the poem insofar as each formal element falls within the range of speaking presence, metrical structure, and poetic lineation popular in the antebellum period. It does, however, ally her with Whitman as a poet of restless revision—a practice facilitated for Dickinson by the fact that during her lifetime no one knew that she wrote poems in radically alternative forms. It is my strong sense that Dickinson would not have protested the standardization of her capitalization, poetic lineation, or punctuation had more of her poems been published during her lifetime. As I discuss in the final chapter, there is no record of protest for such editing of the ten poems she saw published. Moreover, she does too much of this kind of alteration herself, moving back and forth between relatively conventional and unconventional inscriptions of her poems. On the other hand, I feel equally certain that Dickinson would have continued to write these poems out using alternative words, capitalization, punctuation, and lineation as she circulated them or recopied them for her own uses, since the poem did not live for her in any single performance or manifestation of its written form.

5

Becoming a Poet in "turbaned seas"

To an Emigrant, Country is idle except it be his own.

L330, June 1869

His story is told to point the old and dreary moral of the instability of human prosperity. It is, indeed, like a tale of the "Arabian Nights."

James Russell Lowell, 1864

SCHOLARS WRITING on Dickinson's borrowings from popular culture and popular literature have generally treated this phenomenon as an unchanging aspect of her poetry. This may be the case with her enthusiasm for some authors or types of work and for her general interest in popular culture; there are distinct patterns of difference, however, in Dickinson's use of idioms of Orientalism and foreign travel between 1858 and 1886. Travel literature and stories and poems set in foreign lands encouraged Dickinson to measure assumptions and values of Christianity and New England in relation to those of cultures and people elsewhere, particularly the East. Such idiom develops in her early poems and is heightened in the year 1860 by a remarkable focus on foreignness generally, or on moving beyond the known, as a defining characteristic of the poet. As with so many aspects of her writing, both Dickinson's use of images of Asia to express complex desires, critique the world she knew, and describe things she loved, and her characterization of the poet as a traveler change in her later work.[1] This chapter focuses on Dickinson's writing of the early 1860s, when she defines "Exultation" as "the going / Of an inland soul to sea –" (F143 B). In another poem characteristic of this period, the speaker imagines her lover as an "Orient's Apparition," linking the Orient to the "infinite" ("Joy to have merited the Pain –" F739; 1863). Daily events like sunset appear across "Hemisphere[s]": when "The Lady of the Occident / Retire[s]," the "flickering" of her candle is seen "On Ball of Mast in Bosporus –," that is, in the Asian East as well as in Amherst ("The Day undressed – Herself –" F495 A; 1862).[2] Such images were not unusual at the time; Orientalism was in its heyday during the 1850s in the United States. Dickinson both extended this discourse and critiqued it in her poems. She was part of a

118

community that perceived its material pleasures, religious obligations, and republican principles, if not identity itself, in relation to global exchange, including commerce with the several geographic areas understood under the umbrella rubric of the "Orient" or Asia.[3]

Between 1858 and 1881, Dickinson wrote around seventy poems referring to the "Orient" or mentioning people, animals, or products from Asia.[4] Most of these poems, and the most complex of them, were written before 1866, with the highest number between 1860 and 1863, when she also writes several poems of more diffuse allusion to the cluster of tropes associated with the East. Like many of her era, Dickinson imagined South, West, and East Asia as places of extravagant wealth and beauty, capable of satisfying a desirous Westerner's longings. Such images are fully in line with popular narratives about Asia, including what were then thought of as the biblical lands. They are also in line with the great popularity of the *Arabian Nights* in the United States—as noted in Lowell's casual observation quoted as epigraph: any tale about "the instability of human prosperity," magical transformation, or sensuous pleasures may bring the "Arabian Nights" to mind ("The Black Preacher" 467).[5] In 1853, the *Knickerbocker* published an essay called "Orientalism" beginning: "We frame to ourselves a deep azure sky, and a languid, alluring atmosphere; associate luxurious ease with the coffee-rooms and flower-gardens of the Seraglio at Constantinople; with the tapering minarets and gold-crescents of Cairo; with the fountains within and the kiosks without Damascus" (479). Maria Cummins's 1860 novel *El Fureidîs* begins, "Now feasting his eager eye upon the harmonious picture ... the Easternbound traveller acknowledges all his longings satisfied, all his day-dreams realized" (2).[6] Although Dickinson echoes these stereotypes at times, she also writes poems that demonstrate knowledge of the contemporary politics of Asia, critique Western attitudes, and raise questions about racial categorization and liminality.[7] Other poems invoking the East focus on creative self-transformation or fulfillment through a (romanticized) natural, ephemeral, or rare beauty and ability.

News about foreign lands was delivered daily to the Dickinson household through the pages of the *Springfield Republican*—among the nation's most influential and internationally focused newspapers.[8] Dickinson also read analytical commentary on foreign events and places in the *Atlantic* and *Harper's Monthly Magazine*. Books imagining, describing, and translating "other" lands, cultures, and religious scriptures into idioms readily accessible to nineteenth-century Americans were part of the Dickinson family library— including *The Koran* (the first U.S. edition, 1806, translated in 1649 by Alexander Ross), Hiram Bingham's *A Residence of Twenty-one Years in the Sandwich Islands* (1848), David Allen's *India Ancient and Modern* (1856), and Francis L. Hawks's two-volume *Narrative of the Expedition ... to the China Seas and*

Japan, 1852–1854 (1856).[9] Emily teased Austin about his "kindled imagination" from reading the *Arabian Nights* (L19, 1848; L22, 1848), and refers to this text in three later letters (L335, 438, 698, 1869–81). The popularity of these tales of fantastic transformations and riches in the Dickinson household may also be noted from Dickinson's owning sheet music called "Favorite Melodies from the Grand Chinese Spectacle of Aladdin or the Wonderful Lamp."[10] Austin also owned, and Emily marked three passages in, Thomas Moore's popular long poem *Lalla Rookh,* and she read many other Orientalist poems and tales in the family's books and periodicals.[11] Through her poetry, Dickinson participates in the conversation about the Orient carried on in periodicals, literature, and historical or travel narratives.

Foreign names and metaphors of exploration from several countries and continents occur throughout Dickinson's writing: "Soto! Explore thyself!" she writes; "Therein thyself shalt find / The 'Undiscovered Continent' –" (F814 C, 1864). In *The Undiscovered Continent* Suzanne Juhasz writes about the centrality of metaphors of discovery to Dickinson's psychic life, a topic later pursued by Chanthana Chaichit and Cynthia Hallen.[12] Jane Eberwein notes that Dickinson relished the travel writing of Americans abroad ("Siren Alps"). Stimulus to epitomize foreignness through Asia in particular abounded for Dickinson and the citizens of Massachusetts in direct and material forms. In Boston and Salem, trade with Asia flourished, giving rise to multiple cultural ties. As Daniel Lombardo notes, from the 1820s on, Amherst was known for sending missionaries around the world (94); similarly, Mount Holyoke produced a "disproportionate number of graduates" who married missionaries to the East (Schueller 79). Dickinson's friend Abbie Wood moved with her husband to Syria in 1855. Dickinson herself visited the Chinese Museum in Boston in 1846, and commented on the Buddhist concept of self-denial in a letter to Abiah Root.[13] Ronald Zboray and Mary Saracino Zboray describe this museum as espousing "a philosophy of enlightened relativism that invited visitors to see Chinese artifacts and the ways of life they represented on par with their own"; the objects it displayed, its two Chinese guides, and its "atmosphere imbued with politics" "invited visitors to imagine China more as a complex civilization amenable to diplomatic trade relations than as a culturally destitute land ripe for Euro-American conquest."[14] A visit to this museum would have countered Orientalist stereotyping, in other words, although it may well have contributed to fascination with Asia. In Monson, where Dickinson's mother grew up, three Chinese students attended the Academy in 1847 (Sanchez Eppler 302). "Charge to the Heathen, by the Pastor! Front seats reserved for Foreign Lands!" Dickinson writes in mockery to Jane Humphrey in 1855, pleading to her friend "dont let your duty call you 'far hence'" (L180). The *Republican* announced a "Lecture at Holyoke on 'Chinese

Character and Life'" on January 30, 1857; Frazar Stearns, a close friend of Austin's, traveled to India between October 1859 and August 1860; and in 1861 Edward Dickinson spoke at a celebration for the "Inauguration and Naming of Orient House" in West Pelham, a "hotel for invalids and pleasure-seekers"— no doubt thus named to encourage clients to imagine taking the waters there as a form of exotic luxury.[15] Daneen Wardrop writes that in the late 1850s women's "tabletop poetry collections often featured drawings of women in Turkish outfits with other images of eastern exotica interspersed among poems" and "Turkish trousers" was a popular name for bloomers in 1851 and 1852 (196, 141).[16] Brocade, cashmere wool, and silk contributed importantly to an upper-middle-class woman's wardrobe, and Dickinson refers to all three repeatedly, as well as generally to "Fabrics of the East" (F1471, 1878).[17]

Enthusiasm for these aspects of material culture developed in part out of what has been called the "Oriental Renaissance" of the late eighteenth and early nineteenth centuries, when the printing of Sanskrit texts in Europe stimulated an explosion of interest in the cultures of Asia, although American contacts through Asian trade and the publishing industry maintained a high level of interest in Asian cultures and goods independent of this European craze (Schueller 25). Encounters with those who had traveled, news about foreign lands, objects from Asia, and popular Orientalist writing gave Dickinson a geographical vocabulary for exoticism and rare or ephemeral beauty, encouraged speculation about epistemologies of foreignness, and offered narrative models for experiences of radical or fantastic transformation, or inspiration—that "Exultation" of the "inland soul" in entering a sphere overwhelmingly outside its ken. It was also a condition of being she identified with ontologically, as though her increasing isolation after 1860 took her farther from Amherst than any trip she had taken before. As she writes to Higginson in 1869, "To an Emigrant, Country is idle except it be his own. . . . I do not cross my Father's ground to any House or town" (L330). As an "Emigrant," Dickinson identifies as one who has departed from, not arrived at, a point of origin. In some poems, she claims the status of "Exile." As Salman Rushdie writes, "Exile is a dream of glorious return"; it is not to be mistaken for "émigré, expatriate, refugee, immigrant" (212). At a time when famine and oppression forced many populations into mobility and immigration to the United States was increasing, the poet may have been particularly attuned to the emotional burden of emigration. Irish immigration in particular had direct impact on popular culture during the 1840s: Dickinson owned sheet music for "The Lament of the Irish Emigrant" and several Irish tunes, and Murray documents her closeness to the Dickinsons' Irish domestic workers.[18] At least indirectly, Dickinson in her letter identifies with the local population apparently least like her, in being defined as from elsewhere. At the same time, this sympathetic identification is enabled by her perspective as a middle-class, white, well-housed American. Asia and Asians represented a more obscure version of foreignness or difference than the Irish and African Americans she knew in Amherst.

In 1859, Dickinson wrote several poems that involve some element of loss, something that disappears, death, and the changing seasons as geographically distant. Toward the end of the year, she increasingly used international reference or metaphor to describe common phenomena or aspects of life: "Butterflies from St Domingo" (F95), "Velvet people from Vevay –" (F96), sunset as a "Caravan of Red" (F104), "Our lives are Swiss –" (F129). During 1860, Dickinson still uses multiple exclamation marks, emphatic underlining, simple repetition, sentimental diction, and other features of her early writing in her poems.[19] These poems, however, move toward the more complex register, radical metonymies, and formal experimentation of her period of greatest productivity and maturity, voicing less descriptive and more broadly speculative and philosophical concerns. Simultaneously, Dickinson's use of geographic metaphors becomes more pronounced and the idea of foreignness a more important structuring conceit. The preponderance of such language suggests that she may have been stimulated during 1860 by the continuing stream of evidence that she lived in a rapidly changing and precarious world, greatly exacerbated after John Brown's October 1859 attack on Harpers Ferry. From this time on, "Conflict" with the South was increasingly regarded as "Irrepressible"—as the *Republican* announced frequently in headlines. American observers would also have perceived uncertainty and urgency in conflicts around the world, a perception perhaps heightened by national tensions. During this period, Dickinson's references to Asia become complex, detailed, and political.

Some of the most exciting, and probably the most puzzling, news of the late 1850s came from China, Japan, and India. Asian lands once primarily associated with exotic romance were now a regular feature of the spheres of war, politics, and finance. As the *Republican* announced in relation to the laying of the Atlantic telegraph cable in 1858, innovations in communication and transportation were bringing "the world into a nutshell . . . wherever commerce spreads her sails . . . will some time, and soon, be a network of wires . . . transforming the world into a vast community" (7 August 1858).[20] Yet it also reports, "Notwithstanding the multitude of books on China, it is still an unknown country to most of us" (25 July 1859). Asia was frequently in the news, much written about, and largely "unknown." During the Second Anglo-Chinese ("Opium") War (1856–1860), the United States negotiated with China to gain access to more ports and agreement that China would house its ambassador in Beijing. The Indian Uprising or Sepoy Mutiny began in 1857 and continued into 1860. Although the *Republican* was openly Western in its prejudices, it at times sympathized with Asian peoples against European colonizing powers. On 4 April 1857, an article titled "The Chinese—Shall we help fight them?" states that the idea of joining England and France in this impending war "is in gross violation of national independence, and is an especial outrage upon the domestic idea that every people have the right to choose their own institutions. If Great Britain . . . has determined to re-enact in that empire the crimes and cruelties of her conquest of India, let her monopolize the glory and shame of it."[21] Another article refers with equal cynicism to the "very profitable little war" Spain has fought against Morocco (14 April 1860, 1); and a 1 January 1859 article on the battle at Salimpore has the headline "The Butcheries in India." This piece notes that 700 Indian men, women, and children were killed and 300 drowned, but only two Europeans. In 1858, Japan signed the Harris treaty, which began the process of opening that country to foreigners, and in 1860, the Tokugawa Shogunate of Japan sent its first delegation to the United States. Walt Whitman's "A Broadway Pageant (Reception Japanese Embassy, June 16, 1860)" describes the welcome parade for these Japanese visitors in New York: "Comrade Americanos! to us, then, at last, the Orient comes" (*LOG* 1867, 62). Dickinson would have read frequent reports of the visit, including that New York spent nearly $100,000 hosting the embassy, and that the Japanese might visit Boston or even Springfield.[22]

News from Asia was puzzling because of the lag time between when events occurred and when news reached the United States, making even basic accounts unreliable. Generally, in the *Republican,* events in Asia were reported at least a month or two after they occurred, and many reports were partial. A headline one day might be contradicted by a bulletin on the next. On 27 September 1859 a headline read "The New Chinese War," but the article only reported that the French and English claimed they had been treacherously attacked at Peiho while in contrast a letter from China bemoaned British "ill-advised proceedings" in going up the wrong branch of the Peiho river. Daily reports followed, some quoting British and French sources, and some Chinese—with different accounts of the incident and predictions for what would follow. A 3 October account was taken from a 4 July dispatch. Whereas the telegraph made transportation of news within the U.S. relatively quick and reliable, no Atlantic Cable would be successfully in place until 1866, which meant that news even from England arrived with some delay. The frequency of reports from China, Japan, India, and Turkey made these places seem near, while the uncertainty of the news kept one in suspense as to what was happening and what it meant, perhaps supporting stereotypes of Oriental mystery, despite the newspaper's intent to report decisively. The *Republican* also published periodic cultural reports on foreign lands, such as "Female Life in Turkey" (11 April 1857) and "The Wonders of Japan" (21 January 1860). Such cultural reports, like the news, often disrupted popular imagination of a timeless, sensual, and spiritual East by describing events and people in a complex contemporary world.[23] "Railroads in Asia," for example, describes massive construction underway, concluding "One thing is certain, a new era is inaugurated in Asia. The caravan routes . . . will soon be replaced by railway and steam engine." At the same time, they sometimes expressed the prejudices of Orientalism—in this case, through the article's following comment that the "incomparably higher civilization of Christendom" will now have further opportunity to influence "the old homestead of the race" (*SR* 25 August, 1859). Seen in the contexts of both daily news and literary orientalism, some of Dickinson's poems take on distinct political overtones.[24]

The most markedly political of Dickinson's Asia poems refers to a people from the Caucasus who were imagined to define whiteness (and beauty) but whom popular literature and contemporary news represented as Oriental, as Dickinson does in "Some Rainbow – coming from the Fair!" (F162 B, 1860). This poem likens spring flowers and creatures to emigrants, querying: "Whose multitudes are these? / The children of whose turbaned seas – / Or what Circassian Land?" In 1860, the people of the northwest Caucasus (including what is now Chechnya) were embroiled in the Russian-Circassian war of 1763–1864. The final years of this war involved Russian massacres of the Circassians and their forced emigration to various parts of the Ottoman Empire, especially Turkey. Circassians were the focus of myth, literature, and news. Lord Byron's *Don Juan* (1818–24) describes the slave auction of a beautiful Circassian woman; Lucretia Davidson's 1829 "Amir Khan" depicts the story of a romance between the King of Kashmir and a captured Circassian. "An Account of the Panama Rail-Road" describes the concubines or "quasi wives" of foreign residents there as living "as secluded as so many Circassian women in a Grand Turk's seraglio."[25] The *Republican* describes Circassians as "a race of men so vigorous and graceful in form and women so beautiful that eastern nations say they are the original and uncorrupted stock from which all the races of men descended"—a claim repeated almost verbatim three months later.[26] On 6 July 1859, this statement accompanies a news story about the signal success of "the brave Circassian chief, Schamyl" against Russia, "the great power that seeks to subvert their national independence," calling this ongoing struggle a "good example for the world to contemplate." In partial contrast, in "Barbarism and Civilization" Higginson comments that "the Circassians, the purest type of the supreme Caucasian race, have given nothing to history but the courage of their men and the degradation of their women" (52).

Much of the interest in Circassians during the 1850s was connected with the titillating paradox that Circassian "white" women were depicted almost exclusively as enslaved in Turkish harems. On 9 August 1856, the *Republican* reprinted a *London Post* article titled "Horrible Traffic in Circassian Women— Infanticide in Turkey," which details the trade in Circassian slave "girls," noting that there is now such a glut of Circassians on the market that Turkish slave-holders are attempting to sell off their black female slaves at very low prices because they can afford "white slaves."[27] In other *Republican* stories, these "tribal" Circassians are described as believing in "a curious mixture of paganism, Mohammedanism, and Christianity," with Mohammedanism prevailing ("Schamyl, the Hero"). Reports of August and November 1859 and January 1860 tell of Circassian emigrants to Turkey, including a shipwreck killing two or three hundred, and placing the number of emigrants at over 60,000.[28] At the same time, the image of Circassians as fiercely committed to national independence prevailed, as Higginson reveals in a passing analogy in "The Maroons of Jamaica" (1860). The Maroons, he writes, are "the Circassians of the New World . . . black, instead of white; and as the Circassians refused to be transferred from the Sultan to the Czar, so the Maroons refused to be transferred from Spanish dominion to English" (213). To be the child of a "Circassian Land" was to belong to a besieged Muslim people celebrated as heroes, mythologized as exceedingly beautiful, and associated with slavery in Turkish harems.

"Some Rainbow – coming from the Fair!" (F162 B) begins with clear Orientalist imagery:

> Some Rainbow – coming from the Fair!
> Some Vision of the World Cashmere –
> I confidently see!
> Or else a Peacock's purple Train
> Feather by feather – on the plain
> Fritters itself away!

The poem describes an exotic spring landscape: ephemeral as the rainbow, luxurious and rare as wool from Kashmir, and as gorgeously bright as peacocks, native to southern Asia. The poem's continuing description echoes popular association of beautiful flower beds with the Orient, and particularly the sensuality of harems: Dickinson's "Orchis" lures "her old lover."[29] By the second stanza, however, the poet introduces martial imagery into the prototypically oriental "dreamy," "Lethargic," and erotic spring:

> The dreamy Butterflies bestir!
> Lethargic pools resume the whirr
> Of last year's sundered tune!

From some old Fortress on the sun
Baronial Bees – march – one by one –
In murmuring platoon!

The Robins stand as thick today
As flakes of snow stood yesterday –
On fence – and Roof – and Twig!
The Orchis binds her feather on
For her old lover – Don the sun!
Revisiting the Bog!

Without Commander! Countless! Still!
The Regiments of Wood and Hill
In bright detachment stand!
Behold, Whose multitudes are these?
The children of whose turbaned seas –
Or what Circassian Land?

The "multitudes" of flowers, bees, and birds are soldiers of "platoon[s],"
"Regiments," "Without Commander!" (perhaps a sign of their native independence) and "Countless!"—therefore impossible to conquer, or ungovern-
able. One might have thought that such life was lost in the harsh winter, metaphorically a defeat in nature's battles, but they "stand as thick today" as in
previous times—returning or emigrating from "some old Fortress on the sun."
These "Regiments of Wood and Hill" defeat winter; they bring both themselves and "Vision" of softness and color (cashmere and peacocks). Such language implies that the familiar butterflies, bees, robins, and flowers presaging
summer seem exotic after months of winter—like something from a "turbaned" land, with the beauty of the fabled Circassians. On the other hand, the
insistent military language complicates any simple association with timeless
Oriental sensuality; these representatives of spring point directly to the war
for independence waged for years by actual Circassian regiments.[30] Moreover,
the poem's echo of Isaiah's "lost . . . children" of exile seeking a home and the
biblical exclamation, "Behold," introduce the pathos of diaspora.[31]

The double tercets of the poem (886886) support its martial imagery in
the insistence of their quick rhymes and extended sense of return, through
the aabccb rhyme scheme and syntactic closure of each stanza. Lines of the
poem quoted in isolation lose the force of their presence in the poem because the tercets are so compactly structured. In the last stanza, however,
the four exclamatory phrases and concluding three questions also lead to a
sense of open-ended wonder. The speaker's exclamations function less as
points of certainty than as evidence of amazement—as though each were
preceded by the formally awe-invoking "Behold"—and the repeated *oo* and

long *e* sounds of the questions (*Whose,* multi*tudes, these, whose, seas*) contribute to that open wondering. Through its admiring and biblical "Behold," this poem sympathizes with a people for whom spring means a return to literal battle, and who aggressively populate the world (they "march"). Yet such martial immigration brings color and beauty to New England hills and allusion to the children of Israel, not threat of foreign menace. This erotic and martial spring indirectly praises "Mohammedans," described by the *Republican* as "a half civilized race," as apparently indomitable in their continuing military stance and hardy sojourn across "turbaned seas" ("Schamyl, the Hero").[32]

Dickinson also refers to Circassians in 1864. "Color–Caste–Denomination –" (F836) admonishes the living to be as egalitarian as "Death," who with his "Democratic fingers" pays no attention to the shade of the life he takes. Curiously, however, in this 1864 poem about "Color," the only race mentioned is the Circassian: "If Circassian – He is careless – / If He put away / Chrysalis of Blonde – or Umber – / Equal Butterfly – // They emerge from His Obscuring –"; upon resurrection, all emerge "Equal" and with the gorgeous patterns of the butterfly as opposed to the racially hierarchized monotones of human skin. Dickinson's signifiers for "Color" are neither typical nor dichotomous: according to Wardrop, "Blonde" was used to refer to lace that was neither white nor black more often than to hair color in the mid-nineteenth century; it was not yet a common designator for whiteness (184). "Umber," named for its source in Umbria, Italy, is a medium brown. These colors are in between the polarized distinctions of American racism, perhaps suggesting a more accurate depiction of skin tones than is acknowledged by racial stereotype or the multiple shades of beauty in the human "Chrysalis." Similarly, Circassia seems to figure as a racial borderland: a tribal Muslim people of the Caucasian mountains, reputedly the most beautiful in the world, whom Dickinson has previously associated with "turbaned seas."

Schueller argues that Americans were fascinated with southwest Asia because "it was composed of racial and cultural borderlands," giving them an indirect way to face the urgent antebellum racial politics of the United States.[33] In 1866, P. T. Barnum exploits this racial liminality by displaying a "Circassian Beauty" (the first of many) in direct intersection with U.S. racial politics. Over the years, Barnum's Circassian Beauties had as their sole identifying physical characteristics light skin and a distinctive Afro-like or "bushy" hair style (Frost 65–66). This feature was quickly copied by "Circassian" female performers in dime museums and sideshows. Barnum's first "Circassian" was described as having avoided the fate of slavery, but later performers of the "Circassian Beauty" were represented as former slaves, escaped from Turkish harems to find freedom in the U.S.[34] Dickinson's poems predate Barnum's display of Circassians in 1866. Notably, after 1864, Dickinson makes no reference to Circassians—perhaps because of their post-bellum staged notoriety. In "Color – Caste – Denomination –," however, she anticipates the later mythologizing of Circassian racial liminality as associated with whiteness and African American slavery, although she uses this insight to reject distinctions of race and color rather than to sensationalize them.

Dickinson's 1862 "The lonesome for they know not What – / The Eastern Exiles – be –" (F326) may also allude to Circassians—in this case, through a description of the colors of sunrise as crossing an "Amber line" and then striving "in vain" to recross "the purple Moat" and hence return to "Heaven" on "Some Transatlantic Morn –." The poem's conclusion suggests that we are all "Eastern Exiles," all diasporic wanderers taught by "Blessed Ether" to stray from "Heaven" and then incapable of regaining that native land.[35] The poem imagines the East as humanity's mythic place of origin, suggesting that all humans stem from the original exiles, Adam and Eve. At the same time, the word "Transatlantic" shifts this mythic reference pragmatically to the geographical "East" across the Atlantic ocean, and the extravagant colors of sunrise invoke Orientalist associations. The idea, however, that this bright gorgeousness suggests a literally displaced population, moreover a displacement that is typic of all human experience, goes beyond popular representations of the East. Because of ongoing wars and exploitation like the Coolie trade (frequently in the news), Asians were being forced into exile; Dickinson uses this "Eastern Exile[]" as a figure for all mortality, represented daily in the sun's "Transatlantic" journeying.[36]

A poem of 1862 more playfully alludes to political upheaval in an Eastern land. "If you were coming in the Fall," (F356, 1862) reiterates that the speaker would not mind increasingly long periods of waiting for her beloved as long as the period can be known; not-knowing instead constitutes ongoing confrontation with a "Goblin Bee – / That will not state – it's sting." The third stanza of the poem refers to the previous name of an island near Australia colonized by the British:

> If only Centuries, delayed,
> I'd count them on my Hand,
> Subtracting, till my fingers dropped
> Into Van Dieman's Land.

(stanza 3)

In 1856, Van Diemen's Land became a self-governing entity and took the name Tasmania. By claiming that her fingers would fall into a country on the other side of the globe that no longer exists by 1862, Dickinson creates the most extreme case for disappearance possible.[37] She may also play here with the role of the island as a penal colony from 1803 to 1824: her speaker would count time off on her fingers to the point of risking incarceration in a far-away place that sounds vaguely like hell (demon's land) if it assured her beloved's coming in a countable period of time. This poem also suggests that foreignness carries no weight in comparison with the emotional alienation of having no hope of reunion with the beloved "you." "If you were coming" also marks the poet's acquaintance with shifting geo-political boundaries as a matter of casual reference, apt for her psycho-cosmology.

As these examples attest, for Dickinson Orientalism functions as part of a highly complex set of racial, gendered, and nationalist assumptions—as it does generally in the United States in the 1850s and early 1860s. Others have written at length about, as Malini Schueller puts it, "U.S. Orientalism" and there is no need to rehearse that work here, except to say that Dickinson's representation of the East articulates those aspects of U.S. Orientalism that perceive the Orient as an admirable albeit "half-civilized" region, associated with the ageless and eternal, and particularly with nature and natural wealth.[38] Such representation may unconsciously reflect and redirect popular Orientalism, or it may be that Dickinson is actively interested in pondering these associations. The poems themselves do not make this distinction clear. Dickinson makes no reference to the distinctly different gendered associations for Circassian men and women and never represents Orientalized feminine subjects in relation to slavery, although she does allude to female eroticism. As Susan Nance suggests is true generally for American writers during this period, Dickinson's "East" may be most powerfully stimulated by the *Arabian Nights*, a mythical place where magical transformation of beauty and wealth of unimaginable proportions become possible. The *Atlantic* published several Orientalist pieces in the year 1860, beginning with Harriet Prescott (Spofford)'s "The Amber Gods" in January-February. The January issue also contained the long poem "Abdel-Hassan" (anon.), Holmes's "The Professor's Story," which introduces the notion of a "Brahmin caste"—distinguishing New England's natural aristocracy from European legal heredity by using the terms of Asian hierarchy—, and a book review of *Twelve Years of a Soldier's Life in India* by W. S. R. Hodson.[39] Other Orientalist poems appearing in 1860 include "The Water of El Arbain" (Caroline Crane Marsh, February—also published in the *Republican*), "Prince Adeb" (August), and "The Song of Fatima" (Thomas Bailey Aldrich, September). In May 1861, the *Atlantic* published Prescott (Spofford)'s Orientalist poem "Pomegranate-Flowers."[40]

Dickinson gives no evidence of having engaged in the serious reading of Asian scripture and literature, as did her contemporaries Emerson, Whittier, Bayard Taylor, Lydia Maria Child, and Whitman. Unlike Emerson and other transcendentalists, Dickinson is not interested in Asian philosophy and religion as a source of spiritual inspiration or knowledge. Unlike Taylor and

Whittier, she gives little evidence of continuing attention to humanitarian goals—what Marwan Obeidat describes as Whittier's moral desire "to help his fellow men, Christian and Muslim alike, maintain and enjoy their freedom" (89).[41] Unlike Whitman, she is not interested in Asia as a natural partner to or goal of American westward expansion. In extolling the Japanese embassy visit, Whitman describes Asia as "The Originatress . . . the bequeather of poems"; "venerable Asia" is "the all-mother," "rapt with musings, hot with passion, / Sultry with perfume," now meeting the "young" and "ever hot Libertad"—that is, the United States (*LOG* 1867, 62). Dickinson expresses no urges toward an imperialist Manifest Destiny, rarely personifies Asia, and never makes Asia the source or originator of poems—although she does more generally associate both Asia and any travel into the unknown with inspiration or poetry.

Instead, Dickinson's Orientalism borrows from and rewrites the symbolic geographies of her era. While popular geographies portrayed people in relation to stereotyped coordinates of the South, North, East, and West, her representations of Asians were without exception sympathetic, even if romantically or ambivalently so. For examples, S. G. Goodrich's *A Pictorial Geography of the World,* one of her Amherst Academy textbooks, explains "the liberty of Europe, and the slavery of Asia" as stemming from the fact "that Asia has no temperate zone, no intermediate region between very cold and very hot climates. The slaves inhabit the hot, and the conquerors the elevated and cold regions" (891).[42] Every geographical area or people has its stereotype:

> The character of the Arabs is founded upon that of Ishmael. In the desert they are robbers, and in cities cheating is a substitute for robbery. They are, however, very courteous and polite. . . . The Hindoos are gentle, polished, and courteous in their manners; temperate, simple, frugal, industrious, lively, and intelligent. Yet the long oppression of foreign races, and the servile subordination of inferiors to their superiors, often render them treacherous, selfish, and cruel. (925, 946)

When Dickinson writes that "A still – Volcano – Life –" is too "subtle" to be perceived "By natures this side Naples –," she participates in this geographical assigning of attributes (F517; 1863). When she refers to the bee's "jaded" philandering as "His oriental heresies" she similarly participates in this symbology, since the bee is a creature of summer or southern clime (F1562, 1881).[43] Dickinson's more frequent invocation of the Orient as representing that which is most precious and only fleetingly to be possessed, however, departs from these stereotypes, even while remaining parallel to them in its basic romantic orientation. The explicit imagery of exile in "Some Rainbow" and "The lonesome for they know not What –" departs even farther from typical U.S. Orientalism in depicting Asians not as nomadic or steeped in sensual luxuries and not as hermetically sealed off from contemporary civilizations but instead as emigrating across "turbaned seas" to the rest of the world, including Amherst.

The metaphor of "turbaned seas" is in this context particularly significant since it represents the expanse between "home" and foreignness—the sea—as itself "turbaned," oriental, culturally other. To enter into the expanse of the sea is to enter foreignness, perhaps become foreign. This is the assumption behind "Exultation is the going / Of an inland soul to sea –" (F143, 1860). This exultation, however, is the experience only of the "*inland* soul" (my emphasis); the "sailor"—who presumably has a sea-soul—may never feel this "divine intoxication" or release from ordinary inhibitions and boundaries because for him or her the sea is not foreign. In the second stanza, Dickinson presents this intuition of perceptual difference, characteristically, as a question:

> Bred as we, among the mountains,
> Can the sailor understand
> The divine intoxication
> Of the first league out from Land?

As suggested previously, Dickinson's increasing withdrawal from public contact around 1860 may give her sense of all journeying a sharper foreignness and greater "Exultation." This metaphor of the "turbaned" sea may also entice in its maleness, since the turban was traditionally worn by men. "[T]urbaned seas" may invite adventurousness, forbidden liaisons, a promise of new possibilities, as the basis for exultation. Dickinson desires not literal travel but ~travel~ the wealth of greater knowing, or inspiration, or love, realms appropriately ~A~ designated by "turbaned seas," because they will take her "inland soul" beyond its customary bounds.

While some poems reveal concerns with the current political situation of an Eastern land, others point to Dickinson's concerns with the West. "She died at play –" (F141 B), another poem of 1860, invokes Orientalism in an implied critique of Christian beliefs. In this poem, an unnamed subject (probably a butterfly) wanders "o'er the hill" at death: she "Gambolled away / Her lease of spotted hours, / Then sank as gaily as a Turk / Opon a Couch of flowers –." While the poem's second stanza does not follow up this simile, the Orientalist hedonism implied in the subject's death gives it an erotic hue, in clear opposition to the Christian heaven of salvation the poet frequently shunned: in a letter of 1861 Dickinson exclaims "heaven is so cold!" (L234), and in 1862 she writes "I dont like Paradise –" (F437 B). This subject's hours were "spotted," as was all human life to a nineteenth-century Christian; she lived, however, in innocent "Gamboll[ing]," and at death "Her ghost strolled softly o'er the hill –" while her "vestments" became "as the silver fleece –," images evoking purity.

For nature's "spotted" subject, death brings Eastern gaiety, beauty, and sensual pleasure. The point of this analogy would seem to be that such a death has no "sting," but its release from pain is distinctly not Christian.[44] At the same time, this invocation of the "Turk" could only come from stereotype since around 1860 the *Republican* reports only political tension in Turkey. Typical headlines read: "The Turkish Insurrection" (20 October, 1859); "Turkey, The Sick Man of Europe" (12 November 1859); and "Terrible Civil War in Asiatic Turkey" (10 July 1860).[45] As in "Some Rainbow," Dickinson here imagines nature as Oriental, hence the Orient as natural in its "ga[y]" proclivities; logically, then, Christian or other Western restrictions against gaiety are unnatural.

For Dickinson, desire is often more powerful than possession, and joy is precious because it is ephemeral, as she notes in "Delight is as the flight –" (F317, 1862). The distance or inaccessibility of the East—even in relation to factual reporting in the newspaper—makes it the perfect figure of desire, but also of states of inspiration and knowledge that cannot be taken for granted or possessed. "It would never be Common – more – I said –" (F388, 1862), for example, links poetry with the East. This poem's speaker first celebrates a state of exhilaration after her transformation out of the "Common," when she is born by poetic meter rather than "The feet – I former used –." Then, "suddenly" "the Wilderness roll[ed] back / Along my Golden lines –" and she is faced again with the "Sackcloth" of uninspired daily life, questioning, "where my moment of Brocade – / My – drop – of India?" Uncommon moments of poetic inspiration bring wealth resembling the essence of India. Dickinson's "The Spider holds a Silver Ball" (F513, 1863) has often been read as a portrait of an artist, and this ephemeral art is also suggestively Eastern in its connection with pearls: the "dancing" spider "unwinds" "His Yarn of Pearl" (or in a variant "Pursues his pearly strands"), plying these "Tapestries" in "Trade" as he constructs "Continents of Light."[46] The spider functions as diver, fabric artist, and merchant in one.

"Of all the Sounds despatched abroad –" uses an Orientalist metaphor to describe nature's most insubstantial art—the music or "old measure" of the wind "in the Boughs" (F334, 1862). While the wind's music is without lyrics (its "Tune" is "phraseless"), Dickinson claims that these tunes are also "Permitted men – and me –" and are "Inheritance . . . to us – / Beyond the Art to Earn –," perhaps inspiring the rhythms of her poetry. The last stanza then likens the moment of hearing this "solemn" natural music to that when "some Caravan of sound / On Deserts, in the Sky / Had broken Rank – / Then knit – and passed –/ In Seamless Company – ."[47] Like the caravan bringing precious goods to desert dwellers, the wind brings the transitory inspiration of its "Tune" to the poet. Similarly, "By my Window have I for Scenery" (F849, 1864) describes a pine tree as "a Sea – with a Stem –," complete with "Commerce . . . Of Spice," and a "Voice" the speaker associates with "Divine . . . Melody"— again an attribute of the fickle "Wind." "Some Rainbow – coming from the Fair!" (F162) may also associate an Orientalist nature with poetry through the words "tune" and "murmuring": the "Regiments of Wood and Hill . . . resume the whirr / Of last year's sundered tune!" as they return. In these poems, nature's inspirational art or tunes evoke tropes of the East.

The largest cluster of Dickinson's Orientalist poems combines imagery of wealth and desire with narrative fantasy situated, through passing analogy or fully developed scene, in Asia. Five poems written between 1858 and 1862 use the figure of the pearl diver to represent wealth beyond the Western speaker's grasp.[48] In "Her breast is fit for pearls," the speaker acknowledges "I was not a 'Diver'" and is therefore incapable of adorning his or her lover's "breast" appropriately (F121 B, 1859). In "The feet of people walking home" (F16, 1858) the phrase "Pearls are the Diver's farthings, / Extorted from the sea –" initiates two stanzas of analogies presenting "figures" for the distance to "immortality"; pearls are the "farthings" one pays in order to gain "resurrection," and the danger of diving is the cost of gaining such coin, perhaps representing death itself.[49] "*One life* of so much consequence!" similarly places the biblical parable of the "pearl of great price," or heaven, in the context of ocean pearls through the metaphor of diving (F248, 1861). Here the speaker imagines a life "of so much consequence" that she or he "would pay – / My soul's *entire income* –" to obtain it: such a life is "*One Pearl* . . . so signal – / That I would instant dive –" even if it "*cost* me – *just a life!*" Diving for this pearl entails great risk of the unknown to achieve a life of "consequence," but the poem does not tell us if the speaker will take the risk; it merely indicates the speaker's ambition to enter the unknown territory of the "Sea" (again, perhaps representing death) as a route to achieving the desired "*life.*" Because the speaker is willing to pay a life and seeks life, both secular and religious possibilities of interpretation remain in play. As Dickinson writes in "The hallowing of Pain," "All – is the price of All –" (F871, 1864). Following the biblical analogy, pearls typically symbolized purity or virginity (Matthew 13:46; Petrino 141). While "The feet of people walking home –" may also allude to the scriptural pearl, it is noteworthy that Dickinson's focus is on diving, not the pearl, making an activity associated with Asia represent a spiritually and romantically fulfilled life.[50]

"Removed from Accident of Loss / By Accident of Gain" (F417, 1862) pursues an extended analogy with "the Brown Malay," "unconscious . . . Of Pearls in Eastern Waters – / Marked His –," to speculate on the speaker's—or human—unconsciousness of the potential fortune to be discovered in one's local environment. Here the Malay is a figure for humanity, not a figure of contrast to the speaker, and diving again suggests the necessity of risking the unknown in order to achieve the knowledge and wealth fundamental to any creative or significant act. As in "*One life* of so much consequence!," the diving may be entirely psychological: the "Waters" to be tested are private ("Marked His"), but if one has the "power to dream" of what they hold then one might risk the "Accident of Gain" dependent on diving. Even an art like poetry, this figure suggests, requires the "power" to dream and to dive, as well as the discipline and skill to continue diving, if one would potentially reach the "Pearls" or "Riches" of one's own "Waters." The insistent capitals in the stanza introducing the "Brown Malay" (13 of 18 words in the stanza are capitalized) intensifies his allegorical function. There is definite Orientalism in presenting the Malay as a characteristic figure for "slow[ness]" in "conception," but the slowness is shared by the New England speaker who is "as unconscious / As" the Malay.

Much has been written about "The Malay – took the Pearl –" (F451, 1862), but the focus has been on Dickinson's views of slavery and on racism against African Americans, since she refers to the pearl diver as "The Negro" in stanza three.[51] The Asian content of the poem is all but ignored—perhaps because it does not emphasize sensuality, luxuriousness, or beauty. This poem, however, is as close as Dickinson comes to constructing an Oriental tale.

> The Malay – took the Pearl –
> Not – I – the Earl –
> I – feared the Sea – too much
> Unsanctified – to touch –
>
> Praying that I might be
> Worthy – the Destiny –
> The Swarthy fellow swam –
> And bore my Jewel – Home –
>
> Home to the Hut! What lot
> Had I – the Jewel – got –
> Borne on a Dusky Breast –
> I had not deemed a Vest
> Of Amber – fit –
>
> The Negro never knew
> I – wooed it – too –
> To gain, or be undone –
> Alike to Him – One –

Here in dramatic form reminiscent of Robert Browning's "My Last Duchess," the speaking "Earl" ill-temperedly claims the pearl as "my Jewel," petulantly insisting on the unfairness of a lower-class Asian diver's owning what he claims as his own because he wants it (note the repetition of "I," usually isolated for emphasis by dashes). The Earl is, consequently, both a ludicrous and a sympathetic figure—the latter because he stands for unfulfilled desire. The successful Malay is admirable but again ignorant—this time of the speaker's competition for his prize ("The Negro never knew . . ."). The Earl admits his unfitness for winning the pearl, acknowledging "I - feared the Sea - too much" and was "Unsanctified - to touch -" its most precious growth. In contrast, the diver is both a capable man of nature independent of the colonizing Earl's power and stereotypically "unconscious" of the complex longing, inadequacy, and ambition of the white Westerner. The quick aabb rhymes contribute to the brisk narrative flow and underline the speaker's pompousness and fearful desire.

Erkkila argues that this and other poems, like "Color - Caste - Denomination -," "suggest the ways that religious symbolism joins with racial ideology and Western aestheticism to create a perdurable racist *mentality*—a psychology of whiteness" ("Art of Politics" 152). While I agree that Dickinson maintains what is essentially a "psychology of whiteness" I find these poems to be more complex in their negotiation of racial ideologies and stereotype. The widespread fascination with Orientalism and pearl divers makes it likely that Dickinson's association in this group of poems is not primarily with American racial issues: identifying southern and warm eastern climates with emotional fulfillment and, in this case, romantic or sexual desire, Dickinson conflates the Asian and African in opposition to the incapable European aristocrat through an Orientalist idiom. Such idiom directly echoes the language of a story called "Pearl Divers" that Dickinson would have read in *Harper's Monthly Magazine,* June 1851 (46–48)—a periodical to which Lavinia had just begun subscribing and that her big sister would have been sure to check out.[52] In this story, two Malaysian divers compete with each other over the love of a woman; the story's narrator gives her a magnificent pearl and refers to swimming home "to his hut," but is eventually worsted by his rival in the story, who is the better diver.

Pearl divers and pearl oysters appeared frequently in popular Orientalist literature. "Mother of Pearl" in the *Hampshire and Franklin Gazette* features a pearl diver who saves the child of a white couple who can't swim (10 February 1860). The November 1860 *Harper's Monthly* included an informational article on pearl divers called "Pearls and Gems." In a similar essay in the *Atlantic,* James T. Fields states that pearl diving is an ancient activity from the north coast of Africa to India, then relates the story of "a little negro boy in 1560, who obtained his liberty by opening an oyster" because he had found "the rarest of priceless pearls."[53] Dickinson's use of this stock figure focuses on the strength, agility, and success of the diver—characteristics not typically associated with the Orient—with the further twist of making him represent the pursuit of various kinds of value in life, or afterlife. Her diver is unself-consciously capable, in true romantic stereotype, but these Eastern riches are for the most part psychological, not plunderable. This wealth is the Malay's, "His" territorially and legally—as suggested by the insistent capitalization in "Eastern Waters – / Marked His –" (F417). It is imperialistically claimed by the West ("my Jewel," states the Earl) but inaccessible; it can be gained only at great price—again making it the perfect figure for an "inland" soul's ambition and longing.[54]

"Comparisons are never neutral," states Rajagopalan Radhakrishnan. And yet, comparison necessarily catapults one beyond "the safe haven of filiative centrism"; to compare worlds or cultures is to "deterritorialize[]" one's perspective, such that, ideally, "the real motivation behind the comparatist project is the desire and the will for a new knowledge," he writes. Moreover, "a knowledge based on comparison could be more sophisticated, progressive, worldly, and cosmopolitan than a form of knowledge that is secure in its own identity and provenance" (454, 455–56).[55] This is certainly true of Dickinson's implied comparison in poems about the East. While her own perspective remains firmly outside the world of pearl divers, "turbaned seas," or "oriental heresies," she sees the characteristics of such foreignness in the landscape of her own garden, and in psychological characteristics of herself and neighbors as a way to express a deterritorializing "desire and the will for a new knowledge." Dickinson uses symbolic geography in part as a kind of shorthand to give concrete and therefore intensified form to particular aspects of being, but she also uses the implied comparison of metonymy and metaphor to stretch the boundaries of her understanding.

Perhaps as significant as the poems of direct reference to the East are poems of miraculous transformation that may have been inspired by what she herself calls "fabulous" "Oriental Tale[s]" (F1118, 1865). The previously mentioned "It would never be Common – more – I said –" (F388) tells such a story. More obvious is "As if I asked a common alms –" (F14 A, 1858), where the whole focus of the poem is on the instant of unexpected acquisition:

	syllables	
As if I asked a common alms –	8	[Alms,
And in my wondering hand,	6	
A stranger pressed a kingdom –	7	[Stranger Kingdom,
And I – bewildered stand –	6	[I, bewildered, stand –
As if I asked the Orient	8	
Had it for me a morn?	6	[Morn –
And it sh'd lift it's purple dikes	8	[should Dikes
And flood me with the Dawn![56]	6	[And shatter Me with Dawn!

As in a typical magical tale, here a "stranger" presents a humble petitioner not with "common alms" but with "a kingdom" that is also like being "flood[ed]" with "Dawn!" The assonance of the opening "Alms" and closing "Dawn" marks one of the ways this striking poem represents the utter unexpectedness of this gift—as if a daily condition of the skies suddenly rushed into your life with overwhelming force, causing complete disequilibrium. This assonance is echoed in "wondering" and "flood." The power of this flooding is also subtly born out in the repeated *d*s of the poem, all word-end or -middle until the concluding "dikes" and "Dawn."[57] The effect of the shortened third line (making an 8676 stanza, followed by the more predictable 8686) also marvelously represents the moment of shocked realization: "A stranger pressed a kingdom –" creates a pause before the next line's "And I –" because of the line break and consecutive unstressed syllables (uSuSuSu – / uS – . . .), anticipating the speaker's ability to do no more than "bewildered stand." The actual boon accorded this modest speaker is unimportant; the poem presents an analogy to a situation never described—we receive only the "As if." The poem emphasizes instead the gift's glorious unexpectedness, wealth, and beauty, and although Dickinson's use of "Orient" here denotes the East of "morn" it also clearly links the experience with the fabulous quality of Oriental tales.

"I gave Myself to Him –" tells another version of this story: the speaker's gift of herself and taking of "Himself, for Pay" transforms what had previously been no more than a "Fable – in the Isles of spice –" into "The Daily Own – of Love," or something to be enjoyed as real through the sexually charged "Mutual – Risk" and "Sweet Debt" of the partners (F426, 1862).[58] In "A Bird, came down the Walk –" again a simple act of kindness leads to transformation, this time of the object of observation, not the speaker: "I offered him a Crumb, / And he unrolled his feathers, / And rowed him softer Home . . ." (F359 C, 1862). Even the Freudian "In Winter in my Room" (F1742, undated) gives a twist to an Orientalist tale: the speaker is charmed by a snake, independent of any snake charmer. This harmless "Worm" is suddenly "ringed with power" and "Project[s]" himself through "a Rhythm *Slim* / Secreted in his Form / As Patterns swim," exerting a compelling fascination on the hapless and ambivalently desirous speaker. Similarly, the apparently conventional and sentimental love poem "The Daisy follows soft the Sun –" (F161, 1860) concludes not with the Daisy's continued adoration of her powerful lover but with her longing for "the flight – the amethyst –" promised by this master-figure's departure and "Night's possibility!"—clearly a transformation for an earthbound flower. In most of these poems—as in the pearl diver poems—transformation comes only at the price of some "Risk," even it if is only the risk of asking for alms, showing kindness, or reaching out to some other creature.

The tale of transformation, typically associated with love, desire, or salvation, is a core narrative in Dickinson's poems, often associated with judgment day and without any obvious Orientalist association—although it could be that its model is rooted equally in popular (Orientalist) and religious sources, regardless of its particular manifestations in any one poem. In "Title divine – is mine!" the speaker has been elevated by the conferral of an "Acute Degree" resembling but not the same as wifehood (F194, 1861).[59] In "I think I was enchanted," poetry brings transformation of the speaker and all nature through the poet's "Magic" (F627, 1863). "Joy to have merited the Pain –" remembers the lover's presence as "An Orient's Apparition – / Remanded of the Morn –," that is, like a genie's gift; the speaker consequently looks forward to "Paradise," when "Haunting actualize – to last / At least – Eternity –" (F739, 1863). "I'm ceded – I've stopped being Their's –" (F353, 1862) tells the more nuanced tale of transformation that perhaps only the speaker perceives since "before," as a "half unconscious Queen –" she was "Crowned" and she chooses "just a Crown –" to mark her newfound maturity, independence, and consciousness. Attention to the blurring of magic, spiritual transformation, and the transformations of maturity or creativity through common elements of diction and narrative illuminate religious and secular aspects of Dickinson's deep belief in the possibility of change, betterment, liberation, and salvation. One might interestingly explore whether Dickinson's assertion of such possibilities dwindles as the Civil War drags on, or after its conclusion.

Several poems of the late 1850s and early 1860s refer to Eastern things or people in ways commensurate with patterns asserting Eastern wealth, skill, and exile as a figure for all human experience, the possibility of transformation, or as a state preferable to conditions associated with the Christian West. In 1860 alone, the instances are striking.[60] "Tho' my destiny be Fustian –" (F131 B) presents a speaker who "far prefer[s]" "my little Gipsey being" with its "Fustian" (stout, plain cloth) and "sunburnt bosom" to "damask . . . a silver apron" or a "Rosier" bosom, because this hardy "Gipsey being" can withstand "Frosts" and therefore "Bloom Eternally!" This positive identification of the speaker with a gipsy departs radically from the associations of Dickinson's beloved lexicon; Webster defines gipsies as "originat[ing] in Hindoostan," "a race of vagabonds which infest Europe, Africa, and Asia, strolling about and subsisting mostly by theft, robbery and fortune-telling" but also as "a name of slight reproach to a woman; sometimes implying artifice or cunning" (EDL). Dickinson's "little Gipsey being," in contrast, is an honest, unassuming character, neither artificial nor sensual. For the speaker, to be a gipsy is to be comfortable in her natural setting, and therefore to "Bloom" or fulfill her aesthetic and creative possibilities. Steven Hamelman writes that "By its very nature, Orientalism is devoid of sympathy. . . . Orientalism—bidden to create a bravura picture of landscape and indigenous people more or less blissfully busy at work and play—interferes, confirming Western supremacy over anything that the East, even a romanticized version of it, might offer as an alternative" (64). Like Dickinson's pearl diver, this gypsy typifying natural hardihood and "Bloom" would seem to exemplify such blissful busy-ness, but Dickinson presents no conflicting "Western supremacy." Instead—like Emerson in "The Rommany Girl," which Dickinson would have read three years earlier in the *Atlantic*—she praises (and desires) the characteristics of the gypsy over those of European beauty or civilization.[61] This dramatic lyric expresses "my . . . being" rather than admiring picturesqueness in a gypsy "other." As in other poems invoking the East, here the physical otherness of a foreign race directs the reader to psychological or spiritual truths: Dickinson articulates admired aspects of "being" by taking on the voice of a figure generally repugnant to the West.

Other poems of 1860 internalize or naturalize Orientalist tropes as an aspect of human nature. While "cunning Jacob" wrestles "an Angel" or "God" on a site "A little East of Jordan," (F145 B), the poem implies that there are other such "Gymnast[s]," and many critics have read the poem as being about Dickinson's own struggles with the divine.[62] Similarly, one may have a "Gipsey" "being" in any geographical terrain. "Will there really be a 'morning'?" (F148), with its coy questioning of diurnal rhythms, uses associations with the East to mark the miraculous foreignness of "morning" and "Day": the speaker questions whether it is brought from "famous countries / Of which I have never heard?" and calls on "some Scholar," "Sailor," or "Wise Man from the skies" to help with her query—the latter referring apparently both to God and to the tradition of Wise Men from the East at Jesus' birth. The questing speaker is herself a "Pilgrim," the designation for a traveler to holy sites, for a Protestant exclusively associated with the biblical lands. At the playful end of the scale, "A fuzzy fellow, without feet –" makes every caterpillar a creature of Eastern luxury: "when winds alarm the Forest Folk, / He taketh *Damask* Residence – / And struts in sewing silk!" (F171). Damask—the only italicized word in the poem—is silk figured cloth "originally from Damascus" (EDL). In "If I could bribe them by a Rose," the speaker claims she would travel "From Amherst to Cashmere" bringing "every flower that grows" if it would win her the unnamed boon she seeks (F176).[63]

A staggering thirty of the fifty-four poems written during 1860 contain some mention of travel, escape, or of foreign places, language, or people, not including standard tropes of death, time flying, or seasons passing.[64] Although the majority of these references do not mention the East they are noteworthy in establishing the tendency of Dickinson's thinking during this year. "To learn the Transport by the Pain –" (F178 B), Dickinson's most significant poem of this cluster, makes travel the exemplary instance of both education and poetry: when "homesick – homesick feet" stay on "a foreign shore" one is "Haunted by native lands" and feels "sovreign Anguish!" This royal, independent "Anguish" is the condition for "learn[ing] . . . Transport"— evidently both as joy and as poetic ability.[65]

> To learn the Transport by the Pain –   ]thro'
> As Blind Men learn the sun!
> To die of thirst – suspecting
> That Brooks in Meadows run!
>
> To stay the homesick – homesick feet
> Opon a foreign shore –
> Haunted by native lands, the while –
> And blue – beloved Air!
>
> This is the sovreign Anguish!
> This – the signal wo!
> These are the patient "Laureates"
> Whose voices – trained – below –   ] stanza, hushed,
>
> Ascend in ceaseless Carol –   ]Breaks in victorious
> Inaudible, indeed,
> To us – the duller scholars   ]Cornets
> Of the Mysterious Bard!   ]"Band" –

As mentioned in Chapter 3, this poem asserts that the experience of exile or foreignness during the journey of mortal life "below," enables "'Laureates'" to sing, an activity associated with heaven—perhaps in parallel to Dickinson's use of the metaphor of diving for pearls, presumably in some "turbaned" sea, to achieve heavenly "Life." The exile of mortality would seem to teach all people to sing, just as one learns "sun" from blindness and "Transport" from "Pain." The particularity of the experience, however, suggests that not all humans experience such foreignness or "Pain." By apposition, Dickinson defines "These . . . Laureates" as the ones who experience "This" anguish or "signal wo"—both "this" and "signal" suggesting something beyond a norm—a distinction structured through the consecutive line-initial emphasis of "This . . . This . . . These."[66] "Homesick feet," both the daily tread of living away from whatever "home[]" one is "[]sick" for and the (metrical) feet of the Laureates' song, make poetry itself a kind of sojourn (the movement of feet) "Opon a foreign shore –." "Stay[ing]" in foreignness constitutes "train[ing]," which leads Laureates to "ceaseless Carol" (presumably after death). This metaphor in turn suggests that education as well as "Haunt[ing]" is necessary to produce or hear "ceaseless Carol": the keenest "scholars" presumably hear best the music of the "mysterious Bard" (or "'Band'") as well as that sung below. Again, in the poem's dominant tale, God is the "Mysterious Bard"; hence the homesickness we feel is for Heaven, curiously represented as plural "native lands."[67] Even in this reading, however, the dominant trope of the poem presents poetry first as the gift and burden of homesickness for a particular land, one of many, hence of mortality. If one learns from this pain one becomes a poet of earthly stanzas, whether the homesickness is only for heaven or also for some more literal version of "native lands."[68]

In "To learn the Transport by the Pain –" it is not pain itself that transforms but rather our capacity to learn from it, just as it is not the fact of travel but the experience of homesickness that makes a poet. And yet one must travel or there could be no such experience. The very word for joy in this poem—"Transport"—suggests the necessity for voyaging. According to this poem's paradox, joy itself constitutes a moving: Laureates are those who learn from exile to be (further?) transported. Hence the poem suggests a doubled distancing of the poet from "native lands"—both the necessary spiritual exile of the living from God and the more pragmatic travel that defines "home" by its contrast "homesick[ness]." Without the kind of travel that makes one experience being a foreigner, or understanding the strangeness of one's own assumptions and manner in the context of others, there would be no poetry, Dickinson implies. Poetry is, then, the province not of a Keatsian exotic or sensuous fantasy or the supernatural tale (Coleridge's "Rime of the Ancient Mariner") but of a psychological experience of foreignness.

A poem written in 1860 and copied to retain in 1861, "Just lost, when I was saved!" (F132), imagines the same comparative enabling. This poem's highly irregular line lengths (from four to twelve syllables), rhyme pattern, multiple exclamation marks, repeated line beginnings, and stanza structure manifest the speaker's disequilibrium and wonder, especially in the long first and shorter third stanzas.[69]

	rhymes	syllables	
Just lost, when I was saved!	a	6	
Just felt the world go by!	b	6	]heard
Just girt me for the onset with Eternity,	b′	12	
When breath blew back,	c	4	
And on the other side	d	6	
I heard recede the disappointed tide!	d	10	
Therefore, as One returned, I feel,	e	8	
Odd secrets of the line to tell!	e′	8	
Some Sailor, skirting foreign shores –	f	8	]novel
Some pale Reporter, from the awful doors	f	10	
Before the Seal!	e	4	

Next time, to stay!	g	4	
Next time, the things to see	h (b')	6	
By ear unheard –	i	4	
Unscrutinized by eye –	h' (b)	6	
Next time, to tarry,	h (b')	5	
While the Ages steal –	e	5	
Slow tramp the Centuries,	h'(b')	5 or 6	]Tramp the slow
And the Cycles wheel!	e	5	

(F132B)

Here the speaker is "saved" from the brink of death or "Eternity" at sea, but his or her journey to "the line" has made the speaker "Some pale Reporter"— perhaps an allusion to poets such as Bayard Taylor, who sent travel reports to the *Republican*. Like that of an ancient Ishmael or Mariner, the speaker's task is now to "tell" "Odd secrets," to bear witness to what (in the trope of the later poem) seems to have been "Transport" as well as "Pain." Yet, unlike Melville's or Coleridge's protagonists and more like a foreign correspondent, this speaker looks forward to the "Next" voyage: "Next time, to stay! . . . Next time, to tarry" on those "foreign shores" and finally hear and see all that is now "unheard" and "Unscrutinized." The poem's anaphoric syntax and heavily accented line beginnings that describe both the first experience of loss and anticipation of a return to foreignness call attention to the speaker's excitement and almost tell the story of the poem themselves, together with other spondees: "Just lost . . . Just felt . . . Just girt . . . breath blew back . . . Odd secrets . . . Some Sailor . . . Some pale Reporter . . . Next time . . . Next time . . . Next time."

Simply understood, the poem presents death as emigration, following a trial but incomplete scouting voyage: the final migration is then joyfully anticipated as satisfying all curiosity. That reading is partially foiled, however, by the identification of life, not death, as salvation, and "Report[ing]" as its defining act. The poet/speaker is eager not to arrive anywhere (for example, heaven) but to hear and see more; he or she is a sailor who both reports "Odd secrets of the line" and yearns for further travel, even while knowing such travel is analogous to death in isolating the soul from all it has previously known. This poet/speaker has "skirt[ed] foreign shores" without breaking the "awful doors / Before the Seal!" of entry—whether into death or some other ultimately defining emigration or foreignness. Whether travel is the metaphor for death or death/Eternity for travel, the poem associates will to adventure with the imperative "feel[ing] . . . to tell," and that telling bridges the world we know and the unknown where we long to "stay." Poetry, in this 1860 definition, is a kind of journalism—perhaps anticipating Ezra Pound's dictum that poetry should be "news that stays news."

A poem of 1864, "A South Wind – has a pathos / Of individual Voice –" suggests that what Dickinson there calls "foreignhood" may also attract because of its individuality, the kind associated with the peculiarity of "An Emigrant's address," the word "address" punning on directed speech and identifiable place (F883). This individually voiced "pathos" is "The fairer – for the farness – / And for the foreignhood –," the poem concludes, suggesting again that the confrontation with "much not understood" fascinates, attracts. The Dickinson who claims to "see – New Englandly" (F256, 1861) rarely speaks directly from a perspective of racial otherness (as in her gypsy poem). Similarly, the notion of poet as journeyer and journalist is commensurate with poems examined in Chapter 4 that reject the concept of a poet-genius and focus on poetry itself, not the poet, as being of greatest value. These poets "tell"; they relate news; they are not in themselves exceptional since such foreignness is available to anyone willing to risk the voyage of an "inland soul to sea." These poems of the early 1860s, and especially the year 1860, indicate how strongly Dickinson's imagination is fired early in her period of greatest productivity by the psychological experience epitomized in foreign travel, by encounter with the previously unimagined or unknown. Although such psychological encounters are stimulated primarily through print, the words of other "Reporter[s]," Dickinson celebrates their imaginative experience of the unknown or unknowable. There is, as she puts it later, after all, "no Frigate like a Book" (F1286 B, 1873)—unless it is perhaps a newspaper.

After the 1860s, Dickinson perceives the poet less as a potential or psychological traveler and more as everywhere "His Native Land," as she puts it in "The Things that never can come back" (F1564, 1881).[70]

		syllables	beats
The Things that never can come back, are several –	a	11	5
Childhood – some forms of Hope – the Dead –	b	8	4
But Joys like men may sometimes make a Journey	c	11	5
And still abide –	b'	4	2
We do not mourn for Traveler or Sailor –	d	11	4
Their Routes are fair –	d'	4	2
But think – enlarged – of all that they will tell us –	e	11	5
Returning here –	d'	4	2
"Here"! There are typic Heres –	d"	6	3
Foretold Locations –	f	5	2
The Spirit does not stand –	g	6	3
Himself – at whatsoever Fathom	h	9	4
His Native Land –	g	4	2

Now distinctly not a traveler, her speaker is "enlarged" by others' tales, not herself "Transport[ed]" or overcome with "Exultation." Moreover, even the traveler remains unchanged; the "Spirit" "at whatsoever Fathom" remains "Himself . . . His Native Land," hence cannot experience the transformational "Transport" she previously describes. At the same time, Dickinson here again acknowledges the deconstruction of binary oppositions that would divide others from us, native from foreign. Structurally, this poem rocks unevenly between the established or stable ("Himself . . . His Native Land") and inevitable change (the "Things that never can come back"): while the meter is evenly iambic throughout, line lengths vary dramatically following a clear but inconsistent long-short (11/4) pattern—even if one hears the first two lines of the final stanza ("Here"! There are typic Heres – / Foretold Locations –") as a split 11-syllable line. The poem instead seems to circle around the conception of "Here," a word repeated three times and emphasized further through rhyme and off-rhyme (Travel*er*, Sail*or*, *Their, fair*, whatsoev*er*). "Here" is presented as a questionable "Location[]"; "There are typic Heres"—all relative to perception. The Western "here," or Anglo-Euro-centric definitional perspective, is no more "typic" than any other centering vision of the spirit's "Native Land," although it is unquestionably Dickinson's.

After 1865, Dickinson's references to the East are typically more conventional, involving images of wealth and rest, without political allusion, implied cultural critique of Western rigidities, artificiality, and pretension, or a life of prose in contrast to that of poetry.[71] In 1878, "His Mind like Fabrics of the East –" (F1471) presents Asian wealth as "Displayed to the despair" of all but the rare "humble Purchaser"; this wealth is intellectual and clearly admired, but creates "despair." "A Mine there is no Man would own" (F1162, 1869) and "How destitute is he" (F1509, 1879) both associate that which is most valued with "Indies" and "India." The 1881 poem "No Autumn's intercepting Chill" (F1563 C) suggests that death brings "African Exuberance / And Asiatic Rest" to a "Tropic Breast"—revising the early "She died at play –" (F141) to assign gaiety or "Exuberance" to a non-Asian continent. In contrast, the 1865 poem "Always Mine!" (F942) comments "Old, indeed, the East," but then follows this predictable line with an anti-Orientalist assertion of the East's continuing masculine vigor: "Yet upon His Purple Programme / Every Dawn, is first."[72]

That Dickinson would eventually perceive fewer aspects of her world and the challenges of living as invigoratingly foreign, and especially Asian, is reasonable given her increasing seclusion and the longer period of time she has been withdrawn, but even more importantly given the cultural changes in the United States. It is not that daily newspapers contained less foreign news; indeed there was increased political and cultural exchange between

Asian countries and New England in the 1870s and 1880s. Rather, at mid-century, the excitement of encounters with ideas and cultures radically different from her own contributed to the general cultural ferment of the period, in which the world seemed to be changing at a rapid rate and in ways suggesting the possibility of progress, although also the precariousness of a moment of great cultural upheaval. Anne C. Rose describes the 1850s as a period of widespread enthusiasm and assertiveness: "Americans were exuberant about the arts, infatuated with technological progress, enthusiastic once again about personal salvation," and passionately involved in debating new scientific theorems, utopian visions for the improvement of humanity, and theories of personhood (162).[73] Despite the impending political crisis, the late 1850s was a period of cultural and intellectual exhilaration, Rose argues, in part because new modes of communication and transportation made participation in cultural change broadly possible throughout the United States—a result of the "successful establishment of the cultural marketplace" (162)—or what Meredith McGill has less optimistically described as a broad culture of exchange.

This exhilaration was not just middle-class and white. Frederick Douglass, for example, proclaims in an 1848 lecture that "Kingdoms, realms, empires, and republics, roll to and fro like ships upon a stormy sea. . . . Old prejudices are vanishing. The magic power of human sympathy is rapidly healing national divisions, and bringing mankind into the harmonious bonds of common brotherhood."[74] On both sides, the United States entered the Civil War with high idealism over what the war meant and optimism for the future. In the late 1850s and early 1860s, the conjunction of this general social energy with Orientalist fantasies of transformation, the high profile of Asian lands in the news, and her own sense of adventure in starting out on her poetic expedition into unknown waters encouraged Dickinson to represent the East as a complex figure for nature and desire, and as a potential corrective to the decadence and affectation of Western culture. After the Civil War, technology seemed far less promising and idealistic ideologies were suspect, given the slaughter of hundreds of thousands of men through newly invented forms of fire power and under the righteous banners of "liberty" and divine right. The national nostalgic, anti-immigrationist, and (less romantically) racist mood would have been less likely to stimulate imagination of the self as wild, bold, foreign, and powerfully uncivilized, or of nature and beauty as products of foreignness, emigrants from across "turbaned seas."

Dickinson's Orientalist identification with a gypsy or pearl diver was a fantasy, but so was her isolationist pose to Higginson in 1862 of having "my Lexicon – [as] my only companion" and having only the British "Keats – and Mr and Mrs Browning" as poetic influences (L261). While she did not travel, Dickinson understood her New England identity in direct relation to multiple aspects of global exchange, and understood the exploration of previously unknown cultures and seas to be as significant as that of new scientific and philosophical ideas—all of which reached her through the pages of the periodicals delivered to her at home. Knowing that Dickinson participated in popular discourses of foreignness in scores of poems significantly expands our sense of the range and contours of nineteenth-century Orientalism in the United States. Equally important, this participation reveals that Dickinson's references to names or things of, for her, exotic places involve far more complex and globally nuanced thinking about otherness, foreignness, and the properties of selfhood than have been realized. During the early years of her serious writing, Dickinson's understanding of identity and questions about value were stimulated by the daily news.

6

Reading and Writing the Civil War

> So we may, in a certain sense, call this whole war of freedom an acted
> poem, and find a melody of some divine ode in each of its unnumbered
> deeds of heroism and self-sacrifice.
>
> Oliver Wendell Holmes, "The Poetry of the War" 1865

> Poetry is related to music and cadence and therefore to the force of events.
>
> George Oppen, *Selected Poems* 2003 (189)

SCHOLARS HAVE debated the extent to which Dickinson was affected by the
Civil War and responded to it in her poems, from Thomas H. Johnson's famous pronouncement that Dickinson "did not live in history and held no
view of it" (xx) to Shira Wolosky's groundbreaking *Emily Dickinson: A Voice
of War* and several recent essays on particular poems relating to the war.
Without question, the war was the defining historical event of Dickinson's
lifetime.[1] Because the handful of poems Dickinson wrote in unambiguous
response to the war are now well known, this chapter will move from those
texts to others that more subtly echo popular idiom and genres. Notably,
Dickinson circulates none of her explicit war poems and very few of those
intersecting with its issues indirectly.[2] Perhaps she did not want to share such
poems because imagining the situational perspective of a soldier in shock or
pain or dying seemed unseemly, or because the subject matter itself was so
difficult. Or perhaps these poems of experiential perspective interested her
primarily as experiments and she did not want friends to mistake them for
her own experience. Whatever her reasons, Dickinson wrote a number of
poems during the war trying out popular types of war poems or using popular war idiom, and she shared them with no one—just as she did not circulate
the majority of her formally most irregular poems.[3]

Eric Foner writes that in the United States "no aspect of life emerged untouched from the war" (18). The Civil War began in 1861, when Dickinson
was thirty, and ended in 1865, before she turned thirty-five. During these (the war)
years she wrote over half of the poems she would write during her lifetime.
Certainly other personal, local, national, and international events and currents

147

influenced her during these years, and the war itself cannot be understood in isolation from religion, political ideologies, regional loyalties, and social issues like racism and prescribed gender roles. Nonetheless, Dickinson's emotional and intellectual life would have been unimaginably different had she not come to adulthood during the debates over slavery and secession in the 1850s and lived through the Reconstruction Era in the United States. Seven of the ten poems Dickinson published during her life appeared during the war, and three were given to a Union fundraising paper called *Drum Beat* in 1864—perhaps with her consent.[4] More than in any other realm, Dickinson's responses to the Civil War illuminate the complexity of her relationship to the culture and discourse of her moment in that many poems borrowing idioms or tropes of popular war poetry have no obvious connection with the war, in much the way that popular Orientalism takes diffuse form in her early poems.[5] As a whole, her poems responding to war resemble an amalgam of voices or attitudes taking different emotional and philosophical perspectives, often in the form of dramatic lyrics, more than the crafting of any unified response to the conflict or to war generally.[6]

Of course, Dickinson was familiar with death before the war began, but as historian Drew Faust writes, the most widely shared experience of the Civil War was that of death (xiii).[7] Over 620,000 men died during the war; in several battles, there were more than 2,000 casualties a day, and the ten largest battles each ended with 23,000 or more combined casualties. Many more died in prisons or hospitals, including large numbers killed by disease. Moreover, because the beginning of the war coincided with the invention of the telegraph and photography, reports of battles reached all cities and many towns within hours of their occurrence. In response to seeing photographs of the Antietam battlefield, Oliver Wendell Holmes wrote that war is "a repulsive, brutal, sickening, hideous thing" ("Sunbeam" 12). *Harper's Monthly Magazine,* to which Lavinia subscribed, and *Harper's Weekly,* to which Austin and Sue subscribed, contained several lithographs, sketches, and photographs of war scenes, and the *Springfield Republican* and *Franklin and Hampshire Gazette* printed regular lists of the dead and wounded. In such images and through war reporting, death was omnipresent during the war in visual as well as discursive detail.[8]

The Dickinson library contains no volumes of war poems published during the war, but some of the war's most famous poems were published in the *Atlantic*. To mention only a few Dickinson would have read there, Julia Ward Howe's "Battle Hymn of the Republic" leads off the February 1862 issue—a spot of prominence rarely given to a poem.[9] The same issue included Whittier's widely reprinted "At Port Royal. 1861."[10] James Russell Lowell's satirical second series of Biglow Papers ran for several months. In one poem of this sequence, "Mason and Slidell," New Englander Jonathan addresses England's

"John Bull": "The South says *"Poor folks down!"* John, / An *"All men up!"* say we,— / White, yaller, black, an' brown, John: / Now which is your idée?" (February 1862, 270). Emerson's "Boston Hymn" instructs "Pilgrims" to unchain and honor the slaves: "My angel—his name is Freedom, / Choose him to be your king" (February 1863, 227–28). Less famous works repeatedly voiced similar assertions and appeals. For example, "A War Cry" proclaims "Work we want—not words . . . Men to fight, and women to pray for them! / Unclasp their necks then: women! make way for them!" (*SR 15* February 1862). Dickinson's brief "What I can do – I will – / Though it be little as a Daffodil –" (F641, 1863) sounds like an affirmative response to such a call, whether or not it reveals a genuine resolution on Dickinson's part. Her quatrain concludes: "That I cannot – must be / Unknown to possibility –," echoing popular invocations and resolutions. Dickinson also marks two war poems in the *Atlantic,* Oliver Wendell Holmes's "Voyage of the Good Ship Union" (March 1862, 399–400) and Josiah Holland's "The Heart of the War" (August 1864, 241–42).[11]

Dickinson's poems responding directly and indirectly to the war are simultaneously private in that they are not shared and public in that they engage with the most traumatic and influential event of the nineteenth century in the United States. Because they are not circulated, they cannot negotiate her relationship with any particular reader or speak directly to a community, and yet, as Benjamin Friedlander puts it, their "discursive orientation" is "emphatically public" ("Ball's Bluff" 1584). Dickinson herself commented in a letter to the Norcrosses that she "sang off charnel steps" (L298). In some poems, Dickinson is profoundly critical of the self-righteousness of war rhetoric, with its martyrology and strident patriotism, and she does not participate in the widespread celebration of an exaggerated masculinity of valor and strength, express open patriotism, or write about the destiny of the nation. In others, however, she uses the popular war-time discourse of salvation and sentimental registers. Some poems are largely conventional in their language and expressions; others are among her most idiosyncratically original work. The best of these poems develop fully the interplay of aural, structural, and semantic or reflective features examined in earlier chapters. Many of Dickinson's poems most obviously about the war are not successful in this sense, but this indicates neither that she is a good poet only when she is least like the poets of her own time nor that she is at her best when her primary focus is aesthetic. Dickinson was writing around a poem every other day during the war, so it is little wonder that some do not move beyond unconvincing deployment of shared expressions of concern. Keeping war poems only in her private collection of manuscripts may have allowed her the freedom to experiment with a broader range of response than was otherwise possible.

Much writing on the war sacralized the conflict, appealing to God for victory, calling the war itself holy, and heroizing soldiers as martyrs to a sacred cause. In "Voyage of the Good Ship Union," Holmes refers to the flag as "the sacred sign," in a stanza Dickinson marked. In November 1862, Epes Sargent's "The Cabalistic Words" claims that the magical words "BE FREE" are "writ in martyr blood" (*AM* 613). Rose Terry's "The New Sangreal" claims the war as the new "grail": Christ tells the questing soldier, " 'The blood poured out for brothers is my blood; / The flesh for brothers broken is my flesh; / No more in golden chalices I dwell ... Here is the sangreal, here the Holy Quest' " (*AM* September 1863).[12] While Dickinson never suggests that war itself is apocalyptic or sacred, several of her poems present soldiers as sanctified by their sacrifice. "A Sickness of this World it most occasions / When Best Men die." (F993, 1865) presents the dead as "contented" to "forsake" the "World ... For Deity," perhaps referring to soldiers.[13] Similarly, "One Crucifixion is recorded – only –" (F670, 1863) may allude to the war's dead in commenting that "There's newer – nearer Crucifixion / Than" "Our Lord['s]." "Good to have had them lost / For News that they be saved!" (F809 B, 1864) positively asserts that the dead (again, perhaps soldiers) "Shall Stand to Our Right Hand –" although the poem's paradoxical representation of death as "The nearer they departed Us," and claim that the dead stand at "Our," not God's, side suggests some critique of martyr discourse. "Over and over, like a Tune –" (F406, 1862) more conventionally imagines "Drums off the Phantom Battlements" and "Cornets" "too grand / But for the Justified Processions / At the Lord's Right hand."—indicating, as Barrett points out, that those killed in battle are "Justified," and privileged (at the "Right hand") even among the saved. At the same time, this poem's focus is the repeated "Recollection" of such "Drums ... Battlements ... Cornets ... Cadences," as though war haunts us despite that consoling vision of "Justified Processions" ("Drums" 113). In a letter referring to Frazar Stearns's death, Dickinson wholly without irony calls him a "young crusader – too brave that he could fear to die" (L255).

The poem in which Dickinson most obviously employs this rhetoric is written in unambiguous response to the war. In "It feels a shame to be Alive –" she both evokes and disturbs the pieties of war martyrology while expressing the guilty gratitude of a civilian to soldiers.

It feels a shame to be Alive –
When Men so brave – are dead –
One envies the Distinguished Dust –
Permitted – such a Head –

The Stone – that tells defending Whom
This Spartan put away

What little of Him we – possessed
In Pawn for Liberty –

The price is great – Sublimely paid –
Do we deserve – a Thing –
That lives – like Dollars – must be piled
Before we may obtain?

Are we that wait – sufficient worth –
That such Enormous Pearl
As life – dissolved be – for Us –
In Battle's – horrid Bowl?

It may be – a Renown to live –
I think the Men who die –
Those unsustained – Saviors –
Present Divinity –

                                                              (F524, 1863)

In this poem, Dickinson repeats well-known tropes for the war dead: "Distinguished Dust . . . Spartan . . . Liberty . . . Sublimely . . . Renown . . . Saviors . . . Divinity" and the "Pearl" of life are all terms one might expect to find in a popular war poem. The governing metaphor of life as pawned, however, steers the poem's thinking into the unanswerable area of cost and undercuts the romance of patriotic martyrdom. Soldiers are "Saviors" but ominously "unsustained," "Pawn[ing]" their "piled" lives for our "Liberty."[14] This cost is "Sublimely paid –," with "lives" rather than the "Dollars" paid by the wealthy for substitutes to take their place in the draft. Up to this point, Dickinson's poem resembles others. In Holland's "The Heart of the War," for example, a husband guiltily tells his wife that "When I kneel to try to pray, / My thoughts are never free / But cling to those who toil and fight / And die for you and me"; the husband then enlists and the wife becomes a widow. Dickinson marks the last two of these four lines with an x in the margin (242, EDR 546). The third stanza of Dickinson's "It feels a shame to be Alive –," however, pushes its economic logic to an unusual and painful conclusion: "Are we that wait – sufficient worth –"? Does the "Liberty" of "we that wait" justify disregard for the "Pearl" of soldiers' lives "dissolved" in "Battle's – horrid Bowl"?

The logic of much Union war poetry by late 1863 is to justify the war's blood-letting by reference not to the liberty of white civilians but that of slaves. As Lincoln most famously states in his second inaugural address, God "gives to both North and South this terrible war as the woe due to those by whom the offense came" and it may be that war will continue "until all the wealth piled by the bondsman's two hundred and fifty years of unrequited toil shall be sunk, and until every drop of blood drawn with the lash shall be paid by another drawn with the sword."[15] It is unclear whether Dickinson avoids the justification of Northern sacrifice for the liberty of enslaved African Americans out of lack of conviction about emancipation as the key moral charge of the war or because she wishes to press home instead the question of individual responsibility. Perhaps the very possibility of her brother Austin's being drafted raised more urgently for her the question of the "cost" of life and the danger of rhetoric urging sacrificial behavior.[16] Dickinson implies in "It feels a shame" that no cause is worth the hundreds of thousands of deaths caused by the war; but yet, she says, soldiers "Present Divinity." She both acknowledges soldiers' sacrificial bravery and allows her troubling ethical doubt that suffering to this degree can ever be justified to stand. Insofar as this poem both fully engages and directly challenges the logic of war discourse, it is Dickinson's most important war poem.

"It feels a shame" is not the only poem in which Dickinson criticizes the ideology of heroic martyrdom, a genre epitomized by Epes Sargent's "Pro Patria," which relates the life of a soldier who is wounded, recovers, then immediately returns to the battle lines where he is killed, concluding: "He never yields his life too soon, / For country and for right who dies" (*AM* February 1865, 233). In Holland's "The Heart of the War," the husband tells his wife "I'm sure you'd rather have me die / Than not to bear my part"—lines Dickinson also marks with an *x* (242). Howe's "The Flag" urges "All ye that have manhood in you, go, perish for Liberty!" (*AM* April 1863, 443). In apparent caustic response to such urging, Dickinson imagines a soldier wanting to "perish for Liberty!" who is instead forced to live:

> He fought like those Who've nought to lose –
> Bestowed Himself to Balls
> As One who for a further Life
> Had not a further Use –

(F480, stanza 1, 1862)

Yet although, or because, this soldier "Invited Death . . . Death was Coy of Him," Dickinson writes. The poem concludes that this soldier seeking heroic martyrdom "was left alive Because / Of Greediness to die –."[17] How foolish, she implies, to have no "Use" for life.

As I suggest earlier, a more complex poem makes this point affirmatively, albeit without reference to the war. In fall 1862 Dickinson writes:

> A Toad, can die of Light –
> Death is the Common Right   ]mutual –   equal –
> Of Toads and Men –
> Of Earl and Midge

The privilege –
Why swagger, then?
The Gnat's supremacy is large as Thine –

Life – is a different Thing –   ]Another
So measure Wine –
Naked of Flask – Naked of Cask –
Bare Rhine –
Which Ruby's mine?

(F419)

This speaker mockingly addresses someone like that soldier who "Invite[s]" death, or those who "swagger" imagining their glorious "privilege" to die.[18] To idolize men dying in battle constitutes, at some logical extreme, the celebration of death itself as a "privilege." One could think in the twenty-first century of cultures promoting suicide bombers as heroes dying a martyr's death—but this attitude goes back at least to Horace's "'tis sweet and fitting to die for your country," alluded to in Sargent's title "Pro Patria" and frequently in popular poetry. The 1862 "A Midnight Song" gives unusually explicit focus to the violence of such dying: "the country's dower is a gory shower, / Till the red on the banner has blotted the blue. . . . Aye, a nation born / With the blood of its sires on its altar's fires, / Bedews them again with the blood of her sons: / And the world admires while the Truth inspires. / Behold us *men* and our jewels *guns!*"[19] Dickinson chooses a different kind of jewel in asking "Which Ruby's mine?"

"A Toad, can die of Light –" promotes life at its most essential and in ways implying racial equality, as well as condemning heroic martyrdom: "Naked of Flask – Naked of Cask –" there is no difference between rich and poor, women and men, generals and civilians, Confederate and Union soldiers, or a black person and a white. Lincoln's preliminary Emancipation Proclamation was announced as early as 2 August and repeatedly praised in the *Republican* and *Atlantic*, as stated earlier. Dickinson might well have had racial equality in mind in this fall 1862 poem, which implies that we should not wait for what she later calls Death's "Democratic fingers" to value life, regardless of how it is packaged.[20] In "A Toad, can die of Light –," she reminds a culture caught up in the heroism of its generals, soldiers, and battlefields that "Life" not "Death" is what matters; life is "Wine," suggesting the Christian "wine" of communion except that it is everyone's precious "Ruby"; there is a spiritual dimension to all life. As I suggest earlier, wine is also an artisanal product to be enjoyed, savored, suggesting that the value of life is far from intrinsic; it is made, a "Thing." The quality of wine depends upon the luck of natural conditions and the labor of others, as well as the skill of the

vintner. In that sense, the quality of one person's "Bare Rhine" is not independent of another's. In this culture celebrating heroic dying, Dickinson
suggests, we should instead measure "supremacy" through what we make of
our lives.

A poem about defeat similarly questions conventional rhetoric of victory
through a striking portrait of suffering on a battlefield. Here those supposedly contrasting extremes of victory and defeat—like that of friend and
enemy—are profoundly relative. Logically, this speaker may be a soldier
since in "Defeat – today –" he points "Over there –" to the victorious:

> My Portion is Defeat – today –
> A paler luck than Victory –
> Less Paeans – fewer Bells –
> The Drums dont follow Me – with tunes –
> Defeat – a somewhat slower – means –   [something dumber
> More Arduous than Balls –   [difficult –
>
> 'Tis populous with Bone and stain –
> And Men too straight to stoop again –   [bend
> And Piles of solid Moan – ·
> And Chips of Blank – in Boyish Eyes –
> And scraps of Prayer –   [shreds
> And Death's surprise,
> Stamped visible – in stone –
>
> There's somewhat prouder, Over there –   [something
> The Trumpets tell it to the Air –
> How different Victory
> To Him who has it – and the One
> Who to have had it, would have been
> Contenteder – to die –

(F704, 1863)

Defeat is a day's "Portion," paler, slower, more arduous than "Victory" as a
"means" to an unspecified end; victory is "prouder," but this also leaves defeat
its pride. Similarly, soldiers on both sides may be "Content[]" to die—the mo-
mentarily victorious are merely "Contenteder." And these conditions are temporary; defeat is today's "Portion." What is not relative in this poem is the
middle stanza's suffering and death, uncannily presented as a kind of crowd-
ing: defeat is "populous" with "Bone and stain" and "solid Moan"—as though
especially in defeat but also in victory we are individually populated by these
traumatic losses, wherever we stand in relation to the war. This is a personal
experience ("My Portion"), but it suggests a haunting of the nation.[21]

While Dickinson questioned aspects of popular war rhetoric, she also shared
basic concerns with the populations of Amherst, and New England—including

general support for the Union. Her father and brother were active in supporting Amherst's war effort, collecting subscription money to buy uni-
forms, recruiting volunteers, and boosting levels of local support—despite
Austin's later decision to pay a bounty not to fight. Amherst sent more than
the usual number of volunteers into battle early in the war (Wolosky, *Voice of
War* 53). In a letter of 1863, Dickinson mentions "service . . . in Church, for
Our Arms," or Union troops (L 280), and Amherst church bells tolled for Union
victories and defeats.[22] In a town of only 3,000 Dickinson might have known
every soldier who enlisted, was wounded, or died—at least by reputation.

Politically there is no variation in Dickinson's war-time verse: all poems
and letters she writes express attitudes congruent with support of Union ideology, even when they also regret the war's slaughter. The difference between
Dickinson's indeterminate referentiality in poems like "What I can do – I
will –" and political ambivalence is clarified by Nathaniel Hawthorne's 1862
essay, "Chiefly About War-Matters, by a Peaceable Man." Here Hawthorne
tells of a trip to Washington, D.C., Harpers Ferry, and a few military camps
as the ground for broad political and social reflection. Editorial notes, perhaps written by Hawthorne himself to satirize the extremities of Union patriotism, find several aspects of the essay objectionable.[23] When Hawthorne
applauds the hanging of John Brown, the speaker of the notes exclaims: "Can
it be a son of old Massachusetts who utters this abominable sentiment? For
shame!" When Hawthorne justifies Southern response to Northern soldiers by imagining occupying armies in Massachusetts, concluding that
"crowds of honest people" have become "traitors" to the Union out of love
for their region, a note comments that "we . . . are inclined to think [the]
tone [of this passage] reprehensible" (48). And when Hawthorne states
sardonically that even if the South should permanently secede—like Lucifer
and a third of God's angels leaving heaven—"heaven [will be] heaven still," a
long note objects to the premise that the Union would be unchanged by
secession:

> The war can never be allowed to terminate, except in the complete triumph of
> Northern principles. . . . We should be sorry to cast a doubt on the Peaceable Man's
> loyalty, but he will allow us to say that we consider him premature in his kindly
> feelings towards traitors and sympathizers with treason. (61)

Calling "this Rebellion" an "intolerable crime," this note ends with the high
rhetoric of righteousness, unwilling to allow the overtones of Hawthorne's
southern sympathy to stand unmonitored at any point. None of Dickinson's
poems express either of the extremes in Hawthorne's essay and notes. There
is no implicitly pro-southern sympathy and no flag-waving patriotism for
the Union. In this regard, many of her poems could have appeared in the

pages of the *Atlantic* without any notice of discrepancy between their tones and those of other contributors.

Dickinson avoided all openly partisan vocabulary of the war: she never uses the words "Union," "Yankee," "copperhead," "rebel," or any of the popular terms for the conflict: war of rebellion, war of secession, war of the states. She refers to no battles, no generals, writes nothing explicit about slavery or any other of the issues leading to the war, and writes nothing obviously temporal about the war's beginning or its conclusion, although she may write indirectly about Lincoln's assassination.[24] From her poems you cannot guess who is fighting, or even that one side eventually wins this war. Many popular war poems are equally vague. As Alice Fahs writes, "the primacy of individual experience of the war was the focus of much war poetry" and the heroism celebrated was typically that of ordinary, unnamed men and women (92, 116). Moreover, within the pages of particular periodicals and within local communities there was no need to specify which army God favored or to define contentious terms like liberty. Dickinson would have felt no need to identify her sympathies. Consequently while her war poems may be understood universally—that is, as applying equally to Union and Confederate loss—this is not necessarily a statement of political neutrality on her part, since her poetry shared rhetorical ground with poems equally referentially indeterminate but in context clearly pro-Union.

Recent criticism has tended to present Dickinson either as having deep sympathy for the plight of slaves (something she never articulates) or as opposed to the "abolitionist, reformist, and democratizing energies of the time," as Betsy Erkkila puts it (*Wicked Sisters* 46).[25] I see her as falling between these extremes during the war years. Open expressions of class and racial hierarchy are absent from her correspondence and poetry; instead, poems like "The Malay – took the Pearl –" (F451, 1862) and others discussed in Chapter 5 manipulate tropes of difference at times by romantically elevating the racially marked subject above his or her unmarked white Western counterpart and at others through the speaker's identification with a nonwhite subject.[26] Aife Murray argues that Dickinson's views toward the Irish became more sympathetic as she worked closely with Irish servants, beginning in 1856, but that her attitude toward African Americans did not change (*Maid* 169). This may be the case. Dickinson's expressions of hierarchical racial positioning, however, largely disappeared during the period of high political sympathy for enslaved or newly freed African Americans in the North and reappeared only in casual epistolary commentary, with the increased public and national racism following the apparent failure of Reconstruction, and mirroring national trends.[27] The primary examples of Dickinson's racism against the Irish occur in the early 1850s (especially L42, 43, 49) and against blacks in letters written in 1881 (L716, 721).[28] Moreover, as Sandra Runzo points out, Dickinson owns sheet music with explicitly abolitionist language: the Hutchinson Family's "Granite State" includes the repeated lines "Yes, we're friends of emancipation And we'll sing the proclamation 'Till it echoes through our nation" (EDR 469).

Initial opposition to abolitionism followed by gradual or reluctant support was typical in the North. The changing New England barometer on emancipation is demonstrated in the *Republican* in 1862. Moreover, a casual reference by Susan to the "fleet" of Union General Burnside in a March 1862 note indicates that she knew Dickinson kept up with the war news.[29] At the beginning of the year, a letter to the editor asks why the paper is "strongly vehemently against 'emancipation' but it favors 'confiscation' . . . of all slaves of all rebels"; "J. P." responds: "There is just the difference . . . that there is in attaining any end by legal means," namely that confiscation of slaves during war is "a legitimate war measure" whereas immediate emancipation resembles "mob law" (3 January 1862). This is precisely the position taken by Edward Dickinson in 1861, when he declined the Republican nomination for lieutenant governor, denouncing "the heretical dogma that immediate and universal emancipation of slaves should be proclaimed by the government," while still hoping that "in the good providence of God, emancipation [would] be one of the blessed results of the war."[30] On 11 March 1862, the *Republican* strongly supported the proposed Congressional measure to reward border states for voluntarily emancipating their slaves on the grounds that "there will be great moral as well as political advantage in such a position of the general government . . . at the same time declaring slavery to be an evil and disavowing any right to touch it without the consent and invitation of the states in which it exists." On 2 August, the paper equivocally supported Lincoln's preliminary emancipation proclamation: "Many loyal men have doubted the wisdom of undertaking this immense work . . . [but] there is now no other course but to push it through, cost what it may." By 23 September, however, when it printed the proclamation, and in the following day's commentary, it was hailed as the "greatest social and political revolution of the age," "timely . . . thorough . . . just and magnanimous. And it will be sustained by the great mass of the loyal people, North and South."[31]

While there is no hard evidence that the Dickinsons, like other Northerners, had been "daily growing more in favor of this measure," Edward's opposition to emancipation was explicitly constitutional, not moral.[32] He writes to Samuel Mack on 25 April 1863, "I . . . shall be glad to have this war ended—when the rebellion is crushed between the 'upper and the nether millstone'—and not before—when slavery has made its *last squeak,* and when traitors have all 'gone to their places.' "[33] Dickinson's war-time poems imply support for racial equality and declare the urgency of liberty.[34] At the same time, just as she looks at Asia from the perspective of a white Westerner even when criticizing the West, she regards issues of emancipation and equality from the privileged position of a white Northerner, for whom liberty is paramount as a matter of federal politics and personal freedoms rather than of emancipation, even when writing monologues that might be spoken by a (freed) slave. In short, "equality" and "race" remain complex, contradictory, and freighted concepts for her—as for most of her contemporaries.

Civil War poetry exemplified the patterns of fluidity between song and poetry and as generally practiced in the culture of widespread reprinting and borrowing. War poetry circulated broadly through song—like the "Battle Hymn of the Republic" or James Randall's "My Maryland." Poems by Whittier, Holmes, and Longfellow that Dickinson would have read in the *Atlantic* were also set to music. Whittier's "Song of the Negro Boatmen" (a section of "At Port Royal"—*AM* February 1862) was set to music several times.[35] Holmes's "Union and Liberty" (*AM* December 1861) was set to music by Charles E. Kimball. Other poems in the *Atlantic* were published with the name of the hymn tune to which they could be sung immediately following the title, as in "Army-Hymn. *Old Hundred*" or "Parting Hymn. *Dundee*" (June and August 1861). The *Republican* comments on some poems set to music, for example, Henry Ware, Jr.'s "The Triumph of Liberty," which it prints with a note claiming that "The words of this song were written in 1843. . . . It has been set to music for male voices, and is now being distributed through the army" (18 January 1862).[36] As mentioned in Chapter 3, many war poems were also written following the rhythm of well-known songs or poems, and Dickinson herself once made up alternate words to the pastor's homily and choir's song: "when he said 'Our Heavenly Father,' I said 'Oh Darling Sue'. . . . I made up words and kept singing how I loved you, and you had gone, while all the rest of the choir were singing Hallelujahs" (L88). Whether or not Dickinson composed in stanzas following rhythmic tunes, as I argue in Chapter 3, she probably—like her contemporaries—imagined a highly permeable boundary between written and sung lyrics, or verse, and she may well have composed some of her war poems with a distinct tune at least initially in her head.[37] Like Dickinson's, many poems written during the war were composed in personal letters or diaries and never circulated in published form, yet more books were published in 1863 than in any previous year in the United States and the circulation of poetry in periodicals also increased.[38]

What is most striking in this popular enthusiasm for poetry and song is the fluidity of these forms in the public domain: once a poem was published it passed into the common domain and could be used, set, revised, or rewritten freely. In putting Randall's "My Maryland" to music, the Cary sisters altered his refrain to make it fit the music (Erbsen 53). In a Northern example, the Hutchinson family's defining song "The Old Granite State" circulated with multiple lyrics, and was used as a campaign song for Abraham Lincoln (Runzo). The fluidity between poem and song was sometimes so great that poems were known by the name of the composer rather than the lyric's author.[39] The reprinting culture of this period abetted the wildfire distribution of poems and songs that struck a national chord, and encouraged the transformation from one genre to the other, as well as uninhibited borrowing and revising of texts and rhythms. Agnes Leonard copied a section of Ellen Flagg's "Death the Peacemaker" in her poem titled "After the Battle" without attribution. As mentioned previously, the *Republican* even brags about the fact that many of its poems were reprinted elsewhere in praising a poem that had just been set to music (13 February 1860). Dickinson adapts a phrase from minstrelsy and a popular political song in an 1860 letter to Samuel Bowles where she calls herself both "Mrs Jim Crow" and "Bob o' Lincoln" (L223), but she also participates silently in this free-floating circulation of popular song and verse through responses to patterns of popular verse. To my knowledge, she never sets out to compose new words to a particular wartime (or other) song, but the culture in which tunes, rhythms, and phrases were freely borrowed and adapted may have encouraged some of her experimentation with popular idiom and rhythms.[40]

Dickinson comes closest to writing in a popular genre of the war in her nature poems that present war in relation to a natural or sacred order, some adopting traditional Christian attitudes and others imagining nature itself as overwhelmed by the violence of war. As David Cody points out, during the antebellum period many poems depicted the autumn landscape as "the body of Christ, slowly bleeding to death as the natural world reenacts the ritual of purgation" (38). This genre took a different turn during the war, when poets repeatedly noted nature's indifference to the war's "gashes" in "the Nation's heart"—as Della Weeks puts it in "The Wood of Gettysburg"—or used seasonal change as an allegory for the progress of the war (*WFH* 115). Elizabeth Akers's "Spring at the Capital" interweaves descriptions of spring with reflections that "Nature does not recognize / This strife that rends the earth and skies.... When blood her grassy altar wets, / She sends the pitying violets." "Help us to trust," she cries to nature, "that these battle-stains are but the blood-red trouble of the dawn" (*AM* June 1863, 706). Bryant's "My Autumn Walk" begins with "woodlands ruddy with autumn" and a scene of such "beauty" that "tears come into my eyes. // For the wind that sweeps the meadows / Blows out of the far South-west, / Where our gallant men are fighting, / And the gallant dead are at rest" (*AM* January 1865, 20). This is also the vein of Melville's 1866 "Shiloh," with its swallows "Skimming lightly, wheeling still . . . Over the field where April rain / Solaced the parched ones stretched in pain" (*Battle-Pieces* 63).[41]

Dickinson juxtaposes natural beauty with the horror of death in "They dropped like Flakes –" (F545, 1863)—a poem published as "The Battle-Field" in 1890, a title provided by Higginson and demonstrating that he recognized its genre. At this poem's beginning we do not know what "They" are that drop like "Flakes . . . stars . . . [and] Petals from a Rose"—just as other such poems begin with description of a natural scene. The second stanza, however, reveals with quiet poignancy that these multitudinous and unmarked deaths are of men, and concludes with a conventional piety: "They perished in the seamless Grass –" but "God can summon every face" of the dead. "The name – of it – is 'Autumn' – / The hue – of it – is Blood –" (F465, 1862) is almost comically grotesque, with its "Great Globules – in the Alleys –" and graphically open "Artery" and "Vein"—as though the landscape itself were wounded, but its grounding metaphor was familiar in 1862.[42] A sunset becomes "Whole Gulfs – of Red, and Fleets – of Red – / And Crews – of solid Blood –" appearing in "Authorized Arrays," like soldiers in battle who disappear into death just as the sunset daily vanishes (F468, 1862).[43] Fall and sunset are, for obvious reasons, the natural phenomena most often linked with the war's deaths. Less obvious, a poem like "The Birds reported from the South – / A News express to Me –" (F780, 1863) may refer both to the turning seasons and to war news; the poem asserts that once nature becomes "a Mourner, like Myself" then they share "Our Contract / A Wiser Sympathy."

In some poems, Dickinson counters the optimism of natural analogies suggesting that peace or victory are as inevitable as spring. "All but Death, Can be adjusted," she writes bluntly in 1863 (F789). Although this poem acknowledges that "Wastes of Lives – [can be] resown with Colors / By Succeeding Springs –" it implies that "Wastes" in nature lead to regeneration whereas the death of people does not. Apparently only human "Death" is "exempt from Change –." Similarly, in another poem without reference to the war, Dickinson asserts that human chaos or disaster "makes no difference abroad – / The Seasons – fit – the same –" (F686, 1863). Faith Barrett reads such poetry as indicating Dickinson's recognition that the conventions of the romantic lyric poem are inadequate for responding to such a bloody war. If this is the case then many poets of the era discover such limitations since many write such poems.[44] Dickinson and her peers revise the romantic nature poem to demonstrate the unnaturalness of war and its ghastly effects—whether imposing itself on every landscape or invisible in nature's indifferent proliferation of beauty.

A similar genre acknowledges the war but focuses on life's consoling pleasures—particularly art. The speaker of Whittier's "To E. W." mentions the war then "let[s his] fancy stray": "Today, when truth and falsehood speak their words / Through hot-lipped cannon and the teeth of swords . . . I still can hear at times a softer note / Of the old pastoral music round me float" (*AM* May 1863). Holmes's "Shakspeare. April 23, 1864" thanks the bard for providing relief from "this dread hour of Nature's utmost need": "Oh, while our martyrs fall, our heroes bleed, / Keep us to every sweet remembrance true, / Till from this blood-red sunset springs new-born / Our Nation's second morn!" (*AM* June 1864, 763). In "Unto my Books – so good to turn –" (F512, 1863), Dickinson similarly notes that "It may be Wilderness – without – / Far feet of failing Men –" but "within" are "Bells" and "Holiday" when she is comforted by "Kinsmen of the Shelf."

While famous men and battles received lavish attention, the most prolific category of verse in North and South, according to Alice Fahs, emphasized the civilian's heroism or suffering—as in Whittier's famous "Barbara Frietchie" or R. M. Westfield's less famous "The Soldier's Wife." Westfield's speaker extols both soldier and wife: "Oh spirit brave! to lay thy life / Upon a nation's hallowed shrine; / But braver far, the martyr wife, / Who meekly yielded hers in thine" (*SR* 1 February 1862). Because Dickinson never refers to herself as a mother among the many named guises or dramatic perspectives she adopts in her poems (including boy, Czar, Earl, Queen, wife), it is notable that one of her most explicit responses to the war imagines the reunion of a mother and son in heaven. The strong bond between soldiers and their mothers gave rise to an extremely popular subset of sentimental war poems (Fahs 105). In the *Republican,* Dickinson would have read an article honoring William Hunt, a brave soldier and "dutiful son," as "touchingly" demonstrated by a poem he sent home in a letter, "On Guard"; this poem portrays a soldier "At midnight on my lonely beat" envisioning a woman with "silver hair" who "prays for me . . . Till, though the leagues lie far between, / This silent incense of her heart / Steals o'er my soul . . . And we no longer are apart" ("The First of Our Dead," *SR* 11 January 1862). In "Story for the New Year," a dying soldier gives his comrade a bible and says "Take it home to my mother sweet / If you should survive her face to greet; / Tell her that night and morn I prayed / For her, and ever command obeyed" (*SR* 4 January 1862). Other poems encourage mothers to give their sons gladly to the war: "Woman of nerve and thought . . . By you is manhood taught / To meet this supreme hour," writes Annie Fields in "Give" (*AM* May 1863, 643). Lucy Larcom's speaker in "Reenlisted" declares "I cannot hold a musket, but I have a son who can; / And I'm proud for Freedom's sake / To be the mother of a man!" (*AM* May 1864, 630).

Dickinson's "When I was small, a Woman died –" (F518, 1863) emphasizes not the son's heroism, duty, or satisfaction in fighting but his joy to see his mother again: "Today – her Only Boy / Went up from the Potomac – / His face all Victory // To look at her –."[45] Like Fields's and Larcom's mothers, Dickinson's imagined mother takes pride in her son's service, even to the point of being indirectly responsible for it: the "imperial conduct" the poem mentions is "their[s]," not his alone, and both "That Woman and her Boy / Pass back and forth, before my Brain" "proud in Apparition."[46] This is an odd poem for Dickinson because it contains no moments of sharp insight or emotional depth. By representing only the reunion in heaven as imagined by a detached spectator, it provides no moment of mourning for the son and no particular point of pride for the mother or the spectator.

Other poems imagine the death of a beloved man more intimately. "The World – feels Dusty / When We stop to Die –" (F491) borrows war imagery to anticipate easing the death of a beloved on a battlefield, or in comparison with that circumstance: "Flags – vex a Dying face – / But the least Fan / Stirred by a friend's Hand – / Cools – like the Rain –" (F491, 1862). This soldier (or dying man), unlike the heroes of popular patriotic verse, appears to be "vex[ed]," not soothed, by flags, a token of the glory of battle. "Robbed by Death – but that was easy –" (F838, 1864) expresses another trial of those on the home front, namely the suspense of waiting to hear if a loved one has died: it's easy, this speaker claims, to be robbed by death or "Liberty . . . This, too, I endured – / Hint of Glory – it afforded – / For the Brave Beloved –"; in contrast, "Suspense's / Vague Calamity –" when we "Stak[e] our entire [alt: divine –] Possession / On a Hair's result –" is excruciating. The notion that "Liberty" may rob one of life again suggests some critique of national patriotism, in part because its compensating "Hint of Glory" is so minimal and in part because the capitalized alliteration of "Brave Beloved" (or as an alternate "bold Beloved") could be read as slightly mocking. The quality of the language in this poem changes to vivid, arresting metaphors, however, when its focus shifts to suspense. "If He were living – dare I ask – / And how if He be dead –" (F719, 1863) voices the suspense of a woman querying someone about her beloved—a dialogue suggesting the trauma of war deaths, which allowed the grieved no opportunity to tend the dying or even attend a burial. The poem ends with the speaker's response to the feared news: "And He" she asks, " 'Was buried' – 'Buried'! 'He!' / My Life just holds the Trench –." In contrast, although they contain no mention of the war, the unusually long and detailed poems "Although I put away his life –" (F405, 1862) and "I learned – at least – what Home could be –" (F891, 1864) imagine domestic pleasures that "might have been" after a beloved's sudden death. The gendered aspects of both narratives are fully consonant with popular verse—for example, in the later poem, where the speaker imagines a "Task for Both – When Play be done – / Your Problem [alt: labor] – of the Brain – / And mine – some foolisher effect – / A Ruffle – [alt: Thimble] or a Tune –."

"To know just how He suffered – would be dear –" (F688, 1863) presents the related question of how a loved one has died, a topic of great concern to Victorian death culture, where dying was treated as a semi-public ritual. As numerous rule books for the "good" death instructed, ideally a person dies surrounded by family and friends, like the "friend" fanning the dying man's face in "The World – feels Dusty"; the dying individual then utters final words that reveal his or her spiritual readiness to die.[47] Many popular poems described soldiers dying in a comrade's arms, speaking lovingly either of heaven or of their wives or mothers, and anticipating salvation, as in the previously quoted "Story for the New Year." In "The Dying Confederate's Last Words," the speaker says to his "loving comrades dear": "The angels sweetly stand and beckon me to come, / To that bright land of bliss that heavenly realm my home" (Fahs 104). The language of "To know just how He suffered –" moves from the sentimental idiom of "The Dying Confederate's Last Words" to the more idiosyncratic, and from the concerns of popular death culture to more philosophical concerns with dying. The first two stanzas use popular diction and images:

> To know just how He suffered – would be dear –
> To know if any Human eyes were near
> To whom He could entrust His wavering gaze –
> Until it settled broad – on Paradise –   [full –   firm –
>
> To know if He was patient – part content –
> Was Dying as He thought – or different –
> Was it a pleasant Day to die –
> And did the Sunshine face His way –

The last of the poem's six stanzas, however, uses epistemological discourse characteristic of Dickinson's most serious poetry:

> Was he afraid – or tranquil –
> Might He know
> How Conscious Consciousness – could grow –
> Till Love that was – and Love too best to be –
> Meet – and the Junction be Eternity   [mean –

While this poem might seem to be about Jesus, because of its repeated capitalized pronouns (He, His) and lack of martial diction, the huge death tolls of the war by mid-1863 make the context more likely that of a soldier dying without the solace of witnesses, as in "If He were living – dare I ask –" (F719). The opening questions about whether "Human eyes were near," the day was "pleasant," or "Sunshine face[d]" him are typical concerns of a culture that is comforted by knowing if one has died with friendly faces "near."

Dickinson's expressions of concern over several decades about the manner of dying indicate her familiarity with this cultural mode. An 1862 letter asks for details of a relative's death: "You must tell us all you know about dear Myra's going . . . Was Myra willing to leave us all?" (L263). In 1883, she writes Charles H. Clark on the death of his brother, hoping "he was able to speak with you in his closing moment. . . . I am eager to know all you may tell me of those final Days"—a request she repeats in her next letter (L826, 827). In 1885, she writes Forrest Emerson to ask him to enquire about Helen Hunt Jackson's death (ostensibly on Vinnie's behalf): "Should [your friend] know any circumstances of her life's close, would she perhaps lend it to you, that you might lend it to me?" (L1018). In this realm, Dickinson apparently finds the language of sentiment comforting. In 1856, she copies out a highly sentimental poem by James Pierpont in a letter of condolence to Mary Crowell, marking her enthusiasm for it by indicating that she had previously mentioned the poem, sending "the verses of which I spoke one day—I think them very sweet" (L183).[48] "To know just how He suffered –" combines the registers of religious certainty and Victorian death culture with psychological enquiry and philosophical speculation. If one is willing to give any credence to the significance of the manner of dying, then this poem's extended desire for "last" details (was he "patient," was it a "pleasant Day to die," what were his "Wishes," did he speak) lead naturally to the question "Was he afraid," and the closing speculations about love and consciousness.

Once one has considered the possibility that Dickinson writes such dramatic lyrics, some in the voice of a soldier, other poems open up as potentially dramatic. "It was not Death, for I stood up," (F355, 1862) suggests, among its other possible perspectives, the traumatic confusion of a battle survivor.

It was not Death, for I stood up,
And all the Dead, lie down –
It was not Night, for all the Bells
Put out their Tongues, for Noon.

It was not Frost, for on my Flesh   ]Knees
I felt Siroccos – crawl –
Nor Fire – for just my marble feet   ]two
Could keep a Chancel, cool –

And yet, it tasted, like them all,
The Figures I have seen
Set orderly, for Burial,
Reminded me, of mine –

As if my life were shaven,
And fitted to a frame,

And could not breathe without a key,
And 'twas like Midnight, some –

When everything that ticked – has stopped –
And space stares – all around –
Or Grisly frosts – first Autumn morns,
Repeal the Beating Ground –

But, most, like Chaos – Stopless – cool –
Without a Chance, or spar –
Or even a Report of Land –
To justify – Despair.

This poem's power lies in its depiction of a state so awful that it cannot be named, and cannot be understood sufficiently to "justify" the "Despair" it brings. While its speaker might be brought to such a state by various circumstances, such psychological paralysis could well be imagined in relation to the traumatic shock we now understand as following from experiences of extreme violence and near death—conditions repeatedly experienced by soldiers in the Civil War's major battles. A surviving soldier might well look at the dead that "lie down" around him, wonder at the time of day through the smoke of cannon fire, and experience a numbness that is "like Chaos – stopless – cool –." As discussed earlier, the simplicity, almost primitiveness, of the speaker's observations and comparisons could also suggest the utter bafflement, or temporary psychological dislocation, following a battle—what Dickinson elsewhere calls pain's "Element of Blank" (F760). This haunting and brilliant poem contains no perfect rhymes (the closest is "around / Ground," in the penultimate stanza). There are some aural patterns linking one pondered but indeterminate state to another: "Death" and "Dead" anticipate the concluding "Despair," and another sequence gives us "shaven . . . frame . . . space stares" and "spar." Mostly, however, the poem makes us pick our way carefully through its distinctive and disjunctive phrases and sounds, joined primarily by the blank conjunctive "And," all detailing what this state is "not," but therefore also what it is "like." Nothing makes this a war poem, and yet it powerfully evokes a state those who have survived battle might recognize.

A similar state of numbness in "After great pain, a formal feeling comes –" (F372, 1862) is called "Quartz contentment," "the Hour of Lead – / Remembered, if outlived, / As Freezing persons, recollect the Snow – ." This poem might be spoken by a soldier remembering the battle's "Hour of Lead" in addition to the heaviness of pain or grief. "I felt a Funeral, in my Brain," (F340, 1862) uses a striking metaphor to depict a moment of radical dislocation, when "a Plank in Reason" breaks and the soul descends into a kind of living death. Some have argued that this poem responds to Frazar Stearns's death a few months earlier, but it is also imaginable in the voice of a soldier unnerved by witnessing the gruesome deaths and perfunctory funerals of comrades. As Brenda Wineapple points out, this poem echoes Longfellow's "Psalm of Life," which urges readers to "act in the living Present!"—a demand Dickinson herself makes in poems like "A Toad, can die of Light –" (50).[49] Longfellow writes:

> Art is long, and Time is fleeting,
>   And our hearts, though stout and brave,
> Still, like muffled drums, are beating
>   Funeral marches to the grave.

"In the world's broad field of battle, / In the bivouac of Life," Longfellow asserts, one should "Act." Dickinson instead presents that moment when the heart and brain cannot surmount the "Funeral marches" within, although leaving open the possibility for a return to "the living Present!" in her inconclusive final "– then –."

Other poems deploy a dramatic "I" more lightly. The rollicking "Tie the strings to my Life, My Lord, / Then, I am ready to go!" suggests that the speaker could be a newly enlisted soldier as believably as a Christian anticipating salvation, the context most logical given the speaker's address to "My Lord." Lines like "Just a look at the Horses – / Rapid! That will do!" and "Good bye to the Life I used to live . . . kiss the Hills, for me" distinctly echo enlistment poems (F338, 1862).[50] Even if Dickinson imagined the verse only in relation to departure for heaven she borrows clichés and the upbeat tone of the soldier's farewell for her speaker. Another poem with a first-person speaker that may experiment with dramatic war-time narrative echoes poems that presented the war as a period of necessary suffering that would make the United States a more mature, stronger, and truly "free" nation. Adeline Whitney's "Under the Cloud and Through the Sea" posits such a progressive historical perspective: "No mighty birth / But comes by throes of mortal agony; / No man-child among nations of the earth / But findeth baptism in a stormy sea" (AM September 1861, 352). Dickinson's "Let Us play Yesterday –" (F754, 1863) "play[s]" with a cryptic memory that leads the speaker to contrast yesterday's imprisonment in "the Egg-life" and "Manacles" with the wonder of "the new Free" (a category including the speaker), who celebrate liberty as the "last gratitude . . . at night" and "the first Miracle / Let in – with Light –." Yet the last three of the poem's nine stanzas read:

> Can the Lark resume the Shell –
> Easier – for the Sky –

Would'nt Bonds hurt more
Than Yesterday?

Would'nt Dungeons sorer grate
On the Man – free –
Just long enough to taste –
Then – doomed new –

God of the Manacle
As of the Free –
Take not my Liberty
Away from Me –

This speaker concludes with the fear of a return to bondage rather than trust in newly attained freedom.

While the dominant metaphor of "Let Us play Yesterday –" is of imprisonment rather than slavery, and imprisonment figures prominently in gothic antebellum narratives, the language also has a strong resonance with wartime concerns. Like other poems in the progressive historical mode, this poem positions lack of liberty as a condition naturally outgrown, hence unnatural for the mature being: neither the "Girl" nor the metaphorical "Lark" can "resume" its "Bonds" without great injury and pain. Moreover, it identifies God as equally responsible for the enslaved and the free, hence implicitly for black and white populations. God, it implies, will determine the outcome of the war—the linchpin of both Southern and Northern war rhetoric, but here clearly allied with emancipation. This implication is clear not only through the speaker's final plea to God but because there is no other clear "You" in the poem: logically, then, God is the "you" who "troubled the Ellipse" or began the whole process of freeing those previously imprisoned—as part of the natural cycle of bird, human, or national growth.[51] Hence, the poem implies that the individual or nation comes to maturity by gaining its wings, or becoming "Free"—an event echoing the outcome of the revolutionary war and implying that further (or continued) freedom is equally inevitable and just. The certainty of this apparent conclusion is troubled, however, by the speaker's plea at the end of the poem that she not again lose her "Liberty," hence her acknowledgment that neither justice nor logic determines the course of history, and that liberty once gained can be lost. In 1863, only God can know the end of this "untold Tale."

While the speaker of this poem is only possibly a freed slave, an active reader of the daily news like Dickinson might well have reflected on the war's outcome on newly liberated African Americans in 1863, and even more likely on the implications for Massachusetts should the Union lose to a slave-holding power. For her such imagining takes the form of metaphors of slavery or imprisonment rather than of attempts to depict an actual slave's experience or perspective. In "What if I say I shall not wait! / What if I burst the fleshly Gate – / And pass Escaped – to thee!" (F305, 1862) the speaker more extremely presents life itself as analogous to slavery and death to freedom. The poem's middle two tercets read:

What if I file this mortal – off –
See where it hurt me – That's enough –
And step in Liberty!   ]wade

They cannot take me – any more!   ]us
Dungeons can call – and Guns implore –]may
Unmeaning – now – to me –

Here "Liberty" most clearly signifies heaven; it is a geo-spiritual space from which one cannot be retaken because one has moved beyond the "mortal" or "fleshly Gate"; hence it is a place far safer than the North for fleeing slaves. While "Dungeons" evokes European gothic narratives, the line "They cannot take me – any more!" and reference to "Guns" is more suggestive of release from a communally determined bondage and the fugitive slave hunter. The speaker makes no explicit reference to slavery but powerfully represents the pain of imprisonment, the fear of recapture, and the joy of "Escape" into a liberty so tangible one can "wade in" it, using language reminiscent of slave as well as gothic narratives to represent a spiritual escape.[52]

Dickinson addresses the war's ideological issues most directly in "Color – Caste – Denomination –" (F836, 1864)—a poem that does not echo or reflect any existing narrative or rhetorical model. As described in Chapter 5, in this poem the personified Death has "large – Democratic fingers" that "Rub away the Brand" of "Blonde – or Umber," as though skin is merely a "Brand" of public marketing that temporarily identifies us. Whatever the color or caste of the "Chrysalis" that death "put[s] away," individual souls "emerge" from death as "Equal Butterfly," in metaphorical flight and non-racially identified colors rather than in the stereotypical Christian and racially hierarchical "white." While this poem may imply that perfect equality comes only with death's transformations, it is nonetheless consistent with general Union support of Lincoln's emancipation policy and, given the time of its composition, may even respond to the 1864 election campaign, which was a referendum on Lincoln's war policies, including emancipation.

In these poems, Dickinson explores ethical questions or convictions about freedom and equality, especially the horror of losing liberty once it has been gained, using key words that mark the poems as at least peripherally concerned

with contemporary politics of "Color" and "Liberty." In both, she unequivo-
cally condemns dehumanizing, discriminatory marketing or branding and
celebrates freedom. Because Dickinson writes no poems in which she affirms
hierarchical thinking as such, or raced-based discrimination as justifiable,
poems like "Color – Caste – Denomination –" and "Let Us play Yesterday"
seem to express her position on these issues. Through her amorphous "I"
and by omitting contextualizing scenes for her poems' narratives or dia-
logues, Dickinson elides her experience with that of dramatized others,
whether soldiers, civilians, or even potentially freed men and women, making grief, pain, and death itself experiences we share in that we must all face
them. Writing from what seem to be dramatic positions of a soldier, the bereaved, and someone newly freed, she echoes the rhetoric and narratives of
popular poems to try out ways of thinking about grief, pain, and death, and
ways of expressing such feelings effectively.

Dickinson sometimes uses a first-person plural rather than the singular "I"
in poems grieving the death of a loved man, as though she also experiments
with articulating a communal grief, and she indeed writes to the Norcrosses
that "Sorrow seems more general than it did, and not the estate of a few persons, since the war began" (L298, around 1864). As Wolosky writes, "War is
above all the time when community commands and supersedes the self, for
and within larger historical ends"—affecting definitions of selfhood as well as
communal boundaries ("Public and Private" 119). The insistent capitals of
"We Cover Thee – Sweet Face –" (F461, 1862) may stage such blending of personal and communal, or national, sorrow as it "follow[s]" the loved one to the
grave then "reluctant – turn[s] away / To Con Thee o'er and o'er – // And blame
the scanty love / We were Content to show –" while he was living. "It was too
late for Man –" similarly invokes community in noting that although "Creation" was "impotent to help . . . Prayer – remained – Our side –" (F689, 1863).[53]
In another poem of this year, Dickinson speculates on ways that grief may create at least temporary community: "Bereavement in their death to feel / Whom
We have never seen – / A Vital Kinsmanship import / Our Soul and their's
between –" (F756, 1863). In this war metaphorically cast as between brothers,
there is also a "Vital Kinsmanship . . . between" survivors and the slain. "He
gave away his Life –" (F530, 1863) suggests the anticipated domestic response
to a soldier's death, again speaking from the plural perspective of an unidentified community whose task is mourning: "'Tis Our's – to wince – and weep –."
Here "we," like a good neighbor, seem to have witnessed the young man's
"Growth" and his "esteem [alt: estimate] . . . magnified – by Fame –." Yet to
continue, as Dickinson does, that it is also ours to "wonder – and decay" and
to call what may be a soldier's death the *choosing* of "Maturity" departs distinctly from clichés of mourning or consolation.[54]

In some poems, Dickinson echoes popular idiom without using a dramatic speaker or, again, invoking the war specifically. An early recruitment poem by Richard Henry Stoddard states that the South "strike[s] at the life of the State— / Shall the murder be done? / They cry 'We are two!' And you? / *'We are one!'* "[55] Plural singularity is also the theme of Oliver Wendell Holmes's "Union and Liberty," which addresses God, pleading "Thou has united us: who shall divide us? / Keep us, O, keep us, the MANY IN ONE!" (*AM* December 1861, 757). In what may be a light-hearted response to such rhetoric, Dickinson writes "One and One – are One – / Two – be finished using –"; here she rejects mathematics of the "schools" to assert that for "Life – just – Or Death – / Or the Everlasting –" another reckoning is more crucial, perhaps the Union's arithmetic of "e pluribus unum" (F497, 1862). Although this poem points to the unity of love ("More" or "Two" would be "too vast / For the Soul's Comprising –"), the poet may manipulate the frequently invoked mathematics of national federation to assert her preferred union.

"It dont sound so terrible – quite – as it did – / I run it over – 'Dead', Brain – 'Dead'." (F384), written in 1862 in response to the death of Frazar Stearns, expresses gaunt despair and angry cynicism.[56] Although its phrasing contains no predictable idioms, it borrows the word "murder" from patriotic poems like Stoddard's "To the Men of the North and West" and resembles other popular poems in its expression of disbelief about a beloved's death.[57] For example, in Laura C. Redden's "Left on the Battle Field" the speaker exclaims "You are not dead! You are not dead! / God never could will it so – / To craze my brain and break my heart / And shatter my life – I know" (in Hoffman, "Reenacting" 76–77). In her poem, Dickinson's speaker tries out various ways of making the news less "terrible": "Put it in Latin . . . Turn it, a little – full in the face . . . Put the Thought in advance – a Year – / How like 'a fit' – then – / Murder – wear!" In poems suggesting individual or communal response to deaths caused by the war, Dickinson may be expressing an unfocused sorrow by trying out patterns and phrases circulating broadly, placing herself in the dreaded position of grieving for a son, lover, or friend.[58] With Frazar Stearns's death, this position is no longer entirely imagined. More than thinking of the staggering death tolls of the war, his death may have stimulated her to imagine how those in closer relationship to the war dead grieve.

"I wish 'twas plainer, Loo, the anguish in this world. I wish one could be sure the suffering had a loving side," Dickinson writes in response to Stearns's death (L263). Poems like "It feels a shame to be Alive –" (F524), "He fought like those Who've nought to lose –" (F480), and "Whole Gulfs – of Red, and Fleets – of Red –" (F468) express similar skepticism about the cost of such war deaths. An 1871 poem seems to be spoken from the perspective of a victorious soldier, whose "Triumph lasted till the Drums / Had left the Dead alone / And then I dropped my Victory / And chastened stole along / To where the finished Faces / Conclusion turned on me" (F1212)—a reflection indicating that grand ideals do not adequately justify the bloody cost of victory when one is faced with the actual dead, who are "finished" in a "Conclusion" that does not suggest the potential comfort of "Paradise" voiced in other poems in a more popular mode. Most famously, in contrast to the expected choir of angels at a good death, Dickinson writes: "I heard a Fly buzz – when I died –" (F591, 1863); this death involves irritation and hints at coming decay, not ascension to heaven or "that last Onset – when the King / Be witnessed – in the Room –" expected by conventional mourners. More characteristically, in "We pray – to Heaven – / We prate – of Heaven –" (F476, 1862), Dickinson both mocks this death culture, asking "Is Heaven a Place – a Sky – a Tree?," and posits that there is some existence beyond "Location's narrow way." There may be some admonishment and even a pun in this poem's trenchant reminder that "Unto the Dead / There's no Geography – // But State – Endowal – Focus –": this capitalized "State" might be the nation—a concept that is more abstract than geographical, especially in a nation of federated individual "states"—or it might refer to the "State" of the soul; it is definitely not a geographically fixed "Location" like Virginia or Massachusetts.[59] Dickinson may chide her contemporaries for harboring regional loyalties and individuality rather than embracing a communal "State" beyond regional "Geography."

Throughout the war, Northern poetry identifies the Union's cause as "Truth" itself, most famously in Howe's "Battle Hymn," where "truth is marching on" in the form of the Union armies. Howe's "Our Orders" similarly concludes that if the Union's "destiny should fail, / The sun should darken in the sky, . . . And God, and Truth, and Freedom die!"—as Dickinson would have read in the *Atlantic* (July 1861). Adeline Whitney sees "loyal Truth, and holy Trust, / And kingly Strength defying Pain" as born again in the war effort ("Per Tenebras, Lumina," *AM* January 1862, 69). In 1864, Dickinson writes with equal confidence that "The Truth – is stirless –" and therefore "best for confidence"—like a "Body" (or "Giant") that "Stands without a Bone –." Because "Truth stays Herself – and every man / That trusts Her – boldly up –" (F882, 1864), she resembles divinity, through her bodilessness and the possible play on the word "up" at the poem's conclusion. While in this poem Dickinson does not narrow truth to a particular category of thought, by 1864 the word may have been so strongly associated with the morality of the Union war effort in New England that she could take this reading for granted within the poem's interpretive range.

In contrast, "They leave us with the Infinite." (F352 B, 1862) modifies such confidence in divine support in a dramatic lyric. This poem asserts paradigmatically that "whom [the Infinite] foundeth, with his Arm / As Himmaleh, shall stand –" then switches to the chummy soldier-like dialogue of those who must depend not just on the "Infinite" but on each other: "So trust him, Comrade – / You for you, and I, for you and – me / Eternity is ample, / And quick enough, if true."[60] This poem's unusual period at the end of both its first and last lines underlines the necessity of trust: soldiers (or those engaged in any communal battle) have only themselves and God, or the possibility of salvation, to depend on, so better to "trust" even though we cannot know if the promise of an eternal life is "true." "Our journey had advanced –" (F453, 1862) also uses what may be a soldier's voice to hypothesize that beyond "The Forest of the Dead –" lies a certain reward: although "Retreat – was out of Hope –" "Eternity's White Flag – [is] Before – / And God – at every Gate –."[61] As poems like these demonstrate, reading Dickinson's poems in concert with war poems published in widely circulated periodicals reveals that many of her poems adopt the vocabulary, tone, or idiom of popular war poetry.

Dickinson's most lasting contributions to Civil War poetry are her reflections on extremities of grief and pain, such as in "I felt a Funeral" or "After great pain," and her poems taking on major cultural, philosophical, or theological questions raised by this bloody war, such as "My Portion is Defeat – today –" or "A Toad, can die of Light –." In such poems, Dickinson verifies the reality of pain, often deeply psychological whatever the extent of the physical suffering, anticipating not just recent physiological and psychoanalytic knowledge of the brain but also the effects of war trauma, which we are still attempting to come to grips with a century and a half later.[62] As Wolosky puts it, "what emerges [in these poems] is the way the problem of suffering is at once most acutely personal and yet also broadly and fundamentally historical" ("Public and Private" 114).[63] In a previously quoted letter to her Norcross nieces, Dickinson wrote that sorrow is "more general" but also that "if the anguish of others helped with one's own now would be many medicines" (L298, 1864), implying that it does not. At the same time, she seems to find some "medicine" in writing about this sorrow, since her very next comment is that "Every day life feels mightier, and what we have the power to be, more stupendous." Dickinson may have felt the crisis of the historical moment as a stimulus to her own greater "power" or possibilities of being—perhaps another way of understanding her writing "What I can do – I will –" (F641, 1863).

Some of her poems on suffering include military reference. In "Pain – expands the Time –" (F833, 1864), pain both "expands" and "contracts" time: "Ages coil within / The minute Circumference / Of a single Brain –" but pain "contracts – the Time – / Occupied with Shot" or focused on the moment initiating its extremity. The reference to "Shot" suggests the poem may be spoken by a soldier, assuredly one spending a good deal of "Time – / Occupied with" this topic. A poem beginning "If any sink, assure that this, now standing – /

Failed like Themselves – and conscious that it rose –" represents a soldier's "assur[ance]" of life after battle's terror: "Tell," the dead speaker commands, that "Dread, [is] but the Whizzing, before the Ball –" (F616, 1863). Like many of Dickinson's poems on pain and fear, however, this one veers at its end to present a more troubling or complex aspect of dying. This soldier-speaker concludes not with salvation but with release from the army's imperative to violence: "When the Ball enters, enters Silence – / Dying – annuls the power to kill –." Others have no element of popular patriotic or sentimental idiom—for example, "There is a pain – so utter –" (F515, 1863), "Pain – has an Element of Blank –" (F760, 1863), or "Pain has but one Acquaintance" (F1119)—with its legal diction, or "This Merit hath the Worst –" (F844), with its reference to the "Maimed" who at least know that "the Worst" cannot "be again." A lovely and elegiac apostrophe to snow, written early in 1865, may request the "Austere" comfort of the natural world as a requiem following such suffering:

Snow beneath whose chilly softness
Some that never lay
Make their first Repose this Winter
I admonish Thee

Blanket Wealthier the Neighbor
We so new bestow
Than thine Acclimated Creature
Wilt Thou, Austere Snow?   [Russian

(F921, 1865)

Complete with the archaic "Thee" and "Thou," this poem quietly admonishes winter to provide a "Wealthier" than usual comforting of the newly dead.[64]

"Snow beneath whose chilly softness," like several of the poems I mention in this chapter, has no obvious reference to the war, but I believe such poems respond to it in a diffuse way, commenting on popular celebration of martyrdom, reflecting the time's ubiquitous concerns with suffering and death, and portraying soldiers' experiences of defeat or escape, or a bereaved woman's response to her beloved's death in battle. Even the few poems that appear to respond to particular war-related events resist specifying elements. "It dont sound so terrible – quite – as it did –" (F384) makes no mention of Stearns's death, and "When I was small, a Woman died –" (F518), which may have been prompted by the death of her distant cousin Francis H. Dickinson, changes the few details she appears to give of his life story: Francis was killed at Ball's Bluff in Virginia (on the "Potomac" but not in "Maryland"), was not an only child, and his mother died when Dickinson was twenty-three—hardly "small."[65] Individualizing elements do not play a significant role in Dickinson's war verse. We can know, however, that Dickinson wrote some poems in distinct response to the war, was extraordinarily prolific during these years, wrote most of her poems now most frequently anthologized between 1861 and 1865, and circulated almost none of these poems. Given that she circulated only five of the sixty-nine poems I mention in this chapter, only two of which may engage the war even indirectly, these poems would seem less to address any immediate audience and more to function as ways to learn from experiments in communal dialogue about how the deepest feelings, most terrible experiences, and gravest fears can be faced or understood through structures of art.[66]

There are no doubt a number of reasons—none individually sufficient, and none certain—why Dickinson did not share her poems about the war, echoing its idioms, or focused on death and pain. If Dickinson's poems responding even indirectly to the war represent some combination of expression of her experience and her imagining of the suffering of men on battlefields or women losing their most deeply beloved to the war, perhaps they seemed too risky to circulate; perhaps she feared they would reveal more—or might seem to reveal more—about herself than she wished revealed or wanted friends to imagine. Unmailed, such voices could not be mistaken (rightly or wrongly) for her own—although so many poets of her era wrote dramatic lyrics that this may not have been a concern. The power of many of these poems certainly suggests that Dickinson writes at least in part from experience. Perhaps she felt less secure in the dramatic perspectives of these lyrics than in those of the wife, boy, Earl, Queen, or others used more often in her poems and more obviously distinct from herself. Perhaps these poems raised high theosophical, epistemological, and historical anxieties. The multiply circulated "Safe in their Alabaster Chambers –" (F124 B) questions the faith of the "meek members of the Resurrection" through satire, with a light touch and with a variety of second stanzas celebrating the vibrancy of life. In contrast, poems like "After great pain" (F372), "I felt a Funeral, in my Brain," (F340), "It was not Death" (F355), "'Twas like a Maelstrom, with a notch," (F425), "There is a pain – so utter –" (F515), "Pain – has an Element of Blank –" (F760), and many others she did not circulate face with extraordinary forthrightness an experience of suffering so extreme it leads to madness or coma. As she writes in "Inconceivably solemn!" (F414, 1862), the "Pomp," "Pageantry," and "Flags" of the military are "a brave sight–" but they also "Pierce – by the very Press / of Imagery –." While the war alone cannot explain what brought her to such intensity and brilliance during its years, it seems to me that the national crisis, the ongoing suspense of not knowing when or how the war would end and what this would mean for American democracy or daily life in Amherst, and the sorrow of reading repeated death tolls did affect Dickinson profoundly in ways that stimulated a quality and volume of writing she never repeated.

   In her war-time writing, Dickinson shows deep concern for all who lose, whether a battle, liberty, or their lives, and with the textures and tempo of the experience of pain. She could not have written with such fertile genius about the qualities and stages of suspense, pain, and grief without knowing some element of these experiences first-hand. On the other hand, this focus on individual, personal suffering was encouraged by the publication of countless poems expressing such suffering—many written by civilians like herself, taking on various dramatic postures. The outpouring of published poetry on war, death, and grief may have stimulated her own both because she shared in the general sorrow and because it permitted her exploration of these topics in more profound detail than might otherwise have seemed reasonable, even to herself. Cynthia Hogue proposes that Dickinson serves as a witness to war in that she provides a "testament" of its pain and trauma, although she witnesses through literature, periodical reports, and her imagination. Susan Howe writes that "All war is the same" (*My Emily Dickinson* 93). Similarly, at some level, all pain and grief are the same. Just as she both echoes popular verse styles and writes a lyric of extraordinary distinction and diversity, it is Dickinson's genius to write both within the narrative and rhetorical structures of her day in dealing with the Civil War's horrors and to construct narratives and metaphors for exploring the suffering of war so radically unconventional that they continue to take our breath away, a century and a half later. Yet even at the peak of her writing the poems most engaged with this communal discourse of war, Dickinson wrote primarily for herself, or for an audience relegated to a hypothetical future.

Coda: Portrait of a Non-Publishing Poet

A poem is not the end of something.
Elizabeth Willis

Poetry is never a personal possession.
Susan Howe

[Dickinson's] deadline was not publication but immortality.
Shira Wolosky

LIKE MANY others, I believe that during the early 1860s Dickinson entertained the idea of publication, albeit ambivalently—an ambivalence that seems to have reappeared briefly in the 1880s. Had T. W. Higginson responded to her work in 1862 with the same enthusiasm Helen Hunt Jackson did in the 1880s, the story of Dickinson's life might have developed differently. This chapter provides no new thesis for why Dickinson did not publish, but it maps the evidence and conclusions of the earlier chapters of this study in relation to this choice. Not publishing was a choice. As Alfred Habegger states, "Nothing would have been easier for Dickinson than to find a publishing outlet" given her friendships with Samuel Bowles, Josiah Holland, and Higginson and the *Springfield Republican*'s, the *Atlantic Monthly*'s, and Higginson's openness to publishing the work of women writers (389). This choice may not have been conscious at some stages of her life, but it was her own ambivalent or resistant outreach and responses to those who might have helped her publish that determined she would not do so.

A few salient facts modify our understanding of Dickinson as unpublished. First, she knew that the 530 (or more) poems she sent to others were no longer private documents as soon as they left her hands. While I have been stressing that this is a limited number of poems in relation to all she wrote and that after 1865 she circulates a different kind of poem from most of those she has saved previously, it is nonetheless significant that she did circulate more than a quarter of the poems we know she wrote. Susan Dickinson read poems to friends in her parlor; Higginson read and spoke about Dickinson's poems in at least one women's club meeting, in 1875. Melissa White traces the copy of a letter Dickinson sent her Norcross cousins, suggesting that the Norcrosses also shared documents Dickinson mailed them. White concludes that "a significant audience for Dickinson existed in her lifetime, a creation of second and third-hand sharing of Dickinson texts by those who knew her with those who were not acquainted with her directly" (13).[1] Moreover, in her early years of writing, when she seems to have needed encouragement to take her own work seriously, she circulated substantive poems to Sue, Sam Bowles, and Thomas Higginson.

Second, Dickinson also said or read poems aloud informally and spontaneously to a few family members—probably only to her young niece and cousins, since Austin and Vinnie report no such thing, nor does Sue or any other friend her own age.[2] Had Dickinson said or read poems to her immediate family with any frequency this would surely have entered into the stories circulated about the poet—as does her playing music for family and friends. Third, Dickinson knew that ten of her poems were published, most in periodicals where they would be read by many if not most of her acquaintances and all her family. Seven appeared in the *Springfield Republican,* which bragged about the quality of verse it printed and the fact that other papers picked up its poems; in fact, other local papers did reprint some of Dickinson's poems. She did not, nor do we, have any way of knowing how many periodicals across the country reprinted them.[3] What is more to the point, Dickinson knew the customs and the copyright rules of her day: she knew that by sending poems to friends she was putting them into at least one kind of circulation, and that by not protesting vehemently about the publication of the first poem that appeared in the *Republican* she was opening the door to the possibility of others being sent to its editors, printed, and therefore also possibly reprinted. There is no record anywhere of Dickinson protesting the fact of these publications.

Dickinson's infamous letter to Higginson concerns the tenth poem of hers to appear in print and is primarily concerned that he not regard her as dishonest in having claimed she did not publish and then finding a poem in the 14 February 1866 *Republican:* "Lest you meet my Snake and suppose I deceive it was robbed of me – defeated too of the third line by the punctuation. The third and fourth were one – I had told you I did not print . . . If I still entreat you to teach me, are you much displeased?" (L316). This letter sends mixed signals, "entreat[ing]" Higginson to give her the same attention as when he regarded her as completely unpublished yet sending him a clipping of the paper to make sure he does see her "Snake" in print ("A narrow Fellow in the Grass"; see Figure 7); and complaining about one change that alters the syntax and therefore meaning, but not mentioning that her poem had probably been assigned a title, stripped of non-standard capitalization, re-punctuated with commas and periods rather than dashes, and perhaps set into different stanzaic patterns.[4]

Somewhat earlier, about late 1865, Dickinson had copied the poem to retain (S6, F1096 B):

A narrow Fellow in the Grass
Occasionally rides –
You may have met Him – did you not
His notice sudden is –

The Grass divides as with a Comb –
A spotted shaft is seen –
And then it closes at your feet
And opens further on –

He likes a Boggy Acre
A Floor too cool for Corn
Yet when a Boy, and Barefoot –
I more than once at Noon
Have passed, I thought, a Whip lash
Unbraiding in the Sun
When stooping to secure it
It wrinkled, and was gone –

Several of Nature's People
I know, and they know me –
I feel for them a transport
Of cordiality –

But never met this Fellow
Attended, or alone
Without a tighter breathing
And Zero at the Bone –

The two differences in wording between these 1865 and 1866 versions ("sudden" for "instant" in line 2, and "But" for "Yet" in line 21) were probably Dickinson's; an 1872 copy sent to Sue alters the punctuation she used in Set 6 (for example, ending the poem with a period).[5] Moreover, Sue (or whoever submitted the poem to the *Republican*) might have provided the title rather than the paper's editors; the *Republican* very occasionally published poems with no title or a generic title, as did the *Atlantic*.[6] Whatever the source of the changes, it is likely that the copy Dickinson circulated to whatever friend passed it on to the newspaper was not identical to that which appeared in the paper, but she complained only of a single change in punctuation—again evidence that instabilities in textual presentation were not a primary concern. Dickinson also evidently did not mention to Higginson that she has had nine other poems in print by 1866.

In short, Dickinson knew that her work enjoyed some circulation in three forms, and she initiated that circulation in two of them—orally through her renditions to a few family members and in messages sent to friends, who she knew might further circulate them orally, in copies, or by sending her manuscripts to an editor. Her publication in periodicals occurred in the most ephemeral but also most widely circulated print form of her day. As previously mentioned, there is a good possibility that Dickinson herself either sent or allowed three poems to be sent to *Drum Beat,* a Union fundraising paper edited by a friend of the Dickinson family, in 1864.[7] Moreover, she either donated or considered donating one or more poems to the Mission Circle to "'aid unfortunate Children'" in 1880, "[c]hoosing [her] most rudimentary,

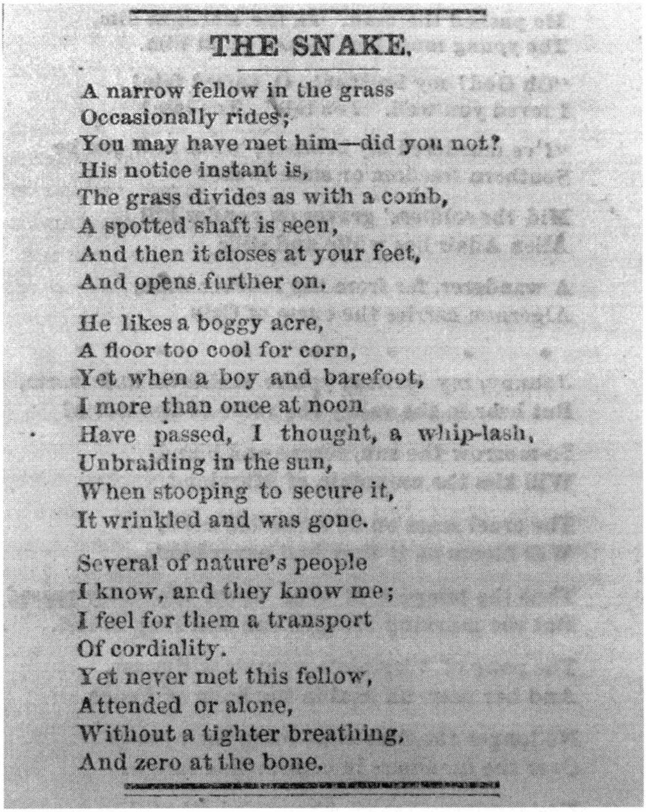

THE SNAKE.

A narrow fellow in the grass
Occasionally rides;
You may have met him—did you not?
His notice instant is,
The grass divides as with a comb,
A spotted shaft is seen,
And then it closes at your feet,
And opens further on.

He likes a boggy acre,
A floor too cool for corn,
Yet when a boy and barefoot,
I more than once at noon
Have passed, I thought, a whip-lash,
Unbraiding in the sun,
When stooping to secure it,
It wrinkled and was gone.

Several of nature's people
I know, and they know me;
I feel for them a transport
Of cordiality.
Yet never met this fellow,
Attended or alone,
Without a tighter breathing,
And zero at the bone.

Figure 7. "The Snake" (F1096, *Springfield Republican* 14 February 1866)

and without criterion" (L676)—a comment indicating that she judged the quality of her poems and was by that point not interested in publishing the more serious or complex during her lifetime—or at least not in the context of missionary aid.

The most significant new information from this study affecting speculation about Dickinson's choice not to publish has to do with her changed patterns of circulating and retaining poems after 1865. Such information, however, is subsidiary to the fact that Dickinson preserved over eleven hundred poems in forty bound fascicles and fifteen unbound sets—booklets that to our knowledge she shared with no friend or family member. The fascicle and set booklets mix many never-circulated poems with poems she did circulate through notes and letters, indicating that they functioned not as a record of unshared poems but of poems she wanted to preserve. This desire to record her poems changed after 1865, when she largely stopped making fair copies, preserving poems instead primarily on scraps of paper that include fragments and drafts. As noted in Chapter 1, she resumed the practice of making booklets sporadically between 1871 and 1875. After 1875, the percentage of poems she sent to friends without preserving a copy for herself increased to around 30.5, in contrast to her earlier general pattern of preserving all but a few of her poems.[8]

To my mind, Dickinson did not regard either her sending or her copying of poems as constituting publication in and of itself.[9] Had this been the case, it would have been logical for her to circulate more of her most serious poems, and not primarily poems of five or fewer lines. Both acts mattered to her, however, in helping to ensure that her poems might be read after her death and in confirming that she was not just a writer of poems but a poet. Keeping poems, in contrast, preserved them for potential later circulation and publication. Martha Dickinson Bianchi reports that Lavinia heard her sister "murmur in her later years, 'Oh, Vinnie, my work, my work!'" and her request to have her papers destroyed was understood by her sister—who would know best—to be no more than the standard request to destroy personal correspondence, an instruction she (unfortunately for us) followed. Like Lavinia, I believe that Dickinson wanted her poetry manuscripts to survive. The fact that she ceased to record her poems in fair copy with any consistency after 1875 suggests that by then she regarded publication of her work as a matter beyond her own energies or immediate ambition. Yet she continued to write extraordinary poems into the last years of her life and engaged in correspondence that would have confirmed her sense that her poems mattered.

As with most complex decisions, no doubt many factors entered into Dickinson's choice not to publish, and these factors would have weighed differently at different points in her life. The evidence of earlier chapters of this study indicates that Dickinson could not have felt that her work was formally so different from the poems of her time that it could not be published, or would predictably have undergone revision of a kind unacceptable to her— that is, beyond the kinds of changes she does not comment on (hence apparently does not object to) in the *Republican*'s publication of her "Snake" and other poems.[10] Many elements of her verse resemble those in poems widely available in antebellum periodicals, anthologies, and volumes of individual poets' work—the Spasmodics, the Azarians (as Henry James called them), and popular poets like Tennyson, the Brownings, and Longfellow. Dickinson also knew that all authors who published or circulated their work in any form submitted it to the possibility of unsupervised revision or editing as well as reprinting. This was a fact of her age.

Meredith McGill refers to the early nineteenth century as dominated by editors in that they determined what was printed and how. Patterns of editorial control and revision like those McGill describes would have been familiar to Dickinson from her textbooks and other aspects of cultural practice, and she participates in such conventions in her own revisional quotation or copying of others' work. Ebenezer Porter acknowledges in the preface to his *Rhetorical Reader* that he silently omits lines or stanzas from several poems (v)— for example, he prints only five of the seven stanzas of Halleck's "Marco Bozzaris," constructing a final "stanza" by linking a quatrain unit from the beginning of Halleck's stanza 6, and five lines from the beginning of stanza 7 with the final four lines of the poem. He also prints excerpts from both Milton and Shakespeare without identifying originating or longer texts. Porter explains such omissions by noting that "to attain *brevity* in each Exercise, the connexion of the writer has sometimes been broken by omissions longer or shorter, without notice" (v). In a popular rhetorical reader Dickinson would probably not have known, William H. McGuffey retitles a Felicia Hemans poem "He Never Smiled Again" as "Henry First after the Death of his Son" and lists it in the Table of Contents as "Henry *the* First *A*fter the Death of his Son," either another variation or a sign of editorial carelessness or indifference to capitalization and use of function words in titles (210, x; my emphasis).[11] Such attitudes perhaps make more sense when one recalls that spelling itself was not entirely standardized during this period.[12] As previously noted, hymns were frequently rewritten to be more concise, and poems were revised by composers when set to music so they would better fit the chosen tune. When Dickinson writes out a copy of John Pierpont's "I cannot make him dead" in a letter in 1856, she is similarly careless or interventionist; Johnson comments in a note that Dickinson's "version is closest to that in *The Sacred Rosary*" (L183), indicating that multiple versions were in circulation and Dickinson's was identical to none of them. Kathryn Wichelns notes Dickinson's (intentional?) misrepresentation of an episode of Henry James's *The Europe-ans* in a letter of 1879 (L619), and Gary Stonum points to her revision of Heathcliff's words in a letter quoting from *Wuthering Heights* (L866; Wichelns 81, Stonum, "Emily's Heathcliff" 25). Domhnall Mitchell demonstrates that even Sue, who knew Dickinson's work best, copied out her poems in ways dif-fering from Dickinson's: she altered punctuation and sometimes assigned a title or changed words.[13] Given such cultural fluidity, Dickinson may well have had no expectation that others would remember or circulate her poems exactly as she inscribed them on any occasion, and seems not to have found such precision important, as long as differing inscriptions did not affect basic syntax. As discussed in Chapter 4, the fact that Dickinson herself changed capitalization, lineation, and punctuation so frequently in writing out her poems suggests that for her the written text did not define the poem. Conse-quently, the possibility of editorial revision of these elements of her writing is not sufficient as an explanation for why Dickinson did not seek publication, much less why her interest decreased after 1865.

The deeply allusive texture of Dickinson's poems and letters, riddled with quotations from or nods to earlier and contemporary literature and events also works against assumptions that she imagined her poetry, or herself as poet, to be functioning beyond the bounds of the culture that enabled this extensive intertextuality. As with all great poets, Dickinson's work differed from that of her contemporaries as much as it resembled it. She was an excep-tional poet, shattering metaphysical, theological, and linguistic complacen-cies or givens, while also very much a poet of her time who wrote brilliantly in ways borrowing from popular forms, using well-known discourses, and sometimes voicing common sentiments. In fact, sometimes the same poems can be read both as formally similar to other poems of the period and as dis-rupting common assumptions or containing metaphors that make the reader "feel physically as if the top of [her] head were taken off" (L342a). Dickinson distinctly felt her marginality in the town of Amherst, but contemporaries of hers like Emerson, Thoreau, and Margaret Fuller also felt themselves to be at odds with the dominant culture and nonetheless published, just as many poets and philosophers in all ages feel acutely their marginality or difference. In other words, she may have felt her difference more powerfully than others would have had she published. Paradoxically, one of the powerful effects of her poems is to make readers feel less alone in their own grief, pain, or other extreme states of being.

Dickinson's repeated portrayal of the invisibility or relative unimportance of the poet similarly works against assumptions that she did not publish be-cause she saw herself as too radical or marginal a writer. Such poems suggest that the personality or genius of the poet matters less than the poem's effect:

"The Poets light but Lamps –/ Themselves – go out –" (F930). Feeling strongly the precariousness of mortality, Dickinson was concerned about the lasting quality of her verse, its fame rather than hers, and she ensured that the great majority of her poems could be read by later generations by inscribing them into booklets between 1858 and 1865 and, sporadically, between 1871 and 1875. Moreover, she wrote poems asserting community, the desire to "tell," and otherwise affirming the social function of poetry, whether as "Message" or "Experiment," even after intensifying her reclusiveness ("This is my letter to the World" [F519], "At Half past Three, a single Bird" [F1099]). In 1880, "The Robin is a Gabriel" (F1520 B) playfully describes its bird-poet as being "Of Transport's Working Classes –"; he entertains "Guests of Perspicacity" but also "covert[ly]" sends ballad-like "Ditties" to cajole and consternate his "Enemy"— presumably everyone who doesn't share his "New England . . . oblique integrity."[14] Similarly, an 1881 poem preserved on a fragment of wrapping paper and never circulated, "The Bird her punctual music brings," describes the "place" of this music as "in the Human Heart" (F1556); as so often, for Dickinson, bird song seems to stand in for poetry. In 1885, within a few days, Dickinson sends two correspondents two lines she did not herself preserve: "A Letter is a joy of Earth – / It is denied the Gods –" (F1672).[15] Many of her late poems are about love—both of those remaining, especially Susan, and in mourning for those now dead. "That Love is all there is / Is all we know of Love, / It is enough, the freight should be / Proportioned to the groove." she writes to Sue, keeping no copy for herself (F1747). Dickinson's messages foreground not the authority or brilliance of the poet but observations or puzzles about the world, thematizing communication or presented as though spoken. That her poems "tell" in her lifetime seems to have mattered less than the possibility of their eventual broader circulation.

Twice in her life, Dickinson reached out to a well-known editor or publisher in response to the possibility of publishing her poems. Both times she writes in so anomalous, coy, and elliptical a fashion that she virtually ensures nothing will come of her overture, leaving it unclear to what extent she deliberately sabotages her effort. The first instance is well known. On 15 April 1862, Dickinson wrote to Higginson to request his opinion of her poems, at a time when she and Sue evidently shared the idea that she might be published and barely a month after the 1 March publication of her first poem in the *Republican*. Had Dickinson in fact wanted to publish, however, she could not have initiated her correspondence with Higginson less persuasively. Higginson's mild suggestion in his second letter that she "delay" to publish was probably based less on his judgment of the quality of the verse she sent and more on the oddity of her highly metaphorical note, the initial inclusion of her name only inside a second envelope, and her outright lie in her second letter (ten days later) that she "had made no verse – but one or two – until this winter" in response to his question about her age. Moreover, her response, "I smile when you suggest that I delay 'to publish,' that being foreign to my thought as firmament to fin," seems definitive in indicating that she has no interest in publication. Higginson has apparently couched the suggestion that she "delay" in words of praise, since Dickinson reports "hav[ing] had few pleasures so deep as your opinion," feeling almost intoxicated with the joy of his "balm," and concluding with the 1858 Orientalist fantasy "As if I asked a common Alms," which describes a "Stranger" magically presenting the speaker with an entire "Kingdom" (F14). Higginson could not have imagined from this response that he had misunderstood her reason for approaching him or that he had disappointed her. The unevenly confiding, apologetic, and imperious manner of these letters would have suggested that their author was gifted but young, insecure, and without professional ambition. There must have been extreme cognitive dissonance for Higginson between the manner of these letters and the extraordinary power of poems Dickinson sent him in 1862, such as "Safe in their Alabaster Chambers –," "Before I got my eye put out –," and "A Bird, came down the Walk –." How might he instead have responded had she written an ordinary business letter informing him that she had written a few hundred poems over the last four years that she felt were worthy of being published and that she had attended Amherst Academy and Mount Holyoke Seminary? A less eccentric letter from her is likely to have made Higginson read her verse differently.

What little we know of Higginson's response, from Dickinson's echoing it in her prose, suggests that she was truly grateful for and encouraged by his words, acknowledged the accuracy of his description of her poems, and rejected suggestions for change in her style. When she writes "You think my gait 'spasmodic' – I am in danger – Sir – You think me 'uncontrolled' – I have no Tribunal" (L265) she could be indicating agreement, as though she were saying "Yes, spasmodic and uncontrolled, in danger of being like the Brownings, Alexander Smith, Tennyson; you are so right." His judgment must to some degree have pleased her, given her great admiration for the frequently condemned Spasmodics. Yet later she acknowledges that his words are also critical, asking if poems are "more orderly" and, whether or not ironically, using the word "improve" (L271). When in the same June 7 letter she writes Higginson that "I could not drop the Bells whose jingling cooled my Tramp" she seems to be apologizing for the extent of her meter and rhyme rather than for her departure from their conventions (L265). "Bells" and "jingling" suggest regularity, as indicated by Emerson's derogatory reference to Poe as the "jingle man." Higginson may have been urging Dickinson to try less metrically loaded forms, like blank verse—a suggestion she clearly rejected.

She was obviously content to follow the rhythmic tunes in her head as they moved from one "jingling" pattern to another, rather than attempting a more standard regularity.[16]

Marianne Moore's early history may provide an illuminating parallel to Dickinson's, although Moore resisted only book publication, not publication altogether, until she was thirty-seven. When Moore was twenty-eight, she told her mother that she had enough poetry for a book and her mother responded, perhaps in partial jest, by calling the work "ephemeral" and suggesting that her daughter publish only "after you've changed your style" (*Letters* 100). Moore did not publish a book of her own for another nine years, four years after H.D. and Bryher had published a volume of her poems—apparently with her collusion but without her formal permission—somewhat like Dickinson's friends, who sent the poems she had given them to newspapers. Neither poet changed her style. The less independent Dickinson (who also could not enjoy Moore's twentieth-century feminist and familial assumptions about the appropriateness of women's work and public status) may well have felt even Higginson's mild suggestion to "delay" as sufficient discouragement, although his praise may also have helped spur her greatest period of productivity. I know of no evidence that Higginson ever again discouraged publication, but he also apparently never said "publish these!"—perhaps mistaking the vehemence of her guise of indifference for sincere lack of interest. H.D. met Moore in college, although they became friends only a decade later, when they learned to know each other as poets. Helen Hunt Jackson knew Dickinson as a girl but only several decades later urged her to publish, in the mid-1870s. Had she and Dickinson re-encountered each other as writers early in Dickinson's writing life rather than near its conclusion, Jackson might have prevailed in encouraging Dickinson to publish, or she might at least have commanded clearer reasons than Higginson for why Dickinson chose not to do so.

In 1882 and 1883, Dickinson again flirted with the possibility of publication. At Jackson's insistent urging, and as Lyndall Gordon rehearses in useful detail, Thomas Niles wrote to Dickinson on 24 April 1882, wishing "that she could be induced to publish a volume of poems." Dickinson responded almost immediately by sending a coy note and a poem that itself strongly implied she was not interested in publication: she sent "How happy is the little Stone," about a stone that doesn't care "about Careers" and delights in its isolation (F1570 E). Discourteously, although not surprisingly, Niles apparently regarded this as an indication of Dickinson's lack of interest in publishing a volume and did not answer. In March 1883, Dickinson reinitiated the correspondence by enquiring about a forthcoming biography of George Eliot; Niles sent her a copy, and she in turn sent him two poems. He thanked her, she sent him a copy of the Brontes' *Poems,* and he returned it, asking a second time for a manuscript of her own poems, a request which she again parried by sending a few more poems. Their correspondence ends here. Gordon reads this exchange as Niles's "outright rejection" of Dickinson's "unwanted offering" of poems, and this might have been Dickinson's interpretation (210). It seems to me, however, that Dickinson twice effectively communicated to Niles that she would send him only isolated poems, not a volume—in response to what would have been a highly unusual repeated solicitation. (How many unpublished authors are invited to publish books by major firms—let alone twice by the same firm?) Perhaps she wanted an editorial courtship, to be wooed to publish—something she could hardly logically have expected. Perhaps she could not imagine herself organizing a "volume" as such for publication, which would presuppose that the fascicles were not organized as publication volumes but instead as a way to keep her records straight—Franklin's surmise. Or perhaps Dickinson could not overcome her own ambivalence about publishing. As Gordon notes, in 1884 Dickinson also refused to see Bleecker Van Wagenen, from Dodd, Mead and Company, when he called (211). By the time Jackson wrote Dickinson that "It is a cruel wrong to your 'day & generation' that you will not" publish, she seems to be set in firm opposition to the idea (L937, 1884). Yet, as Shira Wolosky sagely quips, Dickinson's "deadline was not publication but immortality" ("Public and Private" 130). With over eleven hundred poems copied into sets and booklets, she knew she had preserved a body of work that would last and from which she continued to draw in her correspondence, for example, sending Niles poems written in 1862 ("It sifts from Leaden Sieves –" F291 E), 1864 ("The Wind begun to rock the Grass," F796 E, and "Ample make this Bed –" F804 D), and 1865 ("Further in Summer than the Birds –" F895 E) as well as more recently written poems.[17]

By 1866, Dickinson seems to have been writing serious poetry primarily for herself, as perhaps she always did. Again, turning to Marianne Moore is useful: "It is for himself that the writer writes," Moore claims: "Combine with charmed words certain rhythms and the mind is helplessly haunted." In another essay she claims that one writes "because one has a burning desire to objectify what it is indispensable to one's happiness to express."[18] Dickinson was also "haunted" by the combination of "certain rhythms" and "charmed words" in ways apparently "indispensable to [her] happiness to express." Her impetus to write seems to have been the "burning desire" to articulate feeling, questions, or experience or to take on profound or risky meditations as enabled by meters and stanzas that allow formal without philosophical or logical conclusion. As I suggest in relation to the war, Dickinson may have found it deeply satisfying to experiment with ways to articulate life's profound questions and experience through familiar forms, working from the hymn and popular ballad-style poetry, and using popular idiom—without external confirmation. If she wrote with herself as her most demanding and significant audience and out of the pleasure of the challenge or process, then she was far more psychologically robust as a poet than would appear from portraits that understand her to have written out of ongoing anxieties or crisis. "Haunted," as Moore says, by what she herself calls the "old, odd tunes" that "madden me, with their grief and fun" (L184), Dickinson may have written as a way of engaging in the cultural, political, and philosophical issues of her times, but not with the idea of intervening in them or of speaking directly to her contemporaries.

Already by 1863, Dickinson circulates such a small percentage of her poems that not even Sue could have had an inkling of how many she had compiled, let alone the extraordinary force and emotional depth of the poems she did not share.[19] However significant her periodic inclusion of poems in notes to Sue, Higginson, the Hollands, Sam Bowles, the Norcrosses, and later Jackson, she seems to have been sustained in her writing far beyond what these isolated or cumulative inclusions, or responses to them, could bring.[20] As previously noted, many of her epistemologically, metaphysically, and emotionally most intense poems of the early 1860s were sent to no one and around half the poems she circulated were brief. Starting in around 1862, Dickinson also occasionally circulated only part of a poem. It is also significant that she saves almost none of her own juvenilia. While "On this wondrous sea" (F3) was written in 1853 and then copied into fascicle 1 in 1858, according to Franklin every other poem she recorded in 1858 was almost certainly written that year. Similarly, Dickinson's destruction of drafts through 1865 indicates that she is discarding work she does not want to survive, hence at some level and even if largely unconsciously thinking of posterity.[21] Her late correspondence with Niles about the possibility of publishing seems to have been a flirtation Dickinson found it hard to resist but could not imagine carrying through.[22]

It is striking how abruptly the patterns of Dickinson's writing change after 1865. To summarize: the number of poems she writes drops dramatically: she never again writes as many as fifty poems a year and in several years she writes as few as ten or eleven, after having written a total of 937 poems in the five years from 1861 through 1865. Where she previously retains fair copies of almost all her poems, she now sends an increasing number of poems without keeping a copy and keeps primarily draft-like copies, on fragments or scraps of paper. Similarly, Dickinson moves from writing poems of various lengths and with a wide variety of formal structures to writing an increasing percentage of one-stanza or otherwise very short poems, using fewer distinct (and fewer irregular) metrical and stanzaic structures and more regular

short and common meter. And she begins writing (or saving) more fragments of poems. In short, after 1865, she seems to have lost some of her impetus to write, to experiment with formal structures, and to preserve her work
in organized form.[23] For the remaining twenty-one years of her life, these are
her patterns of production.

practical inferences

It is likely that Dickinson's changing pace of writing and mode of preserving poems are affected by temporary loss of maid service, the end of the war
with its concomitant cultural changes, and the conclusion of her second
long stay in Cambridge for eye treatment—all in 1865. The extremity of these
changes was surely also a result of her perhaps more gradual decision not to
attempt to publish in her lifetime. It seems to me that only this decision makes
sense of the full range of these changes, and of the fact that she wrote fewer
poems and circulated more of them after 1865. Dickinson continued to feel the
imperatives of rhythmic thinking, to write poetry that matters, but not with
the same urgency and intensive innovation. Perhaps by 1865, no longer feeling
herself to be in a moment of "'White Heat'" (F401 C), she began to think about
using poetry differently, leading her to write poems that were at least formally
more accessible. Having preserved more than eleven hundred poems in booklets, perhaps she turned to writing a different kind of poetry to be shared with
a more immediate audience of friends. While Dickinson's idea of the lyric is in
no sense private, her manuscript books contain relatively few poems written in
a context of response to an individual friend, for immediate sharing.[24] Mapping changes in her topics, attitudes toward art, or other aspects of perspective
may illuminate the question of why Dickinson's practices change so distinctly at
this point—as would close attention to whether other aspects of her poetry and
letter writing also undergo changes around 1865. My interest in this study has
been less in explaining Dickinson's behavior or examining changes in her topics and more in identifying the distinct patterns of her writing practices.

Dickinson does write throughout her life about fame, but the topic recurs
more frequently in her late years, perhaps as she wondered more about the
possible reception of her poems by future generations of readers. In 1882, for
example, Dickinson circulated the previously mentioned poem "How happy
is the little stone" (F1570) to Niles, Jackson, Sue, and Higginson.[25] This poem
anthropomorphizes a pebble as not "car[ing] about careers – . . . independent
as the sun" and therefore "bask[ing] alone – / Fulfilling some express Decree /
In casual simplicity –." Here Dickinson may signal that she "Fulfill[s]" her
sense of calling without "career[]," or public commitment to long-term work.
At the very least, it demonstrates that she can imagine a life of apparent
"little"-ness and "simplicity" as "happy." In contrast, a poem composed on a
fragment of a dry goods advertising flier in 1883 asserts first that "To be forgot
by thee / Surpasses Memory" but then claims that the speaker has been

"Raised from oblivion / A single time / To be remembered what – / Worthy to be forgot / My low renown" (F1601), with four variants for the final description of "My . . . renown"—apparently the sticking point for her in thinking about the difference between public fame and private memory. Dickinson mails a one-line or prose version of the poem's final two lines to Jackson, clarifying the syntax but distancing the conclusion's modesty from herself by changing "My" to "their": "To be remembered what? / Worthy to be forgot, is their renown –" (L816). Unlike the "little stone," this speaker does care about "My" exaggeratedly "low [or one, or meek, or wan] renown." The poem, and her letter to Jackson, raise questions of what is, and who or what gives, renown.

In 1863, Dickinson contrasted the fruits of working for "Immortality" or "Time" (F536).

Some – Work for Immortality –
The Chiefer part, for Time –
He – Compensates – immediately –
The former – Checks – on Fame –

Slow Gold – but Everlasting –
The Bullion of Today –
Contrasted with the Currency
Of Immortality –

.

A Beggar – Here and There –
Is gifted to discern
Beyond the Broker's insight –
One's – Money – One's – the Mine –

This uncirculated poem implies that the unexplored "Mine" of immortal fame tops the "Money" of immediate praise—especially with its pun on "Mine," to signal that "Slow Gold" is the artist's or creative "Beggar" 's own, and that which Dickinson herself prefers. In 1863, she presciently and precisely distinguishes the advantage of writing in relation to her immediate world but not "for" any judge or gain from "Time"—or at least, her time.

Three late poems return to definitions of everlasting value but through the narrower contemplation of "fame" or "*public* report, . . . celebrity; renown" as her dictionary defined it (EDL; my emphasis). "Fame is the one that does not stay –" (F1507; 1879) asserts that its "occupant" must ascend "out of sight of estimate" or "die," that is, that fame can be trusted only when it is posthumous. "Fame is a fickle food / Upon a shifting plate" more cynically remarks that it cannot be trusted in any way: "Men eat of it and die" (F1702; undated). Similarly, the brief "Fame is a bee." (F1788; undated) attributes to fame a "song," "sting," and "wing"; it can always depart. As she writes in

1862, it were an "Honor honorless" to be praised by the world if she lacked "Fame of Myself," while "Fame of Myself, to justify," makes "All other Plaudit . . . Superfluous" (F481). This poem, sent to no one—like most of her poems on fame—, suggests that even when she most seriously tests the possibility of extended publication, she regards herself as her own most significant judge and audience. As early as 1862, she seems ambivalently content with the idea that later ages will determine whether her compositions constitute "Slow Gold."

The aspect of publication apparently most distasteful to Dickinson was its publicness, the idea of a "career."[26] Even anonymous publication required negotiation with a press. Moreover, this negotiation linked the author to market economies. Neither were appealing propositions for a well-to-do and ambitious lawyer's daughter, whose seriousness about writing coincided with her increasing reclusiveness. Fiercely determined to protest inequalities of power between God and humanity, or institutions and the individual, Dickinson was uncomfortable with her era's changing gender norms, "sneer[ing]" in one poem at those who imagine a woman's life as "'small'" but unsupportive of the movement for women's rights and uninterested in taking on for herself any public role beyond the domestic sphere ("A solemn thing – it was – I said –" F307). Dickinson eschewed a market-world of public recognition, trusting that a wider audience would come later, when it would no longer disturb her or her family's peace—not guessing the furor that control of her manuscripts would engender for two generations.[27]

Rejection of the market economy is the point of "Publication – is the Auction / Of the Mind of Man –" (F788, 1863), which begins with an oft-quoted unambivalent declaration that although "Poverty" might "be justifying / For so foul a thing" the speaker "would rather" remain unblemished by the economy of publication or the inkiness of print, that is, "White." The explanation for this preference in the final two stanzas, however, is less clear:

> Thought belong to Him who gave it –
> Then – to Him Who bear
> It's Corporeal illustration – sell
> The Royal Air –
>
> In the Parcel – Be the Merchant
> Of the Heavenly Grace –
> But reduce no Human Spirit
> To Disgrace of Price –

In 1863, Dickinson's metaphor of the "Auction," especially given her use of the leading word "White," may have suggested slave auctions: she abhors the "Disgrace" of a "Price" for the "Human Spirit." Because bodies constitute the

"Corporeal illustration" of our soul and "Thought," given to us by God ("Him"), any marketing of our body is in effect a marketing of ourselves, hence assigns price to a "Human Spirit." On the other hand, Dickinson sets up a contrast in which she uses an extraordinarily emphatic enjambment across line and stanza boundaries to suggest that it is acceptable to "sell / The Royal Air – // In the Parcel" or to "Be the Merchant / Of the Heavenly Grace –" "But" not to sell "Human Spirit." The terms of contrast are clear: royal or heavenly versus human "Air . . . Grace . . . Spirit"; it is fine to "sell" the former "But" not the latter. If humans illustrate divine thought through their bodies, perhaps the concept of private property or copyright explains how "Royal Air" might be identified in "Parcel[s]." "Heavenly Grace" may be manifest and therefore marketed through bibles, or through church membership, or missionary societies. In a strong reversal of the dictum to "render unto Caesar the things that are Caesar's" (Matthew 22:21), Dickinson stipulates that that which belongs directly to the divine, or is organized by the church, may be sold. Paradoxically, however, that which God gives us individually to "bear," or "Human Spirit," should be above "Price." This poem is Dickinson's only word about publication per se and therefore it is taken to be final. Yet it may protest too much. By the logic of this poem, there would be no books. Dickinson, however, describes the book as a "Chariot" that "bears the Human Soul" rather than auctioning it ("There is no Frigate like a Book," F1286 B). A book does not enchain; it is a "Bequest of Wings," bringing "Liberty" and making the "Spirit" grow "robust" ("He ate and drank the precious Words –" F1593). Books are "Kinsmen" (F512).

It seems then that Dickinson opposes not the fact of publication but what it would feel like for her to participate in that process: namely, it would feel as though she were exposing her "Spirit" to the public for financial gain. This poem implies that it is not because Dickinson imagined her poems to reveal too much about her personal life but because they revealed too much of her "Human Spirit," the deepest ways she thought about perception and being. Consequently, this is a poem more about how Dickinson thinks than it is about the nineteenth-century publication culture or industry. And if it is the depth of "Human Spirit" revealed in poetry that she feels should not be marketed by the poet him- or herself, this may also explain why she circulates so few of her most challenging poems, even to her most trusted friends, while circulating others that may be more revealing of personal crisis. On the surface of it, this would seem to be true of "Title divine – is mine!" (F194), which she sends to Bowles in 1861; by the time she sends this same seemingly intimate poem to Sue, four years later (in about 1865), the initiating (personal?) impulse would appear to be less important than its general commentary on gender politics and its power as a poem.[28] Or perhaps Dickinson did not

send her poems of most profound psychological and philosophical speculation to anyone because she felt they were too uncertain, too raw as proposi-
tional or expressive thought, even for sharing within the realm of controlled
circulation starting with friends and family. The poet who could write "Publication – is the Auction" would have found it difficult to respond affirmatively and professionally to Thomas Niles's repeated request for a volume
of her poems. On the other hand, as long as she is not the one doing the
exposing—as long as others submit her poems to newspapers, or publish her
poems after her death—she is not in the position of putting her "Spirit" on
the auction block of mercenary exchange.[29] She is just continuing to work
her "Mine," creating "Slow Gold."

Dickinson wrote one poem about publishing and a multitude of poems
about poetry or books as having a kind of power, as being a stimulus to look
or think beyond the known, as comparable to foreign travel and transformation, and as communication. Whatever her reluctance to participate in a market economy of print and exchange, she apparently trusted that at some point
her poetic elegies, speculations, arguments, definitions, queries, riddles, and
expressions of joy in living would find other ears. To return to poems earlier
discussed, she writes "We – tell a Hurt – to cool it –" (F548); "Tell all the truth
but tell it slant –" (F1263); and "as One *returned,* I feel, / Odd secrets of the line
to tell!" (F132 B)—perhaps in punning reference to the "line[s]" of poetry itself.
In "Talk with prudence to a Beggar" (F118) the speaker warns of the power of
"Anecdotes" to overwhelm those who cannot grasp what they long for. "Tell as
a Marksman – were forgotten," she muses, yet he "this Day endures" because of
the repeated "humble story" of his shooting an apple from his son's head—
where a "statelier Tale" of his opposition to tyranny "Scarcely would prevail –"
(F1148). In other poems, Dickinson commands others to "tell" her, asks objects
to communicate for her, or comments on the power of telling—asking "if I
should tell" ("A Murmur in the Trees – to note –" F433) or if "I dare to tell?"
("How the old Mountains" F327). In these poems, poetry participates in the
human exchange of telling.

The word "tell" is used 135 times in Dickinson's poems and "told" an additional 45, exceeded as a verb only by "be," "know," and "see." Among pronouns, "We" exceeds the use of his, he, you, one, him, or she, and "our" and
"us" both fall into her top twenty-five words. "Say" is used one hundred times.
While many of the poems in which these words are used suggest ambivalence
about speaking or propose that some things cannot be said, the accumulated
number of poems invoking telling or saying clearly indicate a writer concerned with the power and ability to communicate—as do the several speech-
based features of the poems and elements of direct or dramatic address. While
Whitman comically and endearingly proclaims "I will not tell everyone but I

will tell you" in a published poem, Dickinson creates a protean quality in her unpublished verse with much the same double-faced intimacy: it can seem to address a particular "you" (whether circulated to one person or several or not at all), or to express only private meditation, and to imply its own imperative "Go tell it" in encouraging the broadest possible audience.

Dickinson's most specific poem on this subject is "'Go tell it' – What a Message –" (F1584, 1882), a poem responding to Simonides' epigram instructing those who pass to "tell" of the Spartans' obedience in fighting to their deaths at the pass of Thermopylae. This was easily the most famous battle of Western history, used frequently to symbolize courage against overwhelming odds.

"Go tell it" – What a Message –
To whom – is specified –
Not murmur – not endearment –
But simply – we obeyed –
Obeyed – a Lure – a Longing?
Oh Nature – none of this –
To Law – said Sweet Thermopylae
I give my dying Kiss –[30]   ]I send –   Convey my dying Kiss –

Simonides' soldiers obey the "Law" of their commander without complaint, seeming even to love it in their strict obedience (giving it their "dying Kiss"). Dickinson's poem perhaps suggests that her nineteenth-century peers ("we") ought similarly not to complain about the strictures of their lives, those "Laws" that determine the degrees of individual sacrifice each must make. At the same time, it suggests that our human, and perhaps spiritual, imperative is to "tell," and it implies other messages closer to her own inclination than obedience to law: namely, murmurs, endearments, and the lures or longings of "Nature." Moving from its initial 7676 structure of broken phrases and fragmentary allusion to its concluding, fuller 7686 rhythm, and final full rhyme (this/Kiss), the poem articulates wonder that verges on incredulity. The last line's repeated long *i* sound (I, my, dying—echoing the previous Thermopyl*ae*), together with the image of the kiss, also emphasizes the personal quality of decision in this obedience. Together, these elements of the poem may punningly indicate that Dickinson would prefer to follow a different "Longing" and give her "dying Kiss" to "Law" in the person of Judge Otis P. Lord, with whom she was at the time exchanging passionate letters.[31]

Yet the poem emphasizes Simonides' message itself, a message passed on only in writing. In parsing the meaning of his message, Dickinson may be anticipating the state of her own poems after her death, preserved only in manuscript books—just as Simonides' epigram was preserved only *in situ* in stone. The preservation, in both cases, enables a message to be passed on. Moreover, Dickinson states that Simonides "specified" "To whom" his message should be told, perhaps suggesting that she hoped for an audience as broad as his fellow Spartans. Dickinson did address her "Sweet – countrymen –" in the 1863 "This is my letter to the World" (F519)—another poem sent to no one.[32] Like the "Message" of extraordinary courage and sacrifice at Thermopylae, Dickinson's poems do not need to be read at the time of their composition for their "Message[s]" to pertain. To borrow, again, from Ezra Pound, while she writes in response of various kinds to her own hour, hers is "news that stays news" (49).

"Good to hide, and hear 'em hunt!" (F945, 1865) also takes communication as its theme, concluding that although it is "Good to know, and not tell –" it is "Best, to know and tell, / Can one find the rare Ear / Not too dull –." Whatever Dickinson made of the abilities and attention of her epistolary readers, I believe that she was convinced that all her preserved poems would eventually be heard by "rare Ear[s]." Perhaps the release of writing and the "Dower" she received from reading her own "Bolts – of Melody!" assured her that her poems were "not the end of something" (as Elizabeth Willis puts it) but a kind of beginning, although she could not have known the extraordinary and worldwide conversations they would stimulate ("Lyric Dissent" 234). Or, as Susan Howe writes, perhaps she felt that "poetry is never a personal possession" (*The Birth-Mark* 147); it is hers to write, and to preserve, but will—if "Slow Gold"—ultimately belong to her readers, or to "Immortality," without requiring her own marketing efforts.

In a little parable she composes to scold Elizabeth Holland for not writing, Dickinson claims to have asked a bird "wherefore sing . . . since nobody *hears*?" She then imagines the bird responding: "One sob in the throat, one flutter of bosom – '*My* business is to *sing*' – and away she rose!" The letter concludes with "cherubim" who, "once, themselves, as patient, listened, and applauded her unnoticed hymn" (L269, "summer 1862?"). Here, using her favored metaphors of poet as songbird and poetry as song, Dickinson imagines the possibility of both a vocation of singing and an applauding audience unperceived by the singer—in addition to more immediately implying that someone must appreciate her letter writing even if Elizabeth doesn't. As I note in Chapter 1, Dickinson borrows the phrase "*My* business is to love" from a novel by Elizabeth's husband. Using this phrase earlier in her letter to Elizabeth indicates her affectionate attentiveness to Josiah's writing. Altering the words to "*My* business is to *sing*" makes the claim her own, just as Dickinson's multiple borrowings from the literature and periodicals of her day are claimed entirely as her own. As she says in a previously quoted letter of the same period to Higginson about a line of "Verse" she had unconsciously borrowed: "I do not let go it, because it is mine" (L271, August 1862). Dickinson eschews the "business" of publishing and the opportunities for broad circulation of her poetry among her "day & generation" (as Jackson puts it), and she dramatically changes her practices of writing and circulating poems during her lifetime. She never, however, abandons her vocation "to *sing*."

APPENDIX A

Poems on the Orient

1858

F14 As if I asked a common alms –	[I asked the Orient]
F16 The feet of people walking home	[Pearls are the Diver's farthings]
F35 Sleep is supposed to be	[East of Eternity]

1859

F98 South winds jostle them –	[passage Cashmere]
F104 A something in a summer's Day	[the East . . . Caravan]
F111 Artists wrestled here!	[a tint Cashmere]
F120 As Watchers hang upon the East –	[Deserts, Amethyst]
F121 Her breast is fit for pearls,	[I was not a "Diver"]

1860

F131 Tho' my destiny be Fustian –	[my little Gipsey being]
F136 Who never lost, are unprepared	[Tamarind]
F141 She died at play –	[as gaily as a Turk]
F145 A little East of Jordan,	
F162 Some Rainbow – coming from the Fair!	[turbaned seas]
F176 If I could bribe them by a Rose	[Amherst to Cashmere]

1861

F201 With thee, in the Desert –	[Tamarind, Leopard]
F206 Least Rivers – docile to some sea. / My Caspian – thee.	
F228 My eye is fuller than my vase –	[East India]
F248 *One life* of so much consequence!	[*Pearl*, dive]

1862

F276 Civilization – spurns – the Leopard!	[the Pard – that left her Asia]
F285 The Love a Life can show Below	[enamors in the East]
F312 I can wade Grief –	[Himmaleh]
F326 The lonesome for they know not What – / The Eastern Exiles	

F333 Many a phrase has the English language –   [Caspian Choirs]
F334 Of all the Sounds despatched abroad –   [Caravan of sound]
F349 He touched me, so I live to know   [Nor Persian]
F352 They leave us with the Infinite.   [Himmaleh]
F356 If you were coming in the Fall,   [Van Dieman's Land]
F388 It would never be Common – more – I said –   [drop – of India]
F410 How sick – to wait – in any place – but thine –   *[spicy isles]*
F417 Removed from Accident of Loss   [Pearls in Eastern Waters]
F418 Your Riches – taught me – Poverty.   [India – all Day]
F426 I gave Myself to Him –   [Fable – in the Isles of spice]
F451 The Malay – took the Pearl –
F460 The Himmaleh was known to stoop
F495 The Day undressed – Herself –   [Bosporus]

1863

F506 Light is sufficient to itself –   [Himmaleh]
F511 He found my Being – set it up –   [bade it to the East]
F513 The Spider holds a Silver Ball   [Yarn of Pearl]
F529 A Dying Tiger – moaned for Drink –
F549 The One that could repeat the Summer Day –   [Orient]
F572 The Day came slow – till Five o'clock –   [Rubies, the East]
F584 We dream – it is good we are dreaming –   [phrase in Egyptian]
F661 Some such Butterfly be seen   [Spice, Foreigners]
F666 I cross till I am weary   [Asiatic Rains]
F696 The Tint I cannot take – is best –   [Bazaar, Cleopatra's Company]
F705 I am ashamed – I hide –   [Cashmere, Pearl]
F716 Shells from the Coast mistaking –   [Pearl, Pearl]
F739 Joy to have merited the Pain –   [Orient's Apparition]
F748 God gave a Loaf to every Bird –   [An Indiaman]
F749 Where Thou art – that – is Home –   [Cashmere, Bands of Spice]
F770 Strong Draughts of Their Refreshing Minds   [The Camel's trait]

1864

F836 Color – Caste – Denomination –   [Circassian]
F846 A Drop fell on the Apple Tree –   [Pearls, Orient]
F849 By my Window have I for Scenery   [Sea, Spice]

1865

F942 Always Mine!   [Old, indeed, the East]
F988 Said Death to Passion   [All His East]
F1064 As the Starved Maelstrom laps the Navies   [Tiger]

F1090 This quiet Dust was Gentlemen and Ladies   [an Oriental Circuit]
F1102 Dew – is the Freshet in the Grass –   [Nature's Caravan]
F1118 Reportless Subjects, to the Quick   [Oriental]

1868

F1147 The Bird did prance – the Bee did play –   [Caspian]

1869

F1162 A Mine there is no Man would own   [Indies]

1872

F1262 Until the Desert knows   [Caspian Fact]

1878

F1462 Brother of Ophir
F1471 His Mind like Fabrics of the East –

1879

F1487 Belshazzar had a Letter
F1488 One of the ones that Midas touched   [splendor of a Burmah]
F1509 How destitute is he   [India]

1881

F1562 His oriental heresies
F1563 No Autumn's intercepting Chill   [Asiatic Rest]

Undated

F1777 To lose thee – sweeter than to gain   [Caspian]

APPENDIX B

Poems Mentioning Travel, Escape, or Foreign Places or People (1860)

Thirty of the fifty-four poems written in 1860 contain some mention of travel, escape, or foreign places or people, not including the tropes of time flying, death, or seasons turning.

F131: Tho' my destiny be Fustian –   [Gipsey being]
F132: Just lost, when I was saved!   [Sailor, foreign shores]
F133: Mute – thy coronation –   [my Vive le roi]
F134: Did the Harebell loose her girdle   [Earl]
F135: A little Bread – A crust – a crumb –   [*Sailor's* business]
F136: Who never lost, are unprepared   [Pizarro, Tamarind]
F140: Bring me the sunset in a cup –   [let me out . . . to fly away]
F141: She died at play –   [as gaily as a Turk]
F142: Cocoon above! Cocoon below!   [Defies imprisonment]
F143: Exultation is the going / Of an inland soul to sea
F144: I never hear the word "Escape
F145: A little East of Jordan,
F146: All overgrown by cunning moss   [Yorkshire hills]
F148: Will there really be a "morning"?   [famous countries, Pilgrim]
F149: Great Caesar! Condescend   [Cato's Daughter]
F152: 'Twas such a little – little boat
F157: I have a King, who does not speak –   [I trudge the day away]
F159: She went as quiet as the Dew   [le Verriere]
F161: The Daisy follows soft the Sun –   [Enamored of . . . the flight]
F162: Some Rainbow – coming from the Fair!   [turbaned seas]
F165: I have never seen 'Volcanoes' –   [Pompeii]
F169: Wait till the Majesty of Death   [Footman, Courtier, royal]
F172: At last – to be identified –   [What Leagues there were]
F173: Except to Heaven, she is nought.   [wide-wandering Bee]
F176: If I could bribe them by a Rose   [Cashmere]
F177: As if some little Arctic flower   [wandering down the Latitudes]
F178: To learn the Transport by the Pain –   [homesick, foreign shore]
F179: If the foolish, call them "*flowers*" –   [Moses, Canaan]
F180: In Ebon Box, when years have flown   [Plucked far away]
F183: I met a King this Afternoon!   [Marquis, Czar, Monarch, transported]

NOTES

1. Reading in Dickinson's Time

1. Others have written about particular kinds of changes in Dickinson's style—with greatest attention, Brita Lindberg-Seyersted but also David Porter and Ralph Franklin. All biographers note changes in topic and style to some extent; Habegger is particularly attentive to such shifts. Among other isolated observations, Martha Nell Smith and Ellen Louise Hart write about changes in Dickinson's letter-writing practices after 1858 (*Open Me Carefully*) and Marta Werner proposes that Dickinson changes her conception of the poem in her later years (*Open Folios*).

2. Domhnall Mitchell and Mary Loeffelholz (*From School to Salon* 131–32) both address this positioning of Dickinson's work as "both residual and emergent," as Mitchell puts it, in *Monarch of Perception* (249). Shira Wolosky calls attention to the gendered paradigms of public and private concerns that block from our sight the poet's full engagement with central elements of her culture, particularly pressures of the world's disorder and the lack of theological justification for the suffering of the Civil War ("Public and Private").

3. Susan Howe similarly writes that Dickinson's "talent was synthetic; she used other writers . . . wherever and whenever she could use them" (*My Emily Dickinson* 28).

4. As evidence of this interest, the *EDJ* published a special issue "Dickinson's Reading" (co-edited by Dan Manheim and Marianne Noble) in spring 2010, and the August 2010 Emily Dickinson International Society conference in Oxford, "'were I Britain born': Dickinson's Transatlantic Connections," included around 90 presentations on aspects of Dickinson's reading, primarily of early and mid-nineteenth-century British and European authors. See also Páraic Finnerty's *Emily Dickinson's Shakespeare*. Considerable work is also being done on her reading of writers in the United States.

5. These stories include Prescott (Spofford)'s "Knitting Sale-Socks" and "The Amber Gods" and Terry (Cooke)'s "Sally Parson's Duty" (*AM* February 1861, January 1860, and November 1857, respectively; see David Cody, "Azarian School" 36–37). Cody argues that Dickinson shared "images, style, and a cultural moment" with writers such as Spofford and Cooke, who were known for their flamboyant fiction and poetry, giving several examples of phrases she borrows from these and similarly "Azarian" writers. Jonathan Morse points out the borrowing from Holland's novel. In another example, Barton Levi Saint Armand notes that in 1862 Dickinson quoted from a eulogy for Frazar Stearns, which itself cited Revelation 7:14, in the poem "Of Tribulation – these are They," (F113). Similarly, she recycles the final lines of Ellery Channing's "A Poet's Hope" in her first two lines of "If my Bark sink / 'Tis to another Sea –" (F1250, 1872).

6. On women publishing in the *Atlantic* see Ellery Sedgwick and my "Pondering 'Liberty.'" According to Elizabeth Young, women generally dominated literary publishing during the Civil War both while the war was in progress and immediately afterward—although her examples are almost exclusively from fiction (5). In the *AM*, Dickinson would have read commentary primarily by men, fiction predominantly by women, and poetry by both women and men.

7. I read Dickinson family copies of the *AM* at the Houghton, from Volume 1 in November 1857 through the end of 1865; the issue for November 1858 is missing. While Dickinson might have read an article in a friend's copy, it is not very likely. Similarly, the fact that pages are cut means only that someone was interested in them, not that Dickinson herself read them.

8. On Dickinson's cut-outs, see Virginia Jackson (*Misery* 141, 229, 168–71); Martha Nell Smith, *Rowing in Eden* (119–21) and "The Poet as Cartoonist"; Socarides 76–77. Werner discusses the cutting of her own texts as a feature of Dickinson's late compositional process (*Open Folios* 31–32).

9. Dickinson also marks a March 1862 *AM* installment of Rebecca Harding Davis's "A Story of To-Day."

10. It is unclear who wrote on Bowles's card; the handwriting is neither his nor Sue's.

11. More than one person writes in these books, and in some cases it is not clear whether the marking is Dickinson's. For example, in *Aurora Leigh* and some other volumes, there is underlining and marking down both sides of some passages rather than Dickinson's usual light pencil lines and *x*s. At other points, the markings clearly differ from Dickinson's (they are squiggly or wavy, and they mark different kinds of passages). Sue (probably) writes verbal responses to texts in a few cases; for example, in Longfellow's 1852 *The Golden Legend*, it seems to be Sue who writes "I don't like this" (EDR 286, 120). Although claims that marks are Dickinson's must be speculative, until someone conducts a thorough investigation of styles of marking in all Dickinson library books, compared with styles of handwriting and Dickinson's known reading, we have only informed scholarly hunches to go on—and even such an investigation could only produce somewhat firmer evidence for supposing. I assume marks are Dickinson's if they correspond in style to marks we know to be hers (such as those in her 1847 edition of Emerson's *Poems*) and if the marked matter corresponds to interests she expresses repeatedly in letters and poems. I come to these conclusions from looking at most of the books containing verse published before 1865 in the Dickinson family library. Almost none of the books extant in the Houghton collection belonged to Dickinson herself; many books we know from letters that she owned have now disappeared.

12. Whenever possible, I quote from the version of poems Dickinson copies into a manuscript book or retains in fair copy, indicated by number and, often, by letter—choosing the first version when she copies a poem into more than one booklet. Where I give only a number, only one copy of the poem is extant or I quote from the copy Franklin labels A. When Dickinson does not retain a fair copy, I mention the source of the poem's text (letter, transcript, or draft).

13. Kristin Kreider points out that Dickinson addresses an envelope to "Samuel Bowles Springfield Massachusetts" via a cut-out from the *SR* (95).

14. In 1865, Dickinson writes 57 poems that are four lines or shorter. In 1870, she writes 15 quatrain or shorter poems out of a total of 28, more than half that year's output. In 1876, 1878, 1879, and 1881–1886, she writes over 30 percent poems with four lines or fewer. These percentages increase if one includes poems of 5 or fewer lines.

15. For example, while from 1860 to 1865 considerably fewer than half of her poems are written in 8686, including poems with lines that vary from this meter, in 1881 all thirteen of her poems in 8686 are fully realized iambic tetrameter/trimeter, and these constitute over half of the twenty-five poems Dickinson wrote that year. Oddly, Dickinson writes virtually no poems in tercets, or in the double-tercet rhythm of another familiar hymn form called Common Particular Meter (886886) between 1866 and 1877, but then returns to the occasional double-tercet during the final eight years of her life.

16. This percentage is higher if we subtract from the 1,789 poems Franklin collects the 141 poems she sent to others but did not herself retain. If we count only the poems Dickinson preserved, before 1866 she had written 66 percent of her poems, around 56 percent of them between 1861 and the end of 1865. These figures assume that Dickinson's undated poems were written after 1865, kept by her, and later lost by others.

17. Franklin asserts that Dickinson typically distinguished poetry from prose in her letters although occasionally when Dickinson sends only a few lines of poetry "they might join the rest as prose" (F page 32); Mitchell has corroborated this assertion by comparing circulated and retained copies of poems (*Measures*). Franklin also speculates that Dickinson wrote impromptu verse in some letters—as in "Would you like Summer? Taste of our's –" (F272)—a poem begun as prose but then written in verse lines and sent to Bowles. Dickinson kept no copy of this playful poem.

18. The record of Dickinson's preservation practices is more strikingly different before and after 1866 if one also distinguishes preservation in clean copy from that on scraps or fragments of paper—"clean copy" here referring to poems deliberately preserved in toto on a clean sheet of stationery, whether or not containing variants or later revisions. Of the 937 poems Dickinson wrote between 1861 and 1865, she saved all but nineteen (before 1861, she kept all but six). Of those 918 preserved, 98 percent are copied into a fascicle or set or written to retain on a full sheet of stationery, that is, they are obviously intentionally preserved. After 1865, the majority of poems are retained on scraps, fragments of paper, or in obviously drafted form. The percentage of poems Dickinson circulated but did not retain increases dramatically after 1875, when she is no longer making sets, from 77.4 percent retained to 69.5—that is, she is not saving an average of 30.5 percent of her poems during her final eleven years.

19. In her early years of keeping manuscript books, Dickinson circulates a greater percentage (although not necessarily a greater number) of poems—reaching almost 41 percent in 1860; she circulates 37.5 percent in 1861 and then the percentage of poems circulated drops significantly until 1866, when she circulates 80 percent of her ten poems. Dickinson circulates one poem written in 1871 twelve years later; all others written after 1865 are circulated within a year or two of their apparent composition. In contrast, Dickinson sends nine poems written before 1866 three or more years after the first extant record of the poem, and some are sent eighteen, nineteen, and twenty-one years

later. These are mostly poems that she sent to multiple recipients, although she also sent poems to more than one person shortly after they were written.

20. While others have argued that Dickinson's is generally a poetic of fragments, silences, hesitation, and visual space, most influentially Susan Howe in *The Birth-mark,* Werner has articulated this argument in specific relation to Dickinson's late years (*Open Folios* and "'A Woe Of Ecstasy'").

21. *Maid* 84–85. Murray is not always careful about generalization based on dates, especially in her fictional recreations representing Dickinson in the kitchen working with Maher. Murray represents the poet at high creative energy after 1869, "for portions of each day, baking and writing" in the kitchen (9). Maher also cannot be considered a primary influence on Dickinson's ear for rhythms and idiom; by 1869, Dickinson has already written two-thirds of her poems. For the now broadly held view that the urgency of the war spurred Dickinson's creativity through 1865, see Wolosky, *A Voice of War.*

22. Similarly, Gordon refers to "off-rhymes" as "unacceptable" in Dickinson's time, although several poets use a variety of slant rhymes in the 1840s and 1850s (54). Fidelia Cooke was the *SR* Literary Editor in 1860–1866. See Habegger 383–84, on Cooke's time at the paper, including his inference that Cooke knew that Dickinson wrote poetry and that she was a friend of Bowles.

23. I am indebted to an exchange with Vivian Pollak for my articulation of this idea (July 20, 2010).

24. Dickinson included poems in 647 letters or messages, following Franklin's reckoning. Those messages, however, contain 117 instances of poems sent to more than one correspondent. Dickinson, then, sent 530 of her poems in or as messages or letters. While she undoubtedly sent other poems in letters that have disappeared, the patterns of her mailing and of her correspondents' preserving her messages make it unlikely that she sent large numbers of additional poems, or more than a few additional serious poems. Most primary recipients of poems seem to have preserved her missives carefully; Higginson, Bowles, the Norcrosses, and Jackson seem to have preserved (or copied, or recorded) every letter received. Sue no doubt did not save every scrap that came from next door but she saved so many small notes and single pages that it is unlikely she would not have saved longer letters or poems. The rest of Dickinson's correspondents received mostly brief occasional poems that came with gifts, in condolence, or about the weather. She undoubtedly sent more poems of this kind than we know about, but having those additional records or figures would not alter our sense of her conception of poetry or its circulation.

25. Mitchell notes that "the majority of Dickinson's lyrics precede and outlive the circumstances of their occasional distribution in letters," demonstrating in a variety of ways that she writes out what she regards as poetry differently from the ways she writes out what she regards as prose (*Measures* 189).

26. As the editors state, Ellen Louise Hart and Martha Nell Smith were the first to make this claim about the genre of Dickinson's letters. In this volume, see also Hart's essay, where she states that "the letters are mixed genre texts" ("Alliteration" 214) and Smith's essay, where she calls manuscripts the "containers in which Dickinson placed

her letters to respective audiences," then stating that to ignore or overlook those containers by printing Dickinson's work "homogenize[s] her various writings so that all letters appear to be of the same ilk, as do all poems" ("A Hazard" 240, 241). A careful survey of the types of letters and letter-poems Dickinson writes, and the types of poems she includes in letters, remains to be undertaken, as Smith implies by her call to avoid homogenization.

27. Tyler Hoffman writes about written orality, or poets committed to writing a poetry that performs speech (*People's Poetry*). His theory leans on both speech-act theory and Judith Butler's theory of language as participating in the performance of identity. Whether read aloud by the poet, distributed privately, or formally published in any variety of editions and kinds of texts, the poem is a performance in each instantiation— although the performance is not necessarily of the poet's identity. Paula Bernat Bennett notes that Browning refers to himself as writing dramatic lyrics, not "dramatic monologue"—a term first used in the twentieth century ("From Browning").

28. The previous poem in Fas 27, "There's been a Death, in the Opposite House," (F547), begins similarly with marked ballad meter in stanza one and then regular 8686 iambic meter—in this case for the rest of the poem. Both "There's been a Death" and "The Black Berry" begin with lines that are ten syllables long and have four beats. The Fas poem following "The Black Berry" also begins with a ten-syllable line, but has definite iambic rhythm and five beats ("The One that could repeat the Summer Day –" F549 B). Of note is the highly unusual beginning ten-syllable line of three poems in a row, a characteristic of either Dickinson's composition or her copying patterns (see Chapter 3).

29. These lines may allude to Malcolm's in *Macbeth,* when he advises against silent suffering. Malcolm says, "Give sorrow words: the grief that does not speak / Whispers the o'er-fraught heart and bids it break" (4.3. 240–41).

30. See Richards, King, and Shoptaw ("Civil War Poetics"). Shoptaw argues that the poem is a "heartfelt" "tribute" to the brave black soldier and "should lay to rest any doubts about Dickinson's allegiance to the causes of abolition and racial equality" (8). In contrast, Richards reads the poem as developing a "meditation on insoluble differences" between support for African Americans and lack of sympathy for their human condition (171–73). Richards's is the most thorough reading of this poem to date, seeing the poem as highly problematic and Dickinson as not "comprehend[ing] the violent scenario she portrays" and unsuccessfully "seek[ing] to experience pity through her vicarious imaginings" (172, 174).

31. For *AM* articles praising the accomplishments or ability of people of color, see C. L. Brace, "The Fruits of Free Labor in the Smaller Islands of the British West Indies" (March 1862); E. H. Derby, "Resources of the South" (October 1862); Rebecca Harding Davis's story "Blind Tom" (November 1862); M. D. Conway, "Benjamin Banneker, the Negro Astronomer" (January 1863); D. A. Wasson, "The Law of Costs" (February 1863); Harriet Beecher Stowe, "Sojourner Truth, The Libyan Sibyl" (April 1863); and several poems promoting emancipation.

32. King points to Dickinson's reference to the "spicy perspective" of the "'Black Berry'" in an 1862 letter to Higginson and argues that this perspective is that of his Black troops, or generally of African Americans (L280); the quotation marks, however,

refer to Higginson's essay "The Procession of Flowers," to which Dickinson explicitly refers in her letter (King, 54).

33. See prizewinning historical analyses by Blight and Eric Foner (also Foner and Joshua Brown's *Forever Free*) on the increasing racism of the Reconstruction and post-Reconstruction eras. The latter's inclusion of several cartoons and illustrations published in popular periodicals following the war illustrates powerfully the kinds of images Dickinson might have seen in the press.

34. An equally possible allusion for a nineteenth-century reader might have been to berry women, who sold berries and herbs from door to door, as described by Lydia Louisa Anna Very in "The Berry Woman" (*Poems* 1856). Very's impoverished berry woman is also described as a Christian martyr. Dickinson's "The Black Berry" may shift focus from the well-known figure of a suffering woman to a masculine thorny berry as itself the sufferer—again insensitive if read as commentary on the poor rather than on the previously enslaved. I am grateful to Domhnall Mitchell for calling Very's poem to my attention. The berry woman was apparently a common figure in New England. Higginson also mentions such women in his biographical sketch of Lydia Maria Child (1868). Dickinson mentions that Lavinia is "trading blackberries" in 1866, L320.

35. For an extremely interesting analysis of minstrel culture and Dickinson's responses to it in several poems, including this one, see Sandra Runzo's chapter "Dickinson and Minstrelsy" in "Nineteenth-Century Popular Culture."

36. There was, however, a more generalized association of people of color (and women) with nature. Wallace Thurman's 1929 novel *The Blacker the Berry* ("the blacker the berry the sweeter the juice"—asserting pride within the African American community in dark skin) gave rise to multiple works playing on this theme, but I have found no evidence of this as a nineteenth-century idiom. Richards reads "As the Starved Maelstrom laps the Navies" (F1064) as using the phrase "Berry of Domingo" to compare African Americans to the poem's flesh-eating tiger "in order to dehumanize the black man" and as evidence of the poet's appropriation of experience she does not understand for solipsistic and aesthetic reasons (174). Richards points to intensely troubling attitudes in these poems, if one reads the allusions as predominantly marking racial distinction. I find there is a more logical, internally consistent way to read them. Nonetheless, Richards is correct in stating that the poems reveal that Dickinson does not have an urgent concern during the war with enslaved or formerly enslaved men and women.

37. Runzo, chap. 3. See also Eric Lott for the argument that blackface minstrelsy constitutes in part an expression of homage to black culture.

38. Dickinson writes "Blue Bird[s]" in L513 (1877) to Higginson, L807 (1883) to Clark, and in poems "We like March" (F1194, 1871), "After all Birds have been investigated and laid aside –" (F1383, 1875), and "A Pang is more conspicuous in Spring" (F1545, 1881). She also titled "Before you thought of Spring" (F1484) as "The Blue bird" when sending it to the Norcrosses, judging from Frances's transcription, and as "Blue Bird" on her own retained copy. Dickinson makes four drafts and two fair copies of "After all Birds" but in each the line "Nature imparts the little Blue Bird" remains the same; similarly, in "We like March" all six copies retain "Blue Birds."

39. Kenneth Price and Ed Folsom write about Dickinson's use of the place name "[San] Domingo" as a vortex word alluding to the slave revolt ("Dickinson, Slavery, and the San Domingo Moment"). Mitchell writes about nineteenth-century class implications associated with wine, beer, hock, and ale in relation to Dickinson's "I taste a liquor never brewed –" ("Ardent Spirits" 207).

40. Several critics read Dickinson's formal structures as coded—for example, David Porter in understanding Dickinson's use of hymn form as indicating rebellion and Annie Finch, who understands Dickinson's rejection of iambic pentameter as similarly rebellious (*The Ghost of Meter*). Paul Crumbley suggests that meter and rhyme indicate the extent to which a speaker's position is or is not conventional (*Winds of Will,* for example, 51, 54, 102).

41. St. Armand initiated such attention in linking Dickinson's material practice to what Emerson called the "portfolio" school of writing. See also Joanne Dobson, Karen Dandurand ("Dickinson and the Public"), and more recently Alexandra Socarides and Melissa White. In the nineteenth century, ministers, lecturers, and others wanting to preserve order among their pages frequently sewed them together.

2. Lyric Strains

1. Charles LaPorte makes the similar claim that academic scholarship has tended to treat nineteenth-century poetic theory in isolation from actual poetic practice (519). See also Yopie Prins ("Historical Poetics" 230, 233–34). Jackson's *Dickinson's Misery* makes this retroprojection one of its primary subjects.

2. Genette argues that lyric is not part of Plato's or Aristotle's taxonomies because they were interested in imitation or narrative and the lyric imitates nothing. Instead, Genette argues, definitions of the lyric depend foundationally upon "modern poetics (which actually, as we will often see, really means *romantic* poetics)" (2).

3. See the brief definition in Christopher Beach (49). Jonathan Arac points out that the notion that "lyric expresses pure subjectivity is very recent historically" (353). In *Radiant Lyre,* the editors David Maker and Ann Townsend claim that the "most abiding subject of all lyric poetry" is time (xv); Maker later defines the lyric in ways typical of post-romantic criticism: as speaking "for the first person, in the present tense—a present toward which lyric always impels any past or future events" and concerned with "radical interiority" (197). Genette defines the lyric according to "modern" criteria as a text that "exposes or expresses" a thought or feeling (30, 31), also citing several romantic thinkers indicating, as he paraphrases, "lyric = subjective" (39).

4. Judy Jo Small notes that "varieties of the lyric too diverse to categorize" were common in Dickinson's era (47). Mary Loeffelholz sees the popularity of Dickinson's poetry in the 1890s as demonstrating that it "assumed a cultural place already prepared to receive it," especially because critics associated "violations of generic decorum with the projects of American literary nationalism" ("Really Indigenous Productions" 184). I return to this idea in Chapter 4. Significantly, Marietta Messmer points out that early female reviewers of Dickinson's work were markedly more enthusiastic than male reviewers ("Critical Reception" 302).

5. See Gary Stonum for an excellent description of the Spasmodics and Dickinson's effective declaration of allegiance to this poetry of sensation and intensity through references to contemporary poets (*Dickinson Sublime* 33–39). Poetry of sensation "might be understood to stimulate response without dictating it"; it stressed provocative imagery, intense or exotic mental states, and an immediacy of impact (39, 37). Much Spasmodic poetry was verse drama, in which the protagonist was a poet. In 1858, Gerald Massey described "spasmodists" poetry as characterized by "sudden transitions" and the "power to startle and surprise"—with particular reference to Robert and Elizabeth Barrett Browning and to Philip James Bailey's "Festus: A Poem." Austin owned a copy of Bailey's "Festus" (1839; 1848 edition). See also Jason R. Rudy, "Spasmodic Poetry."

6. As Cody notes, in several poems Dickinson "celebrated the lush, almost delirious romanticism, propensity for Gothic excess, and quirky, nervous intensity that permeates tales" such as Spofford's and Rose Terry Cooke's, or in poetry like Tennyson's— idolized by Spofford ("Azarian School" 32, 53n.2). Dickinson had strong connections with this type of writing through Higginson's mentoring of Spofford and Cooke (Cody 36), and both women published frequently in the *Atlantic*. Saint Armand comments that "It was [Dickinson's] genius to condense, crystallize, to distill and domesticate [Spofford's] exuberance through the folk form of her verse" (186).

7. After reading what was probably "The Amber Gods," Dickinson asked Sue to "Send me everything she writes"; "it is the only thing I ever read in my life that I didn't think I could have imagined myself!"(Sewall, *Life* 673). Spofford's orientalism may also have influenced Dickinson.

8. Quoted in Cody 56. As he comments, because Dickinson was not publishing, she had no incentive to change her style as public taste moved toward the more realistic ("Azarian School" 78n.5). On the other hand, no one has explored whether her poems become less taken up with gorgeousness, or move closer to realist descriptive techniques, after the mid 1860s. Buckingham also provides evidence of the century's changing norms in "Poetry Readers and Reading," where he writes that "reading expectations for fiction and especially for poetry moved toward increased intimacy, mystery, and sacred personalism" (175) and that the era of the 1890s "sacramentalize[s] poetry reading" thereby situating "the reading experience at the farthest remove from rational explanation. This extreme subjectivizing of imaginative experience claims for poetry reading a world apart from Darwin and Spencer" (173)—quite the opposite of attitudes in Dickinson's day, as demonstrated by the numerous didactic, political, and philosophical poems published in the ante-bellum period and during the war.

9. The relationship of Dickinson's 1890s reviews to aesthetic standards of that era, in contrast to those of the early 1860s, remains largely unstudied.

10. *The Poetic Gift, or, Alphabet in Rhyme* (1844, EDR 439). In this little book Dickinson put large parentheses around "P is for Posies"; she also wrote an arch of names around the illustration and verse "V for the Virtuous Maidens here / Partaking of this Meal": "Miss Wood, Warner, Dickinson, and Hitchcock."

11. Dickinson to Abiah Root, L23, 1848. *The Princess* was published in 1847, shortly before Dickinson wrote this letter. The Dickinson family library contained several volumes of Tennyson. Dickinson mentions Longfellow's "Kavanagh" in two letters (3, 68)

and Longfellow himself in three (56, 619, and 768), in addition to her recommendation of *Evangeline*. These references stem from 1848 to 1882.

12. The volume of Smith's verse was owned by Austin (EDR 205); the Barrett Browning poems are in volumes 1 and 2 of her *Poems,* respectively (EDR 144, owned by Sue). Lowell's *Fable* (also owned by Austin) is marked almost as heavily as *Aurora Leigh* (EDR 293).

13. Eleanor Heginbotham makes the strongest argument I know for understanding the fascicles as deliberately arranged, analyzing poems Dickinson includes in more than one fascicle as evidence that she thereby experiments with constructing alternative contexts. There is very little repetition, however, and no evidence of revision of a fascicle as such.

14. Mill writes that while "eloquence is *heard,* poetry is *over*heard" ("What is Poetry?" 71). Jonathan Culler "take[s] as a point of departure" that "lyric is fundamentally discourse overheard," yet also notes that genre is in part a matter of the expectations we bring to a form (*The Pursuit of Signs* xv, *Structuralist Poetics* 189). In "Why Lyric?" he proposed that the poems we call lyric are still defined by Romantic or Victorian models of subjectivity, address, optative function, and intensified language affect. Jackson similarly argues that we read through theories of the lyric, thereby presupposing characteristics of verse presented to us as lyric (*Misery*).

15. Jackson argues that to regard Dickinson as a lyric poet is to disregard the historical circumstances of the distribution and address of her writing. This claim depends upon a retroprojected definition of the lyric as manifesting "private performances in public, 'sudden flashes' of present-tense immediacy, and utterances addressed to future interpreters" and attention to Dickinson's poems as directly addressed to the immediate interlocutors to whom she sent them (with objects or gifts, or cut-outs)—not noting that most of Dickinson's poems are not circulated (*Misery* 60). In "Bryant, or American Romanticism," Jackson similarly claims that Bryant's use of the Spenserian stanza is not "lyric" (194).

16. Other evidence that lyric continues to be defined in relation to subjectivity, and the poetry of earlier periods, occurs in Hošek and Parker's *Lyric Poetry,* where most essays focus on early modern or nineteenth-century poets; similarly, in a 2005 *PMLA* forum on the lyric, the participants cite only examples from between 1830 and 1930, as Marjorie Perloff points out ("Sound of Poetry" 752). Stephen Burt states that "Lyric poetry . . . consists in short pieces of language (spoken, or sung, or written, or all three) in which the psyche finds the language and the sounds to fit its own internal states; . . . . without any idea of a person whose interior states find language, we do not have a lyric poem" (x–xi).

17. Margaret Homans and Anne Mellor provided strong early arguments about the significance of gender in reading lyric poetry; both assume the poet's subjectivity is key to lyric.

18. "The Poetess Tradition"; see 29, 33, 40, 42 for "flowery"; 9, 14, 16 on "sentimental"; and 27 on imitable form. 5 April 2010.

19. Dickie's argument prefigures Jackson's in formulating a new model for reading the lyric that recognizes how distinct "properties of the lyric" shape social perceptions

of poems; because she defines the lyric differently from Jackson, however, she comes to different conclusions about such reading. Dickie finds that the lyric's brevity and repetition "obstruct readings that are determined by a socially limited understanding of the self or the subject, by view of character as expressed in a cause and effect logic, by an insistence that the poet can be understood by certain representative attitudes" (537). Repetition in the lyric also obstructs "narrative explanation," hence leads not to coherence but to an excess of detail and indeterminateness. In 2008, borrowing from Julia Kristeva, Tyrone Williams repeats the idea that the lyric's "stereotypical history, its historical link to a form of thinking or thought outside the binaries of traditional logic and reason" link it "to the feminine and, more pejoratively, the effete" (2).

20. While my own sense of this discourse is in accord with Bennett's and Wolosky's, the word "poetess" is occasionally used in contexts Dickinson would have known—for example, by Josiah Holland in "Women in Literature" (SR 1858), referring to Elizabeth Barrett Browning as "the greatest poetess of our century"; this article makes several broad generalizations about gender, identifying women's writing with the "ephemeral," experiential, and fanciful (in Loeffelholz, "Mapping the Cultural Field" 157n.8; 141). In contrast, the word "poetess" is rarely used in the AM, for example not once in the year of 1862 and only twice in 1860—once in a piece of fiction and once in a review of Poems by "Miss Murdoch."

21. This felt need continues in the second half of the century, when Francis Gummere strives to masculinize the ballad tradition for American readers and in relation to U.S. history and cultural pressures (see Chapter 4). As Lawrence Buell points out, women were more inclined than men to define themselves as "writers" before the Civil War but they also sustained the practice of literary amateurism because of cultural prescriptions against female professionalism (31, 39). Charles Bernstein may reflect ironically on these anxieties in the title of his collection Girly Man (University of Chicago Press, 2006).

22. Holmes, "Poetry: A Metrical Essay"; this volume belonged to Susan (Poems EDR 77). In this poem, Holmes also moves from a lament that the United States has no heroic national anthem to another theme with the words: "since the lyric dress / Relieves the statelier with its sprightliness / Hear an old song" (21). Here "lyric" seems to include every kind of verse that is not essay-like. The table of contents lists the "Metrical Essay," then "Lyrics," then "Poems added since the first edition." Dickinson may have turned down the corner of the page beginning "The Poet's Lot" (122–23). Another poem in this volume is heavily marked ("To the Portrait of 'A Lady.' In the Athenaeum Gallery," 136–37), but these markings do not appear to be Dickinson's.

23. Dickinson implies that language is "alive" in poetry in her first letter to Higginson (L260) and in "A word is dead" (F278), which claims that words "just begin[] to live" when spoken.

24. This is Juliana Spahr's logic in an online essay, where she notes that "language writing's self-aware roots in modernism and . . . 'inquiry,' rather than confessionalism, felt to me to be a way out of the sad poetess model" ("After Language Poetry" n.p.).

25. Many Dickinson poems use a first-person speaker, usually first-person singular, but that "I" is sometimes explicitly male and at others claims identities not belonging to

the poet, for example, "wife." Those that use no personal pronoun imply a speaker through their distinctive language and perspective; the numerous definition poems are prime examples (see Deppman; Sharon Cameron, *Lyric Time,* and my *Poet's Grammar* 84–87, 90–92, 96–97, 99–101).

26. Agamben 109, 110, 41. Agamben defines the "poem" as "that discourse in which it is possible to oppose a metrical limit . . . to a syntactical limit"—that is, where enjamb-ment may occur (34). His claim that enjambment belongs only to written verse or the "emancipation of the poetic text . . . from all oral performance," however, is unpersua-sive (32). Brilliant metrical poets like Dickinson (or Marianne Moore) play distinctly heard metrical phrases against syntactic units through radical enjambment, across not just lines but stanza breaks and strong rhyming units; in other words, one can also distinctly hear some enjambment. See my "Dickinson's Structured Rhythms" and "'By-Play.'"

27. Such poems, Deppman continues, wrestle with Kantian aesthetic ideals in trying to formulate a complete image or understanding of an idea or experience. They are thought experiments. While he defines poems generally as making it possible "in their presence . . . to reach the key conversational point of being ready to rethink what we know" (25), he sees Dickinson as extraordinary in bringing all aspects of a poem to bear on that project of deliberate difficult thinking.

28. Deppman finds that Isaac Watts's *On the Improvement of the Mind* (a textbook at Amherst Academy and required preliminary text for admission to Mount Holyoke) en-couraged skeptical, open, empirical thinking and tough mental exercises. Watts even cites poetry as an "important source of mental expansion" and elasticization (54–55). Brian Short similarly argues that Dickinson's textbooks at the Amherst Academy and Mount Holyoke encouraged independent and creative thinking. More recently, Scheu-rer argues that Amherst Academy was particularly "modern" in its approach to educa-tion and encouraged participatory learning and original thinking, relative to earlier nineteenth-century standards ("[S]o of course there was Speaking"). Crumbley echoes these conclusions in *Winds of Will,* noting that Parker's *Aids* most strongly encourages innovative writing, among Dickinson's textbooks (76–78).

29. The Amherst Academy used this text during Dickinson's last two and a half years there. According to Frederick Tuckerman and Richard Sewall, Dickinson at-tended from 1840 to 1847, with some terms away for illness and a return to the Academy in fall 1848 (*The Life* 337; Tuckerman 100, 109). Academy catalogues list Dickinson as enrolled in 1841 in the Classical Course and in 1847 in the English Course; she is not listed in 1848, and the Frost Library Special Collections is missing catalogues for 1844–1846. Every catalogue states: "There is connected with the Academy, a Literary Society, which meets weekly in the Academy building, and a valuable Library to which all the students have access" (11–12). Dickinson also recited regularly as part of her lessons: "The whole school are required to attend a Rhetorical Exercise in the Academy Hall, every Wednesday afternoon." Dickinson writes to Annie P. Strong that "I know that I shall lose my character if I don't recite as precisely as the laws of the Medes and Per-sians" in "our examination," suggesting that she was well known for excellence and took pride in recitation (L7, 4 August 1845); Tuckerman 110.

30. A similar hierarchical categorization of verse types occurs in *The Household Book of Poetry*. Dana writes in the preface that "The purpose of this book is to comprise within the bounds of a single volume whatever is truly beautiful and admirable among the minor poems of the English language"; he continues, however, by calling the poems he has collected "immortal productions of genius" and "those on which the unanimous verdict of the intelligent has set the seal of indisputable greatness" (n.p.). The volume contains verse by Shakespeare, Milton, Pope and several now canonical as well as now obscure nineteenth-century British and American poets. "Minor" corresponds to relatively short and non-dramatic, non-narrative verse. Dana stresses that "Especial care has also been taken to give every poem entire and unmutilated, as well as in the most authentic form which could be procured" (n.p.). The Dickinson copy is inscribed "Austin and Sue from Samuel Bowles." Pencil markings and folded pages suggest Dickinson's familiarity with the anthology (EDR 445).

31. Pond/Murray defines melody as a pleasing effect produced on the ear and harmony as a pleasing effect produced by an action of the mind in perceiving proportion between parts of the verse.

32. The uses are 1) in reference to opera; 2) in reference to ancient Greek literature; 3) Holmes's "lyric conception" of a "poet" (March 1858); 4) "Songs of the Sea" describes American fishing ballads and songs as "lyric blessings," suggesting that they give rise to a national poetry (July 1858); 5–11) occur in Halpine's two-part series on English poet Laureates, where from 1693 to 1813 is categorized as the "Lyric" (not "Dramatic" or "Voluntary") period of laureates, and the job of the laureate from 1693 on is said to be to write "formal lyrics" (August-September 1858). Halpine also describes poets as writing a "graceful lyric," "the finest lyric passages in dramatic literature," and as performing at "lyric feasts" in taverns. He mocks Shadwell as writing a "peaceful lyric," and calls Wordsworth incapable of writing a "popular lyric in celebration of notable events" (270, 463). In later *AM* essays, (12–14) the lark is called "a 'feathered lyric'" (August, 1858; 286), a few lines of song are described as the "most melodious and sauciest bits of lyric coquetry to be found" (September 1858; 437), and two questionable lovers appear to their neighbors to be a "lyric match" (October, 1858; 570).

33. Dickinson was given a copy of Emerson's *Poems* (1847) by Benjamin Newton in August 1849 (EDR 21). Several poems in this volume are marked. Deppman links Dickinson's "attraction to Emerson and transcendentalism" with "her commitment to a new poetics, various emphases on the mind as an active, dangerous, and powerful experimental agent, and her idiosyncratic departure from religious orthodoxy" (105; see also 79, 85).

34. In an essay Dickinson cut phrases from, Prescott (Spofford) judges Elizabeth Sheppard as not a "great poet" because "whenever she attempted [verse] its music made her thought shapeless" (767).

35. Poe does refer to the *Iliad* as "a series of lyrics" with "epic intention" (*Selected Writings* 465). As examples of excellent "poetry," he then quotes stanzas or whole poems by Longfellow, Bryant, Tennyson, Byron, Thomas Moore, Thomas Hood, and several other poets, including "Tears, Idle Tears"—a popular anthology piece—from Tennyson's *The Princess*.

36. "Longfellow's Ballads" (*Works* 3:363–74; 366). Poe continues to say that "music . . . is of so vast a moment in Poesy, as *never* to be neglected by him who is truly poetical" (367) and that the idea "that the chief merit of a picture is its *truth,* is an assertion deplorably erroneous" (373).

37. From "Emerson's Meeting with DeQuincey," *Blackwood's Magazine,* April 1894: 480–91; 482.

38. Dickinson uses the word "truth" 25 times in her poetry and "true," "truer" and "truest" an additional 37 times; she uses the word "beauty" 17 times, and "beautiful" and "beauty's" a total of 14. In terms of sheer volume of use, truth would seem to be the more important concept.

39. This is the version Dickinson preserved; Franklin prints the copy she sent to Higginson later in the year in his Reader's Edition.

40. The markings appear to be Dickinson's; this volume of Bryant's *Poems* was given to Sue for Christmas in 1851 by Mary Bernard (EDR 246). See Friedlander's analysis of the quandaries Dickinson's poem raises in "Devious Truths."

41. Porter's *Reader* states outright its intent to "advance[e] the interests of Christian education" (v) and several excerpts in the instructional section come from Milton's *Paradise Lost.* In contrast, the examples section includes 30 (mostly complete) poems.

42. C. D. Wright has written recently on "The New American Ode," noting the ode's traditional hortatory nature, its kinship to hymn and prayer, and its tendency "to give continuous rise to unique and exceptional nonce forms" (289, 294, 287).

43. The general high regard for this poem is suggested by Bryant's reference to it as "the impassioned lyric" whose author will soon join the ranks of other "cherished" poets like Goethe ("Goethe," *Prose Writings* 342).

44. Christopher Warley claims that nineteenth-century British sonnet writers distinguish between convention (social custom) and the individual, leading to the devaluing of "uninspired, rote" writing and praise for "original" writing (20).

45. James Russell Lowell, "The Origin of Didactic Poetry"; Holmes, "The Autocrat of the Breakfast Table" (*AM* November 1857, 110–12; 54); Holmes's "Metrical Essay" also mocks poets who use facile rhymes and poeticisms.

46. What the *Atlantic* regards as "truly . . . original" was not necessarily what twenty-first-century readers might imagine, as Loeffelholz points out in "Really Indigenous Productions" (183). Loeffelholz quotes from reviews published in February and May of 1859 that describe Holland's enormously popular narrative poem *Bitter-Sweet* as disrupting expectations for verse and strikingly "original." Holland's poem combines blank verse with short-lined lyrics, using sections of varying trimeter and tetrameter lines in ways consonant with other writers of the time.

47. *Aurora Leigh* (1856), 171; Sue owned the first U.S. edition (1857, EDR 197). It is probably Dickinson who marks a long passage in this volume urging poets to "represent . . . / Their age, not Charlemagne's," immediately preceding but not including these lines (170–71). She would also have been familiar with Barrett Browning's occasional use of ballad form in "A Drama of Exile" (*Poems,* 1852).

48. For example, Watts uses several slant rhymes (*Psalms carefully suited to the Christian Worship*), as does Emerson in "Threnody" (*power* with *mourn; restore* with *return*)

and Whittier in "To Englishmen" (*us* with *Slaveholders; human* with *common*)—all texts the family owned.

49. Eleven out of forty poems have lines shorter than the pentameter, not counting the ten selections from the Bible. Curiously, one Bible selection is listed under "Poetry" in the table of contents but written out as prose. McGuffy's front pages mention that 43,000 copies of this reader had been sold by 1841, the nineteenth edition.

50. Other Dickinson poems alternating lines of 10 or more syllables with short lines include "Unto like Story – Trouble has enticed me –" (F300, with an 11/4 pattern in stanzas of 8 lines), "It knew no lapse, nor Diminution –" (F568 B, with an 11/2 pattern in its second quatrain), and "Undue Significance a starving man attaches / To Food –" (F626), which contains lines of 13-2-9-4 syllables in its first stanza. Some of Proctor's poems are marked with pencil lines (EDR 405).

51. This volume in the Dickinson library contains some folded pages but no pencil markings (EDR 288).

52. In this poem everything is irregular except the quatrains. Stanzas forms include 8686, 6688, 1010(11)6, and 7887 (roughly 3- and 4-beat lines); rhymes vary from abab to aabb to abcb.

53. For example, the first stanza of "Adeline" rhymes abbcddacbb and the second rhymes ababcdefefaa.

54. EDR 14, owned by Sue. Dickinson echoes lines of Barrett Browning's "Isobel's Child" in later poems—for example, stanza xxxi begins "Can your poet make an Eden / No winter will undo?" (105); in "I reckon – When I count at all –" (F533), the poet's "Summer – lasts a solid Year." Similarly, stanza ix begins "A solemn thing it is to me" (102), echoed in Dickinson's "A solemn thing – it was – I said –" (F307) and perhaps "A Solemn thing within the Soul" (F467). Stanza ix is marked with a light x.

55. This Saturday paper prints a second poem with irregular stanza lengths, "To an old Playmate" by Barry Cornwall; two days earlier, "Some Lines on the Wet Weather" by T. Potts, esq. uses irregular stanza length and rhyme scheme (19 February 1857).

56. For example, in 1857 *Aurora Leigh* is quoted at length on 1 January; Longfellow's "The Slave Singing at Midnight" appears on 10 January; Byron's "Ode to Venice" on 17 January; and Schiller on 21 February.

57. In addition to the great variety of metrical and rhyme patterns and the occasional irregularity in these patterns, many of the poetry volumes owned by the Dickinsons contain frequent use of the dash, including mid-sentence. In Barrett Browning's "Crowned and Wedded," one finds "Long live she!—send up loyal shouts—and true hearts pray between,—"; in "A Vision of Poets" the lines "And patience;—ay, of glorying, / And adoration,—as a king"; these passages are marked with pencil lines, apparently by Dickinson (*Poems* 2. 253, 187). On the widespread use of dashes of inconsistent length and slant in handwritten documents by other writers in the nineteenth century, see Mitchell, *Measures* (61).

58. In "Hearing the Visual Lines," Ellen Louise Hart also writes about the importance of sound to Dickinson's verse—also referring to her schoolbooks, the importance of recitation and elocution to her training, and to elements of her verse like alliteration and rhyme. I do not, however, find Hart's argument for reading Dickinson's handwriting and spaces between words as contributing systematically to the sound of poems

persuasive, since both are manifestly habitual and hence occur whenever she writes anything—despite Hart's assertion that spacing in particular "cannot be accurately described as an 'accidental,' or a 'habit of handwriting'" (363).

59. I use here and throughout a system marking stressed syllables in capital letters and unstressed as small, while indicating the iambic (or other) foot design by designating syllables as belonging to either an (unstressed) "u" or (stressed) "s" position in the line. Hence "S" would designate a syllable in a position assumed to carry stress carrying lexical and/or interpretive relative stress, whereas "s" would indicate a syllable in a position assumed to carry stress that carried only weak stress or was relatively unstressed compared to surrounding syllables in the line. Similarly, "U" would indicate a relatively stressed syllable in a position assumed to be unstressed.

60. In her introduction to *Women Poets in the 21st Century,* Juliana Spahr argues that lyric offers an intimate and interior space of retreat, now being coupled with the more politicized and cultural claims of Language writing (2). In "'Post-Language' Lyric: The Example of Juliana Spahr," Lynn Keller analyses Spahr's recent writing in relation to current post-language experiments with lyric, mentioning Spahr and Claudia Rankine's anthology but also others as collecting this kind of work, such as Cole Swensen and David St. John's *American Hybrid* (Norton, 2009) and Reginald Shepherd's *Lyric Postmodernisms* (Counterpath Press, 2008). The current writing around lyric is prolific and complex, and I do not pretend to summarize its primary contours here.

61. Discussion of the Affiliated Faculty Poetics Group on February 22, 2009, Buffalo, New York. Quoted with permission of Myung Mi Kim.

62. Riley also writes about the "inrush of others' voices" as part of the process of composition (65).

3. Hymn, the "Ballad Wild," and Free Verse

1. Judy Jo Small reviews the critical literature on Dickinson and hymns, including the few scholars who have mentioned the similarity between Dickinson's rhythms and ballad quatrains (41–45). As I do, Small finds that critics exaggerate the influence of hymns on Dickinson's prosody (42). Sandra Runzo writes about the intersection of metrical forms of hymns, ballads, and popular songs in her argument that popular music influenced Dickinson's poetic forms and expression of social public concerns (chap. 2). As she argues, the abolitionist Hutchinson family's songs in particular provided "living illustrations for Dickinson of how to engage a world of struggle in lyric" (ms 17). Dickinson's sheet music collection includes "Bonnie Doon," "The Old American Chair, A Ballad," "The Lament of the Irish Emigrant, A Ballad," "The Rose of Allandale, A Ballad," and "There's a Good Time Coming, Ballad" (EDR 469).

2. For an excellent discussion of poetry written for the page but committed to orality see Tyler Hoffman, *The People's Poetry.*

3. As previously noted, on 15 April 1862, Dickinson famously wrote Higginson to ask "Are you too deeply occupied to say if my Verse is alive?" (L260).

4. Dickinson quotes from Emerson's "Concord Hymn" in an 1875 letter to the Norcrosses. Longfellow titles sections of his 1850 *Poems* "Ballads and Other Poems" and

"Song." Bryant calls six poems "songs" and four "hymns" (*Poems*). Emerson's "Hymn" was first printed as a broadside, as were many contemporary ballads. See Small for reference to the small number of Dickinson's poems that borrow from specific hymns (42, 45). As Small notes, variations on the forms most common in Dickinson's poetry have been popular since the fifteenth century and came back into vogue with the ballad revival—including the poulter's measure (short meter arranged as two lines rather than four) and the romance-six (common particular meter: 886886) (44). In Chapter 6, I discuss poems set to music during the Civil War.

5. In "Contraband Singing," Cohen less persuasively argues that "precisely because popular nineteenth-century songs and poems were not organic, original, or integrated objects but instead derivative, detachable, and disposable, they could circulate widely and effectively among formats, media, and contexts" (298). Poems written by the century's most prestigious writers were also popular and circulated widely, out of the author's control. This did not make the poems themselves less original or unified, but indicates the kind of poetry being written and its interest in speaking directly to a contemporary audience.

6. In contrast, in "On Trisyllabic Feet in Iambic Measure," William Cullen Bryant identifies metrical regularity with children and illiterates—categories associated with traditional ballad singers (Jackson, "Bryant," 196). Bryant's "regularity," however, corresponds to the pattern of beats in a line, not the number of unstressed syllables between beats, suggesting how influential balladic models had already become.

7. Maureen McLane, *Balladeering* 20. McLane contends that the "most original" British romantic poets were strongly influenced by the work of antiquarians who were preserving and theorizing ballads. Susan Dickinson was given a copy of Ossian's *Poems* by her students in 1850, suggesting that they were still popular then. This volume begins with 180 pages of "preliminary discourse and dissertation on the era and poems of Ossian," mostly having to do with questions of these poems' authenticity and rehearsing debates of the previous eighty years. A ballad-style poem by Barrett Browning, "The Poet's Vow," contains several marks in the 1852 *Poems* also owned by Sue (EDR 144).

8. "Goethe found the ballad to be the *Ur-Ei* of genres, the undifferentiated matrix of all subsequent genres," according to Gérard Genette (39).

9. In contrast, detractors saw the traditional ballad form as incompatible with serious poetry. Southey wrote that the form was "incapable of dignity" because of its simplicity of voice (Friedman 294). Barrett Browning has Aurora Leigh reject the ballad form as too slight for her seriousness: "My ballads prospered: but the ballad's race / Is rapid for a poet who bears weights / Of thought and golden image"; in contrast, Aurora comments that a poet can "stand / Like Atlas, in the sonnet" (*Aurora Leigh* 170–71). Others found its form monotonous for long poems and syntactically restrictive, because of its short lines and quatrains (Friedman 294).

10. Cohen also claims that "ballad reading functioned as a dominant model" for reading poetry in the nineteenth-century United States (5).

11. The editor comments about Clark's poem: "We predict that it is one of the ballads that will be sung and become familiar" (*SR* 13 February 1860); "Love me little, love me long" appeared *SR* 3 January 1857.

12. Faith Barrett writes at length about the permeability between songs and poems, arguing that porous borders between these forms and their rapid circulation enabled poets to address broad and diverse audiences and thereby to shape popular understanding of the concept of the nation (*"To Fight Aloud"*). I see this fluidity as significant well before the war begins.

13. Cohen makes this claim in the context of stating that "All the extant descriptions of [Jonathan] Plummer speak of him as though he wrote, sang, and sold ballads but . . . he never wrote any [in traditional ballad form] (so far as I have discovered)" ("Peddler" 26).

14. See Chapter 2 for references to the ballad's rhythms and tales as wild.

15. In "One of the ones that Midas touched" (F1488 D) and "A faded Boy –" (F1549), Dickinson writes of ballads nostalgically, as belonging to the past in the mode of postbellum ballad discourse ("Departing like a Pageant / Of Ballads and of Bards –"— F1488). "Never for Society" refers to the (Scottish) "Border Ballad – / Or Biscayan Hymn –" as "entertain[ing]" (F783).

16. See my "Dickinson and the Ballad" for an argument that Dickinson's use of ballad conventions becomes increasingly complex in the early 1860s and then returns to general expectations for the genre in her late years. This essay reads in detail Dickinson's six poems using the word "ballad."

17. Dickinson sent five lines with a clipping for each line to William Cowper Dickinson in 1852 (L33); see also F Appendix 14.

18. Also, see Lowenberg on the Bertini method (18) and the fact that it is clearly Emily, not Lavinia, who is the musician in the family; in a letter of 1851, Dickinson comments that Vinnie has not yet learned her part of a duet Austin sent them (L71).

19. Leyda I, 367. Leyda places Turner's notes describing these evenings in the spring of 1859, immediately following a note from Emily declining an invitation to spend an evening at Sue's. The poet's note suggests that her failure to attend requires explanation, in other words that she still regularly goes to social evenings next door (L201). In *Emily Dickinson: Face to Face*, Martha Dickinson Bianchi refers to the evening in question as one of "amateur music."

20. "Memorabilia of Mary Lyon," quoted in Small, 49. Here Lyon also reports that "we had been singers in our respective churches at home, and now were pining for our choir-mates and rehearsals" until Mount Holyoke organized its "seminary choirs" for regular practice.

21. In other letters, Dickinson writes Austin late at night about a different kind of family music: Vinnie sleeps, Cousin Emily Norcross sleeps "twice as sound and full twice as sonorous, and there come snatches of music from away in mother's room" (24 December 1851, L66). In an 1853 letter, where she also admits her competitiveness with Austin for writing poetry ("Austin is a Poet"), Emily reports "I shall send you *Village Hymns,* by earliest opportunity. I was just this moment thinking of a favorite stanza of yours." Small also reports that Dickinson had "an auditory relationship" to townspeople in Amherst; Clara Bellinger Green recounts Dickinson saying in 1877 that she knew her and her sister's voices and laughs, and their brother's whistle, from hearing them walk by (Small 51).

22. There is extensive literature on American minstrelsy. For connections of this tradition with Dickinson, see Runzo and Barrett, *To Fight Aloud.*

23. In 1846, Dickinson also mentions having attended a concerto in Boston (L13).

24. Abel 52–53. Carrie Bell Sinclair later wrote new lyrics to the tune, playing off Mc-Carthy's, and within a few months "The Homespun Dress" had also become extremely popular in the South (Abel 123, 52). A scholar who offered a $50 reward for a copy of the complete song and information about its author received around five hundred letters, many from people claiming they had written it (Abel 126–27).

25. See also Alice Fahs 79–80. There is some disagreement about who put the text to music. David Z. Kushner claims that Randall himself set the text to "O Tannenbaum." Fahs claims Hetty Cary set the poem to music, whereas Abel maintains that it was Jennie Cary.

26. Victoria Morgan argues that hymns carry considerably more cultural weight than ballads or songs, and that any poem called a hymn suggests a devotional mode of expression (3–4).

27. St. Armand calls Dickinson's poetry "a Christian Psalmody of questioning and protest" (158). See also Morgan, 26.

28. On Howe, see Barrett, *To Fight Aloud,* and Wolosky, *Poetry and Public Discourse.* Holmes characterized the North and South "each with a sword in his hand, each with a song in its mouth," then uses a familiar conceit to describe the Puritan North's song "John Brown's Body" as a "hymn" but the Cavalier South's "My Maryland" as a "lyric poem, appealing chiefly to local pride and passion" (in Fahs 80). The difference, for Holmes, is patriotic and is meant to reveal a difference in sacredness, or level of serious-ness, not musicality.

29. Other poems refer to the sounds of life as metered, or having rhythmic properties. In "I'm sorry for the Dead – Today –," the speaker pities the dead who cannot hear the "congenial times / Old neighbors have at fences –" or the "Mower's metre" (F582); "The murmuring of Bees has ceased" contemplates "the lower metres of the Year / When Na-ture's laugh is done –" and "Accent fades to interval"—terms suggesting the seasonal fading of fall as well as the distance between musical notes (F1142 A). Similarly, the rail-road engine complains "In horrid – hooting stanza –" (F383), and the "Whippowil . . . everlasting sings" in "Stanzas" (F208 B). Dickinson also puns on metrical feet in several poems. To name just a few: in "To learn the Transport by the Pain –" she refers to "home-sick feet" (F178 B); in "It would never be Common – more – I said-" she writes that "The feet – I former used –" become "Unnecessary . . . As boots – would be – to Birds –" (F388); "I can wade Grief –" claims "the least push of Joy / Breaks up my feet –" in phrases break-ing up the iambic meter (F312); and in "The Soul has Bandaged moments –" the "Fright" places "shackles on the plumed feet" (F360), again creating the doubled association with poetry through the pun on feet and reference to birds. All of life moves in relation to musical and metrical rhythms, as Dickinson represents it in these poems.

30. Morgan 4, 5. In contrast, Susan Stewart argues that Dickinson's disruptions of hymn meter highlight the individuality of the speaker (121). Pollak refers broadly to the "hymn-ballad quatrain" as the "single formal archetype" of her poems (*Anxiety of Gender* 23). As Morgan argues, Dickinson's engagement with hymns goes far beyond her use of

meter. Her family owned copies of *Watts Psalms carefully suited to the Christian Worship* bound in one volume with *Hymns and Spiritual Songs* (1810), *Christian Psalmody in Four Parts* (1817), and *The Psalms, Hymns, and Spiritual Songs of the Reverend Isaac Watts* (1834); *Village Hymns* was also available to the poet at home—as demonstrated by her casual reference to the volume in a letter to Austin (L110). See also Wolosky, "Hymnal Tropes."

31. I also write on the influence of biblical cadence on Dickinson's verse. Mitchell similarly calls attention to Watts's irregular rhyming (*Measures* 227). During the eighteenth century, Watts was regarded as radical for the simplicity and lowness, or colloquial register, of his language. Morgan further points out that Watts was a Dissenter; his late hymns leaned toward Unitarianism (13, 83–118).

32. Manson uses the word "stave" to describe this basic unit as a way to minimize the visual aspect of the stanza; I prefer "stanza," as the word Dickinson uses. His nuanced readings indicate how useful his terminology can be in describing Dickinson's unconventional poetic structures. I discuss visual aspects of Dickinson's writing in Chap. 4.

33. Mabel Loomis Todd wrote in her journal that Dickinson wrote "Elysium is as far as to" (F1590) for her "as [she] sang," and Sewall also speculates that could we know this to be true it would tell us something about Dickinson's method of composition, noting as well that Mabel romantically assumed "the impromptu nature" of the poet's writing (Sewall, *Life* 217–18). The poem is regular 8686 iambic meter in quatrains. According to Franklin, it is unclear whether the extant pencil copy is the one sent to Mabel (F1590).

34. Habegger claims "never" (489); Mitchell notes that Dickinson may twice have sent Susan a copy of "A narrow Fellow in the Grass" (*Measures* 31–32).

35. On Dickinson's use of syntax in counterpoint with metrical rhythms, see my "Dickinson's Structured Rhythms" 395.

36. David Porter, 74; Finch, 13–30; Howe (*My Emily Dickinson*) 23. Morgan also sees "Dickinson's use of hymn metre" as implying "a challenge to the notion that religious faith is 'agreed,' simple and known" (38). As previously noted, Crumbley at times reads conventional metrical form as a guide to the speaker's attitude.

37. *Measures* 226–27. Manson similarly states that Dickinson's "experiments with language do not so much depart from meter as work through meter to discover new forms of poetic experience" (368).

38. Contrary to Ellen Louise Hart and Sandra Chung's claim that "Dickinson wrote 4-beat verse," her preferred form alternates four and three beats, and she more often organizes her lines by accentual-syllabic patterns than by the loosened ballad or beat-count rhythms ("Hearing the Visual Lines" 354). Manson also implies that Dickinson's basic structure is 4-beat in referring to Derek Attridge's "4x4 formation" and Dickinson's "sixteen-beat stave," including "virtual beats" at the end of 3-beat lines as contributing to the structure of the stave (368–90, 371–72). While there are 8686 poems in which there is a distinct syntactic pause at the end of the second and fourth lines, hence the possibility of a virtual beat, in other poems the syntax also breaks after the first and third lines, and in others powerful enjambment overrides all expected breaks, including that between quatrains. Manson is correct, however, in pointing out the complexities of Dickinson's "*metrical grammar*" and how much more work might be done in identifying the nuances of her rhythmic experiments (371).

39. Excellent examples of oral folk poetry using a ballad line are the African American "toasts" collected and analyzed by Bruce Jackson in *Get Your Ass in the Water*. Some of these lines are very long, but they typically have four beats.

40. The preface of *Church Psalmody* has a long section on the appropriate structure for lyric poems, including that "there should be a pause at the end of each line" (vi).

41. The grammar used at Amherst Academy similarly defines "Versification" as "the arrangement of a certain number and variety of syllables, according to certain laws" (Pond's Murray's *Grammar* 201). Francis O'Gorman defines the hymn as "not confusingly rapid or overweighted with thought, and with a clear meaning to each line, even if enjambment is used (and, of course, absolutely metrical)" (*Victorian Poetry* 566).

42. Mitchell gives a similar example from a hymnal of the period, which refers to 8,6; 7,8; 7,6; 6,7; and so on as distinct forms; he also mentions other hymnals using such notation (*Measures* 226–27, and 388–89, notes 19–20). Twenty-first-century hymnals use the same notation. For example the *Chalice Hymnal* has a Metrical Index with entries for forms like "CM 86.86," "44.6 with refrain," or "568.558" (835).

43. Adams links the traditional ballad stanza with "the native accentual four-beat line" of Old English verse. By the mid-sixteenth century, he argues, this line had succumbed to the "control of syllable counts" and syllabic measures became a "shaping feature of the hymns sung in Christian churches" (37–38, 42). In the early nineteenth century, however, the ballad quatrain "began to recover its origins in accentual symmetry" (42). Although he does not say so, this nineteenth-century turn comes with romantic imitation of traditional ballads, as in the example he mentions—Coleridge's "Rime of the Ancient Mariner."

44. Looking only at the first quatrain of the 295 poems Dickinson wrote in 1863, Shoptaw finds "one hundred [poems] in common meter (8686). At a distant second, comprising about one eighth (37) of the total, come the short-metered poems (6686). Another familiar meter, long meter (8888), Dickinson used only six times, each time rhyming it as couplets. There are also three poems in the sestet variation of common meter known as common particular meter (886886)" ("Listening" 39). Although I look at entire poems and although poems that begin with an 8686 quatrain do not always continue in this form, I also find that Dickinson writes one hundred poems in 8686s during 1863 (including poems using split lineation). I count forty-two poems in short meter and four using common particular meter. She also uses less standard forms frequently, namely 7676 quatrains thirteen times and 8585 quatrains fourteen times.

45. Dickinson also uses precise common particular meter in "Musicians wrestle everywhere –" (F229 B), "I should have been too glad, I see –" (F283 C), "Good Night – Which put the Candle out?" (F322 A), "Behind Me – dips Eternity –" (F743), and "Sweet Mountains – Ye tell Me no lie –" (F745), among others. She sometimes writes this form as paired tercets: "What if I say I shall not wait!" (F305), is written in four tercets of 886 syllables in an aab rhyme, with the second stanza in each pair of tercets repeating the "b" rhyme for its end line—in effect recreating the 886886 stanza. Other poems using 886 tercets include "He touched me, so I live to know" (F349—written with tercets and two sestets), "Like Flowers, that heard the news of Dews," (F361), "Because the Bee may blameless hum" (F909—with two stanzas in tercets and one sestet), "I cannot buy it – 'tis

not sold –" (F943), "Dying! To be afraid of thee" (F946 C), and "Unable are the Loved to die" (F951 B).

46. In precise long meter, Dickinson also writes: "Tho' I get home how late – how late –" (F199), "A Wife – at Daybreak – I shall be –" (185 C), "The Martyr Poets – did not tell –" (F665), "My Soul – accused Me – And I quailed –" (F793), and several one-stanza poems, including "Love reckons by itself – alone –" (F812) and "If Blame be my side – forfeit Me –" (F874).

47. *In War Time and Other Poems* (1863) owned by Sue (EDR 418). Dickinson also uses 9898 stanzas in "Trudging to Eden, looking backward," (F1031—with one line of ten rather than nine syllables). "I am afraid to own a Body –" (F1050) provides slight variations on the 9898 pattern, and a handful of earlier poems use a 9898 structure in variant lineation.

48. Longfellow uses the common meter quatrain more often than any other form but his quatrains contain far more trisyllabic substitutions than Dickinson's, hence his line lengths within this basic form are more varied; some stanzas are as much anapestic or dactylic as iambic or trochaic (*Poems*). He also repeatedly uses long meter and a trochaic and catalectic combination of 8787 abab.

49. Poems Dickinson writes in these meters precisely include: in 8585: "Dreams – are well – but Waking's better –" (F449), "Wolfe demanded during Dying" (F482 B), "Autumn – overlooked my Knitting –" (F786), "Bloom opon the Mountain stated –" (F787 C), "All but Death, Can be adjusted" (F789), and "Publication – is the Auction" (F788—with variant lineation in two lines); in 7676: "Faith is a fine invention" (F202 B), "The Soul's Superior instants" (F630 B), "An ignorance a Sunset" (F669), and "They say that 'Time assuages' –" (F861); in 7575: "He who in Himself believes –" (F835), "On the Bleakness of my Lot" (F862 B), and "Revolution is the Pod" (F1044); and in 9595: "How the old Mountains drip with Sunset" (F327) and with some variant lineation "Civilization – spurns – the Leopard!" (F276), "No Bobolink – reverse His Singing" (F766), and "Tell as a Marksman – were forgotten" (F1148). There are a number of forms that Dickinson uses only five or six times over the almost three decades that she preserves her writing.

50. During 1862, out of the 19 poems that use a primarily 6686 quatrain, 9 realize the measure precisely in every stanza; this is almost 48%. In contrast, out of the 94 poems that that are primarily in 8686, only 26 realize the measure without variation in lineation or syllable count, around 28%. In 1863, out of 42 uses of short meter, 22 are consistently realized throughout; in 1864, Dickinson uses this form 13 times, with 10 fully realized. Beginning around 1865, Dickinson varies her stanzaic patterns less frequently. In 1865, she uses short meter 31 times, 25 exactly realized (80%) and common meter 79 times, 61 exactly realized. In 1867–69, 1872–75, and 1878, all her uses of short meter are precisely realized.

51. Manson calls short meter "the most dramatic" manifestation of stanzaic form because "it starts tentatively and then arrives with a bang at the conclusion" (374).

52. Derek Attridge has argued against the use of traditional metrical nomenclature (iambic, trochaic) because of its roots in quantitative verse. For representation of verse that is clearly accentual-syllabic, however, I find its terminology more precise than the language of beats and rising or falling rhythms.

53. Dickinson follows the same opening rhythmic pattern in "Better – than Music!" (F378), where all but three of its twenty-five lines begin with a relative stress and all but two of those twenty-two lines begin with a UsuS rhythm. When the poem settles into the 9/8 accentual syllabic pattern of its final four quatrains, lines one and three end on an unstressed syllable of a polysyllabic word (usually unrhymed), and the 8-syllable fourth line always ends with a monosyllable creating a strong rhyme with the last word of the second line. The last stanza reads:

Let me | not spill – | it's small|est ca|dence –   Us|uS|uS|uS|u
Humming – | for pro|mise – when | alone –   Us|uS|uS|uS
Humming – | until | my faint | Rehear|sal –   Us|uS|uS|uS|u
Drop in | to tune – | around | the Throne – (F378)   Us|uS|uS|uS

54. Dickinson uses several variants in the margins of this poem, including an unusual number of fully variant lines: line 3: Is tipped in Tinsil; 4: By the Setting Sun –; 19: nodding * Acres of Masts are standing; 20: back of Solitude * next to – * At the * After – * Unto; 21: Fashions – baffled –; 24: Powerless to unfold –.

55. One might equally reasonably mark the even-numbered lines as headless iambic, that is, lacking the initial unstressed syllable of the line, as I show in brackets. This makes sense of the lines' concluding rising rhythm and implies different syncopation of foot/word boundaries (*Titian, never*). Catalectic lines make scansion entirely a matter of ear and the larger logic of the poem's patterns.

56. In several other poems, Dickinson moves back and forth between 7676 and 7686 patterns (or 8686 to 7686)—for example, in "This World is not conclusion." (F373). Typically, such poems conclude with a final 86 sequence, which provides a rounder or fuller sense of closure than 76, given our cultural acquaintance with this pattern in songs, hymns, and nursery rhymes. Similarly, poems often begin with a line of eight syllables and then move into a 7686 or 7676 pattern. "These are the Nights that Beetles love –" (F1150), for example, begins 8686, moves into eight lines of 7676 and then concludes with a 7686 pattern. The poem contains no space marking stanzas but its syntax and rhymes indicate four-line units.

57. As sent to Sue, the poem has no stanza division until the last two lines; it also uses all words written as alternatives in the fascicle copy. Dickinson frequently writes a poem in marked stanzas in her manuscript books but not in letters; among the many poems she writes in stanzas in her manuscript books in 1863 but sends to Sue without stanza divisions are F600, 721, 729, 772, 796, 799, 819, 855, and 974; she sends "Except the smaller size –" (F606 A) to Sue in stanzas but not to Higginson. Occasionally she writes poems without stanza division in her retained copies but sends them in marked stanzaic form.

58. Dickinson is not alone in switching stanzaic forms mid poem. Bryant uses three distinct quatrain forms in the 12-line stanzas of "The Greek Partisan," a poem marked in the table of contents of his *Poems*: 6676 8787 and 7787 (178). An anonymously published four-stanza poem, "Ancient Spanish Lyric," alters from a 7777 to an 8787 stanza (*SR* 3 July 1857). See Chapter 2 for other examples.

59. In traditional scansion and enunciation of metrical verse, the words "Heavenly" and "difference" are often pronounced as two syllables (heav'nly, diff'rence) rather than

three, and hence would produce standard trochaic lines in "There's a certain Slant," matching others in the poem. In this case, the first stanza's catalectic lines establish neither a clear iambic nor trochaic base for the poem, leaving it up to the reader's ear whether "Heavenly" requires three syllables (as an iambic line with a feminine ending) or two (as trochaic). Generally in metered verse, the reader knows when to elide syllables of a polysyllabic word in response to the underlying metrical requirement of the verse. Dickinson occasionally marks poetic elision—for example, writing "e'en" in "Take Your Heaven further on –" (F672: "e'en You had seen") and "ne'er" in eight poems, including "Success is counted sweetest" (F112: "those who ne'er succeed"). She also frequently uses the abbreviation " 'Tis." Usually, however, the poem's rhythm determines pronunciation, as in "I think To Live – may be a Bliss" (F757), where "difference" must be pronounced with two syllables ("No numb alarm – lest Difference come –") or "The Spirit is the Conscious Ear –" (F718), where "actually" must be read with all four syllables: "The Spirit is the Conscious Ear – / We actually Hear / When We inspect – that's audible – / That is admitted – Here –"—a wonderful effect in a poem about "audible" inspection. In poems using a looser beat, one might read a polysyllabic word as having more or fewer syllables without disruption to the poem's rhythm. "The Definition of Beauty is" (F797 B) consists of a quatrain alternating four and three beats in a rising rhythm and includes extrametrical unstressed syllables in either all four lines or all but the final line, depending on whether one reads "heav-en" or "heav'n" in line 4: "The Definítion of Béauty ís / That Definítion is nóne – / Of Héaven, éasing Análysís, / Since Héaven and Hé are Ōne." The question of pronunciation does not arise with the first "Heaven" (line three), since here the rising rhythm demands the second, unstressed, syllable.

60. "Most she touched me by her muteness –" (F483) also moves in stages through its stanzaic structures. It begins with two stanzas of alternating trochaic and catalectic 8787; then the third stanza heralds an impending change by ending with a 5-syllable line (8785):

Line #		syllables	beats
9	Not opon her knee to thank me	8	4
10	Sank this Beggar from the Sky –	7	4
11	But the Crumb partook – departed –	8	4
12	And returned on High –	5	3

The remaining two stanzas then move into a 6565 pattern, maintaining the alteration of trochaic and catalectic lines.

61. Dickinson frequently uses shorter concluding lines—in 1862, for example, also in "It dont sound so terrible – quite – as it did –" (F384) and " 'Why do I love' You, Sir?" (F459).

62. While, as Manson point out, there has never been agreement about terminology for prosodic analysis, my preference is to avoid description that declares deficiency or lack. A great many of Dickinson's poems must be considered "metrically deficient when compared to the stave" or do "not achieve the rhythmic completion of stanzaic form" as he puts it; these same poems, however, may create structures that are rhythmically fulfilling in their inconsistency, as Manson also acknowledges (378, 379).

63. In "We dream – it is good we are dreaming –" (F584), line 11, "Lest the Phantasm – prove the mistake –," has an unambiguous four beats (nine syllables); line 5 can also be read as having four beats ("What hárm? Men díe – Extérnallý –") or as having four beats in a row ("Whát hárm? Mén díe –"), giving the line five or more points of stress. Or one could read "What hárm? Men díe – Extérnally –." Lines with several monosyllables and caesurae create the greatest ambiguity in scansion.

64. Other poems written in this loosened balladic meter during 1863 include "The Black Berry – wears a Thorn in his side –" (F548), "It's Coming – the postponeless Creature –" (F556), "If ever the lid gets off my head" (F585), "God is a distant – stately Lover –" (F615), and "Ah, Teneriffe – Receding Mountain –" (F752 B). Poems with rough rhythms that may be influenced by ballad meter include "I'm saying every day" (F575) and "Whatever it is – she has tried it –" (F1200), which begins with a line in ballad meter then moves into shorter iambic lines that either open with or at some point include the chiastic UsuS rhythmic pattern that echoes the consecutive unstressed syllables of line 1.

65. For simplicity of showing ballad structure, I combine the first and sixth lines, which Dickinson split in her Fas 13 copy but not elsewhere. In the copy published in *Drum Beat,* there is in both cases a comma where the fascicle copy begins a new poetic line; in the copy to Higginson, there are no such commas.

66. "If your Nerve, deny you –" (F329) is another poem written in loosened ballad meter that omits rather than adding syllables between stresses. This poem has an approximate 3343 beat measure, although it ends with a 2-beat line.

67. To Sam Bowles, Dickinson writes that Austin's "Brain keeps saying over 'Frazer is killed'," perhaps an impetus for the focus on repetition in her poem (L256).

68. This count of poems in precisely realized meter does not include those in which Dickinson splits or combines metrical lines.

69. Dickinson also mentions Burns or quotes from his "Comin' Thro' the Rye" in L42, 77, and 128, and from Burns's "Gudeen to you Kimmer" in "I had a guinea golden" (F12). "We – Bee and I – live by the quaffing –" (F244) replays a popular broadly comic tone with its "Do we 'get drunk'? . . . Do we 'beat' our 'Wife'?" and concluding pun ("By-Thyme!"). Dickinson also rewrites contemporaries' poems. She composed "It sifts from Leaden Sieves –" (F291 B, late 1862) after Higginson's article "Snow" appeared in the *Atlantic,* bestowing high praise on Emerson's "Snow-Storm" and Lowell's "First Snow-Flake," among other literature describing snow (February 1862, 199). This praise may have challenged Dickinson to try her own hand on the topic. She sends her poem to Susan in 1862, then in a revised version to Higginson in 1871 and to Thomas Niles in 1883. Similarly, in the 1870s Dickinson rewrites James Russell Lowell's "After the Burial" and Higginson's "Decoration" (Loeffelholz, "Dickinson's 'Decoration'" 663–65). Kathryn Wichelns claims that Dickinson "undermines [Lowell's] conventional stylistic elements" but her poem is almost equally conventional in form: Lowell's "After the Burial" is written in loose balladic beats (3s); Dickinson's "One thing of it we borrow" (F1516B—as sent to Higginson with reference to Lowell) maintains three beats except in the penultimate line (a frequent variation for her), and keeps his abcb rhyme scheme. Dickinson keeps a copy of this poem in pencil with the stanzas reversed (94). Jackson reads "I cannot live with You –" (F706) as a rewriting of a scene in *Wuthering Heights* (*Misery* 156–57).

70. Franklin potentially supports this argument in hypothesizing that Dickinson's "composition was generally swift, however much revision occurred at leisure" (13). Although Marta Werner does not write about particular units of composition, she concludes that in her "late writings" Dickinson writes through the experience of "immanence" or "rapt attention"—the "'hearing' of what demands to be written even before one's thoughts have been ordered" (*Open Folios* 21). This also suggests composition in the head, according to what might be a kind of rhythm.

71. Stonum provides an excellent demonstration of this pattern (*Dickinson Sublime* 29). Here an exception may prove the rule: the extreme unusualness of Dickinson's inclusion of a line that floats free of all stanza organization in "I learned – at least – what Home could be –" (F891) underlines the stanzaic basis of her composition. Here there is a line of text between the six-syllable line closing stanza 5 and the eight-syllable line beginning stanza 6, clearly distanced from either of them. This extra-metrical line also does not rhyme.

72. Bianchi writes that "as long ago as 1860 Emily was . . . writing free verse of her own invention" (vii). Susan Howe also makes this claim in *The Birth-mark*.

73. Tupper, *Proverbial Philosophy. A Book of Thoughts and Arguments* (1846), inscribed E. Dickinson (EDR 410).

74. In reference to free verse poems, I use u/U and s/S to mark levels of stress on a four-level scale (uUsS), not expected positions of stress in a given pattern.

75. Other poems foregrounding syntax over rhythmic organization and containing no clear meter for at least a significant number of lines include "It's thoughts – and just One Heart –" (F362 B); "To put this World down, like a Bundle –" (F404)—which varies between complex iambic, catalectic, and the strongly falling rhythm of dactyls; "The Wind did'nt come from the Orchard – today –" (F494 B), which has no regular pattern of syllables or beats; and "For Death – or rather" (F644 B)—which has a rising rhythm but no pattern of line lengths and multiple monosyllables of ambiguous stress.

In other poems, Dickinson establishes a metrical pattern but includes lines markedly irregular in rhythm. For example, in "As Willing lid o'er Weary Eye" (F936) the middle lines of the quatrain disrupt its iambs; in "Conscious am I in my Chamber –" (F773 B), line 7 disrupts the trochaic then catalectic measure through its polysyllabics—"Hospitable intuition"—and the penultimate line falls similarly outside any previous pattern with its internally repeated uSu pattern: "But Instinct estéem Him." "Title divine" (F194; 1861) begins as clearly iambic, moves into a middle section dominated by falling rhythms and more logically scanned as trochaic, then back to catalectic lines with dominantly iambic rhythms in its closing two lines.

76. Werner speculates that during the 1880s Dickinson moves toward the production of fragments, "grammatical breakdown, lack of control, visual parataxis, and aphasia" (*Open Folios* 21).

77. In the early 1860s, Dickinson writes a few paired lines that do not achieve the rhythmic completion of a stanza in letters: for example, "The Juggler's *Hat* her Country is –" (F186), "No Rose, yet felt myself a'bloom," (F190; in a letter draft), "Let others – show this Surry's Grace –" (F290), "Best Gains – must have the Losses' test –" (F499), "Not 'Revelation' – 'tis – that waits," (F500, which Susan transposed as prose), and "Life is death

we're lengthy at," (F502). None of these are copied into manuscript books—perhaps because she did not regard them as poems.

78. Sharon Cameron similarly remarks that "There are frequent instances in Dickinson's definitional poems" where either "the poem's conclusion follows poorly from its beginning" or "a poem's beginning is more forceful than its conclusion" (*Lyric Time* 34).

79. Looking systematically at patterns of revision in Dickinson's poems would be instructive in thinking about her patterns of composition and conception of what constitutes a poem.

80. During the years when she is keeping fair copies of poems and so we know when she is excerpting, Dickinson sends one stanza (or less) of several poems to Susan, including F724, 798, 811, 817, 818, 862, 867, 888, 1120, and 1122; to Higginson, she sends one stanza of F568, 820, 861, 895, and 1350 among others. Before 1863, she does not make a practice of sending parts of poems.

81. A late poem, "The Things that never can come back" (F1564 A), uses a similar structure: (11)8(11)4(11)4(11)4, before moving to shorter lines for the last five lines of the poem—although the first two lines of the final (5-line) stanza might be read as a split 11-syllable line, maintaining the poem's abcb rhyme scheme and giving the final stanza a virtual pattern of (11)694 syllables in line length. Socarides claims that the crucial unit for Dickinson is not the Fas booklet but the sheet; the most significant connections are among poems on the four sides of a single folded sheet of paper (69; 84). It is noteworthy that these groupings I discuss occur within Fas sheets (except when there are more than four poems involved), except for "Four Trees" and "Renunciation" in Fas 37 and the irregular poems from Fas 36—which occur across three sheets. It could also be, however, that Dickinson's decision to bind particular sheets together was affected by the similar structures of poems from one sheet to the next—in other words, further investigation of how formal patterns recur within Dickinson's booklet organization might lead us to different conclusions about her primary units, or primary concerns in copying and binding.

4. Spoken Poetry and the Written Poem

1. *The Voice of the Poet* provides a thorough review of illocutionary or speech-like elements in Dickinson's verse. See also *Poet's Grammar* 104–12.

2. I am indebted to Maria Stuart for calling this essay to my attention, in her paper "Strange English."

3. Hoffman takes the concept of "secondary orality" from Walter Ong, *Orality and Literacy: The Technologizing of the Word* (1982), who distinguishes between the orality of pre-literate societies and a more self-conscious or deliberate use of orality that is based upon or presumes a literate culture, writing, and print. Hoffman writes about poets "committed to an oral poetics" or conceiving poetry as an oral performance (*American Poetry* 11, 10).

4. On the popularity of oratory in the period, see Robert Ferguson, "Hearing Lincoln."

5. The aim of the romantics was to "restore poetry to [its] origins . . . in speech and gesture," McLane writes; "literary" poets of the nineteenth century engaged with "oral

tradition, as well as with the figure of the oral poet" (*Balladeering* 212). Neither McLane nor Newman discusses the use of illocutionary structures in poetry.

6. Robert Weisbuch comments that Dickinson's speaker is "individuated just sufficiently to show that she is one of the 'credulous' . . . to add a note of experiential authority to logic" rather than providing a distinct presence (65).

7. Shira Wolosky's *Poetry and Public Discourse* takes as a primary theme the rhetoric of modesty as a dominant trope of the nineteenth century, for men and women, but especially women. Crumbley's *Winds of Will* demonstrates that Dickinson indirectly articulates political perspectives and positions, with attention to gender. Several feminist critics of the 1980s noted Dickinson's strategic use of apparent innocence as a gendered mode of critiquing, subverting, and sometimes openly challenging authorities, and indeed many speakers using a child voice are distinctly feminine, talking "as Girls do." See, among others, Juhasz, *Feminist Critics* and *The Undiscovered Continent*; Sandra Gilbert and Susan Gubar, *The Madwoman in the Attic*; Barbara Mossberg, *When a Writer Is a Daughter*; Pollak, *Anxiety of Gender*; and my *Poet's Grammar* (154–88).

8. Early discourse on ballads as a manifestation of folk or national voice was spurred by the 1801 political unification of the Kingdom of Great Britain (England and Scotland) with the Kingdom of Ireland, to create the United Kingdom of Great Britain, which gave rise to intense enthusiasm for evidence of distinctive Scottish and Irish cultures.

9. Marietta Messmer calls attention to an 1891 British review of *Poems* that represents "Dickinson's grammar as a symptom of America's uncivilized state" ("Critical Reception" 303).

10. McLane's "The Figure Minstrelsy Makes" reads Trux's essay as sincere in claiming, "It will be a proud day for America when these thirty thousand [negro plantation] songs are collected into several volumes" (Trux 79; McLane 431).

11. Like others writing during the post-war Colonial Revival, Child asserts an Anglo-European common past for the U.S., articulated in ballads drawn from English, Irish, and Scottish sources. As Newman puts it, both Child and Gummere present the ballad as part of a "racialized view" of the "American" past but also as intrinsically American in form "by virtue of the agency it democratically attributes to the individual imagination" as part of a larger "imagined community"—one of Gummere's key concepts (189, 193).

12. Whittier published a volume called *National Lyrics* in 1865—part of the Companion-Poets for the People series published by Ticknor & Fields. On Dickinson and democracy, see Crumbley, *Winds of Will*.

13. Preface to "The Children of the Lord's Supper," by Esaias Tegnér, describing peasant life in Sweden as untouched by modern industry and habits (*Poems* 148). Similar claims were made repeatedly about Scotland—for example, Scotland is called "the land of poesy" in a review of Motherwell's *Minstrelsy, Ancient and Modern* in the end pages of a copy of Tennyson's *In Memoriam* owned by Sue (23); this 1850 copy of *In Memoriam* contains several pencil markings and turned-down pages (EDR 316).

14. See my "Dickinson and the Ballad" for a more complex reading of this poem, suggesting that it in part mocks sentimental nostalgia for a lost era—as though boys no longer whistled and cows were no longer driven to barns.

15. In writing about poetry as an object of exchange, Michael Cohen points out that a "hybrid system of exchanges (economic and bardic, print-mediated and oral, ephemeral and ancient)" supported the broadside production of early nineteenth-century American ballad-mongers as well as the "elite" volumes of verse later imagined to have dominated this period ("Whittier" 13). Cohen does not mention Dickinson.

16. Michael J. Bell's "Ballad Maker's Art" reviews political implications of nineteenth-century associations of the ballad with the "people."

17. I have not been able to find a copy of Lowell's lecture on the ballad given at the Lowell Institute. He does print a summary of this lecture called "The Ballads" in the *Christian Inquirer,* and Michael J. Bell quotes at length from another source in "The Only True Folk Songs." Passages I quote followed by a page number come from Bell's citations. The Houghton Library also has a typescript of lectures on poetry Lowell gave at Harvard, including four with references to ballads (MS Am 183.33). Although Dickinson is unlikely to have read the *Inquirer* summary, the *SR* did report on a lecture Lowell gave in Springfield on 28 February 1855, calling it "a chaste and beautiful essay upon what we would term the Universality of the Poetic element in all enlightened nations and ages of the world." This description emphasizes the element of Lowell's ideas that distinguish them from Child's assumption that modern poets cannot produce heartfelt, deeply pathetic, nationally authentic poetry like that of the ballads.

18. Harvard Lecture 3, "The Spread of Latin – Popular Literature" (MS Am 183.33).

19. "Who's that knockin' at the door" is presented on its front cover "as sung with great applause by William Whitlock" and then at the top of the first page as "composed and sung by" Whitlock; "Old Dan Tucker," is printed "as sung by the Virginia Minstrels." "Our Native Song, A National Refrain" is presented "as Sung with great applause by Mr. H[enry] Russell"—who presumably also wrote the lyrics. "Araby's Daughter" is published as "sung with great applause by Mr. Williamson," followed by the information in smaller type "written by Thomas Moore Esqr." Similarly, "Oh Give Me A Home If In Foreign Land" is "sung by the Harmoneon Family as a Quartette" with secondary billing: "Poetry by Marshall S. Pike."

20. The cover of "The Old Arm Chair, A Ballad" by Henry Russell (music by Holton Olmsted) shows a woman leaning her arm against an arm chair, presumably the song's "I"; "The Lament of the Irish Emigrant, A Ballad," shows a young man with walking stick and cloth bag, leaning against a fence (lyrics by Mrs. Price Blackwood, music by Mrs. Isaac McGaw). Sheet music with minstrel illustrations include "Who's that knockin at the door" from "Whittock's Collection of Ethiopian Melodies" (caricatured performers on a stage, with banjo or dancing) and "Old Dan Tucker" (caricatured African Americans performing stereotypical activities). "The Jolly Raftsman" presents an oval portrait of composer "Old Dan Emmit" surrounded by caricatures of four black musicians playing spoons, fiddle, banjo, and tambourine ("words by Andrew Evans") EDR 469.

21. Stonum argues that the poet eschews "mastery" in her poems, instead presenting unordered scenes to her readers for attention and interpretation (15, 17); she wants to stimulate response, not dictate it (*Dickinson Sublime* 48).

22. See Suzanne Juhasz, "The Big Tease" on this poem (58–59); Dickinson sent a slightly altered version of the poem to Sue. "I reckon – When I count at all –" (F533) similarly

criticizes God's splendors as "too difficult a Grace" and therefore inferior to the products of a casual poet, the kind who would use a word like "reckon."

23. Thomson's *The Seasons* was required reading at Amherst Academy and Mount Holyoke. The line "When Autumn's yellow luster gilds the world" is marked, perhaps by Dickinson, in her mother's 1822 copy; EDR 334 (170). Of the fourteen poems mentioned in the previous three paragraphs, only "I send Two Sunsets," "Essential Oils," "Besides the Autumn poets sing," and "To pile like Thunder" were circulated. Notably, all four were sent to Sue, although the latter was also sent to the Norcrosses and not preserved by Dickinson herself. While I see no evidence that Dickinson and her sister-in-law were engaged in a mutual workshop (as Smith and Hart argue in *Open Me Carefully*), she seems to have shared more of her thinking about poetry with Sue than with anyone else in her early years of preserving poetry.

24. Similarly, Weisbuch observes that Dickinson's child-persona "unconsciously points out crucial inconsistencies" in cultural doctrines (66); like Blake, he comments, she "allows a social critique to grow naturally out of the speaker's innocent questions" (67). Gummere associates Blake with ballads, calling him "the most democratic of poets" and praising the "revolt against the fetters of a regular verse" associated with those "glad democratic days" when poetry attempted to speak the truths of nature (109). A few of Dickinson's many poems using an apparently guileless voice to articulate an adult shrewdness or wisdom include: "Faith is a fine invention" (F202 B), "Over the fence – / Strawberries – grow –" (F271), "I reckon – When I count at all –" (F533), "Of Course – I prayed – / And did God Care?" (F581), "A Thought went up my mind today –" (F731), "Who is the East? / The Yellow Man" (F1085), "The Show is not the Show / But they that go –" (F1270), and "God is indeed a jealous God –" who "cannot bear to see" that we had rather "with each other play" than with "Him" (F1752).

25. According to Linda Freedman, Blake was first published in the United States in 1842 but not well known until the 1890s. Higginson, Christina Rossetti, and an anonymous reviewer compare Dickinson to Blake in the early 1890s (Buckingham, *Reception* 14, 87).

26. As cited in Chapter 3, Parker's *English Composition* defines the ballad as "a rhyming record of some adventure or transaction which is amusing or interesting to the populace, and written in easy and uniform verse" (249).

27. Pollak notes in "Our Emily Dickinsons" that other Dickinson double-gender poems include "I showed her Hights she never saw –" / "He showed me Hights I never saw –" (F346); "The Stars are old, that stood for me –" (F1242); and "Her losses make our Gains ashamed" (or "His losses made . . ." F1602; ms chap. 6, note 68).

28. Similarly she sent "Though the Great Waters sleep," (F1641, 1884) to Sue in relation to Bowles's death, to Catherine Sweetser in reference to the deaths of her own family, to Benjamin Kimball after the death of Otis Lord, and to Abigail Cooper, perhaps responding to the death of Edward Tuckerman. She also preserves a draft and two fair copies of this quatrain. No two of the seven copies are exactly the same.

29. In *Ways of Writing*, David Hall writes that colonial writers understood publishing to be frequently collaborative, and not necessarily as involving the initiative or even knowledge of the author. In this culture, editors and even the copyist or printer were

expected to "improve" the author's text (108). In *Writing for the Street,* Michael Kearns argues that Dickinson rejected publication "mediated through 'editors,'" instead "publishing by manuscript . . . to preserve her ownership while generating symbolic capital" (71, 72).

30. McGill mentions that an 1829 case determined that the content of newspapers was ineligible for copyright (106). Not until 1903 was there a law in the U.S. that strongly identified the published text with its author. See Franklin Appendix 1 for "Poems Published in Dickinson's Lifetime," which includes information on reprinting.

31. The most precise analysis of this practice of Dickinson's occurs in Mitchell's *Measures of Possibility.*

32. To assume that Dickinson intended every aspect of her visual page despite the multiple inconsistencies in her writing out of individual poems also goes against the grain of her contemporaries' assumptions about how to write or read poetry. Such an assumption allows for no run-on lines, imagines Dickinson is inconsistent about capitalization at the beginning of poetic lines, and sees every revision or alternate instantiation of a poem as essentially a new work. This view paradoxically reifies Dickinson's poetic form in ways the poet herself eschews, to the extent that a poem once written out would be untranslatable into any other medium. Such a document cannot participate in a culture of reprinting and would seem opposed to the easy transformation of genre (poem to song) that characterized verse of her era, as well as her uses of the same poems in manuscript books and (sometimes multiple) letters.

Howe's *My Emily Dickinson* has made this argument most influentially. As previously noted, Hart argues that Dickinson composed a "visual line" and that her line division generally substitutes for other forms of emphasis ("Hearing the Visual Lines" 349, 350). She acknowledges that Dickinson's word placement may be "random" and lineation may not be specifically meaningful, but nonetheless finds that it consistently establishes "emphasis and inflection" (352). For counter arguments, see Walter Benn Michaels, *The Shape of the Signifier,* and Mitchell, *Measures.*

33. A metrical line is determined by the metrical norm of a poem; a row of print is a visual unit; I use "poetic line" to distinguish Dickinson's scripted variation of metrical lines, such that a split metrical line constitutes two poetic lines, or a combination of two metrical lines is a single poetic line. Hence a poetic line differs distinctly from a run-on line or row of print.

34. James Longenbach writes that lineation alters patterns of stress, with direct reference to the "equivocal nature" of Dickinson's line (78, 80). While this is indeed the case with free verse, and generally with metrical forms, Dickinson's split metrical lines both typically occur at some kind of syntactic juncture and continue the expected sequence of stress patterns, so that the (unconventional) line break heightens the existing slight pause rather than creating an entirely new one. Read aloud, Dickinson's split (metrical) lines sound metrically regular; seen on the page, one notes the disjunction of the line.

35. Additional poems using split lines in the years 1860–1862 include "What is – 'Paradise' –" (F241), "A Clock stopped –" (F259), "What would I give" (F266), "Again – his

voice" (F274), "This – is the land – the Sunset washes –" (F297), "I know some lonely Houses off the Road" (F311 B), "If I'm lost – now –" (F316), "Put up my lute!" (F324), "Blazing in Gold –" (F321)—written without split lines when sent to Higginson, "Better – than Music!" (F378), "I rose – because He sank –" (F454), "A long – long Sleep –" (F463), and "We pray – to Heaven –" (F476). "Put up my lute!" (F324) begins with a pattern of 558(10)8 rather than (10)8. Less frequent are split lines in the middle of a poem, as in "I prayed, at first, a little Girl," (F546), where the penultimate line of the second stanza is split into two units of four syllables each rather than the expected eight-syllable line.

36. See *Open Me Carefully* 96–100 for this exchange. Franklin notes that the substitution of "cadences" for "cadence" may have been an error. The *SR* publication follows the well-known exchange between Emily and Sue a year earlier (1861), in which Emily wrote two additional versions of the second stanza after Sue indicated that the original second stanza was not as good as the first. Franklin speculates that Dickinson sends Sue the copy printed in the *SR* in 1859, but it would then make little sense for Sue to respond to it critically two years later in 1861.

37. Franklin judges "The" to be capitalized hence definitively beginning a poetic line despite the fact that this row of print is inset from the left margin. Since Dickinson does not inset run-on lines, this marginal indentation on lines 4 and 5 may be another instance of her playing with written form, or it may be an anomaly. She uses distinct marginal indentation (and considerable underlining) in "I reason – Earth is short –" (F403 A) in the copy she sends to Susan but no indentations or underlining in her Fas 20 copy.

38. Again, this line division maintains the iambic rhythm of the poem, the 3-syllable segment having a uSu rhythm and the 5-syllable segment beginning with a stressed syllable (suSuS). In "So much Summer" (F761) the 8585 pattern is written almost entirely using a 4/4 split for the 8-syllable line. In "Although I put away his life –" (F405), Dickinson uses an 8686 or 7686 structure in seven of its eight stanzas but a 76446 in stanza 5. " 'Twas like a Maelstrom, with a notch," (F425) contains the same relatively unusual and suggestive splitting of the third line of an internal stanza into two poetic lines of four syllables each ("And you dropt, lost, / When something broke –"). "I gained it so –" (F639) is structured roughly in two common particular meter (886886) stanzas, except that most 8-syllable lines are split, and Dickinson rhymes on the half lines; the first stanza also omits one 8-syllable line or line-equivalent (4486446). In "Just so – Christ – raps –" (F263), Dickinson splits a final metrical line as 8/2 in her Fas copy: "Heart – I am knocking low / At thee!" By contrast, in a version of this poem sent to Sue, this sentence is written "Heart! I am knocking – low at thee." in one row of print and with a period.

39. The first two stanzas of "Inconceivably solemn! / Things so gay" (F414) also have a basic pentameter norm, written in split lines except for line 5, which is nine syllables long and begins a 3-line stanza, as though it combines two shorter lines. "To love thee Year by Year – / May less appear" is basically a pentameter quatrain written in seven lines, the first six split and the seventh written long: "And so I pieced it, with a flower, now." (F618 B). "That I did always love / I bring three Proof" (F652) similarly uses short lines in 6446 then 6448 arrangement, rhyming abcb, until its last stanza, which has four lines of 5344 syllables, or in effect a tetrameter couplet. Annie Finch writes about

Dickinson's split pentameter lines, finding approximately one hundred split pentameters in Dickinson's verse (23, 24).

40. Combined lines also occur in "As if I asked a common alms –" (F14), which Dickinson wrote in lines of alternating tetrameter and trimeter in 1858 (Fas 1) and in 1862 in a letter to Higginson; in 1884, however, she copied it in rhyming couplets of fourteen syllables in what appears to be a letter that was never mailed.

41. Dickinson marked Bryant's "The Death of the Flowers" with an "X" above the title, by folding the page in half, and by drawing marginal lines down the side of three entire stanzas; "The Conjunction of Jupiter and Venus" is marked with a check in the table of contents. Ferguson's "The Forging of the Anchor" is in John Wilson's *Noctes Ambrosianae*, vol. 3 (New York, 1855; EDR 424), although his name is misspelled as "Fergusson." These poems all contain a line-internal pause after eight syllables.

42. Of course, popular metered verse also divides lines at major syntactic junctures, but free verse has only this mode of organization rather than both meter and syntax.

43. A few other poems contain this kind of reorganization of syntax in a pair of lines without regard to metrical patterning. In "God gave a Loaf to every Bird –" (F748 B), after a first stanza of 8686, the second stanza strongly undercuts the established pattern:

To own it – touch it –	5
Prove the feat – that made the Pellet mine –	9
Too happy – for my Sparrow's chance –	8
For Ampler Coveting –	6

Syntax and meter prescribe line division as "To own it – touch it – Prove the feat / [T]hat made the Pellet mine": "own . . . touch . . . [and] Prove" are syntactically parallel, following the opening infinitive-marker "to." Dickinson, however, clearly indicates a break between "touch it" and "Prove" and no break after "feat" (she uses a second row for writing this longer line, beginning with "the Pellet"). This disruption emphasizes both "touch it" and "Prove" more than standard metrical organization would. More unusually, "Except the smaller size –" (F606A) concludes with a pair of lines that follow word boundaries rather than meter:

The Larger – slower grow –	
And later – hang –	
The Summers of Hesperides	]in
Are long –	

To maintain her metrical organization, Dickinson would have had to break "Hesperides" after the second syllable: the meter would predict "The Summers of Hesper- / ides Are long –." Even without seeing the poem's lineation, one hears the rush across the expected rhythmic boundary created by the word "Hesperides." "Must be a Wo –" (F538) similarly alters a regular 4-syllable line with a 3- and then a 5-syllable line to accommodate the multisyllabic "Even" at the beginning of line 12. The variation is not heard because the poem's iambic rhythm is maintained as is the basic 2-line, 8-syllable unit. Such play with word boundaries across metrical units is the most radical aspect of Dickinson's experimentation with lineation. Not until Marianne Moore breaks words at line-ends ("ac- / cident" in "The Fish") is there similarly extreme tension between word, rhythm, and line.

44. More common are instances where Dickinson uses enjambment rather than the disruption of a metrical pattern, as in "She staked Her Feathers –" (F853), where a new phrase begins at the end of a metrical line ("At home – among the Bellows – As / The Bough where she was born –") or in "A Plated Life – diversified" (F864), where a new sentence begins mid-line at the end of a stanza: ". . . 'tis when // A Value struggle – it exist –."

45. In this case the two instantiations of the poem seem to be alternative versions, since Dickinson makes no marks to indicate she would discard the first. In other poems, she underscores or otherwise marks a preference for one variant—for example in "After great pain," (F372) where she renumbers the lines of the second stanza to indicate a correction—first writing them so that the seventh metrical line was split ("A Wooden way / Regardless grown,"), then renumbering the lines to make the irregular sequence of 84648 syllables per line: "The Feet, mechanical, go round – / A Wooden way / Of Ground, or Air, or Ought – / Regardless grown, / A Quartz contentment, like a stone –." There is only one manuscript of this poem; we cannot know how she might have written it out a second time.

46. Assuming that Sue sent her copy to the *Independent* and that the periodical printing changed no words, Dickinson wrote "strait" rather than "Straight" in line 1, "foreheads" in line 4, and "sure" in line 10 to Sue. To Bowles, Dickinson uses "faces" and "fair" rather than "foreheads" and "sure" but keeps "strait." In Fas 36, she writes "Straight," "foreheads," and "sure," and adds a new alternative for line 2: "steady" for the text's "even" (F187 C).

47. Dickinson also indents the second line of the poem in her Fas copy but not in S7.

48. "Going to Her" constitutes another instance of non-progressive revision; Dickinson clearly changes this poem as is convenient to its use.

49. A lost copy was sent to the Norcrosses and copied out by them for Higginson in 1891. This copy included all twenty lines of the final poem but no stanza divisions, as copied by Frances. This is a rare poem, for which there is evidence Dickinson did not write the first stanza first.

50. This is the copy Dickinson enters into fascicle 34 in 1863, two years after sending the poem to Bowles. Dickinson changes words in five lines between 1861 and 1863, but she changes lineation only once—combining what were initially two lines into: "Who of little Love – know how to starve –." The poem is near others in fascicle 34 written in or verging on free verse, "It dont sound so terrible – quite – as it did –" (F384), "I can wade Grief –" (F312), "I'm saying every day" (F575), and "Four Trees – upon a solitary Acre –" (F778).

51. The one exception to the short and iambic second line of a stanza occurs in stanza 3, where the first two lines have relatively reversed weight: "The Acre gives them – Place – / They – Him – Attention of Passer by –." This reversal is another feature contributing to the irregularity that makes the poem read like free verse. Dickinson uses a more irregular pattern of alternate long and short lines in "Renunciation – is a piercing Virtue –" (F782), "Besides this May" (F976), and "Embarrassment of one another / And

God" (F1057). The first two of these poems approach free verse in the degree to which their extremely varied line lengths create metrical irregularity, although both maintain a basically iambic rhythm throughout. As with almost all of Dickinson's other poems verging on free verse, these were never circulated.

52. Using Michel deCerteau's definition of the "mystic poem," Morgan understands Dickinson's poems to "permit saying," to produce beginnings without endings and therefore provide a "heterologous, liberating space"; multivalent in their relationality, Dickinson's poems destabilize the hierarchy of address assumed in prayer. They are "anti-teleological" (54, 45).

5. Becoming a Poet in "turbaned seas"

1. Yanbin Kang argues that Dickinson's style becomes increasingly Daoist in its brevity, impersonality, and serene combination of opposites in her later years. As Kang notes, Brita Lindberg-Seyersted finds a gradual decrease in Dickinson's use of the first-person singular pronoun in the later poetry, and Christopher Benfey describes Dickinson as having an "Asian aesthetic practice," consisting of compressed miniaturism, spare poetics, a reclusive posture, and the use of impersonal personae. Benfey also regards Dickinson as having what seems like an "instinctive feel" for Zen-like philosophy and the "*wabi* aesthetic" valuing the rough-hewn and flawed, and as having insights on life that seem "deeply Buddhist" (90, 83). My concern in this chapter is how Dickinson uses the idea and models of the "Orient" available to her in the 1840s and 1850s, not the extent to which aspects of her aesthetic resemble Asian philosophy, aesthetics, or spiritual practice. Like Kang's, Benfey's focus is primarily on Dickinson's poetry from the 1870s and 1880s, when there is more exchange between Japan and Amherst. David Reynolds includes discussion of the poet's drawing on sensational and gothic tales, both of which have been linked to Orientalism. An earlier version of part of this chapter was published as "Emily Dickinson's 'turbaned seas'."

2. This version of this line was sent to the Hollands; in Fas 23, Dickinson writes "On Ball of Mast – in Foreign Port –" (F495 B).

3. Paul Giles more generally comments that Dickinson situates her poetry self-consciously "between the local and the global" as a way of "decentering" both Amherst and other parts of the globe (8).

4. This is a conservative estimate, not including every use of words like "pearl" or "East" that also has non-Asian reference and not including biblical place or proper names—Israel, Moses—unless they contain marked geographical orientation (like "A little East of Jordan"). Words or figures that occur repeatedly include "Orient," "Himmaleh" (Himalaya), isles of spice, India, and cashmere. See Appendix A for a list of these poems.

5. Susan Nance argues that the *Arabian Nights* is the primary influence on U.S. Orientalism.

6. On this novel's orientalism, see Steven Hamelman and Schueller, 100–109.

7. Dickinson was not alone in using Asian-based narrative and figures to gain critical purchase on the West. Nance argues that Americans were generally interested in the

East as consumers, not proto-imperialists (11, 21). Bayard Taylor, for example, writes so as to show Americans "how ostensibly authentic experiences of Muslim lands could inform their own identities as cultural relativists and worldly consumers defying bigotry and crudity" (66); Taylor contributed travel writing frequently to the *Republican* and occasionally to the *Atlantic.*

8. The *Republican* contained remarkable international coverage in daily omnibus sections titled "Three" or "Four Days Later from Europe" or "Foreign Matters" and under specific headlines like "Our Minister to China" (12 October 1859), "Ferocity of the War in Morocco" (21 January 1860), or "Anarchy in Eastern Turkey" (26 January 1860). In contrast, the *Hampshire and Franklin Gazette,* to which the Dickinsons also subscribed, contained little international coverage, mostly anecdotal, as part of a personal travel report. For example, a 6 August 1859 front-page article called "Siam," relates "the religious and social customs of this country"; "Japan Among Us" (20 April 1860) gives primary attention to contrasting the dress modes of Japanese and Western women, with titillating reference to the lack of constraint in Japanese women's clothing. While Dickinson sometimes disdained politics, she was a primary reader of the family's newspapers. Subscriptions to the *Republican* and the *Express* stopped during the month after her death (Kirkby 3). For an alternative view, see Shannon Thomas, who regards Dickinson as sharing Emerson's view that news communication technologies impeded the development of the soul, and generally as disdainful of newspapers (69).

9. I include only books published before Dickinson began her serious writing and preservation of poems since later books could not have influenced her writing during the early 1860s. Dickinson may also have read *Mr. Dunn Browne's Experiences in Foreign Parts* (1857)—written by Samuel Fiske, a friend of Austin's.

10. Also called the "Aladdin Quick Step," this sheet music was produced at the Boston Museum; words by S. S. Steele, Esq., music by T. Comer (Boston: Prentiss & Clark, 1847).

11. Dickinson owned sheet music for Moore's "Araby's Daughter," set to music by G. Kiallmark, along with a handful of other non-orientalist songs by Moore (EDR 469); Kiallmark also set to music "Fly to the Desert," an excerpt from *Lalla Rookh,* printed in the *Household Book of Poetry.* There is no evidence that Dickinson read the Qur'an or particular travel books, but she might well have heard her father or brother talk about them, and her father gave her William Lewis Herndon's *Exploration of the Valley of Amazon* (1854), which is inscribed "Miss Emily E. Dickinson from her father . . ." (EDR 65); this suggests that she had some interest in travel books herself. She read Poe and Spofford, both of whose stories and poems contain frequent Orientalist reference. Jay Leyda refers to Austin's copy of *Lalla Rookh,* with its three marked passages, but I have not been able to locate this volume (I:161).

12. Hallen notes Dickinson's multiple allusions to famous explorers; for Dickinson, she argues, to find "land" is to find "the Indies, riches, America, home, death, paradise, language, truth, knowledge, rest, love, and eternity," and to live is to "circumnavigate back and forth from center to circumference in the fragile vessels of our lives" (174–75).

13. 8 September 1846 to Abiah Root (L13). See Hiroko Uno's analysis of this museum visit.

14. Zboray and Zboray (276, 273). They continue: "The museum thus expressed a critical moment of intercultural possibility between . . . vague Orientalist imaginings . . . and the scripted, sensationalistic freakery of P. T. Barnum, who effectively marketed racist stereotypes through his many mid-nineteenth-century exhibits" (272, 273).

15. Frazar Stearns's journal is housed at the Jones Library, Amherst. I am indebted to Tevis Kimball for calling its existence to my attention. Stearns reports looking for his "friend" Edward Dickinson immediately upon his return to Boston (237). The purchase of the lot known as "Orient Springs" is described in Lombardo (306) and by the Massachusetts Historical Commission, at www.pelham-library.org/History%20Room/zAmherst_Road_52.doc.

16. *Harper's Monthly* even prints an article in July 1851 on the chaste "elegant and graceful" practicality of Turkish trousers, in response to a large number of popular cartoons mocking women wearing such apparel (Wardrop 135–36). Sue refers to Abby Sweetser as reveling in her family's "Syrian relics sent over to her by her niece," such as "musky specimens of Arabs and Turks" including peacock feathers, coffee cups, scent bottles, and lentils (in Wardrop 196).

17. According to Elizabeth Petrino, cashmere symbolized transcendence in popular nineteenth-century literature; it was associated with softness and lushness (144).

18. EDR 469. On the Dickinsons' Irish and African American help, see Murray (*Maid* 19). Irish immigration to the United States was at its peak between 1847 and 1854; before 1847, annual immigration was typically below 6,000 a year; between those dates it was over 100,000 a year, reaching the level of 221,253 in 1851, according to Lerner's *Historical Statistics*. Hampshire County had nearly 10 percent foreign-born population in 1850 (35,732 total population, of which 329 was "free colored" and 3,286 was foreign born). In 1850, Boston was 45 percent immigrant: "native" population was 75,322 and "foreigners and their children" 63,466, according to the *7th Census* (DeBow 255, 121). Although Dickinson demonstrates prejudice against the Irish in letters, she typically sympathized with the impoverished and transient in her poems.

19. By simple repetition, I mean the repetition of brief phrases, as in " 'Twas such a little – little boat" (F152, 1860); "homesick – homesick feet" (in "To learn the Transport by the Pain –" F178 B, 1860); the refrain-like repetition in the last line of each tercet "Then dinna care! Then dinna care!" in "Poor little Heart!" (F214, 1861); and "Because – because . . . hunted – hunted . . . They 'noticed' me – they noticed me . . . *listening* – listening . . . Since breaking then – since breaking then –" in "I should not dare to leave my friend," (F234, 1861). Like frequent underlining, this is a stylistic mannerism she largely abandons by the end of 1861.

20. Shannon Thomas's " 'What News must think when pondering' " called this passage to my attention (68). "The Progress of the Electric Telegraph" (*AM* March 1860) similarly claims that the telegraph will bring "all parts of our republic into the closest and most intimate relations of friendship and interest. . . . The highest office of the electric telegraph, in the future, is thus to be the promotion of unity, peace, and good-will among men," later focusing on the international laying of lines and possibilities for communication (290, 291).

21. See also 16 May 1857 for a similar opinion about the war in China as "unhuman."

22. *SR* 3 July 1860; on potential visits to Boston and Springfield, Massachusetts, see 3 May and 25 May1860.

23. Schueller notes the discrepancy between news and travel accounts of contemporary Asian cultures and regions and the focus on traditions and romanticized models of life in much art, fiction, and poetry (147–49); in particular, Orientalist literature ignored colonization and recent wars.

24. To mark the large number of such poems between 1860 and 1863, I give dates for each poem in this chapter.

25. *Harper's Monthly Magazine,* September 1855, 547–51.

26. "Schamyl Still Lives" (*SR* 6 July 1859) and "Schamyl the Hero." In the early nineteenth century, Johann Friedrich Blumenbach theorized that the Circassians were the closest to God's original model of humanity, and thus "the purest and most beautiful whites were the Circassians" (Jordan 222–23).

27. This articles goes into considerable detail about prices, the market, typical purchasers, and racism in Turkey, commenting, for example, that "In Constantinople it is evident that there is a very large number of negresses living and having habitual intercourse with their Turkish masters—yet it is a rare thing to see a *mulatto*. What becomes of the progeny of such intercourse? I have no hesitation in saying that it is got rid of by infanticide, and that there is hardly a family in Stanboul where infanticide is not practiced in such cases as a mere matter of course." See online as printed in the *New York Daily Times* on 6 August 1856: http://chnm.gmu.edu/lostmuseum/lm/311/; and in the CUNY "Lost Museum," Circassian Beauty Archive. http://chnm.gmu.edu/lostmuseum /searchlm.php?function=find&exhibit=star&browse=star.

28. 24 August 1859 "The Russian and Circassian War" and 29 January 1860 (no headline).

29. Schueller notes that flower gardens are a "predictable" feature of U.S. Orientalism (81). Evidence of the pervasive association of flowers with the Orient occurs in Higginson's 1861 description of spring flowers: "Over the meadows spread the regular Chinese-pagodas of the equisetum" ("April Days," 388). Paula Bennett includes Dickinson as among the many nineteenth-century women writers using oriental settings or metaphor to write erotic verse, often through the use of flower imagery (*Public Sphere* 261). She traces the roots of this erotic discourse to the Bible's Canticles and to Sappho's love lyrics—both associated with the Orient. Rebecca Patterson notes that the Evergreens is east of the Homestead and that Dickinson frequently designates Sue as her "East" (157); see also L345. For Patterson, Dickinson's references to India and Cashmere always include allusion to the "passion of love"; parts of the Orient also participate in her association of the South with erotic freedom (161, 188–89).

30. Similarly martial vocabulary in "Their Barricade against the Sky," with its "inference of Mexico," probably refers to the ongoing battles in Mexico, reported on frequently in the *Republican* (F1505, 1879)—although Patterson claims that the poem refers to histories of the Mexican conquest by Spain (146). In "Love & Conquest," Stephanie Browner calls attention to an 1882 letter in which Dickinson refers to a recent event in Egypt (L768).

31. Isaiah 49:20–21: ". . . give place to me that I may dwell. Then shalt thou say in thine heart, Who hath begotten me these, seeing I have lost my children, and am desolate, a

captive, and removing to and fro? and who hath brought up these? Behold, I was left alone." My thanks to Jennifer Leader for identifying this allusion.

32. Although Dickinson writes "The children of whose turbaned seas – / *Or* what Circassian Land" (my emphasis), the Orientalism of the poem links the two.

33. Schueller 78. Nance points out that West and South Asians, including Turks, Persians, and Arabs, were often regarded as "white" (15).

34. Linda Frost argues that as slaves, "white" beauties, and colonial subjects, Circassians blended elements of Victorian True Womanhood with enslaved African American womanhood (66) in representing "endangered-yet-rescued whiteness" (67). At the same time, Circassian women were thoroughly orientalized through their identification with the harem (69). Circassian society was represented as being so unequal that twelve-to-fourteen-year-old girls eagerly anticipated being sold in Istanbul as a way to escape the harsh conditions of their lives in the Caucasus (72). Another analogy in occasional play comparing Circassians to Native Americans suggests the further racial indeterminacy of this people in the Western imagination. According to Thomas Barrett, "Russians sometimes compared the mountain people who resisted Russian encroachment with James Fenimore Cooper's Indian heroes" (76).

35. Dickinson uses a similar figure in "Those fair – fictitious People –" (F369, 1862), where the dead "Esteem[] us – as Exile – / Themself – admitted Home –." Her notion that all people are exiled may also be influenced by Barrett Browning's *A Drama of Exile,* a long poem about Adam and Eve after leaving Eden (*Poems*). Mary Loeffelholz discusses this poem in "Dickinson, and the Servants."

36. "The Coolie Trade" or "Coolie Traffic" appeared periodically as a headline, for example on 6 August 1859 and 29 September 1859. In 1856, the *Republican* reports that Chinese are being sold to "plantations, where they are treated no better than slaves." It continues, however, to report that this "immigration"—a curious word for what it elsewhere describes as kidnapping—"does not diminish the trade in Africans, who are brought in large numbers to Cuba."

37. As Giles comments, Dickinson is interested in Van Diemen's Land as "a spatial correlative to the temporal conception of 'Eternity' "; Giles also calls attention to the fact that Edgar Allan Poe's *Arthur Gordon Pym* (1838) represents Van Diemen's land as a "gothic epiphenomenon" (16).

38. Schueller provides an excellent historical background both of Orientalist writing in the U.S. and of its relation to European Orientalism, as theorized by Edward Said, and international events. As many have pointed out, Said does not include the United States in his survey of Orientalism. U.S. Orientalism shares European attitudes but also sees the ancient civilizations of the East in part as an alternative to European civilization as a philosophical and aesthetic model. Colleen Lye also sees some degree of "exceptionalism" in the ambivalent continuities of " 'negative' and 'positive' stereotypes" in discourse around "America's Asia," because of its "putatively unusual capacity for economic modernity" (3). Zhaoming Qian and Cynthia Stamy discuss U.S. Orientalism as part of American modernism's project to distinguish itself from Europe. Schueller suggests that New England writers in the 1850s have an "indigenous interest in the Far East"

because of the well-developed Asian trade but also want to mark their distinctive participation in the European "Oriental Renaissance" (142–43).

39. As mentioned in Chapter 1, Dickinson wrote Sue enthusiastically about Spofford, marked one passage in Holmes's story, and had her attention called to two other paragraphs of this story by the note on Sam Bowles's calling card.

40. During the Civil War, there is a precipitous drop in the number of essays and poems of Orientalist bent published in the *Atlantic*. The issues through 1861, however, are full of articles, sketches, and verse using the language of Orientalism, often casually in passing—indicating how pervasive such discourse has become. Between 1857 and 1865, almost all essays with reference to Asia or using tropes of Orientalism are cut, suggesting that Dickinson or someone in her family read them.

41. As Obeidat acknowledges, this humanitarian desire is "occasionally colored by . . . cultural misconceptions and stereotypes." Arthur Christy's work remains the primary source of information on Orientalism in Whittier. Dickinson also knew the Orientalist poetry of Bayard Taylor, whose travel writing and poetry influenced Whittier's, according to Christy. Although Taylor's *Romances, Lyrics, and Songs* (Boston, 1852) in the family library contains no marks indicating her use, his "The Soldier and the Pard" might have influenced her "Civilization – spurns – the Leopard!" (F276), and Taylor writes the type of formally innovative and diverse poetry characterizing other of her favorite poets, as noted in Chapter 3. Schueller argues that Emerson increasingly represents Asia as transhistorical and passive in relation to a "westerly movement of civilization" represented by the U.S. (185, 165, 159). Even in his early writing, however, Emerson mapped binaries, in 1845 identifying Europe with "variety, boundary, freedom, and culture" and Asia with "unity, infinity, fate, [and] caste" in his journal (Stamy 12). Dickinson knew several of Emerson's translations of Persian poets, as printed in *May-Day and Other Pieces* (Ticknor and Fields, 1867, inscribed S. H. Dickinson; EDR 155); the volume contains markings and folded pages resembling Dickinson's in other volumes.

42. Patterson points out that Dickinson knew Goodrich's work for children, published under the pseudonym "Peter Parley," to whom she refers twice in poems, "Sic transit gloria mundi" (F2) and "I cant tell you – but you feel it –" (F164). Despite this familiarity with Goodrich/Parley, she departs radically from his attitudes. Patterson includes chapters on "Geography" and "Cardinal Points" without mention of Orientalism or Asian politics.

43. Bennett notes that the linking of southern and "darker" races was common (*Public Sphere* 266). For Dickinson, the southern reference is most often to Italy.

44. Dickinson knew the passage "O death, where is thy sting?" from 1 Corinthians 15:55; she quotes from 1 Corinthians 15 in "'Sown in dishonor'!" (F153), written the same year.

45. Edward Dickinson writes to Emily Norcross early in their courtship letters about his distress that Turkey has successfully invaded the Peloponnese and that Greece will now apparently lose her independence from the Ottoman Empire. Greek "wives and daughters" will now be "doomed to a fate *worse than death*," he writes, calling the Turks

"butchers—these blood-thirsty tyrants—these enemies of the human race. . . . ungodly savages" (*A Poet's Parents* 59–60).

46. The first reading of the spider as a figure for Dickinson as artist is in Gilbert and Gubar, *Madwoman in the Attic.*

47. Patterson argues that Dickinson reads the East as "arid" desert when it occurs in contrast to the West, but otherwise as "oriental wealth and fable" (195); she also understands Dickinson's West—not East—as associated with the "ocean, sea" and "eternity" (198). There is no question that Dickinson longs for the West as a site of immortality in some poems, but the West has no literal referent of foreignness for her as the East does. And for Dickinson, one may go West to arrive at the East.

48. A sixth poem about diving, "I'll clutch – and clutch –" (F385, 1862) involves a speaker seeking diamonds, but the plot of seeking a gift of great wealth and beauty and the sensuality of wearing jewelry are similar; here the speaker calls: "Diamonds – Wait – / I'm diving – just a little late – . . . I'll string you – in fine necklace – / Tiaras – make – . . . I'll show you at the Court – / Bear you – for Ornament / Where Women breathe –."

49. Dickinson copied this poem into Fas 1 and 14; in early 1859, she also sent a copy to Sue. I quote from Fas 1. "I took one Draught of Life –" (F396, 1862) uses a similar economic metaphor: "I paid – / Precisely an existence –" for that "Draught of Life."

50. Pearls are found in other parts of the world, but Dickinson and her contemporaries seemed to associate them with Asia. Patterson points out that Dickinson uses the word "pearl" far more than any other jewel, with thirty-one uses in poems and letters (the next highest is "amber" with twenty-three, then "diamond" with fourteen; 76, 77). Patterson also comments that the pearl is "the most sexually charged" of Dickinson's jewels (80). She does not discuss pearl divers, although she notes that *Othello* includes a reference to a "base Indian" who "threw a pearl away" and that Moore's *Lalla Rookh* also contains a pearl diver (86, 89).

51. Erkkila, "Emily Dickinson and Class"; Pollak, "Poetics of Whiteness"; Bennett, "'The Negro never knew'." Pollak's and Aife Murray's arguments comes closest to mine; Pollak claims that the poem absorbs racial stereotypes conjoining dark skin and phallic power but also figures whiteness as a burden and provides ambivalent critique of imperialism (89–92); Dickinson manipulates race in part, she argues, as a "politically subversive form of self-definition" (89). Murray writes that "if ever there was a Dickinson poem depicting the rightful ascendancy of the poor and the demise of the rich through their own self-admitted weakness and complacency, this is it" (*Maid* 162–63). Patterson refers to this poem as part of a larger argument, briefly developed, that Dickinson identifies herself as "Ethiopian" through repeated references to figures that are "spotted," "tawny," "swarthy" or obviously non-white (151–53).

52. My thanks to Polly Longsworth for calling this story, and the fact of Lavinia's subscription, to my attention.

53. Fields, "Diamonds and Pearls," *AM* March 1861; 371. Patterson imagines that Fields's essay is the source for Dickinson's "Malay" poems (88). Pollak includes an image from the November 1860 *Harper's* essay showing a dark-skinned pearl-diver, hypothesizing that this essay may have inspired Dickinson's "The Malay – took the Pearl"

("Illustrated Chronology" 245). Franklin repeats Johnson's speculation that Dickinson alludes to Robert Browning's "Paracelsus," which refers to "two points in the adventure of the diver," a "beggar" when he dives but "a prince" when "he rises with his pearl" (427). Goodrich's *Pictorial Geography* includes a picture of a pearl oyster in its pages on Asia (880). In the *Republican* a 23 June 1860 report ominously describes Japan itself as being like a pearl in relation to American trade: "Young America and manifest destiny will in the end carry the day; oyster shells once fairly opened rarely close again"—in other words, Japan will not retreat into isolation again. My point is that there were so many popular accounts of pearl divers that it is unlikely Dickinson had any single source.

54. Peter Wollen describes the modernist period's creative ideal as mixing the natural or wild and the artificial as inspired by Orientalism; Dickinson's Orientalism partakes in an idealized naturalism but instead stresses skilled human ability and lack of guile or affectation. According to Wollen, the Russian Ballet stimulated a frenzy of Orientalism in Paris in the 1910s: it was "both 'ultra-natural' (wild, untamed, passionate, chaotic, animal) and 'ultra-artificial' (fantastic, androgynous, bejewelled, decorative, decadent). It was represented as both barbaric and civilized, both wild and refined, both loose and disciplined" (27).

55. As Radhakrishnan summarizes, "The double bind of comparison works thus: on the one hand, operative methodology has to persuade each of the entities implicated in the comparison to reidentify itself with respect to the other; and on the other hand, it has the obligation to 'let each entity be' . . . rather than violate each in the name of the comparison" (461).

56. As written in Fas 1; variants are from a letter sent to Higginson four years later, 7 June 1862.

57. Repeated *d*s occur in: asked, And, wondering, hand, pressed, kingdom, And, bewildered, stand, asked, Had, And, sh'd, And, and flood as well as dikes and Dawn—a total of seventeen words out of the poem's forty-six.

58. In "How sick – to wait – in any place – but thine –" (F410, 1862) the speaker prefers being with "thou" to "the '*spicy isles* –' / And thou – not there –." "I held a Jewel" (F261, 1861) tells a story comparable to "It would never be Common – more – I said –"— where the speaker's riches disappear, leaving only, in the former case, "an Amethyst remembrance." In "Like Flowers, that heard the news of Dews," (F361, 1862) a moment of transformation is described as "The Heaven – unexpected come." "I had a daily Bliss" (F1029, 1865) relates the moment in which that previously "indifferent[ly]" viewed "Bliss" suddenly "Increased beyond my utmost scope."

59. This is one of Dickinson's few important early poems not preserved in her records. She sent a copy to Samuel Bowles without address or signature about 1861 and a copy to Susan signed "Emily" about 1865; I quote from the copy sent to Bowles. It is notable, however, that she either kept a copy of the poem for at least four years before discarding it or that, even having written hundreds of other poems in the meantime, she remembered this one.

60. References to the East and the sea also occur in Dickinson's letters during 1860 and 1861. She writes to Samuel Bowles, "You spoke of the 'East.' I have thought about it

this winter" (L220). She also invites Kate Turner to join her most intimate band of friends: "Dare you dwell in the *East* where we dwell" (L203). In 1861 she tells Bowles that "I pray for your sweet health – to 'Alla' – every morning" and then later "To take the pearl – costs Breath – but then a pearl is not impeached – let it strike the East!" (L241, L242).

61. Emerson's "Rommany Girl" asserts the superiority of her naturalness over "Pale Northern girls!" who "scorn our race" by describing herself, and other gypsies, in relation to natural phenomena of fertility and beauty: "My swarthy tint is in the grain, / The rocks and forest know it real. // The wild air bloweth in our lungs, / The keen stars twinkle in our eyes, / The birds gave us our wily tongues, / The panther in our dances flies." She also turns the tables on these scornful women, claiming "you are Gypsies in a mask, / And I the lady all the while" because no aspect of her appearance is artificial (*AM* November 1857, 46).

62. Richard Ellis suggests that "Perhaps the 'Peniel Hills' are the Pelham Hills visible from the Dickinson Homestead, the poet facing east at sunrise in identification with, yet in opposition to, her Biblical precursor as she rues her own latecomer status" (44).

63. Similarly, Dickinson defines "The Love a Life can show Below" by asserting that it is love that "enamors in the East" (F285 B, 1862); and "Your Riches – taught me – Poverty." imagines the privilege of "look[ing] on You" as "India – all Day" (F418 C, 1862).

64. See Appendix B for a list of these poems. I include "Did the Harebell loose her girdle" (F134) and "I have a King," (F157) in this number because of their significant reference to royalty (although there is no suggestion of travel), but do not include "'Tis so much joy!" with its phrase "O Gun at sea" (F170) or "To fight aloud, is very brave –" (F138) with its reference to fighting unobserved by "nations" and "Country." As a comparison, taking the first one hundred poems of 1863, Dickinson writes twenty-seven poems referring to royalty or foreignness, using the word "sea," or referring to travel beyond the standard tropes of changing seasons and death as distant from life (also not included in the 1860 count). Similarly, taking the two hundred poems written between 1875 and 1881 in sets of one hundred, Dickinson refers to royalty, the foreign, the sea, or travel in fourteen and then eighteen poems (F1352–1452, F1453–1553). As these counts show, reference to the foreign remains a part of her imaginative field but with less urgency than in 1860, when 63 percent of her poems make some such reference.

65. Variants are from a pencil copy sent to Sue in 1860; the primary text is from Fas 8.

66. The unevenness of the poem's meter, in its irregular variation between tetrameter, trimeter, and catalectic lines of five to eight syllables, also points toward "This is the sovereign Anguish! / This – the signal Wo!" as the key element connecting pain and transport, through the brevity of the latter (the only 5-syllable line in the poem) and the parallel line-initial "This."

67. In "Better – than Music!" (F378, 1862), Dickinson uses the same figure: a transformational moment in the speaker's life provides a new "stanza" or "tune" or "strain" that is a "Translation / Of all tunes I knew – and more –" anticipating the music of spiritual afterlife, and life is generally a "Rehearsal" for this more comprehensive "tune."

68. John Burroughs's "Expression" (*AM* November 1860) similarly states: "We cannot know one thing alone; two ideas enter into every distinct act of the understanding . . . we cannot distinguish white without having known black, nor evil without having

known good"; the "whole province of human knowledge . . . hinge[s] upon this principle" (573). "One's capacity for expression is also affected by his experience,—not experience in time and space, but soul-experience,—joy, sorrow, pleasure, pain, love" (576). Giles comments that Dickinson "internalizes the various discourses of geology . . . that were circulating widely in New England," creating textures of "estrangement" that "emerge naturally as inherent conditions of her nineteenth-century universe" (3).

69. Read with the typical elision of "Centuries" as two-syllable, the last two stanzas of the poem could be read as four lines of iambic pentameter rhyming aabb, metrically split. The falling rhythm of "While the Ages steal –" in isolation might seem to disrupt such an iambic base but, as is typical with split metrical lines, it sounds regularly iambic when heard together with the preceding five-syllable line: "Next time, to tarry, / While the Ages steal –" (uSuSu/SuSuS). The first stanza might also be heard as a 4-line unit of (12)(12)1010 rhyming aabb. The second stanza, however, is irregular in any reading of its patterns, calling attention to its definitional claims. Rhymes are marked b/b' where the rhyming is slant. I use the Fas 10 text; variants are from the copy sent to Susan in 1860. Poetic lines are identical in both copies.

70. The copy of this poem that Dickinson sent to Elizabeth Holland does not contain marked stanza breaks but has identical lineation. There is only one variant—"Though" for "But" in line 3. I quote from a fair copy written on stationery with a cake recipe on the opposite side; the poem concludes on a small fragment pinned to the larger sheet.

71. Patterson claims that Dickinson's late poems use such reference as "mere ornament" (152, 157).

72. These poems are preserved, respectively, on two fragments of stationery, pinned together (F1471); in a note to Sue (F1162); and in a retained pencil draft on a fragment of wrapping paper (a second copy was later sent to Susan but is now lost; F1509); and copies sent to Sue and Elizabeth Holland (F1563—I quote from the copy sent to Elizabeth). The 1865 poem (F942) is recorded in S7.

73. Similarly, Kirkby writes that "Dickinson shared with [New England evolutionary theologians] an excitement about the changing view of the world brought about by new scientific discoveries and the speculative possibilities inherent in these discoveries. Dickinson participated in the reconceptualization of the world that was taking place around her" (8).

74. Like the previously cited *SR* article that anticipates the unifying effects of the Atlantic cable, Douglass imagines this new community as partly the effect of technology: "whether the immediate struggle be baptized by the Eastern or Western wave of the waters between us, the water is one. . . . Steam, skill, and lightning, have brought the ends of the earth together" (I.323).

6. Reading and Writing the Civil War

1. This claim is also made by Shira Wolosky, "Public and Private" 103–32. Faith Barrett reviews recent writing on Dickinson and the war in "Dickinson and the Civil War, 1984–2007."

2. Although Dickinson may have circulated some of these poems and they were not saved, it seems unlikely since the correspondents she is most likely to have sent them to were good about preserving her letters: Sue, the Norcrosses, and Higginson.

3. This claim depends, of course, on what poems one considers to be responding to the war. For example, 'The only news I know' (F820), which she sends to Higginson, responds to the war only in its contrast of the speaker's "Bulletins" and "news" from those gripping the nation—that is, hers are not from the front but "From Immortality."

4. As Karen Dandurand explains, this was an important newspaper, professionally edited, with contributions by eminent writers including Holmes, Bryant, and Louisa May Alcott ("Dickinson Civil War Publications"). Dandurand believes that these poems were published "with at least her tacit consent" (22). Habegger is more skeptical, although his evidence stems from a failed appeal of Sue's to submit something of Emily's to another paper (*My Wars* 403).

5. Most criticism focuses either on individual poems or on the poet's personal stance toward the war (or toward slavery or race) in what Benjamin Friedlander aptly refers to as synthesizing narratives ("Ball's Bluff" 1583). Wolosky similarly claims that Dickinson "eschews a visionary grasp of the whole" in responding to the war ("Dickinson's War Poetry" 113). Criticism on individual poems has revolutionized our sense of the poet's religious, personal, and political responses to the war but, as Friedlander points out, tends to smooth away what is contradictory in her rhetoric and ideology. This chapter extends the work of Barrett ("Drums" and "Introduction" *WFH*) in providing further evidence of popular context for Dickinson's war writings, and that of Eliza Richards in seeing poetry and news as "interactive" during the war. Barrett also writes about Dickinson as testing out her responses to the war by representing various situational perspectives ("Drums" 114–15).

6. Although Bennett connects Dickinson's war poems to Browning's dramatic lyrics ("From Browning"), dramatic lyrics were widespread before and during the war. Friedlander also argues that Dickinson's war verse does not necessarily represent lasting or genuine convictions. As he says, Dickinson's "war poems distinguish themselves precisely in their openness to multiple interpretations" or in being "referentially indeterminate" ("Ball's Bluff," 1583, 1584). Stonum makes a similar point in writing about Dickinson's love poems: "reading was experience for her," he notes; her "extravagant literary representations of love" may come from the tradition of love literatures as much as from "personal relations and bodily sensations" ("Emily's Heathcliff" 22).

7. Fahs argues that Civil War poetry engaged in the crucial work of constructing national communities, or nation-building, and of attempting to process grief, especially in the disorienting circumstances of soldiers' deaths far from home and leaving no corporeal trace: no body to claim or grave to visit. Barrett sees Dickinson as participating actively in such nation-building and formation of community response, in *To Fight Aloud*.

8. Renee Bergland claims that war becomes a "visual spectacle" because of these new technologies, although she argues that Dickinson writes about "not seeing the war" (138).

9. Howe's "Battle Hymn" was also printed in the *SR* (16 January 1862). This poem's popularity is demonstrated in the *Republican*'s repetition of the phrase "marching on" from Howe's refrain. A 12 February "EXTRA" proclaims "Burnside still 'Marching

On!' "; on 17 February, "Burnside Marching On" appears as a headline and a story on the capture of Fort Donelson states: "Success still attends the federal arms, and our troops are still 'marching on' to victory and glory." On August 16 one still finds "Burnside Marching On."

10. Other well-known Whittier poems printed in the *AM* include "Astraea at the Capitol. Abolition of Slavery in the District of Columbia, 1862" (June 1862), "The Battle Autumn of 1862" (October 1862), "The Proclamation"—a celebration of the Emancipation Proclamation (February 1863); and "Barbara Frietchie" (October 1863).

11. Furness's "Our Soldiers" asserts that all must do what they can: "God grant that this spirit may obtain among us," "the spirit of all who do with love and zeal whatever their hands find to do, and sigh, not because it is so little, but because it is not better" (*AM* March 1864, 371). Holland's "The Heart of the War" (marked with two faint x's in the margin, EDR 546) appeared when Dickinson was in Cambridge for eye treatment. There is no way of knowing whether she had access to this issue in Cambridge or read it upon her return to Amherst.

12. Sedgwick characterizes rhetoric in the war-time *Atlantic* as generally making soldiers "willing instruments of divine justice" who "imitat[e] Christ's sacrificial death" (93).

13. Wolosky reads "The Martyr Poets – did not tell –" (F665, 1863) as related to this genre of war poems, presenting poets and "Painters" as martyrs seeking "the Art of Peace" in parallel to the soldiers-martyrs who more obviously "wrought their Pang" on battlefields rather than "in syllable" ("Public and Private"125).

14. Wolosky analyses the play on liberty as the right to own property in relation to Dickinson's economic metaphor in this poem ("Public and Private" 121–22). Barrett points out that Dickinson might have read "The Law of Costs" (*AM* February 1863) and traces the economic and political context for this poem ("Drums" 117–19). I am also indebted to conversation with Barrett for this poem's possible connection to the draft riots. Richards cites a poem by Whittier published in the *North American Review* in 1864 that similarly expresses a civilian's sense of guilt in relation to the war dead ("Dickinson and Civil War Media" 159).

15. Lincoln presents these propositions in conditional clauses I have not reproduced here.

16. This poem could not refer to Austin's draft and decision to pay a bounty for a substitute, since he was not drafted until May of 1864; there was a notice of his draft in the *SR* on 14 May (Leyda II, 88); several Amherst College faculty were drafted in 1864, and apparently all furnished a substitute.

17. Dickinson suggests the alternatives: "He gave himself to Balls," "remained alive," and "Urgency –" or "Vehemence to die" rather than "Greediness."

18. As stated in Chapter 3, the poem may also address Christian believers who place desire for a heavenly afterlife above the responsibilities and joys of living. These discourses are in fact related, since the war stimulated conversions, but in 1862 the context of war martyrology would probably have been dominant.

19. Anonymous (*SR* 11 January 1862). This would be the kind of poem Dickinson may parody with the bloodiness of her landscape in "The name – of it – is 'Autumn' –" (F465, written late in 1862), which ends with the tonally peculiar lines: "It sprinkles Bonnets – far

below – / It gathers ruddy Pools – / Then – eddies like a Rose – away – / Opon Vermillion Wheels –." These lines echo the "gory shower" that "Bedews" in "A Midnight Song" but have none of the force of the split vein and artery turning the "hue" of " 'Autumn' " that of "Blood" in her poem's opening lines.

20. A poem written in 1871 makes a similar point more sardonically, with reference to class: "Not any higher stands the Grave / For Heroes than for Men –" the poem begins, then concludes by stating that the "Leisure" of death "equal lulls / The Beggar and his Queen" (F1214)—pointedly reversing the terms of ownership to make the Queen her lowest countryman's possession, rather than him hers.

21. Also alluding to defeat in the context of war is "I should have been too glad, I see," which remarks that "Defeat – whets Victory – they say –" and concludes "Faith bleats to understand" (F283 C, 1862). "There is a flower that Bees prefer –" (F642, 1863) represents the (female) clover as "the Purple Democrat," with a "Public ... Providence ... [and] Progress" analogous to a nation's. This "sturdy" flower is also:

The Bravest – of the Host –
Surrendering – the last –
Nor even of Defeat – aware –
When cancelled by the Frost –

The bravery of the final stanza is that of an individual sacrificing her life ("pro patria"?) with such willingness that neither surrender nor death brings consciousness of "Defeat"—making defeat a subjective experience.

22. See Polly Longsworth for details about enlistment and information about church bells tolling. Leyda quotes the *SR* reporting that Amherst was lax in filling its quotas mid-war but in May 1864 voted to raise the money to fill all past quotas and to provide both the draft substitutes currently needed and fifty more that were anticipated for the coming July (II 88).

23. This is the argument of Randall Fuller, who quotes Emerson saying to a friend that Hawthorne wrote the notes as well as the essay.

24. Shoptaw argues that she writes three elegies to Lincoln, on the basis of her use of words like "Chief" (F993) and "Excellence" (F1013) in poems about the death of a great or important person; also "Step lightly on this narrow spot –" (F1227, 1871) refers to a "name ... told / As far as Cannon dwell," and was written at the time that Lincoln's body was being transferred to the newly completed Lincoln Monument in Springfield. Shoptaw notes that Dickinson sent this elegy to Higginson, who would have understood its reference ("Civil War Poetics" 16–17).

25. According to Erkkila, Dickinson clings to a "royalist dream of rule by heredity and divine right" (*Wicked Sisters* 51). This seems to me an exaggerated response to the evidence, although there is no doubt that Dickinson used such vocabulary. Cynthia Hogue suggests Dickinson's support for slaves' suffering. Pollak argues that Dickinson is "ambivalent about her whiteness" and writes poems that both absorb racial stereotypes and project a "larger vision" of desired hybridity or cancelled racial exclusions ("Poetics of Whiteness" 84, 90, 92).

26. See also Chapter 1 on "The Black Berry – wears a Thorn in his side –" (F548, 1863).

27. Her attitudes may have been changing as early as late 1859 when, after receiving a book by radical abolitionist Theodore Parker, she comments to Mary Bowles that she had heard "he was 'poison.' Then I like poison very well" (L213). Dickinson also read at least one book by Lydia Maria Child, an author her father encouraged his fiancée to read early in their courtship (*Poet's Parents* 16–17).

28. Murray accurately describes Dickinson's comments about the Irish and African Americans as "fairly benign for that time" and as more place-holding and patronizing than derogatory (*Maid* 168–69). William Dean Howells remarks already in 1869 that "the nation had grown tired of racial issues" (Wineapple 175). Martin Griffin writes persuasively about the "war over cultural memory" (2 and passim).

29. Sue responded to the *SR* 1862 publication of "Safe in their Alabaster Chambers –" (F124) with a note saying "It takes as long to start our Fleet as the Burnside" (Leyda II 46).

30. Quoted in Erkkila, from a letter printed *SR* 17 October 1861 ("Art of Politics" 156). Edward Dickinson also gave public speeches in opposition to the extension of slavery and secession when he was in Congress during the 1850s. Coleman Hutchison provides a detailed reading of Edward Dickinson's career and the Whig party.

31. "Confiscation and Emancipation," 2 August 1862; "Proclamation by the President. Emancipation Declared the First of January," 23 September 1862; "The President's Proclamation," 24 September 1862. The *Atlantic* was equally strongly Republican in its loyalties. On the importance of this coverage, see McPherson, *Drawn with the Sword* 78 and Sedgwick 102, 96. Among its regular contributors were abolitionists Whittier, Child, Charles Sumner, Edward Lillie Pierce, and Harriet Beecher Stowe as well as Higginson and Emerson, and by 1862 every issue contained multiple pieces dealing with some aspect of the war or slavery. For example, Emerson writes a four-page encomium in November 1862 ("The President's Proclamation" 638–42), preceded by an equally celebratory essay titled "The Hour and the Man" by C. C. Hazewell (625–30). Before April 1862, when Dickinson first sent him her poems, Higginson had published articles there pronouncing the evils of slavery and necessity of social reform—including one heroizing Nat Turner as a rebel comparable to Eastern European freedom fighters. We know that Dickinson probably read them because she writes Higginson that she has read his "Chapters in the Atlantic" (25 April 1862, L261) and in 1870 she asks about an essay he's written, commenting that it is "perhaps the only one you wrote that I never knew" (L352).

32. A 16 August 1862 *SR* editorial states that "it is true as [Robert Dale Owen] says that the people of the North are daily growing more in favor of this measure" ("Emancipation as a War Policy"). The *Republican* was overly optimistic in assuming that by September 1862 most Unionists supported emancipation even as a pragmatic measure to win the war, but by the time of Lincoln's reelection in 1864 this was the case.

33. Leyda, II, 77. Leyda provides an extensive account of Edward Dickinson's support for the war as well as the many reports in the *Republican* of information following Higginson's activity as Colonel of the first company of black volunteers, beginning in November 1862. He also quotes from George C. Shepard's 24 July 1864 diary, where he

comments that "Mr. E. Dickinson . . . has always been in action *a conservative* or a pro slavery man as I think, but he has now forgotten it"—implying that Shepard sees a change in Edward's attitude, whether or not he is correct in his assessment of Edward's earlier stance (II, 92).

34. The concept of liberty was defined differently in the North and South, and in the North among ardent abolitionists and those opposed to emancipation but pro-Union. In "Pondering 'Liberty'," I argue that Dickinson makes partisan use of this word in some poems. I do agree, however, with Michele Kohler that Dickinson criticizes the antebellum patriotic "reliance on a linear, teleological model of temporality" (22).

35. It was set as "Ol Massa on he trabbels gone," by S. K. Whiting; as "Song of the Negro Boatmen" by J. W. Dadman; as "The Freedman's Song" by Robert Goldbeck; as "The Contrabands" by A. J. Higgins; and as "The 'Contraband' of Port Royal" by Ferdinand Mayer. Cohen notes that this portion of Whittier's poem was, paradoxically, more widely sung than any song by African Americans, although "Let My People Go" (first printed 13 December 1851) "by mid-1862 had become a catchphrase for emancipation" and was sung widely in the North ("Contraband Singing" 282, 283, 286). See www.pdmusic .org/civilwar2.html for a list of Civil War songs, including the author of the lyrics and composer or arranger.

36. Similarly, a poem is introduced as "A Soldier's Dirge, Sung at the Funeral of Capt G. F. Tannat [To Music by George Kingsley]" *SR* 23 August 1862. Under "Literary Gleanings," the *SR* notes that in his "new Hymn for Mothers" Bryant "breathes forth the mother's praise in these sweet lines, that will be read and sung for aye and for aye" (*SR* 8 February 1862). Rewriting and parody were also common. Henry Leigh Hunt's popular "Abou Ben Adhem," was parodied at least twice during the war. Hunt's poem begins: "Abou Ben Adhem (may his tribe increase!) / Awoke one night from a dream of peace, / And saw . . . An angel writing in a book of gold." One parody praises General Butler as "Abou Ben Butler (may his tribe increase!) / Awoke one night down by the old Belize, / And saw . . . A black man shivering in the winter's cold" (Moore 73, 23). Randall's "My Maryland" was rewritten and parodied as "Florida, My Florida," "Michigan, My Michigan," and "Maryland, My Maryland (A Northern Reply)"; see Abel 75 and Kushner. Cohen also notes that "Let My People Go" was widely parodied by 1862 ("Contraband Singing" 286). I am indebted to Bert Barnett for calling several Civil War rewritings, parodies, and song books to my attention.

37. Barrett argues that the confluence of song and poetry affects Dickinson's construction of communal address in her war-time poems (*To Fight Aloud*).

38. According to Fahs, the number of periodicals published "greatly increased" and the circulation of established periodicals was enlarged (57).

39. Thomas Manahan's poem "Brother, Tell Me of the Battle" was most popular as put to music by George F. Root, and Root is typically listed as its author (Miller, "Preface" *WFH* xix).

40. Barrett persuasively argues that "The Gun," published in the 4 July 1863 *Harper's Weekly* stimulates Dickinson to write "My Life had stood – a Loaded Gun –" (F764), but she is not composing to its rhythm.

41. In the *AM* Dickinson would also have read Celia Thaxter 's "The Minute-Guns" (July 1862); Whittier's "The Battle Autumn of 1862" (October 1862), with its lament that "Nature changes not" even in the midst of war and hope that the harvest anticipates the coming of freedom; and Annie Fields's "Waiting," which describes a "note of joy" in Autumn, even though "Under the flowers my soldier lies" (December 1862). Other poems in the *AM* indicate that war hovers in their background but do not refer to it. Whitney's "Per Tenebras, Lumina" compares the changing seasons to human mortality and then concludes "Dear country of our love and pride! / So is thy stormy winter given! / So, through the terrors that betide, / Look up, and hail thy kindling heaven!" (January 1862). See Barrett and Miller, *WFH* for an extensive collection of poems written by Northern and Southern women and men, white and black, during the war.

42. Although the image of an eviscerated landscape is terrible, the over-the-top language may make this poem a parody of other such pieces in the popular press. See my analysis of the poem's complex tonal registers, without regard to the war (*Comic Power* 130–32, 134). Cody argues that this poem refers to a particular New England location— the "Basin" in the White Mountains of New Hampshire.

43. I am indebted to Wolosky's reading of this poem as a "traumatized" sunset (*Voice* 38).

44. Barrett remarks on the "inadequacy of first-person expressive lyric stances to bear witness to suffering on [the] scale" of the Civil War (*To Fight Aloud ms* 6, 40).

45. This is an enjambment that most readers do not notice, reading as if the sentence concludes with "His face all Victory." Maurice Lee reads this poem skeptically, as though Dickinson challenges the fantasy of the convention of reunion in heaven (1127). Because many of her poems anticipate reunion between loved ones in heaven, and other poems represent soldiers as martyrs, however, the elements of the poem Lee reads as critical of popular war culture seem to me instead to be modes Dickinson took at least to some extent seriously. Richards's hypothesis that this poem is written from a Confederate perspective because its use of "Yonder Maryland" suggests proximity to that state also seems to me unpersuasive (169).

46. Alternate wording in Fas 24 makes the "Braveries" in the penultimate line "His": "Braveries, remote as this / In Yonder Maryland –" might be "Braveries, remote as His" or "just sealed" or "proved –/ In Scarlet Maryland –" (F 518). In "A Loyal Woman's No," Lucy Larcom heroizes both soldiers and the women who support them: "Heroes who poured their blood out for the Truth, / Women whose hearts bled, martyrs all unknown, / Here catch the sunrise of immortal youth // On their pale cheeks and consecrated brows!"— both "Heroes" and "Women" are "martyrs, all" and "consecrated" (*AM* December 1863).

47. See Faust 5–11, and Saint Armand 46–59. Saint Armand refers to the "craft of dying" in this period (59) and sees Dickinson as satirizing what he calls the "weeping woman paradigm" and sentimentalized death culture in some poems (50–52).

48. Pierpont's "My Child" includes description of the dead child. As Dickinson writes out the poem (altering punctuation), it includes lines such as: "He lives; . . . In dreams I see him now- / And, on his angel brow, / I see it written—'thou shalt see me *there*!' // Yes, we all live to God! –" (20 April 1856, L183).

49. Longfellow's poem was first published in the *Knickerbocker Magazine*, 1838, and frequently anthologized, as well as included in his *Poems* (1850).

50. An alternative line in Fas 16 provides "Here's a keepsake for the Hills," another typical gesture for the departing soldier, assuming "Hills" functions as a synecdoche for home, or sweetheart (F338).

51. One might criticize this poem for representing African Americans as passive recipients of freedom—merely unhatched fledglings until some "You" stimulates their birth into freedom. The poem is, however, clearly not "about" African Americans, as such, even though its construction of freedom borrows from emancipation discourse. This is one of the places where Dickinson's indeterminate referentiality can be troubling, since a politically engaged reading of the poem desires some sign of concern on her part for the historical realities of slaves' lives.

52. "The Soul has Bandaged moments –" (F360, 1862) and "A Prison gets to be a friend –" (F456, 1862) also involve liberty, but in both cases unambiguously from imprisonment rather than enslavement.

53. Prayer was frequently invoked in poetry as the duty of civilians, especially women.

54. Wolosky argues that although "He gave away his Life –" "concludes with a tribute to heroism and the infinite value of the transfigured individual" it places the community "in a compromised position" in leaving it only to weep, wonder, and decay ("Public and Private" 120).

55. Stoddard's "To the Men of the North and West" appeared in the *Evening Post*, 17 April 1861; rptd *WFH* 47.

56. Here, as previously indicated, Dickinson echoes Austin's words as she reported them in a letter to Bowles: "Austin is chilled – by Frazer's murder – He says – his Brain keeps saying over 'Frazer is killed' – 'Frazer is killed,' just as Father told it – to Him" (L256). Barrett discusses the impact of Stearns's death on Dickinson in *To Fight Aloud*.

57. "Accomplices. Virginia, 1865" (later reprinted as "By the Potomac") by Thomas Bailey Aldrich, includes the lines "[Nature] Sets her birds singing, while she spreads her green / Mantle of velvet where the Murdered lie" (*AM* July 1865). In an essay on Aldrich, Edgar Fawcett calls this sonnet "the most perfect of the few good poems which our late war produced" (*AM* December 1874, 673). In "Pondering 'Liberty'," I described Dickinson's use of the word "murder" as more exceptional than it appears to me now. She uses the word "murder" only three times in her poems, all during the war.

58. Eberwein traces Dickinson's development in learning to write an effective letter of condolence in "Messages of Condolence." One might be able to trace a similar development in poems of consolation, or responding to death.

59. The nation was frequently referred to as the "State," for example, in Holmes, "Choose you this Day whom Ye will Serve," where "tyrants" fear and hate "The self-ruling, chain-breaking, throne-shaking State!" (*AM* March 1863, 288).

60. Other poems perhaps spoken in a soldier's voice include "Afraid! Of whom am I afraid?"—which may take the soldier's boastfulness as a model for fearing neither "Death" nor "Life" nor "Resurrection" (F345); "I read my sentence – steadily –" (F432); and "A Night – there lay the Days between –" (which may be in the voice of a sentry, with

its reference to the "Slow – Night – that must be watched away –" F609). "Did you ever stand in a Cavern's Mouth –" also asks "Did you ever look in a Cannon's face –" and presents the speaker as having to face "The Question of 'To die' –" (F619), hence may suggest a speaking soldier.

61. In an alternate, Dickinson writes "Eternity's cool Flag – in front –" (F453).

62. MacKenzie and Dana's *Wider than the Sky* contains several testimonials and some analysis of ways that Dickinson's poetry continues to help mourners grieve.

63. Judith Butler also makes this point: "the body implies mortality, vulnerability . . . [and hence] has its invariably public dimension" (15).

64. Dickinson also writes two poems about peace, both in 1863: "A Tooth opon Our Peace" (F694) and "I many times thought Peace had come" (F737).

65. Friedlander provides this information, and argues that the poem was written in 1861, not 1863 as Franklin surmises ("Ball's Bluff"). Dickinson may indeed have written with the two 1861 poems in mind that Friedlander cites, but she also read innumerable other battle poems, and she often responded to or rewrote poems years after first reading them. She wrote no other poems directly in reference to the Civil War in 1861 whereas in early 1863 she wrote several that raise similar questions about the extent of God's attention to the war's human loss and pain. The many facts that do not exactly match up suggest that the narrative is largely fictional whenever she wrote it and whether or not she had a particular mother or soldier in mind.

66. Of the five circulated poems I mention here only two are written during the war. Dickinson writes "Safe in their Alabaster Chambers –" (F124) in 1859 and sends it to Sue in 1861; she mails "I should have been too glad, I see –" (F283C, 1862) to the Norcrosses and sends one stanza to Sue; she sends three lines of "The only news I know" (F820) to Higginson in the summer of 1863 as well as writing it into Fas 27; she sends "Not any higher stands the Grave" (F1214, 1871) to Higginson about two years after writing it; and she sends "Step lightly on this narrow spot –" (F1227, 1871; S9) to Higginson, also sending one stanza to Sue. Dickinson makes and signs a fair copy of "Good to have had them lost" (F809), beginning "Sweet, to have had them lost," but does not mail it; and she makes and folds but does not sign or send a fair copy of "They leave us with the Infinite" (F352).

Coda: Portrait of a Non-Publishing Poet

1. Although White does not say so, she seems to mean late in Dickinson's lifetime; we have no evidence of such an audience in the 1860s.

2. First cousin Anna Norcross Swett recalled to her descendants that "'Dickinson would open the window or the curtains and say poetically what she saw outdoors in the garden or a bird or whatever it was'"; according to her granddaughter, Swett "described this experience as observing Dickinson 'talk poetry.'" Louisa Norcross also wrote in 1904 in the *Woman's Journal*: "'I know that Emily Dickinson wrote most emphatic things in the pantry, so cool and quiet, while she skimmed the milk; because I sat on the footstool behind the door, in delight, as she read them to me.'" Martha Dickinson Bianchi similarly reports that Dickinson read her poems aloud in an unpublished biographical narrative "Life Before Last"—referred to in Hart 359. See also Ackmann 123.

3. In fact, new evidence of such potential widespread reprinting has just arisen: "Success is counted sweetest" (F112) was published in the *Brooklyn Daily Union* 27 April 1864, then again in 1878 in *A Masque of Poets,* and in 1882 it was reprinted on the first page of the November issue of the *Amateur Journal,* from Judsonia, Arkansas. My thanks to Lara Cohen for sharing this discovery.

4. As Mitchell notes, we cannot know exactly what the manuscript that was sent to the *Republican* looked like. Mitchell agrees that the emphasis in Dickinson's letter is a concern that Higginson not think her dishonest (*Measures* 33; see 32–48 on this poem).

5. It is also noteworthy that the 1872 copy to Susan, seven years after "The Snake" was published, repunctuates the notorious lines as "You may have met him? Did you not / His notice instant is"—making it unambiguous that a new clause begins with "Did you not." Dickinson also returns to her initial choice of "instant" in line 2 (F1096 C).

6. No title is given 30 July 1859 for what the paper calls "pretty versifications by a Mr. Halifax, another new English poet, written during the Crimean war:—" and several poems are given a generic title like "Song" or "Hymn," or more specifically "Sonnet" or "The Old Hymn"—the latter two by Mrs. A. M. Butterfield (21 January and 10 February 1860). The *AM* also publishes several poems with generic titles such as "Sonnet."

7. See Chapter 6, note 4. The poems she sent this paper had nothing to do with the war and were written considerably earlier: "Flowers – Well – if anybody" (F95 B; 1859), "These are the days when Birds come back –" (F122 C; 1859); and "Blazing in Gold –" (F321 A; 1862).

8. To put this positively, in 1861 Dickinson preserved 91 percent of her poems; between 1862 and 1865, she preserved 98 or 99 percent, or all but one to four poems a year. After 1875, she preserved only an average of 69.5 percent of her poems. For example, in 1879, while Dickinson keeps a fair copy of "A Route of Evanescence" (F1489) as well as mailing this poem to six friends or acquaintances, she does not keep a copy of "Those not live yet" (F1486)—a poem sent to Susan Dickinson using the phrase "Costumeless Consciousness," or " 'Heavenly Father' – take to thee" (F1500), sent to Ned, or "A little overflowing word" (F1501), a longer and not occasional poem addressed "Susan" and signed "Emily" without other comment.

9. In *Rowing in Eden,* Martha Nell Smith argues that Dickinson may regard her circulation of poems as "publication," as distinct from printing (15).

10. Mitchell similarly concludes that "Material signals given by Dickinson's forms of inscription do not support the idea that she was attempting to defamiliarize received certainties about generic boundaries" (*Measures* 187).

11. In *Wicked Sisters,* Betsy Erkkila argues that Barrett Browning inveighs against editorial interference with a writer's work and perhaps all publication. Aurora insists that the poet "will not suffer the best critic known / To step into his sunshine of free thought / And self-absorbed conception and exact / An inch-long swerving of the holy lines"; she contrasts art "for praise or hire" with pure art: "Eschew such serfdom," she directs. Dickinson does not mark these passages.

12. On lexicography during the mid-nineteenth century, see Deppman, chapter 4.

13. *Measures* (71–72, 92–95). Sue also ignored Dickinson's scriptural lineation. As examples of changes in punctuation, see "So set it's Sun in Thee" (F940) and "On this

wondrous sea" (F3)—where she also omits two lines in one transcription. In "Besides the Autumn poets sing" (F123 A) Sue adds a title, changes words, and ignores an underlining. Sue showed the same lack of fidelity to "the aggregate of precise material details embodied in the manuscripts" as Mable Todd and Higginson, Mitchell concludes (95).

14. "The Robin is a Gabriel" was sent to Sarah Tuckerman and to the Norcrosses. A pencil draft containing the first two lines and two later lines remained among Dickinson's papers but not a copy of the entire poem (F1520 B).

15. As sent to Mary and Eben Loomis; to Charles Clark she does not capitalize either "A" or "It" (F1672).

16. In his 1891 essay on Dickinson, Higginson comments that "she was utterly careless of greater irregularities" and that "with her usual naïve adroitness she turns my point" in response to his comments ("Emily Dickinson's Letters," 6). He does not specify what irregularities he has mentioned to her.

17. See Chapter 1, note 18, for these statistics. After 1866, to our knowledge, she sends at most two poems to correspondents three or more years after their composition: in 1883 she may send Todd a poem written in 1871, and in 1883 she sends an 1880 poem to Niles.

18. These phrases are from the essays "Subject, Predicate, Object" and "Idiosyncracy and Technique" (*Complete Prose* 505, 508).

19. In 1858 and 1859, Dickinson mails Sue around a quarter of the poems she is writing, and in 1860 she mails Sue 37 percent of her compositions. Between 1861 and 1865, she mails Sue only between 8 and 17 percent of her compositions (from 10 to 29 poems a year), mostly around 10 percent. From 1866 on, she sends Sue a smaller number of poems (usually from three to eight a year), but these numbers at times constitute around 50 percent of the poems she is writing. Before 1866, Dickinson keeps around 94 percent of the poems sent to Sue but thereafter she keeps only slightly more than half. In the years 1873, 1879, 1881, and 1884, she retains only around 10 percent of the poems sent to Sue.

20. Dickinson begins corresponding with Higginson just six days after Bowles leaves for Europe in 1862, supporting the idea that she required at least a few intelligent, perceptive, and more or less supportive correspondents during the early 1860s.

21. Between 1860 and 1865, only between 1 and 6 poems a year are kept (usually in fair copy) but not bound into a fascicle or set. From 1866 to 1870, she writes a total of 72 poems, 15 of which are sent without a copy being retained and 41 are written on scraps, pinned together, drafted on the same page as other poems, or otherwise indicate that they are not record copies. If one regards the making of fair copies as a sign of Dickinson's intentional preservation, it would seem that only 23 percent of the poems written in these five years are intentionally retained. This is in contrast to the average 97 percent deliberately preserved in the previous six years (1860–1865). After her brief return to making sets, that is, after 1875, Dickinson retains very few poems in fair copy.

22. Others have suggested that nineteenth-century stories about unpublished, unknown writers who became famous after their deaths encouraged Dickinson to think that publication during her lifetime was not necessary for eventual fame. In *Aurora Leigh,* the poet imagines a poem as passed "from hand to hand" to future generations, which finally see its worth (75). In "Really Indigenous Productions," Loeffelholz concludes

that Dickinson "learned from print culture how to be an unpublished manuscript poet" (196). Finnerty writes that Americans romanticized Tennyson as a reclusive and solitary writer associated with the "English wilderness," hence that he provided a model of a poet whose relative solitude enabled him to write. Moreover, Tennyson's famed refusal of cultural dictates and celebrity may have encouraged Dickinson to connect both non-conformity and the "indirect route to fame" (by spurning it during one's lifetime) with "literary immortality" ("'Dreamed of your meeting Tennyson'" 61, 63). In contrast, Michael Kearns understands Dickinson as committed exclusively to "publishing by manuscript" rather than anticipating posthumous publication (42, 72, and passim).

23. Even in the period between 1871 and 1875, when she returns to making sets, she is sporadic in her copying: although she copies thirty-three poems in 1871, she copies only six in 1872, one in 1873, four in 1874, and fourteen in 1875.

24. Franklin asserts that the "unresolved readings" of the poems copied into book-lets and containing variant words or revisions indicate that they "were not intended for others" (20). The fact that Dickinson continues to circulate these poems years after copying them and the fact of their careful preservation at all, however, suggests that she was amenable to their circulation or publication. As I discuss previously, it may also be that Dickinson could well imagine multiple versions of a poem written with variant words, or copied into more than one fascicle, such that she did not feel the need to decide for herself among its possibilities.

25. She kept for herself only a pencil copy written on two fragments of stationery, pinned together, and including a spelling correction and interlined revision; other manuscripts contain alternate wording.

26. Finnerty sees Dickinson as responding negatively to the contemporary cult of celebrity, with its "new degrees of closeness and intimacy" readers desired with their literary idols, feeling that it "denigrated literature and transformed poets into commodities" ("'Dreamed of your meeting Tennyson'" 60).

27. Gordon maps the complex emotional stakes of the various players involved with Dickinson's manuscripts after her death. Although many women published and Dickinson admired some of them extravagantly, there were still cultural and social factors mitigating against the propriety of publishing for middle-class women in the nineteenth century, which Dickinson seems to have felt strongly.

28. This is one of the rare serious poems that Dickinson does not retain. When sending it to Sue, Dickinson adds the line "Tri Victory –" and changes the word "sends" to "gives" (in the line "God sends us Women –"). To Bowles, she adds the message "Here's – what I had to 'tell you' – You will tell no other? Honor – is it's own pawn –" (L250). To Sue, she appends "Emily."

29. Loeffelholz speculates that Dickinson's circulation of poems "accentuates the separation between writer and reader," rather than overcoming such presumed distance ("Master Shakespeare" 46).

30. The fragment of wrapping paper on which this poem was saved also contains a different spelling at the end: "Thermopolae." In a secondary way, "Go tell it" may also allude to Mark 16:15, where Christ instructs his followers "Go ye into all the world, and preach the gospel to every creature" because telling may bring salvation.

31. See Guthrie's "Law, Property, and Provincialism in Dickinson's Poems and Letters to Judge Otis Phillips Lord."

32. Dickinson also uses the adjective "sweet" with "country" in "My country need not change her gown," (F1540, 1880)—a poem she sent to Higginson, requesting his approval to donate it to a charity. The poem refers to the Revolutionary War as still guiding the principles of the United States, referring to "something in their attitude / That taunts her [Great Britain's] bayonet." The poem exists only as published in *Poems,* despite the fact that Dickinson mailed it to Higginson and the Norcrosses, and perhaps also to Todd. She retained no copy of her own.

WORKS CITED

Abel, E. Lawrence. *Singing the New Nation: How Music Shaped the Confederacy 1861–1865.* Mechanicsburg, PA: Stackpole Books, 2000.

Ackmann, Martha. "'I'm Glad I Finally Surfaced': A Norcross Descendent Remembers Emily Dickinson." *EDJ* 5.2 (1996): 120–26.

Adams, Stephen J. *An Introduction to Meters, Verse Forms, and Figures of Speech.* Toronto: Broadview Press, 1997.

Agamben, Giorgio. *The End of the Poem: Studies in Poetics.* Translated by Daniel Heller-Roazen. Stanford: Stanford University Press, 1999.

Arac, Jonathan. "Afterword: Lyric Poetry and the Bounds of New Criticism." In *Lyric Poetry: Beyond New Criticism,* edited by Chaviva Hošek and Patricia Parker, 345–55. Ithaca: Cornell University Press, 1985.

Atlantic Monthly. Review of James R. Lowell's *Fresh Hearts that Failed Three Thousand Years Ago. AM* 5.32 (1860): 759.

———. Review of John G. Whittier's *Home Ballads and Poems. AM* 6.37 (November 1860): 637–39.

Attridge, Derek. *Poetic Rhythm: An Introduction.* Cambridge: Cambridge University Press, 1995.

Barrett, Faith. "'Drums off the Phantom Battlements': Dickinson's War Poems in Discursive Context." In Smith and Loeffelholz, *Companion.* 107–32.

———. "Introduction." In *WFH.* 1–22.

———."Public Selves and Private Spheres: Studies of Emily Dickinson and the Civil War, 1984–2007." *EDJ* 16.1 (2007): 92–104.

———. *"To Fight Aloud is Very Brave": American Poetry and the Civil War.* Amherst: University of Massachusetts Press, 2012.

Barrett, Thomas. "Southern Living (In Captivity): The Caucasus in Russian Popular Culture." *Journal of Popular Culture* 31.4 (1998): 75–93.

Barrett Browning, Elizabeth. *Aurora Leigh* 1856; New York: St. Francis & Co., 1857.

———. *Poems.* 2 vols. New York: C. S. Francis & Co., 1852.

Beach, Christopher. *Introduction to 20th-Century American Poetry.* New York: Cambridge University Press, 2003.

Bell, Michael J. "'No Borders to the Ballad Maker's Art': Francis James Child and the Politics of the People." *Western Folklore* 47.4 (1988): 285–307.

———. "'The Only True Folk Songs We Have in English': James Russell Lowell and the Politics of the Nation." *Journal of American Folklore* 108.428 (1995): 131–55.

Benfey, Christopher. "'A Route of Evanescence': Emily Dickinson and Japan." *EDJ* 16.2 (2007): 81–93.

Bennett, Paula Bernat. "From Browning to the American Civil War: Dickinson and the American Dramatic Monologue." Paper presented at "'Were I Britain born': Dickinson's Transatlantic Connections," Oxford, Eng., August 2010.

———. "'The Negro never knew': Emily Dickinson and Racial Typology in the Nineteenth Century." *Legacy* 19.1 (2002): 53–61.

———. *Poets in the Public Sphere: The Emancipatory Project of American Women's Poetry, 1800–1900.* Princeton: Princeton University Press, 2003.

Bergland, Renee. "The Eagle's Eye: Dickinson's View of Battle." In Smith and Loeffelholz, *Companion.* 133–56.

Bianchi, Martha Dickinson. *Emily Dickinson: Face to Face.* New York: Houghton Mifflin, 1932.

Blight, David. *Race and Reunion: The Civil War in American Memory.* Cambridge: Harvard University Press, 2001.

Bloch, Julia. "Lyric Descent: A Soft Polemic." *P/Queue* 7 (2010): 33–40.

Browner, Stephanie. "Love & Conquest: The Erotics of Colonial Discourse in Emily Dickinson's Poems and Letters." Dickinson Electronic Archive, Classroom Electric.

Bryant, William Cullen. *Poems.* Philadelphia: Carey and Hart, 1849.

———. *Prose Writings,* edited by Parke Godwin. New York: D. Appleton, 1884.

Buckingham, Willis. "Poetry Readers and Reading in the 1890s: Emily Dickinson's First Reception." In *Readers in History: Nineteenth-Century American Literature and the Contexts of Response,* edited by James L. Machor, 164–79. Baltimore: John Hopkins University Press, 1993.

———, ed. *Emily Dickinson's Reception in the 1890s: A Documentary History.* Pittsburgh: University of Pittsburgh Press, 1989.

Buell, Lawrence. *New England Literary Culture: From Revolution through Renaissance.* New York: Cambridge University Press, 1989.

Burt, Stephen. *Close Calls with Nonsense: Reading New Poetry.* Minneapolis: Graywolf, 2009.

Butler, Judith. "Violence, Mourning, Politics." *Studies in Gender and Sexuality* 4.1 (2003): 9–37.

Cameron, Sharon. *Choosing Not Choosing: Dickinson's Fascicles.* Chicago: University of Chicago Press, 1993.

———. *Lyric Time: Dickinson and the Limits of Genre.* Baltimore: Johns Hopkins University Press, 1979.

Capps, Jack. *Emily Dickinson's Reading, 1846–1886.* Cambridge: Harvard University Press, 1966.

Chaichit, Chanthana. "Emily Dickinson Abroad: The Paradox of Seclusion." *EDJ* 5.2 (1996): 162–68.

Chalice Hymnal. St. Louis: Chalice Press, 1995.

Child, Francis James. "Ballad Poetry." In *Johnson's Universal Cyclopedia.* 464–68. New York: Appleton, 1874.

Christy, Arthur. "Orientalism in New England: Whittier." *American Literature* 1.4 (1930): 372–92.

———. "The Orientalism of Whittier." *American Literature* 5.3 (1933): 247–57.

Cody, David. "Blood in the Basin: The Civil War in Emily Dickinson's 'The name of it is Autumn'." *EDJ* 12.1 (2003): 25–52.

———. "'When one's soul is at a white heat': Dickinson and the Azarian School." *EDJ* 19.1 (2010): 30–59.

Cohen, Michael. "Contraband Singing: Poems and Songs in Circulation during the Civil War." *American Literature* 82.2 (2010): 271–304.

———. "Peddlars, Poems, and Local Culture: The Case of Jonathan Plummer, a 'Balladmonger' in Nineteenth-Century New England." *ESQ* 54.5 (2008): 9–32.

———. "Whittier, Ballad Reading, and the Culture of Nineteenth-Century Poetry." *Arizona Quarterly* 64.3 (2008): 1–29.

Crumbley, Paul. *Inflections of the Pen: Dash and Voice in Emily Dickinson*. Lexington: University Press of Kentucky, 1997.

———. *Winds of Will: Emily Dickinson and the Sovereignty of Democratic Thought*. Tuscaloosa: University of Alabama Press, 2010.

Culler, Jonathan. *The Pursuit of Signs: Semiotics, Literature, Deconstruction*. Ithaca: Cornell University Press, 1981.

———. *Structuralist Poetics: Structuralism, Linguistics, and the Study of Literature*. Ithaca: Cornell University Press, 1975.

———. "Why Lyric?" Paper presented at "Genre," The English Institute, Cambridge, Massachusetts, September 2009.

Cummins, Maria. *El Fureidîs*. Boston: Ticknor and Fields, 1860.

Curtis, George W. "Longfellow." *AM* 12.73 (December 1863): 760–76.

Cushman, Stephen. *Fictions of Form in American Poetry*. Princeton: Princeton University Press, 1993.

Dana, Charles A., ed. *The Household Book of Poetry*. New York: D. Appleton, 1860.

Dandurand, Karen. "Dickinson and the Public." In *Dickinson and Audience,* edited by Martin Orzeck and Robert Weisbuch, 255–77. Ann Arbor: University of Michigan Press, 1996.

———. "New Dickinson Civil War Publications." *American Literature* 56.1 (1984): 17–27.

DeBow, J. D. B., ed. *7th Census of the United States, Compendium*. Vol. 4. New York: Norman Ross Publishing Co., 1990.

Deppman, Jed. *Trying to Think with Emily Dickinson*. Amherst: University of Massachusetts Press, 2008.

Dickie, Margaret. "Dickinson's Discontinuous Lyric Self." *American Literature* 60.4 (1988) 537–53.

Dickinson, Edward, and Emily Norcross. *A Poet's Parents: The Courtship Letters of Emily Norcross and Edward Dickinson,* edited by Vivian R. Pollak. Chapel Hill: University of North Carolina Press, 1988.

Dickinson, Emily. *The Letters of Emily Dickinson,* edited by Thomas H. Johnson and Theodora Ward. 3 vols. Cambridge: Belknap Press/Harvard University Press, 1958.

————. *The Poems of Emily Dickinson,* edited by Ralph Waldo Franklin. 3 vols. Cambridge: Belknap Press/Harvard University Press, 1998.

————. *Open Me Carefully: Emily Dickinson's Intimate Letters to Susan Huntington Dickinson,* edited by Ellen Louise Hart and Martha Nell Smith. Ashfield, MA: Paris Press, 1998.

Dimock, Wai Chee. "Genres as Fields of Knowledge." *PMLA* 122.5 (2007): 1377–89.

Dobson, Joanne. *Dickinson and the Strategies of Reticence.* Bloomington: Indiana University Press, 1989.

Douglass, Frederick. "The Revolution of 1848." In *The Life and Writings of Frederick Douglass: Early Years, 1817–1849.* Edited by Philip S. Foner. 5 vols. New York: International Publishers, 1950.

Duncan, Robert. *The H. D. Book.* Edited by Michael Boughn and Victor Coleman. Berkeley: University of California Press, 2011 [1961].

Eberwein, Jane Donahue. *Dickinson: Strategies of Limitation.* Amherst: University of Massachusetts Press, 1985.

————. "Messages of Condolence: 'more Peace than Pang'." In *Reading Emily Dickinson's Letters,* edited by Jane Donahue Eberwein and Cindy MacKenzie. 100–125. Amherst: University of Massachusetts Press, 2009.

————. "'Siren Alps': The Lure of Europe for American Writers." *EDJ* 5.2 (1996): 176–82.

————, and Cindy MacKenzie, eds. *Reading Emily Dickinson's Letters.* Amherst: University of Massachusetts Press, 2009.

Eliot, T. S. *Collected Poems, 1909–1962.* New York: Harcourt, Brace, 1991.

Ellis, Richard. "A little East of Jordan": Human-Divine Encounter in Dickinson and the Hebrew Bible." *EDJ* 8.1 (1999): 36–58.

Emerson, Ralph Waldo. *Essays and Lectures,* edited by Joel Porte. New York: Library of America, 1983..

————. *Poems.* Boston: James Munroe, 1847.

Erbsen, Wayne. *Rousing Songs & True Tales of the Civil War.* Native Ground Music, 1999.

Erkkila, Betsy. "Dickinson and the Art of Politics." In *A Historical Guide to Emily Dickinson,* edited by Vivian Pollak, 133–74. New York: Oxford University Press, 2004.

————. "Emily Dickinson and Class." *American Literary History* 4.1 (1992): 1–27.

————. *Wicked Sisters: Women Poets, Literary History, and Discord.* New York: Oxford University Press, 1992.

Esdale, Logan. "Dickinson's Epistolary 'Naturalness.'" *EDJ* 14.1 (2005): 1–23.

Fahs, Alice. *The Imagined Civil War: Popular Literature of the North and South 1861–1865.* Chapel Hill: University of North Carolina Press, 2001.

Faust, Drew Gilpin. *This Republic of Suffering: Death and the American Civil War.* New York: Knopf, 2008.

Ferguson, Robert. "Hearing Lincoln and the Making of Eloquence." *American Literary History* 21.4 (2009): 687–724.

Finch, Annie. *The Ghost of Meter: Culture and Prosody in American Free Verse.* Ann Arbor: University of Michigan Press, 2000.

Finnerty, Páraic. "'Dreamed of your meeting Tennyson in Ticknor and Fields': A Transatlantic Encounter with Britain's Poet Laureate." *EDJ* 20.1 (2011): 56–77.

————. *Emily Dickinson's Shakespeare.* Amherst: University of Massachusetts Press, 2006.

Fisher, Aileen, and Olive Rabe. *We Dickinsons.* New York: Atheneum, 1965.

Fliegelman, Jay. *Declaring Independence: Jefferson, Natural Language, and the Culture of Performance.* Stanford: Stanford University Press, 1993.

Foner, Eric. *Reconstruction: America's Unfinished Revolution, 1863–1877.* New York: Harper and Row, 1988.

————, and Joshua Brown. *Forever Free: The Story of Emancipation and Reconstruction.* New York: Knopf, 2005.

Freedman, Linda. "Dickinson's 'wonderful Blakean gift.'" Paper presented at "'Were I Britain born': Dickinson's Transatlantic Connections," Oxford, UK, August 2010.

Friedlander, Benjamin. "Devious Truths." *EDJ* 18.1 (2009): 32–43.

————. "Emily Dickinson and the Battle of Ball's Bluff." *PMLA* 124.5 (2009): 1582–99.

Friedman, Albert. *The Ballad Revival: Studies in the Influence of Popular on Sophisticated Poetry.* Chicago: University of Chicago Press, 1961.

Frost, Linda. *Never One Nation: Freaks, Savages, and Whiteness in U.S. Popular Culture 1850–1877.* University of Minnesota Press, 2005.

Genette, Gérard. *The Architext* (1979), trans. Jane E. Lewin. Berkeley: University of California Press, 1992.

Gilbert, Sandra, and Susan Gubar. *The Madwoman in the Attic: The Woman Writer and the Nineteenth-Century Literary Imagination.* New Haven: Yale University Press, 1978.

Giles, Paul. "'The Earth reversed her Hemispheres': Dickinson's Global Antipodality." *EDJ* 20.1 (2011): 1–21.

Goodrich, S. G. *A Pictorial Geography of the World.* Boston: C. D. Strong, 1841.

Gordon, Lyndall. *Lives Like Loaded Guns: Emily Dickinson and Her Family's Feuds.* New York: Viking 2010.

Griffin, Martin. *Ashes of the Mind: War and Memory in Northern Literature: 1865–1900.* Amherst: University of Massachusetts Press, 2009.

Griswold, Rufus W., ed. *Readings in American Poetry.* New York: John C. Ricker, 1843.

Gummere, Francis. *Democracy and Poetry.* Boston: Houghton Mifflin, 1911.

Guthrie, James. "Law, Property, and Provincialism in Dickinson's Poems and Letters to Judge Otis Phillips Lord." EDJ 5.1 (1996): 27–44.

Habegger, Alfred. *My Wars Are Laid Away in Books: The Life of Emily Dickinson.* Paperback ed. New York: Modern Library, 2002.

Hall, David. *Ways of Writing: The Practice and Politics of Text-Making in Seventeenth-Century New England.* Philadelphia: University of Pennsylvania Press, 2008.

Hallen, Cynthia. "Brave Columbus, Brave Columba: Emily Dickinson's Search for Land." *EDJ* 5.2 (1996): 169–75.

Halpine, Charles. "Daphnaides, Or the English Laurel." *AM* 2.11 (September 1858): 452–65.

Hamelman, Steven. "Orientalism and Sympathy in Maria Susanna Cummins's *El Fureidis.*" *Legacy* 25.1 (2008): 62–82.

Hart, Ellen Louise. "Alliteration, Emphasis, and Spatial Prosody in Dickinson's Manuscript Letters." In *Reading Emily Dickinson's Letters,* edited by Jane Donahue Eberwein and Cindy MacKenzie. 213–38. Amherst: University of Massachusetts Press, 2009.

———. "Hearing the Visual Lines: How Manuscript Study Can Contribute to an Understanding of Dickinson's Prosody." In Smith and Loeffelholz, *Companion*. 348–67.

Hawthorne, Nathaniel. "Chiefly About War-Matters, by a Peaceable Man." *AM* 10.57 (July 1862): 43–61.

Heginbotham, Eleanor. *Reading the Fascicles of Emily Dickinson: Dwelling in Possibilities*. Columbus: Ohio State University Press, 2003.

Hejinian, Lyn. *The Language of Inquiry*. Berkeley: University of California Press, 2000.

Higginson, Thomas Wentworth. "April Days." *AM* 7.42 (April 1861): 385–95.

———."Barbarism and Civilization." *AM* 7.39 (January 1861): 51–62.

———. "Emily Dickinson's Letters." *AM* 68.408 (October 1891): 444–56.

———. "Preface." *Poems* by Emily Dickinson, iii–vi. Boston, Roberts Brothers, 1890.

———. "Lydia Maria Child." In *Eminent Women of the Age*. 38–65. Hartford, CT: S. M. Betts & Co., 1868.

———. "Negro Spirituals." *AM* 19.116 (June 1867): 685–94.

———. "The Maroons of Jamaica." *AM* 5.28 (February 1860): 213–22.

Hoffman, Tyler. *American Poetry in Performance: From Walt Whitman to Hip Hop*. Ann Arbor: University of Michigan Press, 2011.

———. "Reenacting Civil War Poetry." In *Teaching Nineteenth-Century American Poetry*, edited by Paula Bernat Bennett and Karen Kilcup. 67–81. New York: MLA, 2007.

Hogue, Cynthia. " 'lives – like Dollars': Dickinson and the Poetics of Witness." *EDJ* 15.2 (2006): 40–46.

Holmes, Oliver Wendell. "The Autocrat of the Breakfast Table." *AM* 1.5 (March 1858): 614–25.

———. "Doings of the Sunbeam." *AM* 12.69 (July 1863): 1–12.

———. *Poems*. 1848. Boston: William D. Ticknor & Co, 1851.

———. "The Poetry of the War." Lecture delivered Boston, November 21, 1865. Huntington Library 55327. San Marino, CA.

———. "The Professor's Story." *AM* 5.27–7.42 (January 1860–April 1861).

Homans, Margaret. *Women Writers and Poetic Identity*. New Haven: Yale University Press, 1980.

Hošek, Chaviva, and Patricia Parker, eds. *Lyric Poetry: Beyond New Criticism*. Ithaca: Cornell University Press, 1985.

Howe, Julia Ward. *Words for the Hour*. Boston: Ticknor and Fields, 1857.

Howe, Susan. *The Birth-Mark: Unsettling the Wilderness in American Literary History*. Middletown, CT: Wesleyan University Press, 1993.

———. *My Emily Dickinson*. New York: New Directions, 1985; reissued 2007.

Hutchison, Coleman. " 'Eastern Exiles': Dickinson, Whiggery and War." *EDJ* 13.2 (2004) 1–26.

Huyssen, Andreas. *After the Great Divide: Modernism, Mass Culture, Postmodernism*. Bloomington: Indiana University Press,1986.

Jackson, Bruce. *Get Your Ass in the Water and Swim Like Me: African American Narrative Poetry from Oral Tradition*. Cambridge: Harvard University Press, 1974.

Jackson, Virginia. "Bryant, or American Romanticism." In *The Traffic in Poems: Nineteenth-century Poetry Exchange,* edited by Meredith McGill. 185–204. New Brunswick, NJ: Rutgers University Press, 2008.

——. *Dickinson's Misery: A Theory of Lyric Reading.* Princeton: Princeton University Press, 2005.

Jordan, Winthrop. *White over Black.* Chapel Hill: University of North Carolina Press, 1968.

Juhasz, Suzanne. "The Big Tease." In *Comic Power in Emily Dickinson,* by Suzanne Juhasz, Cristanne Miller, and Martha Nell Smith. 26–62. Austin: University of Texas Press, 1993.

——, ed. *Feminist Critics Read Emily Dickinson.* Bloomington: Indiana University Press, 1983.

——. *The Undiscovered Continent: Emily Dickinson and the Space of the Mind.* Bloomington: Indiana University Press, 1983.

Kang, Yanbin. "Dickinson's Hummingbirds, Circumference, and Chinese Poetics." *EDJ* 20.2 (2011): 61–68.

Kearns, Michael. *Writing for the Street, Writing in the Garrett: Melville, Dickinson, and Private Publication.* Columbus: Ohio State University Press, 2010.

Keller, Lynn. "'Post-Language' Lyric: The Example of Juliana Spahr." *Chicago Review* 55.3–4 (2010): 74–83.

——, and Cristanne Miller. "Gender and Poetry." *The Princeton Encyclopedia of Poetics.* Princeton: Princeton University Press, 2012.

King, Wesley. "The White Symbolic of Emily Dickinson." *EDJ* 18.1 (2009): 44–68.

Kirkby, Joan. "'[W]e thought Darwin had thrown "the Redeemer" away': Darwinizing with Emily Dickinson." *EDJ* 19.1 (2010): 1–29.

Kohler, Michelle. "Dickinson and the Poetics of Revolution." *EDJ* 19.2 (2010): 20–47.

Kreider, Kristin. "'Scrap,' 'Flap,' 'Strip,' 'Stain,' 'Cut': The Material Poetics of Emily Dickinson's Later Manuscripts Pages." *EDJ* 19.2 (2010): 67–103.

Kushner, David Z. "Reflections on the State Songs of Florida." *Min-Ad: Israel Studies in Musicology Online* (2007): n.p.

LaPorte, Charles. "Post-Romantic Ideologies and Victorian Poetic Practice, or, the Future of Criticism at the Present Time." *Victorian Poetry* 41.4 (2003): 519–25.

Lee, Maurice. "Writing through the War: Melville and Dickinson after the Renaissance." *PMLA* 115.5 (2000): 1124–28.

Lerner, William, compiled under his direction. *Historical Statistics of the United States: Colonial Times to 1970.* Part I. Washington, DC. Bureau of the Census, 1975.

Leyda, Jay, ed. *The Years and Hours of Emily Dickinson.* New Haven: Yale University Press, 1960.

Lindberg-Seyersted, Brita. *The Voice of the Poet: Aspects of Style in the Poetry of Emily Dickinson.* Cambridge: Harvard University Press, 1968.

Loeffelholz, Mary. "Dickinson's 'Decoration.'" *ELH* 72.3 (2005): 663–89.

——. *From School to Salon: Reading Nineteenth-Century American Women's Poetry.* Princeton: Princeton University Press, 2004.

————. "Mapping the Cultural Field: *Aurora Leigh* in America." In *The Traffic in Poems: Nineteenth-Century Poetry Exchange,* edited by Meredith McGill. 139–59. New Brunswick, NJ: Rutgers University Press, 2008.

————. "Master Shakespeare, Mrs. Browning, Miss Dickinson, and the Servants." *EDJ* 20.1 (2011): 34–55.

————. "Really Indigenous Productions: Emily Dickinson, Josiah Holland, and Nineteenth-Century Popular Verse." In Smith and Loeffelholz, *Companion.* 183–204.

Lombardo, Daniel. *A Hedge Away: The Other Side of Emily Dickinson's Amherst.* Amherst: Daily Hampshire Gazette, 1997.

Longenbach, James. *The Art of the Poetic Line.* Minneapolis: Graywolf, 2008.

Longfellow, Henry W. *Poems.* 1851.

Longsworth, Polly. "Brave among the Bravest: Amherst in the Civil War." *Amherst College Quarterly* (1999): 25–31.

Lott, Eric. *Blackface, White Noise: Jewish Immigrants in the Hollywood Melting Pot.* Berkeley: University of California Press, 1996.

Lowell, James Russell. "The Ballad." *Christian Inquirer.* 3 May 1855: 4.

————. "The Black Preacher. A Breton Legend." *AM* 13.78 (April 1864): 465–67.

Lowenberg, Carlton. *Musicians Wrestle Everywhere: Emily Dickinson and Music.* Berkeley: Fallen Leaf Press, 1992.

Lye, Colleen. *America's Asia: Racial Form and American Literature, 1893–1945.* Princeton: Princeton University Press, 2005.

MacKenzie, Cindy, and Barbara Dana, eds. *Wider than the Sky: Essays and Meditations on the Healing Power of Emily Dickinson.* Kent. OH: Kent State University Press, 2007.

Maier, Carol. "Love Unfaithful but True: Reflections on *Amor infiel. Emily Dickinson por Nuria Amat.*" *EDJ* 18.2 (2009): 77–93.

Maker, David, and Ann Townsend. "Introduction." In *Radiant Lyre: Essays on Lyric Poetry.* Minneapolis: Graywolf, 2007.

————. " 'I'm Nobody': Lyric Poetry and the Problem of People." In Maker and Townsend, *Radiant Lyre.* 197–218.

Mandell, Laura. "Introduction to the Poetess Archive," "About the Poetess." "Uses of the Archive." *Poetess Archive Journal* (March 2010). www.poetessarchive.com/.

————. "The Poetess Tradition." *Romanticism on the Net.* Nos. 29–30 (2003). www.erudit .org/revue/ron/2003/v/n29-30/007712ar.html.

Manheim, Daniel, and Marianne Noble, eds. "Emily Dickinson's Reading." Special Issue, *EDJ* 19.1 (2010).

Manson, Michael. " 'The Thews of Hymn': Dickinson's Metrical Grammar." In Smith and Loeffelholz, *Companion.* 368–90.

Mason, Lowell, and David Greene. *Church Psalmody: A Collection of Psalms and Hymns Adapted to Public Worship.* 1831.

Massey, Gerald. "Poetry—The Spasmodists." *North British Review* 28 (February 1858). Reprinted www.gerald-massey.org.uk/massey/cpr_the_spasmodists.htm.

McGill, Meredith. *American Literature and the Culture of Reprinting, 1834–1853.* Philadelphia: University of Pennsylvania Press, 2003.

McGuffy, William H., ed. *The Eclectic 4th Reader: containing Elegant Extracts in Prose and Poetry, from the best American and English Writers.* Cincinnati, OH: Truman & Smith, 1841.

McLane, Maureen. *Balladeering, Minstrelsy, and the Making of British Romantic Poetry.* New York: Cambridge University Press, 2008.

——. "The Figure Minstrelsy Makes: Poetry and Historicity." *Critical Inquiry* 29.3 (2003): 429–53.

McPherson, James. *Drawn with the Sword: Reflections on the American Civil War.* New York: Oxford University Press, 1996.

Mellor, Anne. *Romanticism and Gender.* London: Routledge, 1993.

Melville, Herman. *Battle-Pieces and Aspects of the War.* New York: Harper and Brothers, 1866.

Messmer, Marietta. "Dickinson's Critical Reception." In *The Emily Dickinson Handbook,* edited by Gudrun Grabher, Roland Hagenbüchle, and Cristanne Miller, 299–322. Amherst: University of Massachusetts Press, 1998.

——. *A Vice for Voices: Reading Emily Dickinson's Correspondences.* Amherst: University of Massachusetts Press, 2001.

Michaels, Walter Benn. *The Shape of the Signifier: 1967 to the End of History.* Princeton: Princeton University Press, 2004.

Mill, John Stuart. "What is Poetry?" 1833. In *Dissertations and Discussions Political, Philosophical, and Historical.* London: Adamant, Elibron Classics, 2005.

Miller, Cristanne. "'By-Play': The Radical Rhythms of Marianne Moore." *Foreign Literature Studies* (Wuhan China) 30.6 (2008): 20–33.

——. "Dickinson and the Ballad." *Genre* (forthcoming 2012).

——. "Dickinson's Structured Rhythms." In Smith and Loeffelholz, *Companion.* 391–414.

——. *Emily Dickinson: A Poet's Grammar.* Cambridge: Harvard University Press, 1987.

——. "Emily Dickinson's 'turbaned seas'." In *Cambridge Companion to Nineteenth-Century American Poetry,* edited by Kerry Charles Larson. Cambridge University Press, forthcoming.

——."Pondering 'Liberty': Emily Dickinson and the Civil War." In *American Vistas and Beyond: A Festschrift for Roland Hagenbüchle,* edited by Marietta Messmer and Josef Raab, 45–64. Trier: Wissenschaftlicher Verlag Trier, 2002.

——. "Preface." In *WFH,* xv–xxii.

Mitchell, Domhnall. "Ardent Spirits: Temperance in Emily Dickinson's Writing." *EDJ* 15.2 (2006): 95–112.

——. *Emily Dickinson: Monarch of Perception.* Amherst: University of Massachusetts Press, 2000.

——. *Measures of Possibility: Emily Dickinson's Manuscripts.* University of Massachusetts Press, 2005.

Moore, Frank. *The Civil War in Song and Story.* New York: P. F. Collier, 1889.

Moore, Marianne. *Becoming Marianne Moore: Early Poems, 1907–1924,* edited by Robin G. Schulze. Berkeley: University of California Press, 2002.

——. *Complete Prose.* edited by Patricia C. Willis. New York: Viking, 1986.

——. *A Marianne Moore Reader.* New York: Viking, 1965.

————. *Selected Letters of Marianne Moore,* edited by Bonnie Costello, Celeste Goodridge, and Cristanne Miller. New York: Knopf, 1997.

Morgan, Victoria. *Emily Dickinson and Hymn Culture: Tradition and Experience.* Surrey, UK: Ashgate, 2010.

Morse, Jonathan. "Conduct Book and Serf: Emily Dickinson Writes a Word," *EDJ* 16.1 (2007): 53–72.

Mossberg, Barbara. *Emily Dickinson: When a Writer Is a Daughter.* Bloomington: Indiana University Press, 1982.

Murray, Aife. *Maid as Muse: How Servants Changed Emily Dickinson's Life and Language.* Concord: University of New Hampshire Press, 2009.

Nance, Susan. *How the Arabian Nights Inspired the American Dream.* Chapel Hill: University of North Carolina Press, 2009.

Nettleton, Asahel. *Village Hymns.* New York: E. Sands and Mahlon Day, 1838.

Newman, Steve. *Ballad Collection, Lyric, and the Canon: The Call of the Popular from the Restoration to the New Criticism.* Philadelphia: University of Pennsylvania Press, 2007.

Obeidat, Marwan. *American Literature and Orientalism.* Berlin: Klaus Schwarz Verlag, 1998.

O'Gorman, Francis, ed. *Victorian Poetry: An Annotated Anthology.* Oxford: Blackwell, 2004.

Oppen, George. *Selected Poems,* edited by Robert Creeley. New York: New Directions, 2003.

"Orientalism." *Knickerbocker* 41 (1853): 479–96.

Parker, Richard Green. *Aids to English Composition.* New York: Harper & Brothers, 1844–45.

Patterson, Rebecca. *Emily Dickinson's Imagery.* Amherst: University of Massachusetts Press, 1979.

Paulin, Tom. "Introduction." *Faber Book of Vernacular Verse.* London: Faber & Faber, 1990.

Perloff, Marjorie. "Language Poetry and the Lyric Subject." *Critical Inquiry* 25.3 (1999): 405–34.

————, and Craig Dworkin. "The Sound of Poetry / The Poetry of Sound: The 2006 MLA Presidential Forum." *PMLA* 123.3 (May 2008): 749–61.

Petrino, Elizabeth. *Emily Dickinson and Her Contemporaries: Women's Verse in America 1820–1885.* University Press of New England, 1998.

Poe, Edgar Allan. *Selected Writings of Edgar Allan Poe,* edited by Edward H. David. New York: Houghton Mifflin, 1956.

————. *The Works of the Late Edgar Allan Poe,* edited by Nathaniel P. Willis, James R. Lowell, and Rufus Griswold. 3 vols. New York: J. S. Redfield, 1850–1856.

Pollak, Vivian. *Dickinson: The Anxiety of Gender.* Ithaca: Cornell University Press, 1984.

————. "Dickinson and the Poetics of Whiteness." *EDJ* 9.2 (2000): 84–95.

————, ed. *A Historical Guide to Emily Dickinson.* New York: Oxford University Press, 2004. "Illustrated Chronology" 235–354.

————. "Our Emily Dickinsons." Book manuscript in progress.

Pond, Enoch. The abridged, improved, and adapted edition of Lindley Murray's *System of English Grammar*. Worcester: Dorr, Howland, 1835.

Porter, David. *The Art of Emily Dickinson's Early Poetry*. Cambridge: Harvard University Press, 1966.

Porter, Ebenezer. *Rhetorical Reader*. Andover, NY: Gould and Newman, 1841.

Pound, Ezra. *ABC of Reading*. London: Faber & Faber, 1934.

Prescott (Spofford), Harriet E. "The Author of 'Charles Auchester'." *AM* 9.56 (June 1862): 763–76.

Price, Kenneth, and Ed Folsom. "Dickinson, Slavery, and the San Domingo Moment." Classroom Electric, www.classroomelectric.org/volume1/folsomprice/index.html.

Prins, Yopie. "Historical Poetics, Dysprosody, and *The Science of English Verse*." *PMLA* 123.1 (2008): 229–34.

———. *Victorian Sappho*. Princeton: Princeton University Press, 1999.

Qian, Zhaoming. *Orientalism and Modernism: The Legacy of China in Pound and Williams*. Durham, NC: Duke University Press, 1995.

Radhakrishnan, Rajagopalan. "Why Compare?" *New Literary History* 40 (2009): 453–71.

Reed, Brian. "Grammar Trouble." *Boundary2* 36.3 (2009): 133–58.

Reynolds, David. "Emily Dickinson and Popular Culture." In *Cambridge Companion to Emily Dickinson,* edited by Wendy Martin. 167–90. New York: Cambridge University Press, 2006.

Richards, Eliza. "'How News Must Feel When Traveling': Dickinson and Civil War Media." In Smith and Loeffelholz, *Companion*. 157–79.

Riley, Denise. *The Words of Selves: Identification, Solidarity, Irony*. Stanford: Stanford University Press, 2000.

Rose, Anne C. *Voices of the Marketplace: American Thought and Culture, 1830–1860*. Boston: Twayne, 1995.

Rubin, Joan. *Songs of Ourselves: The Uses of Poetry in America*. Cambridge: Harvard University Press, 2007.

Rudy, Jason R. "On Cultural Neoformalism, Spasmodic Poetry, and the Victorian Ballad." *Victorian Poetry* 41.4 (2003): 590–96.

Runzo, Sandra. "Emily Dickinson and Nineteenth-Century Popular Culture." Book manuscript in progress.

Rushdie, Salman. *The Satanic Verses* 1988; New York: Random House, 2008.

Saint Armand, Barton Levi. *Emily Dickinson and Her Culture: The Soul's Society*. New York: Cambridge University Press, 1984.

Sanchez Eppler, Karen. "Copying and Conversion: A Connecticut Friendship Album from 'a Chinese Youth.'" *American Quarterly* (2007): 301–39.

Scheurer, Erika. "'Near, but remote': Emily Dickinson's Epistolary Voice." *EDJ* 4.1 (1995): 86–107.

———. "'[S]o of course there was Speaking and Composition – ': Dickinson's Early Schooling as a Writer." *EDJ* 18.1 (2009): 1–21.

Schueller, Malini Johar. *U.S. Orientalisms: Race, Nation, and Gender in Literature, 1790–1890*. Ann Arbor: University of Michigan Press, 1998.

Scott, Sir Walter. "Essay on Imitations of the Ancient Ballad," 1830. www.walterscott.lib
.ed.ac.uk/works/poetry/apology/essay.html.

Sedgwick, Ellery. *The Atlantic Monthly, 1857–1909: Yankee Humanism at High Tide and Ebb.* Amherst: University of Massachusetts Press, 1994.

Sewall, Richard. "Emily Dickinson's Perfect Audience." In *Dickinson and Audience,* edited by Martin Orzeck and Robert Weisbuch. 201–13. Ann Arbor: University of Michigan Press, 1996.

———. *The Life of Emily Dickinson.* Cambridge: Harvard University Press, 1974.

Shoptaw, John. "Dickinson's Civil War Poetics: From the Enrollment Act to the Lincoln Assassination." *EDJ* 19.2 (2010): 1–20.

———. "Listening to Dickinson." *Representations* 86 (2004): 20–52.

———. "Lyric Cryptography." *Poetics Today* 21.1 (2000): 221–62.

Short, Brian. "Emily Dickinson and the Scottish New Rhetoric," *EDJ* 4.2 (1996): 261–66.

Silliman, Ron, and Carla Harryman, Lyn Hejinian, Steve Benson, Bob Perelman, Barrett Watten. "Aesthetic Tendency and the Politics of Poetry: A Manifesto." *Social Text* 19/20 (Autumn 1988): 261–75.

Small, Judy Jo. *Positive as Sound: Emily Dickinson's Rhyme.* Athens: University of Georgia Press, 1990.

Smith, Martha Nell. "A Hazard of a Letter's Fortunes: Epistolarity and the Technology of Audience in Emily Dickinson's Correspondences." In *Reading Emily Dickinson's Letters,* edited by Jane Donahue Eberwein and Cindy MacKenzie. 239–56. Amherst: University of Massachusetts Press, 2009.

———."The Poet as Cartoonist." In *Comic Power in Emily Dickinson,* by Suzanne Juhasz, Cristanne Miller, and Martha Nell Smith. Austin: University of Texas Press, 1993.

———. *Rowing in Eden: Reading Emily Dickinson.* Austin: University of Texas Press, 1992.

———, and Mary Loeffelholz, eds. *Companion to Emily Dickinson's Poetry.* London: Blackwell, 2007. Abbreviated elsewhere as Smith and Loeffelholz, *Companion.*

Socarides, Alexandra. "Rethinking the Fascicles: Dickinson's Writing, Copying, and Binding Practices." *EDJ* 15.2 (2006): 69–94.

Spahr, Juliana. "After Language Poetry." Ubu Web Papers. *OEI* 7–8 (2001): n.p.

———, and Claudia Rankine. *Women Poets in the 21st Century: Where Lyric Meets Language.* Middletown, CT: Wesleyan University Press, 2002.

Springfield Republican. "Schamyl, the Hero." 11 October 1859.

Stamy, Cynthia. *Marianne Moore and China: Orientalism and a Writing of America.* New York: Oxford University Press, 1999.

Stewart, Susan. *Poetry and the Fate of the Senses.* Chicago: University of Chicago Press, 2002.

Stonum, Gary. *The Dickinson Sublime.* Madison: University of Wisconsin Press, 1990.

———. "Emily's Heathcliff: Metaphysical Love in Dickinson and Bronte." *EDJ* 20.1 (2011): 22–32.

Stuart, Maria. "Strange English: Reading Paulin Reading Dickinson." Paper presented at "'Were I Britain born': Dickinson's Transatlantic Connections." Oxford, Eng., August 2010.

Symonds, W. L. "The Carnival of the Romantic." *AM* 6.34 (August 1860): 129–41.

Tedlock, Dennis. "Toward a Poetics of Polyphony and Translatability." In *Close Listening,* edited by Charles Bernstein. 178–99. New York: Oxford University Press, 1998.

Thomas, Shannon L. "'What News must think when pondering': Emily Dickinson, The *Springfield Daily Republican,* and the Poetics of Mass Communication." *EDJ* 19.1 (2010): 60–79.

Thoreau, Henry David. *Walden; or, Life in the Woods.* Boston: Ticknor & Fields, 1854.

Tocqueville, Alexis de. *Democracy in America.* 2 vols., translated by Henry Reeve. New York: J. & H. G. Langley, 1840.

Trux, J. J. "Negro Minstrelsy—Ancient and Modern." *Putnam's Monthly Magazine* 5.25 (1855): 72–75.

Tuckerman, Frederick. *Amherst Academy 1814–1861.* Amherst, 1929.

Twain, Mark. [Samuel Clemens]. *The Adventures of Huckleberry Finn.* 1885. Berkeley: University of California Press, 1985.

Uno, Hiroko. "Emily Dickinson's Encounter with the East." *EDJ* 17.1 (2008): 43–67.

Vogelius, Christa. "'Paralyzed, with gold -': Dickinson's Poetics of Photography." *EDJ* 18.2 (2009): 21–37.

Wardrop, Daneen. *Emily Dickinson and the Labor of Clothing.* Durham: University of New Hampshire Press, 2009.

Warley, Christopher. *Sonnet Sequences and Social Distinction in Renaissance England.* New York: Cambridge University Press, 2005.

Wasson, David Atwood. "Whittier." *AM* 13.77 (March 1864): 331–39.

Weisbuch, Robert. *Emily Dickinson's Poetry.* Chicago: University of Chicago Press, 1975.

Werner, Marta. *Open Folios: Scenes of Reading, Surfaces of Writing.* Ann Arbor: University of Michigan Press, 1995.

———. "'A Woe Of Ecstasy': On the Electronic Editing of Emily Dickinson's Late Fragments." *EDJ* 16.2 (2007): 25–52.

White, Melissa. "Letter to the Light: Discoveries in Dickinson's Correspondence." *EDJ* 16.1 (2007): 1–26.

Whitman, Walt. *Leaves of Grass.* 1855, 1860, 1867. Whitman Archive. http://whitmanarchive.org/published/LG/1855/whole.html.

Whittier, John Greenleaf. *Whittier on Writers and Writing: The Uncollected Critical Writing of John Greenleaf Whittier,* edited by Edwin H. Cady and Harry H. Clark, 1950. Syracuse: Syracuse University Press, 1971.

Wichelns, Kathryn. "Emily Dickinson's Henry James," *EDJ* 20.1 (2011): 77–99.

Williams, Tyrone. "Problems and Promises of Actually Existing Cross-Cultural Poetics." *XCP: Cross Cultural Poetics* 20 (2008). http://xcp.bfn.org/.

Willis, Elizabeth. "Lyric Dissent." *Boundary 2* 36.3 (Fall 2009): 229–34.

Wineapple, Brenda. *White Heat: The Friendship of Emily Dickinson and Thomas Wentworth Higginson.* New York: Knopf, 2008.

Wollen, Peter. "Fashion/Orientalism/The Body." *new formations* 1 (1987): 5–34.

Wolosky, Shira. *Emily Dickinson: A Voice of War.* New Haven: Yale University Press, 1984.

———. "Emily Dickinson's War Poetry: The Problem of Theodicy." *Massachusetts Review* 25.1 (1984): 22–41.

————. *Poetry and Public Discourse in Nineteenth-Century America.* London: Palgrave, 2010.

————. "Public and Private in Emily Dickinson's Poetry." *A Historical Guide to Emily Dickinson,* edited by Vivian R. Pollak. 103–32. New York: Oxford University Press, 2004.

————. "Rhetoric or Not: Hymnal Tropes in Emily Dickinson and Isaac Watts." *New England Quarterly* 61.2 (1988): 214–32.

Worcester, Samuel. *The Psalms, Hymns, and Spiritual Songs of the Rev. Isaac Watts.* Boston: Crocker & Brewster, 1834.

Wordsworth, William, and Samuel Taylor Coleridge. *Lyrical Ballads,* edited by W. J. B. Owen. London: Oxford University Press, 1969.

Wright, C. D. "The New American Ode." *Antioch Review* 47.3 (1989): 287–96.

Young, Elizabeth. *Disarming the Nation: Women's Writing and the American Civil War.* Chicago: University of Chicago Press, 1999.

Zboray, Ronald, and Mary Saracino Zboray. "Between 'Crockery-dom' and Barnum: Boston's Chinese Museum, 1845–1847." *American Quarterly* 56.2 (2004): 271–307.

GENERAL INDEX

Agamben, Giorgio, 27, 213n26
Arabian Nights, 119–20, 129, 236n5
Atlantic Monthly, 3–4, 10, 22, 96, 119, 129, 135, 176, 204n6, 210n6; marking/cutting in, 4–5, 149; poetry in, 9, 33, 158, 171, 178, 215n46; politics of, 15, 148, 153, 155–56, 247n12, 249n31

ballad, 3, 6, 17, 23–26, 28, 29, 49–81, 82, 183, 187; as national, 87–88, 222n43; and orality, 82, 84, 89, 222n39; and Romantic poetry, 50–51, 83–84, 88–89, 160; speakers, 14, 83–94, 97, 116–17. *See also* meter
Barrett, Faith, 2, 150, 160, 219n12, 246n5, 246n7, 247n14, 250n37n40, 251n44
Barrett Browning, Elizabeth, 3, 4, 9, 22, 35, 212n20, 216n57, 218n7, 240n35; *Aurora Leigh*, 23, 33, 215n47, 218n9, 254n11; ED's poems on, 37–38, 54, 90, 91, 138
Bennett, Paula Bernat, 2, 25, 207n27, 239n39, 241n43, 246n6
Bianchi, Martha Dickinson, 180, 219n19, 227n42, 253n2
Blake, William, 50, 92, 231nn24–25
Blight, David, 15, 208n33
Bowles, Samuel, 4, 176, 206n22, 255n20; letters/poems sent to, 12, 92, 112, 159, 177, 187, 191, 205n17, 243–44n60
Bryant, William Cullen, 26, 31, 50, 108, 211n15, 214n35, 215n43, 250n36; on meter, 218n6; poems marked by ED, 34, 59, 91, 215n40, 224n58, 234n41; and war, 159, 246n4
Burns, Robert, 50, 74, 226n69
Butler, Judith, 207n27, 253n63

Cameron, Sharon, 116, 228n78
Child, Francis James, 58, 87, 89
Child, Lydia Maria, 129, 208n34, 249n27
Civil War, 3, 49, 53–54, 138, 145, 204n6; New England politics, 157; and racism, 15, 147–48, 156, 158
Civil War poetry, 4, 17, 45, 51, 54; ED's soldier speakers, 154, 164–66, 171–73; martyrology,

14, 45, 149–54, 173; mothers/wives in, 161–63; nature in, 16, 159–60, 173; and slavery/freedom, 14–17, 151–52, 156–58, 166–69, 207n30. *See also* music
Cody, David, 159, 203n5, 210n6n8, 251n42
Cohen, Michael, 50, 51, 218n5n10, 219n13, 230n15, 250n35n36
Coleridge, Samuel Taylor, 23, 50, 141, 142, 222n43
Crumbley, Paul, 2, 209n40, 213n28, 229n7

Deppman, Jed, 2, 13, 27–28, 30, 85, 213n27n28, 214n33, 254n12
Dickie, Margaret, 25, 211–12n19
Dickinson, Austin, 53, 54, 120, 148, 152, 219n21, 226n67, 247n16; books owned by, 210n5, 211n12, 214n30, 237n11
Dickinson, Edward, 30, 52, 53, 95, 121, 237n11, 249n27; books owned by, 5, 60; and politics, 155, 157, 241n45, 249n30, 249–50n33
Dickinson, Emily: circulation of poems, 1–3, 7–8, 10–13, 17–18, 95–96, 116, 147, 149, 158, 174, 176–80, 187–88, 191–92, 195; composition of poems, 7, 8, 12, 51, 56–57, 74–75, 78–80; cutting/marking, 4–6, 204n13, 214n34; dating of poems, 6–9, 187; as musician, 52–54; poetry as aural/performative, 12–13, 37–46, 49, 83–84, 94, 97, 116, 177, 179; publication during lifetime, 98–101, 148, 176–81, 183–87, 191–92; and race, 14–17, 119, 126–30, 133–36, 138–39, 158, 167–69; reception in 1890s, 21–22, 210n8, 231n5; revision of poems, 10, 11, 12, 79, 84, 96, 111–14, 117, 181–82, 205n18, 227n70; schoolbooks, 27–28, 32–34, 59, 130, 181, 243n53; sheet music owned, 15, 87, 230nn19–20; and textual instability, 10, 82–84, 96–97, 101, 112–14, 116; unusual qualities of verse, 2–3, 9–10, 17–18, 20, 36, 48, 80–81, 182
Dickinson, Emily Norcross, 5, 54, 120, 231n23

273

INDEX OF POEMS

277